The Iliads of Homer by Homer

Translated from the Greek by George Chapman

George Chapman was born at Hitchin in Hertfordshire in about 1559. There is some evidence that Chapman attended Oxford University but did not obtain a degree, but the evidence is rather scant.

During the first part of the early 1590s Chapman was in Europe, in military action in the Low Countries fighting under the famed English general Sir Francis Vere.

It is from this period that his earliest published works are found including the obscure philosophical poems The Shadow of Night (1594) and Ovid's Banquet of Sense (1595).

By the end of the 1590s, Chapman had become a successful playwright, working for the Elizabethan Theatrical entrepreneur, Philip Henslowe, and later for the Children of the Chapel.

From 1598 he published his translation of the Iliad in installments. In 1616 the complete Iliad and Odyssey appeared in The Whole Works of Homer, the first complete English translation, which until Alexander Pope's, was the most popular in the English language and was the entry point for most English readers of these magnificent poems.

The great Ben Jonson was also using Chapman's talents in the play Eastward Ho (1605), co-written with John Marston. Both Chapman and Jonson landed in jail over some satirical references to the Scots in the play but both were quick to say that Marston was the culprit.

Chapman also wrote one of the most successful masques of the Jacobean era, The Memorable Masque of the Middle Temple and Lincoln's Inn, performed on February 15th, 1613. Another masque, The Masque of the Twelve Months, performed on Twelfth Night 1619 is also now given as Chapman's.

George Chapman died in London on May 12th, 1634 having lived his latter years in poverty and debt. He was buried at St Giles in the Fields.

Index of Contents

THE ILIADS OF HOMER THE EPISTLE DEDICATORY

TO THE IMMORTAL MEMORY OF THE INCOMPARABLE HEROE, HENRY, PRINCE OF WALES.

Thy tomb, arms, statue, all things fit to fall
At foot of Death, and worship funeral,
Form hath bestow'd; for form is nought too dear.
Thy solid virtues yet, eterniz'd here,
My blood and wasted spirits have only found
Commanded cost, and broke so rich a ground,
Not to inter, but make thee ever spring,
As arms, tombs, statues, ev'ry earthy thing,
Shall fade aid vanish into fume before.
What lasts thrives least; yet wealth of soul is poor,
And so 'tis kept. Not thy thrice-sacred will,
Sign'd with thy death, moves any to fulfil
Thy just bequests to me. Thou dead, then I
Live dead, for giving thee eternity.

Ad Famam

To all times future this time's mark extend,
Homer no patron found, nor Chapman friend.
Ignotus nimis omnibus,
Sat notus moritur sibi.

TO THE HIGH BORN PRINCE OF MEN, HENRY, THRICE ROYAL INHERITOR TO THE UNITED KINGDOMS OF GREAT BRITAIN, ETC.

Since perfect happiness, by Princes sought,
Is not with birth born, nor exchequers bought,
Nor follows in great trains, nor is possest
With any outward state, but makes him blest
That governs inward, and beholdeth there
All his affections stand about him bare,
That by his pow'r can send to Tower and death
All traitorous passions, marshalling beneath
His justice his mere will, and in his mind
Holds such a sceptre as can keep confin'd
His whole life's actions in the royal bounds
Of virtue and religion, and their grounds
Takes in to sow his honours, his delights,
And cómplete empire; you should learn these rights,
Great Prince of men, by princely precedents,
Which here, in all kinds, my true zeal presents
To furnish your youth's groundwork and first state,
And let you see one godlike man create
All sorts of worthiest men, to be contriv'd
In your worth only, giving him reviv'd
For whose life Alexander would have giv'n
One of his kingdoms; who (as sent from heav'n,
And thinking well that so divine a creature
Would never more enrich the race of nature)
Kept as his crown his works, and thought them still
His angels, in all pow'r to rule his will;
And would affirm that Homer's poesy
Did more advance his Asian victory,
Than all his armies. O! 'tis wond'rous much,
Though nothing priz'd, that the right virtuous touch
Of a well-written soul to virtue moves;
Nor have we souls to purpose, if their loves
Of fitting objects be not so inflam'd.
How much then were this kingdom's main soul maim'd,
To want this great inflamer of all pow'rs
That move in human souls! All realms but yours

Are honour'd with him, and hold blest that state
That have his works to read and contemplate:
In which humanity to her height is rais'd,
Which all the world, yet none enough, hath prais'd;
Seas, earth, and heav'n, he did in verse comprise,
Out-sung the Muses, and did equalize
Their king Apollo; being so far from cause
Of Princes' light thoughts, that their gravest laws
May find stuff to be fashion'd by his lines.
Through all the pomp of kingdoms still he shines,
And graceth all his gracers. Then let lie
Your lutes and viols, and more loftily
Make the heroics of your Homer sung,
To drums and trumpets set his angel's tongue,
And, with the princely sport of hawks you use,
Behold the kingly flight of his high muse,
And see how, like the phœnix, she renews
Her age and starry feathers in your sun,
Thousands of years attending ev'ry one
Blowing the holy fire, and throwing in
Their seasons, kingdoms, nations, that have been
Subverted in them; laws, religions, all
Offer'd to change and greedy funeral;
Yet still your Homer, lasting, living, reigning,
And proves how firm truth builds in poet's feigning.
A prince's statue, or in marble carv'd,
Or steel, or gold, and shrin'd, to be preserv'd,
Aloft on pillars or pyramides,
Time into lowest ruins may depress;
But drawn with all his virtues in learn'd verse,
Fame shall resound them on oblivion's hearse,
Till graves gasp with her blasts, and dead men rise.
No gold can follow where true Poesy flies.
Then let not this divinity in earth,
Dear Prince, be slighted as she were the birth
Of idle fancy, since she works so high;
Nor let her poor disposer, Learning, lie
Still bed-rid. Both which being in men defac'd,
In men with them is God's bright image ras'd;
For as the Sun and Moon are figures giv'n
Of his refulgent Deity in heav'n,
So Learning, and, her light'ner, Poesy,
In earth present His fiery Majesty.
Nor are kings like Him, since their diadems
Thunder and lighten and project brave beams,
But since they His clear virtues emulate,
In truth and justice imaging His state,
In bounty and humanity since they shine,

Than which is nothing like Him more divine;
Not fire, not light, the sun's admiréd course,
The rise nor set of stars, nor all their force
In us and all this cope beneath the sky,
Nor great existence, term'd His treasury;
Since not for being greatest He is blest,
But being just, and in all virtues best.
What sets His justice and His truth best forth,
Best Prince, then use best, which is Poesy's worth;
For, as great princes, well inform'd and deck'd
With gracious virtue, give more sure effect
To her persuasions, pleasures, real worth,
Than all th' inferior subjects she sets forth;
Since there she shines at full, hath birth, wealth, state,
Pow'r, fortune, honour, fit to elevate
Her heav'nly merits, and so fit they are,
Since she was made for them, and they for her;
So Truth, with Poesy grac'd, is fairer far,
More proper, moving, chaste, and regular,
Than when she runs away with untruss'd Prose;
Proportion, that doth orderly dispose
Her virtuous treasure, and is queen of graces;
In Poesy decking her with choicest phrases,
Figures and numbers; when loose Prose puts on
Plain letter-habits makes her trot upon
Dull earthly business, she being mere divine;
Holds her to homely cates and harsh hedge-wine,
That should drink Poesy's nectar; ev'ry way
One made for other, as the sun and day,
Princes and virtues. And, as in spring,
The pliant water mov'd with anything
Let fall into it, puts her motion out
In perfect circles, that move round about
The gentle fountain, one another raising;
So Truth and Poesy work; so Poesy, blazing
All subjects fall'n in her exhaustless fount,
Works most exactly, makes a true account
Of all things to her high discharges giv'n,
Till all be circular and round as heav'n.
And lastly, great Prince, mark and pardon me:—
As in a flourishing and ripe fruit-tree,
Nature hath made the bark to save the bole,
The bole the sap, the sap to deck the whole
With leaves and branches, they to bear and shield
The useful fruit, the fruit itself to yield
Guard to the kernel, and for that all those,
Since out of that again the whole tree grows;
So in our tree of man, whose nervy root

Springs in his top, from thence ev'n to his foot
There runs a mutual aid through all his parts,
All join'd in one to serve his queen of arts, [1]
In which doth Poesy like the kernel lie
Obscur'd, though her Promethean faculty
Can create men and make ev'n death to live,
For which she should live honour'd, kings should give
Comfort and help to her that she might still
Hold up their spirits in virtue, make the will
That governs in them to the pow'r conform'd,
The pow'r to justice, that the scandals, storm'd
Against the poor dame, clear'd by your fair grace,
Your grace may shine the clearer. Her low place,
Not showing her, the highest leaves obscure.
Who raise her raise themselves, and he sits sure
Whom her wing'd hand advanceth, since on it
Eternity doth, crowning virtue, sit.
All whose poor seed, like violets in their beds,
Now grow with bosom-hung and hidden heads;
For whom I must speak, though their fate convinces
Me worst of poets, to you best of princes.
By the most humble and faithful implorer for all
the graces to your highness eternized by your divine Homer.
George Chapman.

[1] *Queen of arts—the soul.*

TO THE SACRED FOUNTAIN OF PRINCES, SOLE EMPRESS OF BEAUTY AND VIRTUE, ANNE, QUEEN OF ENGLAND, ETC.

With whatsoever honour we adorn
Your royal issue, we must gratulate you,
Imperial Sovereign; who of you is born
Is you, one tree make both the bole and bow.
If it be honour then to join you both
To such a pow'rful work as shall defend
Both from foul death and age's ugly moth,
This is an honour that shall never end.
They know not virtue then, that know not what
The virtue of defending virtue is;
It comprehends the guard of all your State,
And joins your greatness to as great a bliss.
Shield virtue and advance her then, great Queen,
And make this book your glass to make it seen.
Your Majesty's in all subjection most
humbly consecrate,

GEORGE CHAPMAN.

Lest with foul hands you touch these holy rites,
And with prejudicacies too profane,
Pass Homer in your other poets' slights,
Wash here. In this porch to his num'rous fane,
Hear ancient oracles speak, and tell you whom
You have to censure. First then Silius hear,
Who thrice was consul in renowned Rome,
Whose verse, saith Martial, nothing shall out-wear.

SILIUS ITALICUS, LIB. XIII. 777

He, in Elysium having cast his eye
Upon the figure of a youth, whose hair,
With purple ribands braided curiously,
Hung on his shoulders wond'rous bright and fair,
Said: "Virgin, what is he whose heav'nly face
Shines past all others, as the morn the night;
Whom many marvelling souls, from place to place,
Pursue and haunt with sounds of such delight;
Whose count'nance (were't not in the Stygian shade)
Would make me, questionless, believe he were
A very God?" The learned virgin made
This answer: "If thou shouldst believe it here,
Thou shouldst not err. He well deserv'd to be
Esteem'd a God; nor held his so-much breast
A little presence of the Deity,
His verse compris'd earth, seas, stars, souls at rest;
In song the Muses he did equalize,
In honour Phœbus. He was only soul,
Saw all things spher'd in nature, without eyes,
And rais'd your Troy up to the starry pole."
Glad Scipio, viewing well this prince of ghosts,
Said: "O if Fates would give this poet leave
To sing the acts done by the Roman hosts,
How much beyond would future times receive
The same facts made by any other known!
O blest Æacides, to have the grace
That out of such a mouth thou shouldst be shown
To wond'ring nations, as enrich'd the race
Of all times future with what he did know!

Thy virtue with his verse shall ever grow."
Now hear an Angel sing our poet's fame,
Whom fate, for his divine song, gave that name.

ANGELUS POLITIANUS, IN NUTRICIA

More living than in old Demodocus,
Fame glories to wax young in Homer's verse.
And as when bright Hyperion holds to us
His golden torch, we see the stars disperse,
And ev'ry way fly heav'n, the pallid moon
Ev'n almost vanishing before his sight;
So, with the dazzling beams of Homer's sun,
All other ancient poets lose their light.
Whom when Apollo heard, out of his star,
Singing the godlike act of honour'd men,
And equalling the actual rage of war,
With only the divine strains of his pen,
He stood amaz'd and freely did confess
Himself was equall'd in Mæonides.
Next hear the grave and learned Pliny use
His censure of our sacred poet's muse.
Plin. Nat. Hist. lib. 7. cap. 29.
Turned into verse, that no prose may come near Homer.
Whom shall we choose the glory of all wits,
Held through so many sorts of discipline
And such variety of works and spirits,
But Grecian Homer, like whom none did shine
For form of work and matter? And because
Our proud doom of him may stand justified
By noblest judgments, and receive applause
In spite of envy and illiterate pride,
Great Macedon, amongst his matchless spoils
Took from rich Persia, on his fortunes cast,
A casket finding, full of precious oils,
Form'd all of gold, with wealthy stones enchas'd,
He took the oils out, and his nearest friends
Ask'd in what better guard it might be us'd?
All giving their conceits to sev'ral ends,
He answer'd: "His affections rather choos'd
An use quite opposite to all their kinds,
And Homer's books should with that guard be serv'd,
That the most precious work of all men's minds
In the most precious place might be preserv'd.
The Fount of Wit was Homer, Learning's Sire,
And gave antiquity her living fire."

Volumes of like praise I could heap on this,
Of men more ancient and more learn'd than these,
But since true virtue enough lovely is
With her own beauties, all the suffrages
Of others I omit, and would more fain
That Homer for himself should be belov'd,
Who ev'ry sort of love-worth did contain.
Which how I have in my conversion prov'd
I must confess I hardly dare refer
To reading judgments, since, so gen'rally,
Custom hath made ev'n th' ablest agents err [1]
In these translations; all so much apply
Their pains and cunnings word for word to render
Their patient authors, when they may as well
Make fish with fowl, camels with whales, engender,
Or their tongues' speech in other mouths compell.
For, ev'n as diff'rent a production
Ask Greek and English, since as they in sounds
And letters shun one form and unison;
So have their sense and elegancy bounds
In their distinguish'd natures, and require
Only a judgment to make both consent
In sense and elocution; and aspire,
As well to reach the spirit that was spent
In his example, as with art to pierce
His grammar, and etymology of words.
But as great clerks can write no English verse, [2]
Because, alas, great clerks! English affords,
Say they, no height nor copy; a rude tongue,
Since 'tis their native; but in Greek or Latin
Their writs are rare, for thence true Poesy sprung;
Though them (truth knows) they have but skill to chat in,
Compar'd with that they might say in their own;
Since thither th' other's full soul cannot make
The ample transmigration to be shown
In nature-loving Poesy; so the brake
That those translators stick in, that affect
Their word-for-word traductions (where they lose
The free grace of their natural dialect,
And shame their authors with a forcéd gloss)
I laugh to see; and yet as much abhor [3]
More license from the words than may express
Their full compression, and make clear the author;
From whose truth, if you think my feet digress,
Because I use needful periphrases,
Read Valla, Hessus, that in Latin prose,
And verse, convert him; read the Messines
That into Tuscan turns him; and the gloss

Grave Salel makes in French, as he translates;
Which, for th' aforesaid reasons, all must do;
And see that my conversion much abates
The license they take, and more shows him too,
Whose right not all those great learn'd men have done,
In some main parts, that were his commentors.
But, as the illustration of the sun
Should be attempted by the erring stars,
They fail'd to search his deep and treasurous heart;
The cause was, since they wanted the fit key
Of Nature, in their downright strength of Art. [4]
With Poesy to open Poesy:
Which, in my poem of the mysteries
Reveal'd in Homer, I will clearly prove;
Till whose near birth, suspend your calumnies,
And far-wide imputations of self-love.
'Tis further from me than the worst that reads,
Professing me the worst of all that write;
Yet what, in following one that bravely leads,
The worst may show, let this proof hold the light.
But grant it clear; yet hath detraction got
My blind side in the form my verse puts on;
Much like a dung-hill mastiff, that dares not
Assault the man he barks at, but the stone
He throws at him takes in his eager jaws,
And spoils his teeth because they cannot spoil.
The long verse hath by proof receiv'd applause
Beyond each other number; and the foil,
That squint-ey'd Envy takes, is censur'd plain;
For this long poem asks this length of verse,
Which I myself ingenuously maintain
Too long our shorter authors to rehearse.
And, for our tongue that still is so impair'd [5]
By travelling linguists, I can prove it clear,
That no tongue hath the Muse's utt'rance heir'd
For verse, and that sweet music to the ear
Strook out of rhyme, so naturally as this;
Our monosyllables so kindly fall,
And meet oppos'd in rhyme as they did kiss;
French and Italian most immetrical,
Their many syllables in harsh collision
Fall as they break their necks; their bastard rhymes
Saluting as they justled in transition,
And set our teeth on edge; nor tunes, nor times
Kept in their falls; and, methinks, their long words
Shew in short verse as in a narrow place
Two opposites should meet with two-hand swords
Unwieldily, without or use or grace.

Thus having rid the rubs, and strow'd these flow'rs
In our thrice-sacred Homer's English way,
What rests to make him yet more worthy yours?
To cite more praise of him were mere delay
To your glad searches for what those men found
That gave his praise, past all, so high a place;
Whose virtues were so many, and so crown'd
By all consents divine, that, not to grace
Or add increase to them, the world doth need
Another Homer, but ev'n to rehearse
And number them, they did so much exceed.
Men thought him not a man; but that his verse
Some mere celestial nature did adorn;
And all may well conclude it could not be,
That for the place where any man was born,
So long and mortally could disagree
So many nations as for Homer striv'd,
Unless his spur in them had been divine.
Then end their strife and love him, thus receiv'd,
As born in England; see him over-shine
All other-country poets; and trust this,
That whosesoever Muse dares use her wing
When his Muse flies, she will be truss'd by his,
And show as if a bernacle should spring
Beneath an eagle. In none since was seen
A soul so full of heav'n as earth's in him.
O! if our modern Poesy had been
As lovely as the lady he did limn,
What barbarous worldling, grovelling after gain,
Could use her lovely parts with such rude hate,
As now she suffers under ev'ry swain?
Since then 'tis nought but her abuse and Fate,
That thus impairs her, what is this to her
As she is real, or in natural right?
But since in true Religion men should err
As much as Poesy, should the abuse excite
The like contempt of her divinity,
And that her truth, and right saint-sacred merits,
In most lives breed but rev'rence formally,
What wonder is't if Poesy inherits
Much less observance, being but agent for her,
And singer of her laws, that others say?
Forth then, ye moles, sons of the earth, abhor her,
Keep still on in the dirty vulgar way,
Till dirt receive your souls, to which ye vow,
And with your poison'd spirits bewitch our thrifts.
Ye cannot so despise us as we you;
Not one of you above his mole-hill lifts

His earthy mind, but, as a sort of beasts,
Kept by their guardians, never care to hear
Their manly voices, but when in their fists
They breathe wild whistles, and the beasts' rude ear
Hears their curs barking, then by heaps they fly
Headlong together; so men, beastly giv'n,
The manly soul's voice, sacred Poesy,
Whose hymns the angels ever sing in heav'n,
Contemn and hear not; but when brutish noises,
For gain, lust, honour, in litigious prose
Are bellow'd out, and crack the barbarous voices
Of Turkish stentors, O, ye lean to those,
Like itching horse to blocks or high may-poles;
And break nought but the wind of wealth, wealth, all
In all your documents; your asinine souls,
Proud of their burthens, feel not how they gall.
But as an ass, that in a field of weeds
Affects a thistle, and falls fiercely to it,
That pricks and galls him, yet he feeds, and bleeds,
Forbears a while, and licks, but cannot woo it
To leave the sharpness; when, to wreak his smart,
He beats it with his foot, then backward kicks,
Because the thistle gall'd his forward part;
Nor leaves till all be eat, for all the pricks,
Then falls to others with as hot a strife,
And in that honourable war doth waste
The tall heat of his stomach, and his life;
So in this world of weeds you worldlings taste
Your most-lov'd dainties, with such war buy peace,
Hunger for torment, virtue kick for vice,
Cares for your states do with your states increase,
And though ye dream ye feast in Paradise,
Yet reason's daylight shews ye at your meat
Asses at thistles, bleeding as ye eat.

THE PREFACE TO THE READER

Of all books extant in all kinds, Homer is the first and best. No one before his, Josephus affirms; nor before him, saith Velleius Paterculus, was there any whom he imitated, nor after him any that could imitate him. And that Poesy may be no cause of detraction from all the eminence we give him, Spondanus (preferring it to all arts and sciences) unanswerably argues and proves; for to the glory of God, and the singing of his glories, no man dares deny, man was chiefly made. And what art performs this chief end of man with so much excitation and expression as Poesy; Moses, David, Solomon, Job, Esay, Jeremy, etc. chiefly using that to the end abovesaid? And since the excellence of it cannot be obtained by the labour and art of man, as all easily confess it, it must needs be acknowledged a Divine infusion. To prove which in a word, this distich, in my estimation, serves something nearly:

Great Poesy, blind Homer, makes all see
Thee capable of all arts, none of thee.

For out of him, according to our most grave and judicial Plutarch, are all Arts deduced, confirmed, or illustrated. It is not therefore the world's vilifying of it that can make it vile; for so we might argue, and blaspheme the most incomparably sacred. It is not of the world indeed, but, like truth, hides itself from it. Nor is there any such reality of wisdom's truth in all human excellence, as in Poets' fictions. That most vulgar and foolish receipt of poetical licence being of all knowing men to be exploded, accepting it, as if Poets had a tale-telling privilege above others, no Artist being so strictly and inextricably confined to all the laws of learning, wisdom, and truth, as a Poet. For were not his fictions composed of the sinews and souls of all those, how could they defy fire, iron, and be combined with eternity? To all sciences therefore, I must still, with our learned and ingenious Spondanus, refer it, as having a perpetual commerce with the Divine Majesty, embracing and illustrating all His most holy precepts, and enjoying continual discourse with His thrice perfect and most comfortable Spirit. And as the contemplative life is most worthily and divinely preferred by Plato to the active, as much as the head to the foot, the eye to the hand, reason to sense, the soul to the body, the end itself to all things directed to the end, quiet to motion, and eternity to time; so much prefer I divine Poesy to all worldly wisdom. To the only shadow of whose worth, yet, I entitle not the bold rhymes of every apish and impudent braggart, though he dares assume anything; such I turn over to the weaving of cobwebs, and shall but chatter on molehills (far under the hill of the Muses) when their fortunatest self-love and ambition hath advanced them highest. Poesy is the flower of the Sun, and disdains to open to the eye of a candle. So kings hide their treasures and counsels from the vulgar, ne evilescant (saith our Spond.). We have example sacred enough, that true Poesy's humility, poverty, and contempt, are badges of divinity, not vanity. Bray then, and bark against it, ye wolf-faced worldlings, that nothing but honours, riches, and magistracy, nescio quos turgidè spiratis (that I may use the words of our friend still) qui solas leges Justinianas crepatis; paragraphum unum aut alterum, pluris quàm vos ipsos facitis, etc. I (for my part) shall ever esteem it much more manly and sacred, in this harmless and pious study, to sit till I sink into my grave, than shine in your vainglorious bubbles and impieties; all your poor policies, wisdoms, and their trappings, at no more valuing than a musty nut. And much less I weigh the frontless detractions of some stupid ignorants, that, no more knowing me than their own beastly ends, and I ever (to my knowledge) blest from their sight, whisper behind me vilifyings of my translation, out of the French affirming them, when both in French, and all other languages but his own, our with-all-skill-enriched Poet is so poor and unpleasing that no man can discern from whence flowed his so generally given eminence and admiration. And therefore (by any reasonable creature's conference of my slight comment and conversion) it will easily appear how I shun them, and whether the original be my rule or not. In which he shall easily see, I understand the understandings of all other interpreters and commentors in places of his most depth, importance, and rapture. In whose exposition and illustration, if I abhor from the sense that others wrest and wrack out of him, let my best detractor examine how the Greek word warrants me. For my other fresh fry, let them fry in their foolish galls, nothing so much weighed as the barkings of the puppies, or foisting hounds, too vile to think of our sacred Homer, or set their profane feet within their lives' length of his thresholds. If I fail in something, let my full performance in other some restore me; haste spurring me on with other necessities. For as at my conclusion I protest, so here at my entrance, less than fifteen weeks was the time in which all the last twelve books were entirely new translated. No conference had with anyone living in all the novelties I presume I have found. Only some one or two places I have showed to my worthy and most learned friend, M. Harriots, for his censure how much mine own weighed; whose judgment and knowledge in all kinds, I know to be incomparable and bottomless, yea, to be admired as much, as his most blameless life, and the right sacred expense of his time, is to be honoured and reverenced. Which affirmation of his clear unmatchedness in all manner of learning I make in contempt of that nasty objection often thrust upon me,—that he that will judge must know more than he of whom he judgeth; for so a man should know neither God nor himself. Another right learned, honest, and entirely loved friend of mine, M. Robert Hews, I must needs put into my confess'd conference touching Homer, though very little more than that I had with M. Harriots. Which two, I protest, are all, and preferred to all. Nor charge I their authorities with, any allowance of my general labour, but only of those one or two places, which for instances of my innovation, and how it showed to them, I imparted. If any tax me for too much periphrasis or circumlocution in some places, let them read Laurentius Valla, and Eobanus Hessus, who either use such shortness as cometh nothing home to Homer, or, where they shun that fault, are ten parts more paraphrastical than I. As for example, one place I will trouble you (if you please) to confer with the original, and one interpreter for all. It is in the end of the third book, and is Helen's speech to Venus fetching her to Paris from seeing his cowardly combat with Menelaus; part of which speech I will here cite:

Οὕνεκα δὴ νῦν δῖον Ἀλέξανδρον Μενέλαος
Νικήσας, etc.

For avoiding the common reader's trouble here, I must refer the more Greekish to the rest of the speech in Homer, whose translation ad verbum by Spondanus I will here cite, and then pray you to confer it with that which followeth of Valla.

Quoniam verò nunc Alexandrum Menelaus
Postquam vicit, vult odiosam me domum abducere,
Propterea verò nunc dolum (seu dolos) cogitans advenisti?
Sede apud ipsum vadens, deorum abnega vias,
Neque unquam tuis pedibus revertaris in cœlum,
Sed semper circa eum ærumnas perfer, et ipsum serva
Donec te vel uxorem faciat, vel hic servam, etc.
Valla thus:

Quoniam victo Paride, Menelaus me miseram est reportaturus ad lares, ideo tu, ideo falsâ sub imagine venisti, ut me deciperes ob tuam nimiam in Paridem benevolentiam: eò dum illi ades, dum illi studes, dum pro illo satagis, dum illum observas atque custodis, deorum commercium reliquisti, nec ad eos reversura es ampliùs: adeò (quantum suspicor) aut uxor ejus efficieris, aut ancilla, etc.

Wherein note if there be any such thing as most of this in Homer; yet only to express, as he thinks, Homer's conceit, for the more pleasure of the reader, he useth this overplus, dum illi ades, dum illi studes, dum pro illo satagis, dum ilium observas, atque custodis, deorum commercium reliquisti. Which (besides his superfluity) is utterly false. For where he saith reliquisti deorum commercium, Helen saith, θεῶν δ᾽ἀπόειπε κελεύθους, deorum auten abnega or abnue, vias, ἀπείπειν (vel ἀποείπειν as it is used poetically) signifying denegare or aonuere; and Helen (in contempt of her too much observing men) bids her renounce heaven, and come live with Paris till he make her his wife or servant; scoptically or scornfully speaking it; which both Valla, Eobanus, and all other interpreters (but these ad verbum) have utterly missed. And this one example I thought necessary to insert here, to show my detractors that they have no reason to vilify my circumlocution sometimes, when their most approved Grecians, Homer's interpreters generally, hold him fit to be so converted. Yet how much I differ, and with what authority, let my impartial and judicial reader judge. Always conceiving how pedantical and absurd an affectation it is in the interpretation of any author (much more of Homer) to turn him word for word, when according to Horace and other best lawgivers to translators) it is the part of every knowing and judicial interpreter, not to follow the number and order of words, but the material things themselves, and sentences to weigh diligently, and to clothe and adorn them with words, and such a style and form of oration, as are most apt for the language in which they are converted. If I have not turned him ill any place falsely (as all other his interpreters have in many, and most of his chief places) if I have not left behind me any of his sentences, elegancy, height, intention, and invention, if in some few places (especially in my first edition, being done so long since, and following the common tract) I be something paraphrastical and faulty, is it justice in that poor fault (if they will needs have it so) to drown all the rest of my labour? But there is a certain envious windsucker, that hovers up and down, laboriously engrossing all the air with his luxurious ambition, and buzzing into every ear my detraction, affirming I turn Homer out of the Latin only, etc. that sets all his associates, and the whole rabble of my maligners on their wings with him, to bear about my impair, and poison my reputation. One that, as he thinks, whatsoever he gives to others, he takes from himself; so whatsoever he takes from others, he adds to himself. One that in this kind of robbery doth like Mercury, that stole good and supplied it with counterfeit bad still. One like the two gluttons, Philoxenus and Gnatho, that would still empty their noses in the dishes they loved, that no man might eat but themselves. For so this castrill, with too hot a liver, and lust after his own glory, and to devour all himself, discourageth all appetites to the fame of another. I have stricken, single him as you can. Nor note I this, to cast any rubs or plashes out of the particular way of mine own estimation with the world; for I resolve this with the wilfully obscure:

Sine honore vivam, nulloque numero ero.

Without men's honours I will live, and make
No number in the manless course they take.

But, to discourage (if it might be) the general detraction of industrious and well-meaning virtue, I know I cannot too much diminish and deject myself; yet that passing little that I am, God only knows, to Whose ever-implored respect and comfort I only submit me. If any further edition of these my silly endeavours shall chance, I will mend what is amiss (God assisting me) and amplify my harsh Comment to Homer's far more right, and mine own earnest and ingenious love of him. Notwithstanding, I know, the curious and envious will never sit down satisfied. A man may go over and over, till he come over and over, and his pains be only his recompense, every man is so loaded with his particular head, and nothing in all respects perfect, but what is perceived by few. Homer himself hath met with my fortune, in many maligners; and therefore may my poor self put up without motion. And so little I will respect malignity, and so much encourage myself with mine own known strength, and what I find within me of comfort and confirmance (examining myself throughout with a far more jealous and severe eye than my greatest enemy, imitating this:

Judex ipse sui totum se explorat ad unguem, etc.)

that after these Iliads, I will (God lending me life and any meanest means) with more labour than I have lost here, and all unchecked alacrity, dive through his Odysseys. Nor can I forget here (but with all hearty gratitude remember) my most ancient, learned, and right noble friend, M. Richard Stapilton, first most desertful mover in the frame of our Homer. For which (and much other most ingenious and utterly undeserved desert) God make me amply his requiter; and be his honourable family's speedy and full restorer. In the mean space, I entreat my impartial and judicial Reader, that all things to the quick he will not pare, but humanely and nobly pardon defects, and, if he find anything perfect, receive it unenvied.

Of his country and time, the difference is so infinite amongst all writers, that there is no question, in my conjecture, of his antiquity beyond all. To which opinion, the nearest I will cite, Adam Cedrenus placeth him under David's and Solomon's rule; and the Destruction of Troy under Saul's. And of one age with Solomon, Michael Glycas Siculus affirmeth him. Aristotle (in tertio de Poeticâ) affirms he was born in the isle of Io, begot of a Genius, one of them that used to dance with the Muses, and a virgin of that isle compressed by that Genius, who being quick with child (for shame of the deed) came into a place called Ægina, and there was taken of thieves, and brought to Smyrna, to Mæon king of the Lydians, who for her beauty married her. After which, she walking near the flood Meletes, on that shore being overtaken with the throes of her delivery, she brought forth Homer, and instantly died. The infant was received by Mæon, and brought up as his own till his death, which was not long after. And, according to this, when the Lydians in Smyrna were afflicted by the Æolians, and thought fit to leave the city, the captains by a herald willing all to go out that would, and follow them, Homer, being a little child, said he would also ὁμηρεῖν (that is, sequi); and of that, for Melesigenes, which was his first name, he was called Homer. These Plutarch.

The varieties of other reports touching this I omit for length; and in place thereof think it not unfit to insert something of his praise and honour amongst the greatest of all ages; not that our most absolute of himself needs it, but that such authentical testimonies of his splendour and excellence may the better convince the malice of his maligners.

First, what kind of person Homer was, saith Spondanus, his statue teacheth, which Cedrenus describeth. The whole place we will describe that our relation may hold the better coherence, as Xylander converts it. "Then was the Octagonon at Constantinople consumed with fire; and the bath of Severus, that bore the name of Zeuxippus, in which there was much variety of spectacle, and splendour of arts; the works of all ages being conferred and preserved there, of marble, rocks, stones, and images of brass; to which this only wanted, that the souls of the persons they presented were not in them. Amongst these master-pieces and all-wit-exceeding workmanships stood Homer, as he was in his age, thoughtful and musing, his hands folded beneath his bosom, his beard untrimm'd and hanging down, the hair of his head in like sort thin on both sides before, his face with age and cares of the world, as these imagine, wrinkled and austere, his nose proportioned to his other parts, his eyes fixed or turned up to his eyebrows, like one blind, as it is reported he was." (Not born blind, saith Vell. Paterculus, which he that imagines, saith he, is blind of all senses.) "Upon his under-coat he was attired with a loose robe, and at the base beneath his feet a brazen chain hung." This was the statue of Homer, which in that conflagration perished. Another renowned statue of his, saith Lucian in his Encomion of Demosthenes, stood in the temple of Ptolemy, on the upper hand of his own statue. Cedrenus likewise remembereth a library in the palace of the king, at Constantinople, that contained a thousand a hundred and twenty books, amongst which there was the gut of a dragon of an hundred and twenty foot long, in which, in letters of gold, the Iliads and Odysseys of Homer were inscribed; which miracle, in Basiliscus the Emperor's time, was consumed with fire.

For his respect amongst the most learned, Plato in Ione calleth him ἄριστον καὶ θειότατον τῶν ποιητῶν, Poeta rum omnium et præstantissimum et divinissimum; in Phædone, θεῖον ποιητὴν, divinum Poetam; and in Theætetus, Socrates citing divers of the most wise and learned for confirmation of his there held opinion, as Protagoras, Heraclitus, Empedocles, Epicharmus, and Homer, who, saith Socrates, against such an army, being all led by such a captain as Homer, dares fight or resist, but he will be held ridiculous? This for Scaliger and all Homer's envious and ignorant detractors. Why therefore Plato in another place banisheth him with all other poets out of his Commonwealth, dealing with them like a Politician indeed, use men, and then cast them off, though Homer he thinks fit to send out crowned and anointed, I see not, since he maketh still such honourable mention of him, and with his verses, as with precious gems, everywhere enchaceth his writings. So Aristotle continually celebrateth him. Nay, even amongst the barbarous, not only Homer's name, but his poems have been recorded and reverenced. The Indians, saith Ælianus (Var. Hist. lib. xii. cap. 48) in their own tongue had Homer's Poems translated and sung. Nor those Indians alone, but the kings of Persia. And amongst the Indians, of all the Greek poets, Homer being ever first in estimation; whensoever they used any divine duties according to the custom of their households and hospitalities, they invited ever Apollo and Homer. Lucian in his Encomion of Demosth. affirmeth all Poets celebrated Homer's birthday, and sacrificed to him the first fruits of their verses. So Thersagoras answereth Lucian, he used to do himself. Alex. Paphius, saith Eustathius, delivers Homer as born of Egyptian parents, Dmasagoras being his father, and Æthra his mother, his nurse being a certain prophetess and the daughter of Oris, Isis' priest, from whose breasts, oftentimes, honey flowed in the mouth of the infant. After which, in the night, he uttered nine several notes or voices of fowls, viz. of a swallow, a peacock, a dove, a crow, a partridge, a redshank, a stare, a blackbird, and a nightingale; and, being a little boy, was found playing in his bed with nine doves. Sibylla being at a feast of his parents was taken with sudden fury, and sung verses whose beginning was Δμασαγ ὁρα πολύνικε; polynice, signifying much victory, in which song also she called him μεγάκλεα, great in glory, and στεφανίτην, signifying garland-seller, and commanded him to build a temple to the Pegridarij, that is, to the Muses. Herodotus affirms that Phæmius, teaching a public school at Smyrna, was his master; and Dionysius in his 56th Oration saith, Socrates was Homer's scholar. In short, what he was, his works show most truly; to which, if you please, go on and examine him.

FOOTNOTES

[1] Of Translation, and the natural difference of Dialects necessarily to be observed in it.

[2] Ironicè.

[3] The necessary nearness of Translation to the example.

[4] The power of Nature above Art in Poesy.

[5] Our English language above all others for Rhythmical Poesy.

THE FIRST BOOK OF HOMER'S ILIADS

THE ARGUMENT

Apollo's priest to th' Argive fleet doth bring
Gifts for his daughter, pris'ner to the king;
For which her tender'd freedom he entreats;
But, being dismiss'd with contumelious threats,
At Phœbus' hands, by vengeful pray'r, he seeks

To have a plague inflicted on the Greeks.
Which had; Achilles doth a council cite,
Embold'ning Calchas, in the king's despite;
To tell the truth why they were punish'd so.
From hence their fierce and deadly strife did grow.
For wrong in which Æacides so raves,
That goddess Thetis, from her throne of waves
Ascending heav'n, of Jove assistance won,
To plague the Greeks by absence of her son,
And make the general himself repent
To wrong so much his army's ornament.
This found by Juno, she with Jove contends;
Till Vulcan, with heav'n's cup, the quarrel ends.

ANOTHER ARGUMENT

Alpha the prayer of Chryses sings:
The army's plague: the strife of kings.
Achilles' baneful wrath resound, O Goddess, that impos'd
Infinite sorrows on the Greeks, and many brave souls los'd.
From breasts heroic; sent them far to that invisible cave
That no light comforts; and their limbs to dogs and vultures gave;
To all which Jove's will gave effect; from whom first strife begun
Betwixt Atrides, king of men, and Thetis' godlike son.
What god gave Eris their command, and op'd that fighting vein?
Jove's and Latona's son: who fir'd against the king of men,
For contumély shown his priest, infectious sickness sent
To plague the army, and to death by troops the soldiers went.
Occasion'd thus: Chryses, the priest, came to the fleet to buy,
For presents of unvalu'd price, his daughter's liberty;
The golden sceptre and the crown of Phœbus in his hands
Proposing; and made suit to all, but most to the commands
Of both th' Atrides, who most rul'd. "Great Atreus' sons," said he,
"And all ye well-greav'd Greeks, the gods, whose habitations be
In heav'nly houses, grace your pow'rs with Priam's razéd town,
And grant ye happy conduct home! To win which wish'd renown
Of Jove, by honouring his son, far-shooting Phœbus, deign
For these fit presents to dissolve the ransomable chain
Of my lov'd daughter's servitude." The Greeks entirely gave
Glad acclamations, for sign that their desires would have
The grave priest reverenc'd, and his gifts of so much price embrac'd.
The Gen'ral yet bore no such mind, but viciously disgrac'd
With violent terms the priest, and said:—"Dotard! avoid our fleet,
Where ling'ring be not found by me; nor thy returning feet
Let ever visit us again; lest nor thy godhead's crown,
Nor sceptre, save thee! Her thou seek'st I still will hold mine own,
Till age deflow'r her. In our court at Argos, far transferr'd

From her lov'd country, she shall ply her web, and see prepar'd 1]
With all fit ornaments my bed. Incense me then no more,
But, if thou wilt be safe, be gone." This said, the sea-beat shore,
Obeying his high will, the priest trod off with haste and fear;
And, walking silent, till he left far off his enemies' ear,
Phœbus, fair hair'd Latona's son, he stirr'd up with a vow,
To this stern purpose: "Hear, thou God that bear'st the silver bow,
That Chrysa guard'st, rul'st Tenedos with strong hand, and the round
Of Cilia most divine dost walk! O Sminthëus! if crown'd
With thankful off'rings thy rich fane I ever saw, or fir'd
Fat thighs of oxen and of goats to thee, this grace desir'd
Vouchsafe to me: pains for my tears let these rude Greeks repay,
Forc'd with thy arrows." Thus he pray'd, and Phœbus heard him pray,
And, vex'd at heart, down from the tops of steep heav'n stoop'd; his bow,
And quiver cover'd round, his hands did on his shoulders throw;
And of the angry Deity the arrows as he mov'd
Rattled about him. Like the night he rang'd the host, and rov'd
(Apart the fleet set) terribly; with his hard-loosing hand
His silver bow twang'd; and his shafts did first the mules command,
And swift hounds; then the Greeks themselves his deadly arrows shot.
The fires of death went never out; nine days his shafts flew hot
About the army; and the tenth, Achilles called a court
Of all the Greeks; heav'n's white-arm'd Queen (who, ev'rywhere cut short,
Beholding her lov'd Greeks, by death) suggested it; and he
(All met in one) arose, and said: "Atrides, now I see
We must be wandering again, flight must be still our stay,
If flight can save us now, at once sickness and battle lay
Such strong hand on us. Let us ask some prophet, priest, or prove
Some dream-interpreter (for dreams are often sent from Jove)
Why Phœbus is so much incens'd; if unperformed vows
He blames in us, or hecatombs; and if these knees he bows
To death may yield his graves no more, but off'ring all supply
Of savours burnt from lambs and goats, avert his fervent eye,
And turn his temp'rate." Thus, he sat; and then stood up to them
Calchas, surnam'd Thestorides, of augurs the supreme;
He knew things present, past, to come, and rul'd the equipage
Of th' Argive fleet to Ilion, for his prophetic rage
Giv'n by Apollo; who, well-seen in th' ill they felt, propos'd
This to Achilles: "Jove's belov'd, would thy charge see disclos'd
The secret of Apollo's wrath? then cov'nant and take oath
To my discov'ry, that, with words and pow'rful actions both,
Thy strength will guard the truth in me; because I well conceive
That he whose empire governs all, whom all the Grecians give
Confirm'd obedience, will be mov'd; and then you know the state
Of him that moves him. When a king hath once mark'd for his hate
A man inferior, though that day his wrath seems to digest
Th' offence he takes, yet evermore he rakes up in his breast
Brands of quick anger, till revenge hath quench'd to his desire

The fire reservéd. Tell me, then, if, whatsoever ire
Suggests in hurt of me to him, thy valour will prevent?"
Achilles answer'd: "All thou know'st speak, and be confident;
For by Apollo, Jove's belov'd, (to whom performing vows,
O Calchas, for the state of Greece, thy spirit prophetic shows
Skills that direct us) not a man of all these Grecians here,
I living, and enjoy'ng the light shot through this flow'ry sphere,
Shall touch thee with offensive hands; though Agamemnon be
The man in question, that doth boast the mightiest empery
Of all our army." Then took heart the prophet unreprov'd,
And said: "They are not unpaid vows, nor hecatombs, that mov'd
The God against us; his offence is for his priest impair'd
By Agamemnon, that refus'd the present he preferr'd,
And kept his daughter. This is cause why heav'n's Far-darter darts
These plagues amongst us; and this still will empty in our hearts
His deathful quiver, uncontain'd till to her lovéd sire
The black-eyed damsel be resign'd; no rédemptory hire
Took for her freedom,-not a gift, but all the ransom quit,
And she convey'd, with sacrifice, till her enfranchis'd feet
Tread Chrysa under; then the God, so pleas'd, perhaps we may
Move to remission." Thus, he sate; and up, the great in sway,
Heroic Agamemnon rose, eagérly bearing all;
His mind's seat overcast with fumes; an anger general
Fill'd all his faculties; his eyes sparkled like kindling fire,
Which sternly cast upon the priest, thus vented he his ire:
"Prophet of ill! for never good came from thee towards me
Not to a word's worth; evermore thou took'st delight to be
Offensive in thy auguries, which thou continu'st still,
Now casting thy prophetic gall, and vouching all our ill,
Shot from Apollo, is impos'd since I refus'd the price
Of fair Chryseis' liberty; which would in no worth rise
To my rate of herself, which moves my vows to have her home,
Past Clytemnestra loving her, that grac'd my nuptial room
With her virginity and flow'r. Nor ask her merits less
For person, disposition, wit, and skill in housewif'ries.
And yet, for all this, she shall go, if more conducible
That course be than her holding here. I rather wish the weal
Of my lov'd army than the death. Provide yet instantly
Supply for her, that I alone of all our royalty
Lose not my winnings. 'Tis not fit. Ye see all I lose mine
Forc'd by another, see as well some other may resign
His prise to me." To this replied the swift-foot, god-like, son
Of Thetis, thus: "King of us all, in all ambition
Most covetous of all that breathe, why should the great-soul'd Greeks
Supply thy lost prise out of theirs? Nor what thy av'rice seeks
Our common treasury can find; so little it doth guard
Of what our ras'd towns yielded us; of all which most is shar'd,
And giv'n our soldiers; which again to take into our hands

Were ignominious and base. Now then, since God commands,
Part with thy most-lov'd prise to him; not any one of us
Exacts it of thee, yet we all, all loss thou suffer'st thus,
Will treble, quadruple, in gain, when Jupiter bestows
The sack of well-wall'd Troy on us; which by his word he owes."
"Do not deceive yourself with wit," he answer'd, "god-like man,
Though your good name may colour it; 'tis not your swift foot can
Outrun me here; nor shall the gloss, set on it with the God,
Persuade me to my wrong. Wouldst thou maintain in sure abode
Thine own prise, and slight me of mine? Resolve this: if our friends,
As fits in equity my worth, will right me with amends,
So rest it; otherwise, myself will enter personally
On thy prise, that of Ithacus, or Ajax, for supply;
Let him on whom I enter rage. But come, we'll order these
Hereafter, and in other place. Now put to sacred seas
Our black sail; in it rowers put, in it fit sacrifice;
And to these I will make ascend my so much envied prise,
Bright-cheek'd Chryseis. For conduct of all which, we must choose
A chief out of our counsellors. Thy service we must use,
Idomenëus; Ajax, thine; or thine, wise Ithacus;
Or thine, thou terriblest of men, thou son of Peleüs,
Which fittest were, that thou might'st see these holy acts perform'd
For which thy cunning zeal so pleads; and he, whose bow thus storm'd
For our offences, may be calm'd." Achilles, with a frown,
Thus answer'd: "O thou impudent! of no good but thine own
Ever respectful, but of that with all craft covetous,
With what heart can a man attempt a service dangerous,
Or at thy voice be spirited to fly upon a foe,
Thy mind thus wretched? For myself, I was not injur'd so
By any Trojan, that my pow'rs should bid them any blows;
In nothing bear they blame of me; Phthia, whose bosom flows
With corn and people, never felt impair of her increase
By their invasion; hills enow, and far-resounding seas,
Pour out their shades and deeps between; but thee, thou frontless man,
We follow, and thy triumphs make with bonfires of our bane;
Thine, and thy brother's, vengeance sought, thou dog's eyes, of this Troy
By our expos'd lives; whose deserts thou neither dost employ
With honour nor with care. And now, thou threat'st to force from me
The fruit of my sweat, which the Greeks gave all; and though it be,
Compar'd with thy part, then snatch'd up, nothing; nor ever is
At any sack'd town; but of fight, the fetcher in of this,
My hands have most share; in whose toils when I have emptied me
Of all my forces, my amends in liberality,
Though it be little, I accept, and turn pleas'd to my tent;
And yet that little thou esteem'st too great a continent
In thy incontinent avarice. For Phthia therefore now
My course is; since 'tis better far, than here t' endure that thou
Should'st still be ravishing my right, draw my whole treasure dry,

And add dishonour." He replied: "If thy heart serve thee, fly;
Stay not for my cause; others here will aid and honour me;
If not, yet Jove I know is sure; that counsellor is he
That I depend on. As for thee, of all our Jove-kept kings
Thou still art most my enemy; strifes, battles, bloody things,
Make thy blood-feasts still. But if strength, that these moods build upon,
Flow in thy nerves, God gave thee it; and so 'tis not thine own,
But in his hands still. What then lifts thy pride in this so high?
Home with thy fleet, and Myrmidons; use there their empery;
Command not here. I weigh thee not, nor mean to magnify
Thy rough-hewn rages, but, instead, I thus far threaten thee:
Since Phœbus needs will force from me Chryseis, she shall go;
My ships and friends shall waft her home; but I will imitate so
His pleasure, that mine own shall take, in person, from thy tent
Bright-cheek'd Briseis; and so tell thy strength how eminent
My pow'r is, being compar'd with thine; all other making fear
To vaunt equality with me, or in this proud kind bear
Their beards against me." Thetis' son at this stood vex'd, his heart
Bristled his bosom, and two ways drew his discursive part;
If, from his thigh his sharp sword drawn, he should make room about
Atrides' person, slaught'ring him, or sit his anger out,
And curb his spirit. While these thoughts striv'd in his blood and mind,
And he his sword drew, down from heav'n Athenia stoop'd, and shin'd
About his temples, being sent by th' ivory-wristed Queen,
Saturnia, who out of her heart had ever loving been,
And careful for the good of both. She stood behind, and took
Achilles by the yellow curls, and only gave her look
To him appearance; not a man of all the rest could see.
He turning back his eye, amaze strook every faculty;
Yet straight he knew her by her eyes, so terrible they were,
Sparkling with ardour, and thus spake: "Thou seed of Jupiter,
Why com'st thou? To behold his pride, that boasts our empery?
Then witness with it my revenge, and see that insolence die
That lives to wrong me." She replied: "I come from heav'n to see
Thy anger settled, if thy soul will use her sov'reignty
In fit reflection. I am sent from Juno, whose affects
Stand heartily inclin'd to both. Come, give us both respects,
And cease contention; draw no sword; use words, and such as may
Be bitter to his pride, but just; for, trust in what I say,
A time shall come, when, thrice the worth of that he forceth now,
He shall propose for recompense of these wrongs; therefore throw
Reins on thy passions, and serve us." He answer'd "Though my heart
Burn in just anger, yet my soul must conquer th' angry part,
And yield you conquest. Who subdues his earthly part for heav'n,
Heav'n to his pray'rs subdues his wish." This said, her charge was given
Fit honour; in his silver hilt he held his able hand,
And forc'd his broad sword up; and up to heav'n did re-ascend
Minerva, who, in Jove's high roof that bears the rough shield, took

Her place with other deities. She gone, again forsook
Patience his passion, and no more his silence could confine
His wrath, that this broad language gave: "Thou ever steep'd in wine,
Dog's face, with heart but of a hart, that nor in th' open eye
Of fight dar'st thrust into a prease, nor with our noblest lie
In secret ambush! These works seem too full of death for thee;
'Tis safer far in the open host to dare an injury
To any crosser of thy lust. Thou subject-eating king!
Base spirits thou govern'st, or this wrong had been the last foul thing
Thou ever author'dst; yet I vow, and by a great oath swear,
Ev'n by this sceptre, that, as this never again shall bear [2]
Green leaves or branches, nor increase with any growth his size,
Nor did since first it left the hills, and had his faculties
And ornaments bereft with iron; which now to other end
Judges of Greece bear, and their' laws, receiv'd from Jove, defend;
(For which my oath to thee is great); so, whensoever need
Shall burn with thirst of me thy host, no pray'rs shall ever breed
Affection in me to their aid, though well-deserved woes
Afflict thee for them, when to death man-slaught'ring Hector throws
Whole troops of them, and thou torment'st thy vex'd mind with conceit
Of thy rude rage now, and his wrong that most deserv'd the right
Of all thy army." Thus, he threw his sceptre 'gainst the ground,
With golden studs stuck, and took seat. Atrides' breast was drown'd
In rising choler. Up to both sweet-spoken Nestor stood,
The cunning Pylian orator, whose tongue pour'd forth a flood
Of more-than-honey-sweet discourse; two ages were increas'd
Of divers-languag'd men, all born in his time and deceas'd,
In sacred Pylos, where he reign'd amongst the third-ag'd men
He, well-seen in the world, advis'd, and thus express'd it then:
"O Gods! Our Greek earth will be drown'd in just tears; rapeful Troy,
Her king, and all his sons, will make as just a mock, and joy,
Of these disjunctions; if of you, that all our host excel
In counsel and in skill of fight, they hear this. Come, repel
These young men's passions. Y' are not both, put both your years in one,
So old as I. I liv'd long since, and was companion
With men superior to you both, who yet would ever hear
My counsels with respect. My eyes yet never witness were,
Nor ever will be, of such men as then delighted them;
Pirithous, Exadius, and god-like Polypheme,
Cæneus, and Dryas prince of men, Ægean Theseüs,
A man like heav'n's immortals form'd; all, all most vigorous,
Of all men that ev'n those days: bred; most vig'rous men, and fought
With beasts most vig'rous, mountain beasts, (for men in strength were nought
Match'd with their forces) fought with them, and bravely fought them down
Yet ev'n with these men I convers'd, being call'd to the renown
Of their societies, by their suits, from Pylos far, to fight
In th' Apian kingdom; and I fought, to a degree of might
That help'd ev'n their mights, against such as no man now would dare

To meet in conflict; yet ev'n these my counsels still would hear,
And with obedience crown my words. Give you such palm to them;
'Tis better than to wreath your wraths. Atrides, give not stream
To all thy pow'r, nor force his prise, but yield her still his own,
As all men else do. Nor do thou encounter with thy crown,
Great son of Peleus, since no king that ever Jove allow'd
Grace of a sceptre equals him. Suppose thy nerves endow'd
With strength superior, and thy birth a very goddess gave,
Yet he of force is mightier, since what his own nerves have
Is amplified with just command of many other. King of men,
Command thou then thyself; and I with my pray'rs will obtain
Grace of Achilles to subdue his fury; whose parts are
Worth our entreaty, being chief check to all our ill in war."
"All this, good father," said the king, "is comely and good right;
But this man breaks all such bounds; he affects, past all men, height;
All would in his pow'r hold, all make his subjects, give to all
His hot will for their temp'rate law; all which he never shall
Persuade at my hands. If the gods have giv'n him the great style
Of ablest soldier, made they that his licence to revile
Men with vile language?" Thetis' son prevented him, and said:
"Fearful and vile I might be thought, if the exactions laid
By all means on me I should bear. Others command to this,
Thou shalt not me; or if thou dost, far my free spirit is
From serving thy command. Beside, this I affirm (afford
Impression of it in thy soul): will not use my sword
On thee or any for a wench, unjustly though thou tak'st
The thing thou gav'st; but all things else, that in my ship thou mak'st
Greedy survey of, do not touch without my leave; or do,—
Add that act's wrong to this, that these may see that outrage too,—
And then comes my part; then be sure, thy blood upon my lance
Shall flow in vengeance." These high terms these two at variance
Us'd to each other; left their seats; and after them arose
The whole court. To his tents and ships, with friends and soldiers, goes
Angry Achilles. Atreus' son the swift ship launch'd, and put
Within it twenty chosen row'rs, within it likewise shut
The hecatomb t' appease the God; then caus'd to come aboard
Fair-cheek'd Chryseis; for the chief, he in whom Pallas pour'd
Her store of counsels, Ithacus, aboard went last; and then
The moist ways of the sea they sail'd. And now the king of men
Bade all the host to sacrifice. They sacrific'd, and cast
The offal of all to the deeps; the angry God they grac'd
With perfect hecatombs; some bulls, some goats, along the shore
Of the unfruitful sea, inflam'd. To heav'n the thick fumes bore
Enwrapped savours. Thus, though all the politic king made shew
Respects to heav'n, yet he himself all that time did pursue
His own affections; the late jar, in which he thunder'd threats
Against Achilles, still he fed, and his affections' heats
Thus vented to Talthybius, and grave Eurybates,

Heralds, and ministers of trust, to all his messages.
"Haste to Achilles' tent; where take Briseis' hand, and bring
Her beauties to us. If he fail to yield her, say your king
Will come himself, with multitudes that shall the horribler
Make both his presence, and your charge, that so he dares defer."
This said, he sent them with a charge of hard condition.
They went unwillingly, and trod the fruitless sea's shore; soon
They reach'd the navy and the tents, in which the quarter lay
Of all the Myrmidons, and found the chief Chief in their sway
Set at his black bark in his tent. Nor was Achilles glad
To see their presence; nor themselves in any glory had
Their message, but with rev'rence stocd, and fear'd th' offended king,
Ask'd not the dame, nor spake a word. He yet, well knowing the thing
That caus'd their coming, grac'd them thus: "Heralds, ye men that bear
The messages of men and gods, y' are welcome, come ye near.
I nothing blame you, but your king; 'tis he I know doth send
You for Briseis; she is his. Patroclus, honour'd friend,
Bring forth the damsel, and these men let lead her to their lord.
But, heralds, be you witnesses, before the most ador'd,
Before us mortals, and before your most ungentle king,
Of what I suffer, that, if war ever hereafter bring
My aid in question, to avert any severest bane
It brings on others, I am 'scus'd to keep mine aid in wane,
Since they mine honour. But your king, in tempting mischief, raves,
Nor sees at once by present things the future; how like waves
Ills follow ills; injustices being never so secure
In present times, but after-plagues ev'n then are seen as sure;
Which yet he sees not, and so soothes his present lust, which, check'd,
Would check plagues future; and he might, in succouring right, protect
Such as fight for his right at fleet. They still in safety fight,
That fight still justly." This speech us'd, Patroclus did the rite
His friend commanded, and brought forth Briseis from her tent,
Gave her the heralds, and away to th' Achive ships they went.
She sad, and scarce for grief could go. Her love all friends forsook,
And wept for anger. To the shore of th' old sea he betook
Himself alone, and casting forth upon the purple sea
His wet eyes, and his hands to heav'n advancing, this sad plea
Made to his mother; "Mother! Since you brought me forth to breathe
So short a life, Olympius had good right to bequeath
My short life honour; yet that right he doth in no degree,
But lets Atrides do me shame, and force that prise from me
That all the Greeks gave." This with tears he utter'd, and she heard,
Set with her old sire in his deeps, and instantly appear'd
Up from the grey sea like a cloud, sate by his side, and said:
"Why weeps my son? What grieves thee?
Speak, conceal not what hath laid
Such hard hand on thee, let both know." He, sighing like a storm,
Replied: "Thou dost know. Why should I things known again inform?

We march'd to Thebes, the sacred town of king Eëtion,
Sack'd it, and brought to fleet the spoil, which every valiant son
Of Greece indifferently shar'd. Atrides had for share
Fair-cheek'd Chryseis. After which, his priest that shoots so far,
Chryses, the fair Chryseis' sire, arriv'd at th' Achive fleet,
With infinite ransom, to redeem the dear imprison'd feet
Of his fair daughter. In his hands he held Apollo's crown,
And golden sceptre; making suit to ev'ry Grecian son,
But most the sons of Atreüs, the others' orderers,
Yet they least heard him; all the rest receiv'd with rev'rend ears
The motion, both the priest and gifts gracing, and holding worth
His wish'd acceptance. Atreus' son yet (vex'd) commanded forth
With rude terms Phœbus' rev'rend priest; who, angry, made retreat,
And pray'd to Phœbus, in whose grace he standing passing great
Got his petitión. The God an ill shaft sent abroad
That tumbled down the Greeks in heaps. The host had no abode
That was not visited. We ask'd a prophet that well knew
The cause of all; and from his lips Apollo's prophecies flew,
Telling his anger. First myself exhorted to appease
The anger'd God; which Atreus' son did at the heart displease,
And up he stood, us'd threats, perform'd. The black-eyed Greeks sent home
Chryseis to her sire, and gave his God a hecatomb.
Then, for Briseis, to my tents Atrides' heralds came,
And took her that the Greeks gave all. If then thy pow'rs can frame
Wreak for thy son, afford it. Scale Olympus, and implore
Jove (if by either word, or fact, thou ever didst restore
Joy to his griev'd heart) now to help. I oft have heard thee vaunt,
In court of Peleus, that alone thy hand was conversant
In rescue from a cruel spoil the black-cloud-gath'ring Jove,
Whom other Godheads would have bound (the Pow'r whose pace doth move
The round earth, heav'n's great Queen, and Pallas); to whose bands
Thou cam'st with rescue, bringing up him with the hundred hands
To great Olympus, whom the Gods call Briarëus, men
Ægæon, who his sire surpass'd, and was as strong again,
And in that grace sat glad by Jove. Th' immortals stood dismay'd
At his ascension, and gave free passage to his aid.
Of all this tell Jove; kneel to him, embrace his knee, and pray,
If Troy's aid he will ever deign, that now their forces may
Beat home the Greeks to fleet and sea; embruing their retreat
In slaughter; their pains pay'ng the wreak of their proud sov'reign's heat;
And that far-ruling king may know, from his poor soldier's harms
His own harm falls; his own and all in mine, his best in arms."
Her answer she pour'd out in tears: "O me, my son," said she,
"Why brought I up thy being at all, that brought thee forth to be
Sad subject of so hard a fate? O would to heav'n, that since
Thy fate is little, and not long, thou might'st without offence
And tears perform it! But to live, thrall to so stern a fate
As grants thee least life, and that least so most unfortunate,

Grieves me t' have giv'n thee any life. But what thou wishest now,
If Jove will grant, I'll up and ask; Olympus crown'd with snow
I'll climb; but sit thou fast at fleet, renounce all war, and feed
Thy heart with wrath, and hope of wreak; till which come, thou shalt need
A little patience. Jupiter went yesterday to feast
Amongst the blameless Æthiops, in th' ocean's deepen'd breast,
All Gods attending him; the twelfth, high heav'n again he sees,
And then his brass-paved court I'll scale, cling to his pow'rful knees,
And doubt not but to win thy wish." Thus, made she her remove,
And left wrath tyring on her son, for his enforcèd love.
Ulysses, with the hecatomb, arriv'd at Chrysa's shore;
And when amidst the hav'n's deep mouth, they came to use the oar,
They straight strook sail, then roll'd them up, and on the hatches threw;
The top-mast to the kelsine then, with halyards down they drew;
Then brought the ship to port with oars; then forked anchor cast;
And, 'gainst the violence of storm, for drifting made her fast.
All come ashore, they all expos'd the holy hecatomb
To angry Phœbus, and, with it, Chryseis welcom'd home;
Whom to her sire, wise Ithacus, that did at th' altar stand,
For honour led, and, spoken thus, resign'd her to his hand:
"Chryses, the mighty king of men, great Agamemnon, sends
Thy lov'd seed by my hands to thine; and to thy God commends
A hecatomb, which my charge is to sacrifice, and seek
Our much-sigh-mix'd woe his recure, invok'd by ev'ry Greek."
Thus he resign'd her, and her sire receiv'd her highly joy'd.
About the well-built altar, then, they orderly employ'd
The sacred off'ring, wash'd their hands, took salt cakes; and the priest,
With hands held up to heav'n, thus pray'd: "O thou that all things seest,
Fautour of Chrysa, whose fair hand doth guard fully dispose
Celestial Cilia, governing in all pow'r Tenedos,
O hear thy priest, and as thy hand, in free grace to my pray'rs,
Shot fervent plague-shafts through the Greeks, now hearten their affairs
With health renew'd, and quite remove th' infection from their blood."
He pray'd; and to his pray'rs again the God propitious stood.
All, after pray'r, cast on salt cakes, drew back, kill'd, flay'd the beeves,
Cut out and dubb'd with fat their thighs, fair dress'd with doubled leaves,
And on them all the sweetbreads' prick'd, The priest, with small sere wood,
Did sacrifice, pour'd on red wine; by whom the young men stood,
And turn'd, in five ranks, spits; on which (the legs enough) they eat
The inwards; then in giggots cut the other fit for meat,
And put to fire; which roasted well they drew. The labour done,
They serv'd the feast in, that fed all to satisfaction.
Desire of meat and wine thus quench'd, the youths crown'd cups of wine
Drunk off, and fill'd again to all. That day was held divine,
And spent in pæans to the Sun, who heard with pleasèd ear;
When whose bright chariot stoop'd to sea, and twilight hid the clear,
All soundly on their cables slept, ev'n till the night was worn.
And when the lady of the light, the rosy-finger'd Morn,

Rose from the hills, all fresh arose, and to the camp retir'd.
Apollo with a fore-right wind their swelling bark inspir'd.
The top-mast hoisted, milk-white sails on his round breast they put,
The mizens strooted with the gale, the ship her course did cut
So swiftly that the parted waves against her ribs did roar;
Which, coming to the camp, they drew aloft the sandy shore,
Where, laid on stocks, each soldier kept his quarter as before.
But Peleus' son, swift-foot Achilles, at his swift ships sate,
Burning in wrath, nor ever came to councils of estate
That make men honour'd, never trod the fierce embattled field,
But kept close, and his lov'd heart pin'd, what fight and cries could yield
Thirsting at all parts to the host, And now, since first he told
His wrongs to Thetis, twelve fair morns their ensigns did unfold,
And then the ever-living gods mounted Olympus, Jove
First in ascension. Thetis then, remember'd well to move
Achilles' motion, rose from sea, and, by the morn's first light,
The great heav'n and Olympus climb'd; where, in supremest height
Of all that many-headed hill, she saw the far-seen son
Of Saturn, set from all the rest, in his free seat alone.
Before whom, on her own knees fall'n, the knees of Jupiter
Her left hand held, her right his chin, and thus she did prefer
Her son's petition: "Father Jove! If ever I have stood
Aidful to thee in word or work, with this imploréd good,
Requite my aid, renown my son, since in so short a race
(Past others) thou confin'st his life. An insolent disgrace
Is done him by the king of men; he forc'd from him a prise
Won with his sword. But thou, O Jove, that art most strong, most wise,
Honour my son for my sake; add strength to the Trojans' side
By his side's weakness in his want; and see Troy amplified
In conquest, so much, and so long, till Greece may give again
The glory reft him, and the more illustrate the free reign
Of his wrong'd honour." Jove at this sate silent; not a word
In long space pass'd him. Thetis still hung on his knee, implor'd
The second time his help, and said: "Grant, or deny my suit,
Be free in what thou dost; I know, thou canst not sit thus mute
For fear of any; speak, deny, that so I may be sure,
Of all heav'n's Goddesses 'tis I, that only must endure
Dishonour by thee." Jupiter, the great cloud-gath'rer, griev'd
With thought of what a world of griefs this suit ask'd, being achiev'd,
Swell'd, sigh'd, and answer'd: "Works of death thou urgest. O, at this
Juno will storm, and all my pow'rs inflame with contumelies.
Ever she wrangles, charging me in ear of all the Gods
That I am partial still, that I add the displeasing odds
Of my aid to the Ilians. Begone then, lest she see;
Leave thy request to my care; yet, that trust may hearten thee
With thy desire's grant, and my pow'r to give it act approve
How vain her strife is, to thy pray'r my eminent head shall move;
Which is the great sign of my will with all th' immortal states;

Irrevocable; never fails; never without the rates
Of all pow'rs else; when my head bows, all heads bow with it still
As their first mover; and gives pow'r to any work I will."
He said; and his black eyebrows bent; above his deathless head
Th' ambrosian curls flow'd; great heav'n shook: and both were severéd,
Their counsels broken. To the depth of Neptune's kingdom div'd
Thetis from heav'n's height; Jove arose; and all the Gods receiv'd
(All rising from their thrones) their Sire, attending to his court.
None sate when he rose, none delay'd the furnishing his port
Till he came near; all met with him, and brought him to his throne.
Nor sate great Juno ignorant, when she beheld alone
Old Nereus' silver-footed seed with Jove, that she had brought
Counsels to heav'n; and straight her tongue had teeth in it, that wrought
This sharp invective: "Who was that (thou craftiest counsellor
Of all the Gods) that so apart some secret did implore?
Ever, apart from me, thou lov'st to counsel and decree
Things of more close trust than thou think'st are fit t' impart to me.
Whatever thou determin'st, I must ever be denied
The knowledge of it by thy will." To her speech thus replied
The Father both of men and Gods: "Have never hope to know
My whole intentions, though my wife; it fits not, nor would show
Well to thine own thoughts; but what fits thy woman's ear to hear,
Woman, nor man, nor God, shall know before it grace thine ear.
Yet what, apart from men and Gods, I please to know, forbear
T' examine, or inquire of that." She with the cow's fair eyes,
Respected Juno, this return'd: "Austere king of the skies,
What hast thou utter'd? When did I before this time inquire,
Or sift thy counsels? Passing close you are still. Your desire
Is serv'd with such care, that I fear you can scarce vouch the deed
That makes it public, being seduc'd by this old sea-god's seed,
That could so early use her knees, embracing thine. I doubt,
The late act of thy bowéd head was for the working out
Of some boon she ask'd; that her son thy partial hand would please
With plaguing others." "Wretch!" said he, "thy subtle jealousies
Are still exploring; my designs can never 'scape thine eye,
Which yet thou never canst prevent. Thy curiosity
Makes thee less car'd for at my hands, and horrible the end
Shall make thy humour. If it be what thy suspects intend,
What then? 'Tis my free will it should; to which let way be giv'n
With silence. Curb your tongue in time; lest all the Gods in heav'n
Too few be and too weak to help thy punish'd insolence,
When my inaccessible hands shall fall on thee." The sense
Of this high threat'ning made her fear, and silent she sate down,
Humbling her great heart. All the Gods in court of Jove did frown
At this offence giv'n; amongst whom heav'n's famous artizan,
Ephaistus, in his mother's care, this comely speech began:
"Believe it, these words will breed wounds, beyond our pow'rs to bear,
If thus for mortals ye fall out. Ye make a tumult here

That spoils our banquet. Evermore worst matters put down best.
But, mother, though yourself be wise, yet let your son request
His wisdom audience. Give good terms to our lov'd father Jove,
For fear he take offence again, and our kind banquet prove
A wrathful battle. If he will, the heav'nly Light'ner can
Take you and toss you from your throne; his pow'r Olympian
Is so surpassing. Soften then with gentle speech his spleen,
And drink to him; I know his heart will quickly down again."
This said, arising from his throne, in his lov'd mother's hand
He put the double-handed cup, and said: "Come, do not stand
On these cross humours, suffer, bear, though your great bosom grieve,
And lest blows force you; all my aid not able to relieve
Your hard condition, though these eyes behold it, and this heart
Sorrow to think it. 'Tis a task too dang'rous to take part
Against Olympius. I myself the proof of this still feel.
When other Gods would fain have help'd, he took me by the heel,
And hurl'd me out of heav'n. All day I was in falling down;
At length in Lemnos I strook earth. The likewise-falling sun
And I, together, set; my life almost set too; yet there
The Sintii cheer'd and took me up." This did to laughter cheer
White-wristed Juno, who now took the cup of him, and smil'd.
The sweet peace-making draught went round, and lame Ephaistus fill'd
Nectar to all the other Gods. A laughter never left
Shook all the blesséd deities, to see the lame so deft
At that cup service. All that day, ev'n till the sun went down,
They banqueted, and had such cheer as did their wishes crown.
Nor had they music less divine; Apollo there did touch
His most sweet harp, to which, with voice, the Muses pleas'd as much.
But when the sun's fair light was set, each Godhead to his house
Address'd for sleep, where ev'ry one, with art most curious,
By heav'n's great both-foot-halting God a sev'ral roof had built.
Ev'n he to sleep went, by whose hand heav'n is with lightning gilt,
High Jove, where he had us'd to rest when sweet sleep seiz'd his eyes;
By him the golden-thron'd Queen slept, the Queen of deities.

THE END OF THE FIRST BOOK.

[1] *"See my bed made," it may be Englished. The word is ἀντιόωσαν, which signifies contra stantem as standing of one side opposite to another on the other side; which yet others translate capessentem et adornantem; which since it shows best to a reader, I follow.*

[2] *This simile Virgil directly translates.*

THE SECOND BOOK OF HOMER'S ILIADS

THE ARGUMENT

Jove calls a vision up from Somnus' den
To bid Atrides muster up his men.
The King, to Greeks dissembling his desire,
Persuades them to their country to retire.
By Pallas' will, Ulysses stays their flight:
And wise old Nestor heartens them to fight.
They take their meat; which done, to arms they go,
And march in good array against the foe.
So those of Troy; when Iris, from the sky,
Of Saturn's son performs the embassy.

ANOTHER ARGUMENT

Beta the dream and synod cites;
And catalogues the naval knights.
The other Gods, and knights at arms, all night slept; only Jove
Sweet slumber seiz'd not; he discours'd how best he might approve
His vow made for Achilles' grace, and make the Grecians find
His miss in much death. All ways cast, this counsel serv'd his mind
With most allowance; to despatch a harmful Dream to greet
The king of men, and gave this charge: "Go to the Achive fleet,
Pernicious Dream, and, being arriv'd in Agamemnon's tent,
Deliver truly all this charge. Command him to convent
His whole host arm'd before these tow'rs; for now Troy's broad-way'd town
He shall take in; the heav'n-hous'd Gods are now indiff'rent grown:
Juno's request hath won them; Troy now under imminent ills
At all parts labours." This charge heard, the Vision straight fulfils;
The ships reach'd, and Atrides' tent, in which he found him laid,
Divine sleep pour'd about his pow'rs. He stood above his head
Like Nestor, grac'd of old men most, and this did intimate:
"Sleeps the wise Atreus' tame-horse son? A councillor of state
Must not the whole night spend in sleep, to whom the people are
For guard committed, and whose life stands bound to so much care.
Now hear me, then, Jove's messenger, who, though far off from thee,
Is near thee yet in ruth and care, and gives command by me
To arm thy whole host. Thy strong hand the broad-way'd town of Troy
Shall now take in; no more the Gods dissentiously employ
Their high-hous'd powers; Juno's suit hath won them all to her;
And ill fates overhang these tow'rs, address'd by Jupiter.
Fix in thy mind this, nor forget to give it action, when
Sweet sleep shall leave thee." Thus, he fled; and left the king of men
Repeating in discourse his dream, and dreaming still, awake,
Of pow'r, not ready yet for act. O fool, he thought to take
In that next day old Priam's town; not knowing what affairs
Jove had in purpose, who prepar'd, by strong fight, sighs and cares
For Greeks and Trojans. The Dream gone, his voice still murmured

About the king's ears; who sate up, put on him in his bed
His silken inner weed, fair, new; and then in haste arose,
Cast on his ample mantle, tied to his soft feet fair shoes,
His silver-hilted sword he hung about his shoulder, took
His father's sceptre never stain'd, which then abroad he shook,
And went to fleet. And now great heav'n Goddess Aurora scal'd,
To Jove, and all Gods, bringing light; when Agamemnon call'd
His heralds, charging them aloud to call to instant court
The thick-hair'd Greeks. The heralds call'd; the Greeks made quick resort.
The Council chiefly he compos'd of old great-minded men,
At Nestor's ships, the Pylian king. All there assembled then,
Thus Atreus' son begun the court: "Hear, friends: A Dream divine,
Amidst the calm night in my sleep, did through my shut eyes shine,
Within my fantasy. His form did passing naturally
Resemble Nestor; such attire, a stature just as high.
He stood above my head, and words thus fashion'd did relate:
'Sleeps the wise Atreus' tame-horse son? A councillor of state
Must not the whole night spend in sleep, to whom the people are
For guard committed, and whose life stands bound to so much care.
Now hear me then, Jove's messenger, who, though far off from thee,
Is near thee yet in love and care, and gives command by me
To arm thy whole host. Thy strong hand the broad-way'd town of Troy
Shall now take in; no more the Gods dissentiously employ
Their high-hous'd pow'rs; Saturnia's suit hath won them all to her;
And ill fates over-hang these tow'rs, address'd by Jupiter.
Fix in thy mind this.' This express'd, he took wing and away,
And sweet sleep left me. Let us then by all our means assay
To arm our army; I will first (as far as fits our right)
Try their addictions, and command with full-sail'd ships our flight;
Which if they yield to, oppose you." He sate, and up arose
Nestor, of sandy Pylos king, who, willing to dispose
Their counsel to the public good, propos'd this to the state:
"Princes and Councillors of Greece, if any should relate
This vision but the king himself, it might be held a tale,
And move the rather our retreat; but since our General
Affirms he saw it, hold it true, and all our best means make
To arm our army." This speech us'd, he first the Council brake;
The other sceptre-bearing States arose too, and obey'd
The people's Rector. Being abroad, the earth was overlaid
With flockers to them, that came forth, as when of frequent bees
Swarms rise out of a hollow rock, repairing the degrees
Of their egression endlessly, with ever rising new
From forth their sweet nest; as their store, still as it faded, grew,
And never would cease sending forth her clusters to the spring,
They still crowd out so; this fleck here, that there, belabouring
The loaded flow'rs; so from the ships and tents the army's store
Troop'd to these princes and the court, along th' unmeasur'd shore;
Amongst whom, Jove's ambassadress, Fame, in her virtue shin'd,

Exciting greediness to hear. The rabble, thus inclin'd,
Hurried together; uproar seiz'd the high court; earth did groan
Beneath the settling multitude; tumult was there alone.
Thrice-three vocif'rous heralds rose, to check the rout, and get
Ear to their Jove-kept governors; and instantly was set
That huge confusion; ev'ry man set fast, the clamour ceas'd.
Then stood divine Atrides up, and in his hand compress'd
His sceptre, th' elaborate work of fi'ry Mulciber,
Who gave it to Saturnian Jove; Jove to his messenger;
His messenger, Argicides, to Pelops, skill'd in horse;
Pelops to Atreus, chief of men; he, dying, gave it course
To prince Thyestes, rich in herds; Thyestes to the hand
Of Agamemnon render'd it, and with it the command
Of many isles, and Argos all. On this he leaning, said:
"O friends, great sons of Danaus, servants of Mars, Jove laid
A heavy curse on me, to vow, and bind it with the bent
Of his high forehead; that, this Troy of all her people spent,
I should return; yet now to mock our hopes built on his vow,
And charge ingloriously my flight, when such an overthrow
Of brave friends I have authored. But to his mightiest will
We must submit us, that hath raz'd, and will be razing still,
Men's footsteps from so many towns; because his pow'r is most,
He will destroy most. But how vile such and so great an host
Will show to future times, that, match'd with lesser numbers far,
We fly, not putting on the crown of our so-long-held war,
Of which there yet appears no end! Yet should our foes and we
Strike truce, and number both our pow'rs; Troy taking all that be
Her arm'd inhabitants, and we, in tens, should all sit down
At our truce banquet, ev'ry ten allow'd one of the town
To fill his feast-cup; many tens would their attendant want;
So much I must affirm our pow'r exceeds th' inhabitant.
But their auxiliáry bands, those brandishers of spears,
From many cities drawn, are they that are our hinderers,
Not suff'ring well-rais'd Troy to fall. Nine years are ended now,
Since Jove our conquest vow'd; and now, our vessels rotten grow,
Our tackling falls; our wives, young sons, sit in their doors and long
For our arrival; yet the work, that should have wreak'd our wrong,
And made us welcome, lies unwrought. Come then, as I bid, all
Obey, and fly to our lov'd home; for now, nor ever, shall
Our utmost take-in broad-way'd Troy." This said, the multitude
Was all for home; and all men else that what this would conclude
Had not discover'd. All the crowd was shov'd about the shore,
In sway, like rude and raging waves, rous'd with the fervent blore
Of th' east and south winds, when they break from Jove's clouds, and are borne
On rough backs of th' Icarian seas: or like a field of corn
High grown, that Zephyr's vehement gusts bring eas'ly underneath,
And make the stiff up-bristled ears do homage to his breath;
For ev'n so eas'ly, with the breath Atrides us'd, was sway'd

The violent multitude. To fleet with shouts, and disarray'd,
All rush'd; and, with a fog of dust, their rude feet dimm'd the day;
Each cried to other, "Cleanse our ships, come, launch, aboard, away."
The clamour of the runners home reach'd heav'n; and then, past fate,
The Greeks had left Troy, had not then the Goddess of estate
Thus spoke to Pallas: "O foul shame, thou untam'd seed of Jove,
Shall thus the sea's broad back be charg'd with these our friends' remove,
Thus leaving Argive Helen here, thus Priam grac'd, thus Troy,
In whose fields, far from their lov'd own, for Helen's sake, the joy
And life of so much Grecian birth is vanish'd? Take thy way
T' our brass-arm'd people, speak them fair, let not a man obey
The charge now giv'n, nor launch one ship." She said, and Pallas did
As she commanded; from the tops of heav'n's steep hill she slid,
And straight the Greeks' swift ships she reach'd; Ulysses (like to Jove
In gifts of counsel) she found out; who to that base remove
Stirr'd not a foot, nor touch'd a ship, but griev'd at heart to see
That fault in others. To him close the blue-eyed Deity
Made way, and said: "Thou wisest Greek, divine Laertes' son,
Thus fly ye homewards to your ships? Shall all thus headlong run?
Glory to Priam thus ye leave, glory to all his friends,
If thus ye leave her here, for whom so many violent ends
Have clos'd your Greek eyes, and so far from their so loved home.
Go to these people, use no stay, with fair terms overcome
Their foul endeavour, not a man a flying sail let hoice."
Thus spake she; and Ulysses knew 'twas Pallas by her voice,
Ran to the runners, cast from him his mantle, which his man
And herald, grave Eurybates, the Ithacensian
That follow'd him, took up. Himself to Agamemnon went,
His incorrupted sceptre took, his sceptre of descent,
And with it went about the fleet. What prince, or man of name,
He found flight-giv'n, he would restrain with words of gentlest blame:
"Good sir, it fits not you to fly, or fare as one afraid,
You should not only stay yourself, but see the people staid.
You know not clearly, though you heard the king's words, yet his mind;
He only tries men's spirits now, and, whom his trials find
Apt to this course, he will chastise, Nor you, nor I, heard all
He spake in council; nor durst press too near our General,
Lest we incens'd him to our hurt. The anger of a king
Is mighty; he is kept of Jove, and from Jove likewise spring
His honours, which, out of the love of wise Jove, he enjoys."
Thus he the best sort us'd; the worst, whose spirits brake out in noise,
He cudgell'd with his sceptre, chid, and said: "Stay, wretch, be still,
And hear thy betters; thou art base, and both in pow'r and skill
Poor and unworthy, without name in council or in war.
We must not all be kings. The rule is most irregular,
Where many rule. One lord, one king, propose to thee; and he,
To whom wise Saturn's son, hath giv'n both law and empery
To rule the public, is that king." Thus ruling, he restrain'd

The host from flight; and then again the Council was maintain'd
With such a concourse, that the shore rung with the tumult made;
As when the far-resounding sea doth in its rage invade
His sandy confines, whose sides groan with his involvéd wave,
And make his own breast echo sighs. All sate, and audience gave.
Thersites only would speak all. A most disorder'd store
Of words he foolishly pour'd out, of which his mind held more
Than it could manage; any thing, with which he could procure
Laughter, he never could contain. He should have yet been sure
To touch no kings; t' oppose their states becomes not jesters' parts.
But he the filthiest fellow was of all that had deserts
In Troy's brave siege; he was squint-ey'd, and lame of either foot;
So crook-back'd, that he had no breast; sharp-headed, where did shoot
(Here and there spers'd) thin mossy hair. He most of all envíed
Ulysses and Æacides, whom still his spleen would chide.
Nor could the sacred King himself avoid his saucy vein;
Against whom since he knew the Greeks did vehement hates sustain,
Being angry for Achilles' wrong, he cried out, railing thus:
"Atrides, why complain'st thou now? What would'st thou more of us?
Thy tents are full of brass; and dames, the choice of all, are thine,
With whom we must present thee first, when any towns resign
To our invasion. Want'st thou then, besides all this, more gold
From Troy's knights to redeem their sons, whom to be dearly sold
I or some other Greek must take? Or would'st thou yet again
Force from some other lord his prise, to soothe the lusts that reign
In thy encroaching appetite? It fits no prince to be
A prince of ill, and govern us, or lead our progeny
By rape to ruin. O base Greeks, deserving infamy,
And ills eternal! Greekish girls, not Greeks, ye are! Come, fly
Home with our ships; leave this man here to perish with his preys,
And try if we help'd him or not; he wrong'd a man that weighs
Far more than he himself in worth; he forc'd from Thetis' son,
And keeps his prise still. Nor think I that mighty man hath won
The style of wrathful worthily; he's soft, he's too remiss;
Or else, Atrides, his had been thy last of injuries."
Thus he the people's Pastor chid; but straight stood up to him
Divine Ulysses, who, with looks exceeding grave and grim,
This bitter check gave: "Cease, vain fool, to vent thy railing vein
On kings thus, though it serve thee well; nor think thou canst restrain,
With that thy railing faculty, their wills in least degree;
For not a worse, of all this host, came with our King than thee,
To Troy's great siege; then do not take into that mouth of thine
The names of kings, much less revile the dignities that shine
In their supreme states, wresting thus this motion for our home,
To soothe thy cowardice; since ourselves yet know not what will come
Of these designments, if it be our good to stay, or go.
Nor is it that thou stand'st on; thou revil'st our Gen'ral so,
Only because he hath so much, not giv'n by such as thou

But our heroës. Therefore this thy rude vein makes me vow
(Which shall be curiously observ'd) if ever I shall hear
This madness from thy mouth again, let not Ulysses bear
This head, nor be the father call'd of young Telemachus,
If to thy nakedness I take and strip thee not, and thus
Whip thee to fleet from council; send, with sharp stripes, weeping hence
This glory thou affect'st to rail." This said, his insolence
He settled with his sceptre; strook his back and shoulders so
That bloody wales rose. He shrunk round; and from his eyes did flow
Moist tears, and, looking filthily, he sate, fear'd, smarted, dried
His blubber'd cheeks; and all the prease, though griev'd to be denied
Their wish'd retreat for home, yet laugh'd delightsomely, and spake
Either to other: "O ye Gods, how infinitely take
Ulysses' virtues in our good! Author of counsels, great
In ord'ring armies, how most well this act became his heat,
To beat from council this rude fool! I think his saucy spirit,
Hereafter, will not let his tongue abuse the sov'reign merit,
Exempt from such base tongues as his." Thus spake the people; then
The city-razer Ithacus stood up to speak again,
Holding his sceptre. Close to him gray-eyed Minerva stood,
And, like a herald, silence caus'd, that all the Achive brood
(From first to last) might hear and know the counsel; when, inclin'd
To all their good, Ulysses said: "Atrides, now I find
These men would render thee the shame of all men; nor would pay
Their own vows to thee, when they took their free and honour'd way
From Argos hither, that, till Troy were by their brave hands rac'd,
They would not turn home. Yet, like babes, and widows, now they haste
To that base refuge, 'Tis a spite to see men melted so
In womanish changes; though 'tis true, that if a man do go
Only a month to sea, and leave his wife far off, and he,
Tortur'd with winter's storms, and toss'd with a tumultuous sea,
Grows heavy, and would home. Us then, to whom the thrice-three year
Hath fill'd his revoluble orb since our arrival here,
I blame not to wish home much more; yet all this time to stay,
Out of our judgments, for our end; and now to take our way
Without it, were absurd and vile. Sustain then, friends; abide
The time set to our object; try if Calchas prophesied
True of the time or not. We know, ye all can witness well,
(Whom these late death-conferring fates have fail'd to send to hell)
That when in Aulis, all our fleet, assembled with a freight
Of ills to Ilion and her friends, beneath the fair grown height
A platane bore, about a fount, whence crystal water flow'd,
And near our holy altar, we upon the Gods bestow'd
Accomplish'd hecatombs; and there appear'd a huge portent,
A dragon with a bloody scale, horrid to sight, and sent
To light by great Olympius; which, crawling from beneath
The altar, to the platane climb'd, and ruthless crash'd to death
A sparrow's young, in number eight, that in a top-bough lay

Hid under leaves; the dam the ninth, that hover'd every way,
Mourning her lov'd birth, till at length, the serpent, watching her,
Her wing caught, and devour'd her too. This dragon, Jupiter,
That brought him forth, turn'd to a stone, and made a pow'rful mean
To stir our zeals up, that admir'd, when of a fact so clean
Of all ill as our sacrifice, so fearful an ostent
Should be the issue. Calchas, then, thus prophesied th' event
'Why are ye dumb-strook, fair-hair'd Greeks? Wise Jove is he hath shown
This strange ostent to us. 'Twas late, and passing lately done,
But that grace it foregoes to us, for suff'ring all the state
Of his appearance (being so slow) nor time shall end, nor fate.
As these eight sparrows, and the dam (that made the ninth) were eat
By this stern serpent; so nine years we are t' endure the heat
Of rav'nous war, and, in the tenth, take-in this broad-way'd town.'
Thus he interpreted this sign; and all things have their crown
As he interpreted, till now. The rest, then, to succeed
Believe as certain. Stay we all, till, that most glorious deed
Of taking this rich town, our hands are honour'd with." This said,
The Greeks gave an unmeasur'd shout; which back the ships repaid
With terrible echoes, in applause of that persuasion
Divine Ulysses us'd; which yet held no comparison
With Nestor's next speech, which was this: "O shameful thing! Ye talk
Like children all, that know not war. In what air's region walk
Our oaths, and cov'nants? Now, I see the fit respects of men
Are vanish'd quite; our right hands giv'n, our faiths, our counsels vain,
Our sacrifice with wine, all fled in that profanéd flame
We made to bind all; for thus still we vain persuasions frame,
And strive to work our end with words, not joining stratagemes
And hands together, though, thus long, the pow'r of our extremes
Hath urg'd us to them. Atreus' son, firm as at first hour stand!
Make good thy purpose; talk no more in councils, but command
In active field. Let two or three, that by themselves advise,
Faint in their crowning; they are such as are not truly wise;
They will for Argos, ere they knew if that which Jove hath said
Be false or true. I tell them all, that high Jove bow'd his head,
As first we went aboard our fleet, for sign we should confer
These Trojans their due fate and death; almighty Jupiter
All that day darting forth his flames, in an unmeasur'd light,
On our right hand. Let therefore none once dream of coward flight,
Till (for his own) some wife of Troy he sleeps withal, the rape
Of Helen wreaking, and our sighs enforc'd for her escape.
If any yet dare dote on home, let his dishonour'd haste
His black and well-built bark but touch, that (as he first disgrac'd
His country's spirit) fate, and death, may first his spirit let go.
But be thou wise, king, do not trust thyself, but others. Know
I will not use an abject word. See all thy men array'd
In tribes and nations, that tribes tribes, nations may nations, aid.
Which doing, thou shalt know what chiefs, what soldiers, play the men,

And what the cowards; for they all will fight in sev'ral then,
Easy for note. And then shalt thou, if thou destroy'st not Troy,
Know if the prophecy's defect, or men thou dost employ
In their approv'd arts want in war, or lack of that brave heat
Fit for the vent'rous spirits of Greece, was cause to thy defeat."
To this the king of men replied: "O father, all the sons
Of Greece thou conquer'st in the strife of consultations.
I would to Jove, Athenia, and Phœbus, I could make,
Of all, but ten such counsellors; then instantly would shake
King Priam's city, by our hands laid hold on and laid waste.
But Jove hath order'd I should grieve, and to that end hath cast
My life into debates past end. Myself, and Thetis' son,
Like girls, in words fought for a girl, and I th' offence begun.
But if we ever talk as friends, Troy's thus deferréd fall
Shall never vex us more one hour. Come then, to victuals all,
That strong Mars all may bring to field. Each man his lance's steel
See sharpen'd well, his shield well lin'd, his horses meated well,
His chariot carefully made strong, that these affairs of death
We all day may hold fiercely out. No man must rest, or breath;
The bosoms of our targeteers must all be steeped in sweat;
The lancer's arm must fall dissolv'd; our chariot-horse with heat
Must seem to melt. But if I find one soldier take the chace,
Or stir from fight, or fight not still fix'd in his enemy's face,
Or hid a-ship-board, all the world, for force, nor price, shall save
His hated life, but fowls and dogs be his abhorréd grave."
He said; and such a murmur rose, as on a lofty shore
The waves make, when the south wind comes, and tumbles them before
Against a rock, grown near the strand which diversely beset
Is never free, but, here and there, with varied uproars beat.
All rose then, rushing to the fleet, perfum'd their tents, and eat;
Each off'ring to th' immortal gods, and praying to 'scape the heat
Of war and death. The king of men an ox of five years' spring
T' almighty Jove slew, call'd the peers; first Nestor; then the king
Idomenёus; after them th' Ajaces; and the son
Of Tydeus; Ithacus the sixth, in counsel paragon
To Jove himself. All these he bade; but at-a-martial-cry
Good Menelaus, since he saw his brother busily
Employ'd at that time, would not stand on invitation,
But of himself came. All about the off'ring over-thrown
Stood round, took salt-cakes, and the king himself thus pray'd for all:
"O Jove, most great, most glorious, that, in that starry hall,
Sitt'st drawing dark clouds up to air, let not the sun go down,
Darkness supplying it, till my hands the palace and the town
Of Priam overthrow and burn; the arm, on Hector's breast
Dividing, spoiling with my sword thousands, in interest
Of his bad quarrel, laid by him in dust, and eating earth."
He pray'd; Jove heard him not, but made more plentiful the birth
Of his sad toils, yet took his gifts. Pray'rs past, cakes on they threw;

The ox then, to the altar drawn, they kill'd, and from him drew
His hide, then cut him up, his thighs; in two hewn, dubb'd with fat,
Prick'd on the sweetbreads, and with wood, leaveless, and kindled at
Apposéd fire, they burn the thighs; which done, the inwards, slit,
They broil'd on coals and eat; the rest, in giggots cut, they spit,
Roast cunningly, draw, sit, and feast; nought lack'd to leave allay'd
Each temp'rate appetite; which serv'd, Nestor began and said:
"Atrides, most grac'd king of men, now no more words allow,
Nor more defer the deed Jove vows. Let heralds summon now
The brazen-coated Greeks, and us range ev'rywhere the host,
To stir a strong war quickly up." This speech no syllable lost;
The high-voic'd heralds instantly he, charg'd to call to arms
The curl'd-head Greeks; they call'd; the Greeks straight answer'd their alarms.
The Jove-kept kings, about the king all gather'd, with their aid
Rang'd all in tribes and nations. With them the gray-eyed Maid
Great Ægis (Jove's bright shield) sustain'd, that can be never old,
Never corrupted, fring'd about with serpents forg'd of gold,
As many all suffic'd to make an hundred fringes, worth
An hundred oxen, ev'ry snake all sprawling, all set forth
With wondrous spirit. Through the host with this the Goddess ran,
In fury casting round her eyes, and furnish'd ev'ry man
With strength, exciting all to arms, and fight incessant. None
Now lik'd their lov'd homes like the wars. And as a fire upon
A huge wood, on the heights of hills, that far off hurls his light;
So the divine brass shin'd on these thus thrusting on for fight,
Their splendour through the air reach'd heav'n. And as about the flood
Caïster, in an Asian mead, flocks of the airy brood,
Cranes, geese, or long-neck'd swans, here, there, proud of their pinions fly,
And in their falls layout such throats, that with their spiritful cry
The meadow shrieks again; so here, these many-nation'd men
Flow'd over the Scamandrian field, from tents and ships; the din
Was dreadful that the feet of men and horse beat out of earth.
And in the flourishing mead they stood, thick as the odorous birth
Of flow'rs, or leaves bred in the spring; or thick as swarms of flies
Throng then to sheep-cotes, when each swarm his erring wing applies
To milk dew'd on the milk-maid's pails; all eagerly dispos'd
To give to ruin th' Ilians. And as in rude heaps clos'd,
Though huge goatherds are at their food, the goatherds eas'ly yet
Sort into sundry herds; so here the chiefs in battle set
Here tribes, here nations, ord'ring all. Amongst whom shin'd the king,
With eyes like lightning-loving Jove, his forehead answering,
In breast like Neptune, Mars in waist. And as a goodly bull
Most eminent of all a herd, most wrong, most masterful,
So Agamemnon, Jove that day made overheighten clear
That heav'n-bright army, and preferr'd to all th' heroës there.
Now tell me, Muses, you that dwell in heav'nly roofs, (for you
Are Goddesses, are present here, are wise, and all things know,
We only trust the voice of fame, know nothing,) who they were

That here were captains of the Greeks, commanding princes here.
The multitude exceed my song, though fitted to my choice
Ten tongues were, harden'd palates ten, a breast of brass, a voice
Infract and trump-like; that great work, unless the seed of Jove,
The deathless Muses, undertake, maintains a pitch above
All mortal pow'rs. The princes then, and navy that did bring
Those so inenarrable troops, and all their soils, I sing.

THE CATALOGUE OF THE GRECIAN SHIPS AND CAPTAINS

Peleüs, and Leitus, all that Bœotia bred,
Arcesilaus, Clonius, and Prothoenor led;
Th' inhabitants of Hyria, and stony Aulida,
Schæne, Scole, the hilly Eteon, and holy Thespia,
Of Græa, and great Mycalesse, that hath the ample plain,
Of Harma, and Ilesius, and all that did remain
In Eryth, and in Eleon, in Hylen, Peteona,
In fair Ocalea, and, the town well-builded, Medeona,
Copas, Eutresis, Thisbe, that for pigeons doth surpass,
Of Coroneia, Haliart, that hath such store of grass,
All those that in Platæa dwelt, that Glissa did possess,
And Hypothebs, whose well-built walls are rare and fellowless,
In rich Onchestus' famous wood, to wat'ry Neptune vow'd,
And Arne, where the vine-trees are with vig'rous bunches bow'd,
With them that dwelt in Midea, and Nissa most divine,
All those whom utmost Anthedon did wealthily confine.
From all these coasts, in general, full fifty sail were sent;
And six score strong Bœotian youths in ev'ry burthen went.
But those who in Aspledon dwelt, and Minian Orchomen,
God Mars's sons did lead (Ascalaphus and Ialmen)
Who in Azidon Actor's house did of Astyoche come;
The bashful maid, as she went up into the higher room,
The War-god secretly compress'd. In safe conduct of these,
Did thirty hollow-bottom'd barks divide the wavy seas.
Brave Schedius and Epistrophus, the Phocian captains were,
(Naubolida-Iphitus' sons) all proof 'gainst any fear;
With them the Cyparissians went, and bold Pythonians,
Men of religious Chrysa's soil, and fat Daulidians,
Panopæans, Anemores, and fierce Hyampolists;
And those that dwell where Cephisus casts up his silken mists;
The men that fair Lilæa held, near the Cephisian spring;
All which did forty sable barks to that designment bring.
About th' entoil'd Phocensian fleet had these their sail assign'd;
And near to the sinister wing the arm'd Bœotians shin'd.
Ajax the less, Oïleus' son, the Locrians led to war;
Not like to Ajax Telamon, but lesser man by far,
Little he was, and ever wore a breastplate made of linne,
But for the manage of his lance he gen'ral praise did win.

The dwellers of Caliarus, of Bessa, Opoën,
The youths of Cynus, Scarphis, and Augias, lovely men,
Of Tarphis, and of Thronius, near flood Boagrius' fall;
Twice-twenty martial barks of these, less Ajax sail'd withal.
Who near Eubœa's blesséd soil their habitations had,
Strength-breathing Abants, who their seats in sweet Eubœa made,
The Histiæans rich in grapes, the men of Chalcida,
The Cerinths bord'ring on the sea, of rich Eretria,
Of Dion's highly-seated town, Charistus, and of Styre,
All these the duke Alphenor led, a flame of Mars's fire,
Surnam'd Chalcodontiades, the mighty Abants' guide,
Swift men of foot, whose broad-set backs their trailing hair did bide,
Well-seen in fight, and soon could pierce with far extended darts
The breastplates of their enemies, and reach their dearest hearts.
Forty black men of war did sail in this Alphenor's charge.
The soldiers that in Athens dwelt, a city builded large,
The people of Eristhius, whom Jove-sprung Pallas fed,
And plenteous-feeding Tellus brought out of her flow'ry bed;
Him Pallas placed in her rich fane, and, ev'ry ended year,
Of bulls and lambs th' Athenian youths please him with off'rings there;
Mighty Menestheus, Peteus' son, had their divided care;
For horsemen and for targeteers none could with him compare,
Nor put them into better place, to hurt or to defend;
But Nestor (for he elder was) with him did sole contend;
With him came fifty sable sail. And out of Salamine
Great Ajax brought twelve sail, that with th' Athenians did combine.
Who did in fruitful Argos dwell, or strong Tiryntha keep,
Hennion, or in Asinen whose bosom is so deep,
Trœzena, Eïon, Epidaure where Bacchus crowns his head,
Ægina, and Maseta's soil, did follow Diomed,
And Sthenelus, the dear-lov'd son of famous Capaneus
Together with Euryalus, heir of Mecisteus,
The king of Talæonides; past whom in deeds of war,
The famous soldier Diomed of all was held by far.
Four score black ships did follow these. The men fair Mycene held,
The wealthy Corinth, Cleon that for beauteous site excell'd,
Aræthyrea's lovely seat, and in Ornia's plain,
And Sicyona, where at first did king Adrastus reign,
High-seated Gonoëssa's towers, and Hyperisius,
That dwelt in fruitful Pellenen, and in divine Ægius,
With all the sea-side borderers, and wide Helice's friends,
To Agamemnon ev'ry town her native birth commends,
In double-fifty sable barks. With him a world of men
Most strong and full of valour went, and he in triumph then
Put on his most resplendent arms, since he did over-shine
The whole heroic host of Greece, in pow'r of that design.
Who did in Lacedæmon's rule th' unmeasur'd concave hold,
High Pharis, Sparta, Messe's tow'rs, for doves so much extoll'd,

Bryseia's and Augia's grounds, strong Laa, Oetylon,
Amyclas, Helos' harbour-town, that Neptune beats upon,
All these did Menelaus lead (his brother, that in cries
Of war was famous). Sixty ships convey'd these enemies
To Troy in chief, because their king was chiefly injur'd there,
In Helen's rape, and did his best to make them buy it dear.
Who dwelt in Pylos' sandy soil, and Arene the fair,
In Thryon, near Alpheus' flood, and Aepy full of air,
In Cyparisscus, Amphigen, and little Pteleon,
The town where all the Iliots dwelt, and famous Doreon,
Where all the Muses, opposite, in strife of poesy,
To ancient Thamyris of Thrace, did use him cruelly,
(He coming from Eurytus' court, the wise Œchalian king,)
Because he proudly durst affirm he could more sweetly sing
Than that Pierian race of Jove; who, angry with his vaunt,
Bereft his eyesight, and his song, that did the ear enchant,
And of his skill to touch his harp disfurnishéd his hand.
All these in ninety hollow keels grave Nestor did command.
The richly-blest inhabitants of the Arcadian land
Below Cyllene's mount (that by Epytus' tomb did stand)
Where dwelt the bold near-fighting men, who did in Phæneus live,
And Orchomen, where flocks of sheep the shepherds clust'ring drive,
In Ripe, and in Stratié, the fair Mantinean town,
And strong Enispe, that for height is ever weather-blown,
Tegea, and in Stymphalus, Parrhasia strongly wall'd,
All these Alcæus' son to field (king Agapenor) call'd;
In sixty barks he brought them on, and ev'ry bark well-mann'd
With fierce Arcadian's, skill'd to use the utmost of a band.
King Agamemnon, on these men, did well-built ships bestow
To pass the gulfy purple sea, that did no sea rites know.
They, who in Hermin, Buphrasis, and Elis, did remain,
What Olen's cliffs, Alisius, and Myrsin did contain,
Were led to war by twice-two dukes (and each ten ships did bring,
Which many vent'rous Epians did serve for burthening,)
Beneath Amphimachus's charge, and valiant Thalpius,
(Son of Eurytus-Actor one, the other Cteatus,)
Diores Amaryncides the other did employ,
The fourth divine Polixenus (Agasthenes's joy).
The king of fair Angeiades, who from Dulichius came,
And from Echinaus' sweet isles, which hold their holy frame
By ample Elis region, Meges Phylides led;
Whom duke Phyleus, Jove's belov'd, begat, and whilome fled
To large Dulichius, for the wrath that fir'd his father's breast.
Twice-twenty ships with ebon sails were in his charge address'd.
The warlike men of Cephale, and those of Ithaca,
Woody Neritus, and the men of wet Crocylia,
Sharp Ægilipa, Samos' isle, Zacynthus sea inclos'd,
Epirus, and the men that hold the continent oppos'd,

All these did wise Ulysses lead, in counsel peer to Jove;
Twelve ships he brought, which in their course vermilion sterns did move.
Thoas, Andremon's well-spoke son, did guide th' Ætolians well,
Those that in Pleuron, Olenon, and strong Pylene dwell,
Great Chalcis, that by sea-side stands, and stony Calydon;
(For now no more of Œneus' sons surviv'd; they all were gone;
No more his royal self did live, no more his noble son
The golden Meleager now, their glasses all were run)
All things were left to him in charge, th' Ætolians' chief he was,
And forty ships to Trojan wars the seas with him did pass.
The royal soldier Idomen did lead the Cretans stout,
The men of Gnossus, and the town Gortyna wall'd about,
Of Lictus, and Miletus' tow'rs, of white Lycastus' state,
Of Phæstus, and of Rhytius, the cities fortunate.
And all the rest inhabiting the hundred towns of Crete;
Whom warlike Idomen did lead, co-partner in the fleet
With kill-man Merion. Eighty ships with them did Troy invade.
Tlepolemus Heraclides, right strong and bigly made,
Brought nine tall ships of war from Rhodes, which haughty Rhodians mann'd,
Who dwelt in three dissever'd parts of that most pleasant land,
Which Lyndus and Jalissus were, and bright Camirus, call'd.
Tlepolemus commanded these, in battle unappall'd;
Whom fair Astyoche brought forth, by force of Hercules,
Led out of Ephyr with his hand, from river Selleës,
When many towns of princely youths he levell'd with the ground.
Tlepolem, in his father's house (for building much renown'd)
Brought up to headstrong state of youth, his mother's brother slew,
The flow'r of arms, Licymnius, that somewhat aged grew;
Then straight he gather'd him a fleet, assembling bands of men,
And fled by sea, to shun the threats' that were denouncéd then
By other sons and nephews of th' Alciden fortitude.
He in his exile came to Rhodes, driv'n in with tempests rude.
The Rhodians were distinct in tribes, and great with Jove did stand,
The King of men and Gods, who gave much treasure to their land.
Nirëus, out of Syma's hav'n three well-built barks did bring;
Nirëus, fair Aglaia's son, and Charopes' the king;
Nirëus was the fairest man that to fair Ilion came
Of all the Greeks, save Peleus' son, who pass'd for gen'ral frame;
But weak this was, not fit for war, and therefore few did guide.
Who did in Cassus, Nisyrus, and Crapathus, abide,
In Co, Eurypylus's town, and in Calydna's soils,
Phidippus and bold Antiphus did guide to Trojan toils,
(The sons of crownéd Thessalus, deriv'd from Hercules)
Who went with thirty hollow ships well-order'd to the seas.
Now will I sing the sackful troops Pelasgian Argos held,
That in deep Alus, Alopé, and soft Trechina dwell'd,
In Phthia, and in Hellade where live the lovely dames,
The Myrmidons, Hellenians, and Achives, rob'd of fames;

All which the great Æacides in fifty ships did lead.
For these forgat war's horrid voice, because they lack'd their head
That would have brought them bravely forth; but now at fleet did lie
That wind-like user of his feet, fair Thetis' progeny,
Wroth for bright-cheek'd Briseis' loss, whom from Lyrnessus' spoils
(His own exploit) he brought away as trophy of his toils,
When that town was depopulate; he sunk the Theban tow'rs;
Myneta, and Epistrophus, he sent to Pluto's bow'rs,
Who came of king Evenus' race, great Helepiades;
Yet now he idly lives enrag'd, but soon must leave his ease.
Of those that dwelt in Phylace, and flow'ry Pyrason
The wood of Ceres, and the soil that sheep are fed upon
Iton, and Antron built by sea, and Pteleus full of grass,
Protesilaus, while he liv'd, the worthy captain was,
Whom now the sable earth detains; his tear-torn-facéd spouse
He woeful left in Phylace, and his half-finish'd house;
A fatal Dardan first his life, of all the Greeks, bereft,
As he was leaping from his ship; yet were his men unleft
Without a chief, for though they wish'd to have no other man
But good Protesilay their guide, Podarces yet began
To govern them, (Iphitis' son, the son of Phylacus)
Most rich in sheep, and brother to short-liv'd Protesilaus,
Of younger birth, less, and less strong, yet serv'd he to direct
The companies, that still did more their ancient duke affect.
Twice-twenty jetty sails with him the swelling stream did take.
But those that did in Pheres dwell, at the Bœbeian lake,
In Bœbe, and in Glaphyra, Iaolcus builded fair,
In thrice-six ships to Pergamus did through the seas repair,
With old Admetus' tender son, Eumelus, whom he bred
Of Alcest, Pelius' fairest child of all his female seed.
The soldiers that before the siege Methone's vales did hold,
Thaumacie, flow'ry Melibœ, and Olison the cold,
Duke Philoctetes governéd, in darts of finest sleight;
Sev'n vessels in his charge convey'd their honourable freight,
By fifty rowers in a bark, most expert in the bow;
But he in sacred Lemnos lay, brought miserably low
By torment of an ulcer grown with Hydra's poison'd blood,
Whose sting was such, Greece left him there in most impatient mood;
Yet thought they on him at his ship and choos'd, to lead his men,
Medon, Oïleus' bastard son, brought forth to him by Rhen.
From Tricce, bleak Ithomen's clifts, and hapless Oechaly,
(Eurytus' city, rul'd by him in wilful tyranny,)
In charge of Æsculapius' sons, physician highly prais'd,
Machaon, Podalirius, were thirty vessels rais'd.
Who near Hyperia's fountain dwelt, and in Ormenius,
The snowy tops of Titanus, and in Asterius,
Evemon's son, Eurypylus, did lead into the field;
Whose towns did forty black-sail'd ships to that encounter yield.

Who Gyrton, and Argissa, held, Orthen, and Elon's seat,
And chalky Oloössone, were led by Polypœte,
The issue of Pirithous, the son of Jupiter.
Him the Athenian Theseus' friend Hippodamy did bear,
When he the bristled savages did give Ramnusia,
And drove them out of Pelius, as far as Æthica.
He came not single, but with him Leonteus, Coron's son,
An arm of Mars, and Coron's life Cenëus' seed begun.
Twice-twenty ships attended these. Gunëus next did bring
From Cyphus twenty sail and two; the Enians following;
And fierce Peræbi, that about Dodon's frozen mould
Did plant their houses; and the men that did the meadows hold,
Which Titaresius decks with flow'rs and his sweet current leads
Into the bright Penëus, that hath the silver heads,
Yet with his admirable stream doth not his waves commix,
But glides aloft on it like oil; for 'tis the flood of Styx,
By which th' immortal Gods do swear. Teuthredon's honour'd birth,
Prothous, led the Magnets forth, who near the shady earth
Of Pelius, and Penëion, dwelt; forty revengeful sail
Did follow him. These were the dukes and princes of avail
That came from Greece. But now the man, that overshin'd them all,
Sing, Muse; and their most famous steeds to my recital call,
That both th' Atrides followéd. Fair Pheretiades
The bravest mares did bring by much; Eumelius manag'd these,
Swift of their feet as birds of wing, both of one hair did shine,
Both of an age, both of a height, as measur'd by a line,
Whom silver-bow'd Apollo bred in the Pierian mead,
Both slick and dainty, yet were both in war of wondrous dread.
Great Ajax Telamon for strength pass'd all the peers of war,
While vex'd Achilles was away; but he surpass'd him far.
The horse that bore that faultless man were likewise past compare;
Yet lay he at the crook'd-stern'd ships, and fury was his fare,
For Atreus' son's ungracious deed, his men yet pleas'd their hearts
With throwing of the holéd stone, with hurling of their darts,
And shooting fairly on the shore; their horse at chariots fed
On greatest parsley, and on sedge that in the fens is bred.
His princes' tents their chariots held, that richly cover'd were.
His princes, amorous of their chief, walk'd storming here and there
About the host, and scorn'd to fight: their breaths as they did pass
Before them flew, as if a fire fed on the trembling grass;
Earth under-groan'd their high-rais'd feet, as when offended Jove,
In Arime, Typhœius with rattling thunder drove
Beneath the earth; in Arime, men say, the grave is still,
Where thunder tomb'd Typhœius, and is a monstrous hill;
And as that thunder made earth groan, so groan'd it as they past,
They trod with such hard-set-down steps, and so exceeding fast.
To Troy the rainbow-girded Dame right heavy news relates
From Jove, as all to council drew in Priam's palace-gates,

Resembling Priam's son in voice, Polites, swift of feet;
In trust whereof, as sentinel, to see when from the fleet
The Grecians sallied, he was set upon the lofty brow
Of aged Æsyetes' tomb; and this did Iris show:
"O Priam, thou art always pleas'd with indiscreet advice,
And fram'st thy life to times of peace, when such a war doth rise
As threats inevitable spoil. I never did behold
Such and so mighty troops of men, who trample on the mould
In number like Autumnus' leaves, or like the marine sand,
All ready round about the walls to use a ruining hand.
Hector, I therefore charge thee most, this charge to undertake.
A multitude remain in Troy, will fight for Priam's sake,
Of other lands and languages; let ev'ry leader then
Bring forth well-arm'd into the field his sev'ral bands of men."
Strong Hector knew a Deity gave charge to this assay,
Dismiss'd the council straight; like waves, clusters to arms do sway;
The ports are all wide open set; out rush'd the troops in swarms,
Both horse and foot; the city run with sudden-cried alarms.
A column stands without the town, that high his head doth raise,
A little distant, in a plain trod down with divers ways,
Which men do Batieia call, but the Immortals name
Myrine's famous sepulchre, the wondrous active dame.
Here were th' auxiliary bands, that came in Troy's defence,
Distinguish'd under sev'ral guides of special excellence.
The duke of all the Trojan pow'r great helm-deck'd Hector was,
Which stood of many mighty men well-skill'd in darts of brass.
Æneas of commixéd seed (a Goddess with a man,
Anchises with the Queen of love) the troops Dardanian
Led to the field; his lovely sire in Ida's lower shade
Begat him of sweet Cyprides; he solely was not made
Chief leader of the Dardan pow'rs, Antenor's valiant sons,
Archilochus and Acamas, were joind companions.
Who in Zelia dwelt beneath the sacred foot of Ide,
That drank of black Æsepus' stream, and wealth made full of pride,
The Aphnii, Lycaon's son, whom Phœbus gave his bow,
Prince Pandarus did lead to field. Who Adrestinus owe,
Apesus' city, Pityæ, and mount Tereiës,
Adrestus and stout Amphius led; who did their sire displease,
(Merops Percosius, that excell'd all Troy in heav'nly skill
Of futures-searching prophecy) for, much against his will,
His sons were agents in those arms; whom since they disobey'd,
The fates, in letting slip their threads, their hasty valours stay'd.
Who in Percotes, Practius, Arisba, did abide,
Who Sestus and Abydus bred, Hyrtacides did guide;
Prince Asius Hyrtacides, that, through great Selees' force,
Brought from Arisba to that fight the great and fiery horse.
Pylæus, and Hippothous, the stout Pelasgians led,
Of them Larissa's fruitful soil before bad nourishéd;

These were Pelasgian Pithus' sons, son of Teutamidas.
The Thracian guides were Pirous, and valiant Acamas,
Of all that the impetuous flood of Hellespont enclos'd.
Euphemus, the Ciconian troops, in his command dispos'd,
Who from Trœzenius-Ceades right nobly did descend.
Pyræchmes did the Pæons rule, that crookéd bows do bend;
From Axius, out of Amydon, he had them in command,
From Axius, whose most beauteous stream still overflows the land.
Pylæmen with the well-arm'd heart, the Paphlagonians led,
From Enes, where the race of mules fit for the plough is bred.
The men that broad Cytorus' bounds, and Sesamus, enfold,
About Parthenius' lofty flood, in houses much extoll'd,
From Cromna and Ægialus, the men that arms did bear,
And Erythinus situate high, Pylæmen's soldiers were.
Epistrophus and Dius did the Halizonians guide,
Far-fetch'd from Alybe, where first the silver mines were tried.
Chromis, and augur Ennomus, the Mysians did command,
Who could not with his auguries the strength of death withstand,
But suffer'd it beneath the stroke of great Æacides,
In Xanthus; where he made more souls dive to the Stygian seas.
Phorcys, and fair Ascanius, the Phrygians brought to war,
Well train'd for battle, and were come out of Ascania far.
With Methles, and with Antiphus, (Pylæmen's sons) did fight
The men of Meïon, whom the fen Gygæa brought to light,
And those Meionians that beneath the mountain Tmolus sprung.
The rude unletter'd Caribæ, that barbarous were of tongue,
Did under Nastes' colours march, and young Amphimachus,
(Nomion's famous sons) to whom, the mountain Phthirorus
That with the famous wood is crown'd, Miletus, Mycales
That hath so many lofty marks for men that love the seas,
The crooked arms Mæander bow'd with his so snaky flood,
Resign'd for conduct the choice youth of all their martial brood.
The fool Amphimachus, to field, brought gold to be his wrack,
Proud-girl-like that doth ever bear her dow'r upon her back;
Which wise Achilles mark'd, slew him, and took his gold in strife,
At Xanthus' flood; so little Death did fear his golden life.
Sarpedon led the Lycians, and Glaucus unreprov'd,
From Lycia, and the gulfy flood of Xanthus far remov'd.

THE END OF THE SECOND BOOK.

THE THIRD BOOK OF HOMER'S ILIADS

THE ARGUMENT

Paris, betwixt the hosts, to single fight,

Of all the Greeks, dares the most hardy knight.
King Menelaus doth accept his brave,
Conditioning that he again should have
Fair Helena, with all she brought to Troy,
If he subdu'd; else Paris should enjoy
Her, and her wealth, in peace. Conquest doth grant
Her dear wreath to the Grecian combatant;
But Venus to her champion's life doth yield
Safe rescue, and conveys him from the field
Into his chamber, and for Helen sends,
Whom much her lover's foul disgrace offends;
Yet Venus for him still makes good her charms,
And ends the second combat in his arms.

ANOTHER ARGUMENT

Gamma the single fight doth sing
'Twixt Paris and the Spartan king.
When ev'ry least commander's will best soldiers had obey'd,
And both the hosts were rang'd for fight, the Trojans would have fray'd
The Greeks with noises, crying out, in coming rudely on;
At all parts like the cranes that fill, with harsh confusion,
Of brutish clangés all the air, and in ridiculous war
(Eschewing the unsuffer'd storms, shot from the winter's star)
Visit the ocean, and confer the Pygmei soldiers' death.
The Greeks charg'd silent, and like men, bestow'd their thrifty breath
In strength of far-resounding blows, still entertaining care
Of either's rescue, when their strength did their engagements dare.
And as, upon a hill's steep tops, the south wind pours a cloud,
To shepherds thankless, but by thieves that love the night, allow'd,
A darkness letting down, that blinds a stone's cast off men's eyes;
Such darkness from the Greeks' swift feet (made all of dust) did rise.
But, ere stern conflict mix'd both strengths, fair Paris stept before
The Trojan host; athwart his back a panther's hide he wore,
A crookéd bow, and sword, and shook two brazen-headed darts;
With which well-arm'd, his tongue provok'd the best of Grecian hearts
To stand with him in single fight. Whom when the man, wrong'd most
Of all the Greeks, so gloriously saw stalk before the host;
As when a lion is rejoic'd, (with hunger half forlorn,)
That finds some sweet prey, as a hart, whose grace lies in his horn,
Or sylvan goat, which he devours, though never so pursu'd
With dogs and men; so Sparta's king exulted, when he viewed
The fair-fac'd Paris so expos'd to his so thirsted wreak,
Whereof his good cause made him sure. The Grecian front did break,
And forth he rush'd, at all parts arm'd, leapt from his chariot,
And royally prepar'd for charge. Which seen, cold terror shot
The heart of Paris, who retir'd as headlong from the king

As in him he had shunn'd his death. And as a hilly spring
Presents a serpent to a man, full underneath his feet,
Her blue neck, swoln with poison, rais'd, and her sting out, to greet
His heedless entry, suddenly his walk he altereth,
Starts back amaz'd, is shook with fear, and looks as pale as death;
So Menelaus Paris scar'd; so that divine-fac'd foe
Shrunk in his beauties. Which beheld by Hector, he let go
This bitter check at him; "Accurs'd, made but in beauty's scorn,
Impostor, woman's man! O heav'n, that thou hadst ne'er been born,
Or, being so manless, never liv'd to bear man's noblest state,
The nuptial honour! Which I wish, because it were a fate
Much better for thee than this shame. This spectacle doth make
A man a monster. Hark! how loud the Greeks laugh, who did take
Thy fair form for a continent of parts as fair. A rape
Thou mad'st of nature, like their queen. No soul, an empty shape,
Takes up thy being; yet how spite to ev'ry shade of good
Fills it with ill! for as thou art, thou couldst collect a brood
Of others like thee, and far hence fetch ill enough to us,
Ev'n to thy father; all these friends make those foes mock them thus
In thee, for whose ridiculous sake so seriously they lay
All Greece, and fate, upon their necks. O wretch! Not dare to stay
Weak Menelaus? But 'twas well; for in him thou hadst tried
What strength lost beauty can infuse, and with the more grief died
To feel thou robb'dst a worthier man, to wrong a soldier's right.
Your harp's sweet touch, curl'd locks, fine shape, and gifts so exquisite,
Giv'n thee by Venus, would have done your fine dames little good,
When blood and dust had ruffled them, and had as little stood
Thyself in stead; but what thy care of all these in thee flies
We should inflict on thee ourselves. Infectious cowardice
In thee hath terrified our host; for which thou well deserv'st
A coat of tombstone, not of steel in which, for form, thou serv'st."
To this thus Paris spake, (for form, that might inhabit heav'n)
"Hector, because thy sharp reproof is out of justice giv'n,
I take it well; but though thy heart, inur'd to these affrights,
Cuts through them as an axe through oak, that more us'd more excites
The workman's faculty, whose art can make the edge go far,
Yet I, less practis'd than thyself in these extremes of war,
May well be pardon'd, though less bold; in these your worth exceeds,
In others mine. Nor is my mind of less force to the deeds
Requir'd in war, because my form more flows in gifts of peace.
Reproach not, therefore, the kind gifts of golden Cyprides.
All heav'n's gifts have their worthy price; as little to be scorn'd
As to be won with strength, wealth, state; with which to be adorn'd,
Some men would change state, wealth, or strength. But, if your martial heart
Wish me to make my challenge good, and hold it such a part
Of shame to give it over thus, cause all the rest to rest,
And, 'twixt both hosts, let Sparta's king and me perform our best
For Helen and the wealth she brought; and he that overcomes,

Or proves superior any way, in all your equal dooms,
Let him enjoy her utmost wealth, keep her, or take her home;
The rest strike leagues of endless date, and hearty friends become;
You dwelling safe in gleby Troy, the Greeks retire their force
T' Achaia, that breeds fairest dames, and Argos, fairest horse."
He said, and his amendsful words did Hector highly please,
Who rush'd betwixt the fighting hosts, and made the Trojans cease,
By holding up in midst his lance. The Grecians noted not
The signal he for parley used, but at him fiercely shot,
Hurl'd stones, and still were leveling darts. At last the king of men,
Great Agamemnon, cried aloud: "Argives! for shame, contain;
Youths of Achaia, shoot no more; the fair-helm'd Hector shows
As he desir'd to treat with us." This said, all ceas'd from blows,
And Hector spake to both the hosts: "Trojans, and hardy Greeks,
Hear now what he that stirr'd these wars, for their cessation seeks.
He bids us all, and you, disarm, that he alone may fight
With Menelaus, for us all, for Helen and her right,
With all the dow'r she brought to Troy; and he that wins the day,
Or is, in all the art of arms, superior any way,
The queen, and all her sorts of wealth, let him at will enjoy;
The rest strike truce, and let love seal firm leagues 'twixt Greece and Troy."
The Greek host wonder'd at this brave; silence flew ev'rywhere;
At last spake Sparta's warlike king: "Now also give me ear,
Whom grief gives most cause of reply. I now have hope to free
The Greeks and Trojans of all ills, they have sustain'd for me,
And Alexander, that was cause I stretch'd my spleen so far.
Of both then, which is nearest fate, let his death end the war;
The rest immediately retire, and greet all homes in peace.
Go then (to bless your champion, and give his pow'rs success)
Fetch for the Earth, and for the Sun (the Gods on whom ye call)
Two lambs, a black one and a white, a female and a male;
And we another, for ourselves, will fetch, and kill to Jove.
To sign which rites bring Priam's force, because we well approve
His sons perfidious, envious, and (out of practis'd bane
To faith, when she believes in them) Jove's high truce may profane.
All young men's hearts are still unstaid; but in those well-weigh'd deeds
An old man will consent to pass things past, and what succeeds
He looks into, that he may know, how best to make his way
Through both the fortunes of a fact, and will the worst obey."
This granted, a delightful hope both Greeks and Trojans fed,
Of long'd-for rest from those long toils, their tedious war had bred.
Their horses then in rank they set, drawn from their chariots round,
Descend themselves, took off their arms, and plac'd them on the ground,
Near one another; for the space 'twixt both the hosts was small.
Hector two heralds sent to Troy, that they from thence might call
King Priam, and to bring the lambs, to rate the truce they swore.
But Agamemnon to the fleet Talthybius sent before,
To fetch their lamb; who nothing slack'd the royal charge was giv'n.

Iris, the rain-bow, then came down, ambassadress from heav'n,
To white-arm'd Helen. She assum'd at ev'ry part the grace
Of Helen's last love's sister's shape, who had the highest place
In Helen's love, and had to name Laodice, most fair
Of all the daughters Priam had, and made the nuptial pair
With Helicaon, royal sprout of ole Antenor's seed.
She found queen Helena at home, at work about a weed,
Wov'n for herself; it shin'd like fire, was rich, and full of size,
The work of both sides being alike; in which she did comprise
The many labours warlike Troy and brass-arm'd Greece endur'd
For her fair sake, by cruel Mars and his stern friends procur'd.
Iris came in in joyful haste, and said; "O come with me,
Lov'd nymph, and an admiréd sight of Greeks and Trojans see,
Who first on one another brought a war so full of tears,
Ev'n thirsty of contentious war. Now ev'ry man forbears,
And friendly by each other sits, each leaning on his shield,
Their long and shining lances pitch'd fast by them in the field,
Paris, and Sparta's king, alone must take up all the strife;
And he that conquers only call fair Helena his wife."
Thus spake the thousand-colour'd Dame, and to her mind commends
The joy to see her first espous'd, her native tow'rs, and friends;
Which stirr'd a sweet desire in her: to serve the which she hied,
Shadow'd her graces with white veils, and (though she took a pride
To set her thoughts at gaze, and see, in her clear beauty's flood,
What choice of glory swum to her yet tender womanhood)
Season'd with tears her joys to see more joys the more offence,
And that perfection could not flow from earthly excellence.
Thus went she forth, and took with her her women most of name,
Æthra, Pitthëus' lovely birth, and Clymene, whom fame
Hath for her fair eyes memoris'd. They reach'd the Scæn Tow'rs,
Where Priam sat, to see the fight, with all his counsellors;
Panthous, Lampus, Clytius, and stout Hicetaon,
Thymœtes, wise Antenor, and profound Ucalegon;
All grave old men; and soldiérs they had been, but for age
Now left the wars; yet counsellors they were exceeding sage.
And as in well-grown woods, or trees, cold spiny grasshoppers
Sit chirping, and send voices out, that scarce can pierce our ears
For softness, and their weak faint sounds; so, talking on the tow'r,
These seniors of the people sat; who when they saw the pow'r
Of beauty, in the queen, ascend ev'n those cold-spirited peers,
Those wise and almost wither'd men, found this heat in their years,
That they were forc'd (though whispéring) to say: "What man can blame
The Greeks and Trojans to endure, for so admir'd a dame,
So many mis'ries, and so long? In her sweet count'nance shine
Looks like the Goddesses. And yet (though never so divine)
Before we boast, unjustly still, of her enforcéd prise,
And justly suffer for her sake, with all our progenies,
Labour and ruin, let her go; the profit of our land

Must pass the beauty." Thus, tough these could bear so fit a hand
On their affections, yet, when all their gravest powers were us'd,
They could not choose but welcome her, and rather they accus'd
The Gods than beauty; for thus spake the most-fam'd king of Troy:
"Come, lovéd daughter, sit by me and take the worthy joy
Of thy first husband's sight, old friends, and princes near allied,
And name me some of these brave Greeks, so manly beautified.
Come, do not think I lay the wars, endur'd by us, on thee,
The Gods have sent them, and the tears in which they swum to me.
Sit then, and name this goodly Greek, so tall, and broadly spread,
Who than the rest, that stand by him, is higher by the head;
The bravest man I ever saw, and most majestical,
His only presence makes me think him king amongst them all."
The fairest of her sex replied: Most rev'rend father-in-law,
Most lov'd, most fear'd, would some ill death had seiz'd me, when I saw
The first mean why I wrong'd you thus: that I had never lost
The sight of these my ancient friends, of him that lov'd me most,
Of my sole daughter, brothers both, with all those kindly mates,
Of one soil, one age, born with me, though under diff'rent fates!
But these boons envious stars deny; the memory of these
In sorrow pines those beauties now, that then did too much please;
Nor satisfy they your demand, to which I thus reply:
That's Agamemnon, Atreus' son, the great in empery;
A king, whom double royalty doth crown, being great and good,
And one that was my brother-in-law, when I contain'd my blood,
And was more worthy; if at all I might be said to be,
My being being lost so soon in all that honour'd me."
The good old king admir'd, and said: "O Atreus' blesséd son,
Born unto joyful destinies, that hast the empire won
Of such a world of Grecian youths, as I discover here!
I once march'd into Phrygia, that many vines doth bear,
Where many Phrygians I beheld, well-skill'd in use of horse,
That of the two men, like two Gods, were the commanded force,
Otrëus, and great Mygdonus, who on Sangarius' sands
Set down their tents with whom myself, for my assistant bands,
Was number'd as a man in chief; the cause of war was then
Th' Amazon dames, that in their facts affected to be men.
In all there was a mighty pow'r, which yet did never rise
To equal these Achaian youths, fat have the sable eyes."
Then (seeing Ulysses next) he said: "Lov'd daughter, what is he
That, lower than great Atreus' son; seems by the head to me,
Yet, in his shoulders and big breast, presents a broader show?
His armour lies upon the earth; he up and down doth go,
To see his soldiers keep their ranks, and ready have their arms,
If, in this truce, they should be tried by any false alarms.
Much like a well-grown bell-wether, or feltred ram, he shows,
That walks before a wealthy flock of fair white-fleeced ewes."
High Jove and Leda's fairest seed to Priam thus replies:

"This is the old Laertes' son, Ulysses, call'd the wise;
Who, though unfruitful Ithaca was made his nursing seat,
Yet knows he ev'ry sort of sleight, and is in counsels great."
The wise Antenor answer'd her: "'Tis true, renownéd dame;
For, some times past, wise Ithacus to Troy a legate came,
With Menelaus, for your cause; to whom I gave receipt
As guests, and welcom'd to my house, with all the love I might.
I learn'd the wisdom of their souls, and humours of their blood;
For when the Trojan council met, and these together stood,
By height of his broad shoulders had Atrides eminence,
Yet, set, Ulysses did exceed, and bred more reverence.
And when their counsels and their words they wove in one, the speech
Of Atreus' son was passing loud, small, fast, yet did not reach
To much, being naturally born Laconical; nor would
His humour lie for anything, or was, like th' other, old;
But when the prudent Ithacus did to his counsels rise,
He stood a little still, and fix'd upon the earth his eyes,
His sceptre moving neither way, but held it formally,
Like one that vainly doth affect. Of wrathful quality,
And frantic (rashly judging him) you would have said he was,
But when, out of his ample breast he gave his great voice pass,
And words that flew about our ears, like drifts of winter's snow,
None thenceforth might contend with him, tho' nought admir'd for show."
The third man, aged Priam mark'd, was Ajax Telamon,
Of whom he ask'd: "What lord is that, so large of limb and bone,
So rais'd in height, that to his breast I see there reacheth none?"
To him the Goddess of her sex, the large-veil'd Helen, said:
"That Lord is Ajax Telamon, a bulwark in their aid.
On th' other side stands Idomen, in Crete of most command,
And round about his royal sides his Cretan captains stand;
Oft hath the warlike Spartan king giv'n hospitable due
To him within our Lacene court, and all his retinue.
And now the other Achive dukes I gen'rally discern;
All which I know, and all their names could make thee quickly learn.
Two princes of the people yet, I nowhere can behold,
Castor, the skilful knight on horse and Pollux, uncontroll'd
For all stand-fights, and force of hand; both at a burthen bred;
My natural brothers; either here they have not followéd
From lovely Sparta, or, arriv'd within the sea-born fleet,
In fear of infamy for me, in broad field shame to meet."
Nor so; for holy Tellus' womb inclos'd those worthy men
In Sparta, their belovéd soil. The voiceful heralds then
The firm agreement of the Gods through all the city ring;
Two lambs, and spirit-refreshing wine (the fruit of earth) they bring,
Within a goat-skin bottle clos'd; Idæus also brought
A massy glitt'ring bowl, and cups, that all of gold were wrought;
Which bearing to the king, they cried: "Son of Laomedon
Rise, for the well-rode peers of Troy, and brass-arm'd Greeks, in

one,
Send to thee to descend the field, that they firm vows may make;
For Paris, and the Spartan king, must fight for Helen's sake,
With long-arm'd lances; and the man that proves victorious,
The woman, and the wealth she brought, shall follow to his house;
The rest knit friendship, and firm leagues; we safe in Troy shall dwell,
In Argos and Achaia they, that do in dames excel."
He said; and Priam's aged joints with chilléd fear did shake,
Yet instantly he bade his men his chariot ready make.
Which soon they did, and he ascends. He takes the reins, and guide
Antenor calls; who instantly mounts to his royal side,
And, through the Scæan ports to field, the swift-foot horse they drive.
And when at them of Troy and Greece the aged lords arrive,
From horse, on Troy's well-feeding soil, 'twixt both the hosts they go.
When straight up-rose the king of men, up-rose Ulysses too,
The heralds in their richest coats repeat (as was the guise)
The true vows of the Gods (term'd theirs, since made before their eyes)
Then in a cup of gold they mix the wine that each side brings,
And next pour water on the hands of both the kings of kings.
Which done, Atrides drew his knife, that evermore he put
Within the large sheath of his sword; with which away he cut
The wool from both fronts of the lambs, which (as a rite in use
Of execration to their heads, that brake the plighted truce)
The heralds of both hosts did give the peers of both; and then,
With hands and voice advanc'd to heav'n, thus pray'd the king of men:
"O Jove, that Ida dost protect, and hast the titles won
Most glorious, most invincible; aid thou all-seeing Sun,
All-hearing, all-recomforting; Floods; Earth; and Pow'rs beneath,
That all the perjuries of men chastise ev'n after death!
Be witnesses, and see perform'd the hearty vows we make.—
If Alexander shall the life of Menelaus take,
He shall from henceforth Helena, with all her wealth, retain,
And we will to our household Gods, hoise sail, and home again.
If, by my honour'd brother's hand, be Alexander slain,
The Trojans then shall his forc'd queen, with all her wealth, restore,
And pay convenient fine to us, aid ours for evermore.
If Priam and his sons deny to pay his, thus agreed,
When Alexander shall be slain; or that perfidious deed,
And for the fine, will I fight here, till dearly they repay,
By death and ruin, the amends, that falsehood keeps away."
This said, the throats of both the lambs cut with his royal knife,
He laid them panting on the earth, till, quite depriv'd of life,
The steel had robb'd them of their strength; then golden cups they crown'd,
With wine out of a cistern drawn; which pour'd upon the ground,
They fell upon their humble knees to all the Deities,
And thus pray'd one of both the hosts, that might do sacrifice:
"O Jupiter, most high, most great, and all the deathless Pow'rs!
Who first shall dare to violate the late sworn oaths of ours,

So let the bloods and brains of them, and all they shall produce,
Flow on the stain'd face of the earth, as now this sacred juice;
And let their wives with bastardice brand all their future race."
Thus pray'd they; but, with wish'd effects, their pray'rs Jove did not grace;
When Priam said: "Lords of both hosts, I can no longer stay
To see my lov'd son try his life, and so must take my way
To wind-exposéd Ilion. Jove yet and heav'n's high States
Know only, which of these must now pay tribute to the Fates."
Thus, putting in his coach the lambs, he mounts and reins his horse;
Antenor to him; and to Troy, both take their speedy course.
Then Hector, Priam's martial son, stepp'd forth, and met the ground,
With wise Ulysses, where the blows of combat must resound;
Which done, into a helm they put two lots, to let them know
Which of the combatants should first his brass-pil'd jav'lin throw;
When all the people standing by, with hands held up to heav'n,
Pray'd Jove the conquest might not be by force or fortune giv'n,
But that the man, who was in right the author of most wrong,
Might feel his justice, and no more these tedious wars prolong,
But, sinking to the house of death, leave them (as long before)
Link'd fast in leagues of amity, that might dissolve no more.
Then Hector shook the helm that held the equal dooms of chance,
Look'd back, and drew; and Paris first had lot to hurl his lance,
The soldiers all sat down enrank'd, each by his arms and horse
That then lay down and cool'd their hoofs. And now th' allotted course
Bids fair-hair'd Helen's husband arm; who first makes fast his greaves
With silver buckles to his legs; then on his breast receives
The curets that Lycaon wore (his brother) but made fit
For his fair body; next his sword he took, and fasten'd it,
All damask'd, underneath his arm; his shield then grave and great
His shoulders wore; and on his head his glorious helm he set,
Topp'd with a plume of horse's hair, that horribly did dance,
And seem'd to threaten as he mov'd; at last he takes his lance,
Exceeding big, and full of weight, which he with ease could use.
In like sort, Sparta's warlike king himself with arms indues.
Thus arm'd at either army both, they both stood bravely in,
Possessing both hosts with amaze, they came so chin to chin,
And, with such horrible aspécts, each other did salute.
A fair large field was made for them; where wraths, for hugeness mute,
And mutual, made them mutually at either shake their darts
Before they threw. Then Paris first with his long jav'lin parts;
It smote Atrides' orby targe, but ran not through the brass,
For in it (arming well the shield) the head reflected was.
Then did the second combatant apply him to his spear,
Which ere he threw, he thus besought almighty Jupiter:
"O Jove! Vouchsafe me now revenge, and that my enemy,
For doing wrong so undeserv'd, may pay deservedly
The pains he forfeited; and let these hands inflict those pains,
By conqu'ring, ay, by conqu'ring dead, him on whom life complains;

That any now, or anyone of all the brood of men
To live hereafter, may with fear from all offence abstain,
Much more from all such foul offence to him that was his host,
And entertain'd him as the man whom he affected most."
This said, he shook and threw his lance; which strook through Paris' shield,
And, with the strength he gave to it, it made the curets yield,
His coat of mail, his breast, and all, and drove his entrails in,
In that low region where the guts in three small parts begin;
Yet he, in bowing of his breast, prvented sable death.
This taint he follow'd with his sword, drawn from a silver sheath,
Which lifting high, he strook his helm full where his plume did stand,
On which it piecemeal brake, and fell from his unhappy hand.
At which he sighing stood, and star'd upon the ample sky,
And said: "O Jove, there is no God giv'n more illiberally
To those that serve thee than thyself, why have I pray'd in vain?
I hop'd my hand should have reveng'd, the wrongs I still sustain,
On him that did them, and still dares their foul defence pursue;
And now my lance hath miss'd his end, my sword in shivers flew,
And he 'scapes all." With this, again he rush'd upon his guest,
And caught him by the horse-hair plume, that dangled on his crest,
With thought to drag him to the Greeks; which he had surely done,
And so, besides the victory, had wondrous glory won,
(Because the needle-painted lace, with which his helm was tied
Beneath his chin, and so about his dainty throat implied,
Had strangled him;) but that, in time, the Cyprian seed of Jove
Did brake the string, with which was lin'd that which the needle wove,
And was the tough thong of a steer; and so the victor's palm
Was, for so full a man-at-arms, only an empty helm.
That then he swung about his head, and cast among his friends,
Who scrambled, and took 't up with shouts. Again then he intends
To force the life-blood of his foe, and ran on him amain,
With shaken jav'lin; when the Queen, that lovers loves, again [1]
Attended, and now ravish'd him from that encounter quite,
With ease, and wondrous suddenly; for she, a Goddess, might.
She hid him in a cloud of gold, and never made him known,
Till in his chamber, fresh and sweet, she gently set him down,
And went for Helen; whom she found in Scæa's utmost height,
To which whole swarms of city dames had climb'd to see the sight.
To give her errand good success, she took on her the shape
Of beldame Græa, who was brought by Helen, in her rape,
From Lacedæmon, and had trust in all her secrets still,
Being old, and had (of all her maids) the main bent of her will,
And spun for her her finest wool. Like her, Love's Empress came,
Pull'd Helen by the heav'nly veil, and softly said: "Madame,
My lord calls for you, you must needs make all your kind haste home;
He's in your chamber, stays, and longs; sits by your bed; pray come,
'Tis richly made, and sweet; but he more sweet, and looks so clear,
So fresh, and movingly attir'd, that, seeing, you would swear

He came not from the dusky fight, but from a courtly dance,
Or would to dancing." This she made a charm for dalliance;
Whose virtue Helen felt, and knew, by her so radiant eyes,
White neck, and most enticing breasts, the deified disguise.
At which amaz'd, she answer'd her: "Unhappy Deity!
Why lov'st thou still in these deceits to wrap my phantasy?
Or whither yet, of all the towns giv'n to their lust beside,
In Phrygia, or Mæonia, com'st thou to be my guide,
If there (of divers-languag'd men thou hast, as here in Troy,
Some other friend to be my shame; since here thy latest joy
By Menelaus now subdu'd, by him shall I be borne
Home to his court, and end my life in triumphs of his scorn?
And, to this end, would thy deceits my wanton life allure?
Hence, go thyself to Priam's son and all the ways abjure
Of Gods, or godlike-minded dames, nor ever turn again
Thy earth-affecting feet to heav'n but for his sake sustain
Toils here; guard, grace him endlessly, till he requite thy grace
By giving thee my place with him; or take his servant's place,
If, all dishonourable ways, your favours seek to serve
His never-pleas'd incontinence; I better will deserve,
Than serve his dotage now. What shame were it for me to feed
This lust in him; all honour'd dames would hate me for the deed!
He leaves a woman's love so sham'd, and shows so base a mind,
To feel nor my shame nor his own; griefs of a greater kind
Wound me than such as can admit such kind delights so soon."
The Goddess, angry that, past shame, her mere will was not done,
Replied: "Incense me not, you wretch, lest, once incens'd, I leave
Thy curs'd life to as strange a hate, as yet it may receive
A love from me; and lest I spread through both hosts such despite,
For those plagues they have felt for thee, that both abjure thee quite,
And setting thee in midst of both, turn all their wraths on thee,
And dart thee dead; that such a death may wreak thy wrong of me."
This strook the fair dame with such fear, it took her speech away,
And, shadow'd in her snowy veil, she durst not but obey;
And yet, to shun the shame she fear'd, she vanish'd undescried
Of all the Trojan ladies there, for Venus was her guide.
Arriv'd at home, her women both fell to their work in haste;
When she, that was of all her sex the most divinely grac'd,
Ascended to a higher room, though much against her will,
Where lovely Alexander was, being led by Venus still.
The laughter-loving Dame discen'd her mov'd mind by her grace,
And, for her mirth sake, set a stool, full before Paris' face,
Where she would needs have Helen sit; who, though she durst not choose
But sit, yet look'd away for all the Goddess' pow'r could use,
And used her tongue too, and to chide whom Venus sooth'd so much,
And chid, too, in this bitter kind: "And was thy cowardice such,
So conquer'd, to be seen alive? O would to God, thy life
Had perish'd by his worthy hand, to whom I first was wife!

Before this, thou wouldst glorify thy valour and thy lance,
And, past my first love's, boast them far. Go once more, and advance
Thy braves against his single pow'r; this foil might fall by chance.
Poor conquer'd man! 'Twas such a chance, as I would not advise
Thy valour should provoke again. Shun him, thou most unwise,
Lest next, thy spirit sent to hell, thy body be his prise."
He answer'd: "Pray thee, woman, cease, to chide and grieve me thus.
Disgraces will not ever last. Look on their end. On us
Will other Gods, at other times, let fall the victor's wreath,
As on him Pallas put it now. Shall our love sink beneath
The hate of fortune? In love's fire, let all hates vanish. Come,
Love never so inflam'd my heart; no, not when, bringing home
Thy beauty's so delicious prise, on Cranaë's blest shore
I long'd for, and enjoy'd thee first." With this he went before,
She after, to the odorous bed. While these to pleasure yield,
Perplex'd Atrides, savage-like, ran up and down the field,
And ev'ry thickest troop of Troy, and of their far-call'd aid,
Search'd for his foe, who could not be by any eye betray'd;
Nor out of friendship (out of doubt) did they conceal his sight,
All hated him so like their deaths, and ow'd him such despite.
At last thus spake the king of men: "Hear me, ye men of Troy,
Ye Dardans, and the rest, whose pow'rs you in their aids employ.
The conquest on my brother's part, ye all discern is clear,
Do you then Argive Helena, with all her treasure here,
Restore to us, and pay the mulct, that by your vows is due,
Yield us an honour'd recompense, and, all that should accrue
To our posterities, confirm; that when you render it,
Our acts may here be memoris'd." This all Greeks else thought fit.

[1] When the Queen, etc.-This place Virgil imitateth.

THE END OF THE THIRD BOOK.

THE ARGUMENT

The Gods in council, at the last, decree
That famous Ilion shall expugnéd be;
And that their own continu'd faults may prove
The reasons that have so incenséd Jove,
Minerva seeks, with more offences done
Against the lately injur'd Atreus' son,
(A ground that clearest would make seen their sin)
To have the Lycian Pandarus begin.
He ('gainst the truce with sacred cov'nants bound)

Gives Menelaus a dishonour'd wound,
Machaon heals him. Agamemnon then
To mortal war incenseth all his men.
The battles join; and, in the heat of fight,
Cold death shuts many eyes in endless night.

ANOTHER ARGUMENT

In Delta is the Gods' Assize;
The truce is broke; wars freshly rise.
Within the fair-pav'd court of Jove, he and the Gods conferr'd
About the sad events of Troy; amongst whom minister'd
Bless'd Hebe nectar. As they sat, and did Troy's tow'rs behold,
They drank, and pledg'd each other round in full-crown'd cups of gold.
The mirth at whose feast was begun by great Saturnides
In urging a begun dislike amongst the Goddesses,
But chiefly in his solemn queen, whose spleen he was dispos'd
To tempt yet further, knowing well what anger it inclos'd,
And how wives' angers should be us'd. On which, thus pleas'd, he play'd:
"Two Goddesses there are that still give Menelaus aid,
And one that Paris loves. The two that sit from us so far
(Which Argive Juno is, and She that rules in deeds of war,)
No doubt are pleas'd to see how well the late-seen fight did frame;
And yet, upon the adverse part, the laughter-loving Dame
Made her pow'r good too for her friend; for, though he were so near
The stroke of death in th' others' hopes, she took him from them clear.
The conquest yet is questionless the martial Spartan king's.
We must consult then what events shall crown these future things,
If wars and combats we shall still with even successes strike,
Or as impartial friendship plant on both parts. If ye like
The last, and that it will as well delight as merely please
Your happy deities, still let stand old Priam's town in peace,
And let the Lacedæmon king again his queen enjoy."
As Pallas and Heav'n's Queen sat close, complotting ill to Troy,
With silent murmurs they receiv'd this ill-lik'd choice from Jove;
'Gainst whom was Pallas much incens'd, because the Queen of Love
Could not, without his leave, relieve in that late point of death
The son of Priam, whom she loath'd; her wrath yet fought beneath
Her supreme wisdom, and was curb'd; but Juno needs must ease
Her great heart with her ready tongue, and said; "What words are these,
Austere, and too-much-Saturn's son? Why wouldst thou render still
My labours idle, and the sweat of my industrious will
Dishonour with so little pow'r? My chariot-horse are tir'd
With posting to and fro for Greece, and bringing banes desir'd
To people must'ring Priamus, and his perfidious sons;
Yet thou protect'st, and join'st with them whom each just Deity shuns.
Go on, but ever go resolv'd all other Gods have vow'd

To cross thy partial course for Toy, in all that makes it proud."
At this, the cloud-compelling Jove a far-fetch'd sigh let fly,
And said: "Thou fury! What offence of such impiety
Hath Priam or his sons done thee, that, with so high a hate,
Thou shouldst thus ceaselessly desire to raze and ruinate
So well a builded town as Troy? I think, hadst thou the pow'r,
Thou wouldst the ports and far-stretch'd walls fly over, and devour
Old Priam and his issue quick, and make all Troy thy feast,
And then at length I hope thy wrath and tiréd spleen would rest;
To which run on thy chariot, that nought be found in me
Of just cause to our future jars. In this yet strengthen thee,
And fix it in thy memory fast, this if I entertain
As peremptory a desire to level with the plain
A city where thy lovéd live, stand not betwixt my ire
And what it aims at, but give way, when thou hast thy desire;
Which now I grant thee willingly, although against my will.
For not beneath the ample sun, and heav'n's star-bearing hill,
There is a town of earthly men so honour'd in my mind
As sacred Troy; nor of earth's kings as Priam and his kind,
Who never let my altars lack rich feast of off'rings slain,
And their sweet savours; for which grace I honour them again."
Dread Juno, with the cow's fair eyes, replied: "Three towns there are
Of great and eminent respect, both in my love and care;
Mycene, with the broad highways; and Argos, rich in horse;
And Sparta; all which three destroy, when thou envi'st their force,
I will not aid them, nor malign thy free and sov'reign will,
For if I should be envious, and set against their ill,
I know my envy were in vain, since thou art mightier far.
But we must give each other leave, and wink at either's war.
I likewise must have pow'r to crown my works with wishéd end,
Because I am a Deity, and did from thence descend
Whence thou thyself, and th' elder born; wise Saturn was our sire;
And thus there is a two-fold cause that pleads for my desire,
Being sister, and am call'd thy wife; and more, since thy command
Rules all Gods else, I claim therein a like superior hand.
All wrath before then now remit, and mutually combine
In either's empire; I, thy rule, and thou, illustrate, mine;
So will the other Gods agree, and we shall all be strong.
And first (for this late plot) with speed let Pallas go among
The Trojans, and some one of them entice to break the truce
By off'ring in some treach'rous wound the honour'd Greeks abuse."
The Father both of men and Gods agreed, and Pallas sent,
With these wing'd words, to both the hosts: "Make all haste, and invent
Some mean by which the men of Troy, against the truce agreed,
May stir the glorious Greeks to arms with some inglorious deed."
Thus charg'd he her with haste that did, before, in haste abound,
Who cast herself from all the heights, with which steep heav'n is crown'd.
And as Jove, brandishing a star, which men a comet call,

Hurls out his curled hair abroad, that from his brand exhals
A thousand sparks, to fleets at sea, and ev'ry mighty host,
Of all presages and ill-haps a sign mistrusted most;
So Pallas fell 'twixt both the camps, and suddenly was lost,
When through the breasts of all that saw, she strook a strong amaze
With viewing, in her whole descent, her bright and ominous blaze.
When straight one to another turn'd, and said: "Now thund'ring Jove
(Great Arbiter of peace and arms) will either stablish love
Amongst our nations, or renew such war as never was."
Thus either army did presage, when Pallas made her pass
Amongst the multitude of Troy; who now put on the grace
Of brave Laodocus, the flow'r of old Antenor's race,
And sought for Lycian Pandarus, a man that, being bred
Out of a faithless family, she thought was fit to shed
The blood of any innocent, and break the cov'nant sworn;
He was Lycaon's son, whom Jove into a wolf did turn
For sacrificing of a child, and yet in arms renown'd
As one that was inculpable. Him Pallas standing found,
And round about him his strong troops that bore the shady shields;
He brought them from Æsepus' flood, let through the Lycian fields;
Whom standing near, she whisper'd thus: "Lycaon's warlike son,
Shall I despair at thy kind hands to have a favour done?
Nor dar'st thou let an arrow fly upon the Spartan king?
It would be such a grace to Troy, and such a glorious thing,
That ev'ry man would give his gift; but Alexander's hand
Would load thee with them, if he could discover from his stand
His foe's pride strook down with thy shaft, and he himself ascend
The flaming heap of funeral. Come, shoot him, princely friend;
But first invoke the God of Light, that in thy land was born,
And is in archers' art the best that ever sheaf hath worn,
To whom a hundred first-ew'd lambs vow thou in holy fire,
When safe to sacred Zelia's tow'rs thy zealous steps retire."
With this the mad gift-greedy man Minerva did persuade,
Who instantly drew forth a bow, most admirably made
Of th' antler of a jumping goat bred in a steep upland,
Which archer-like (as long before he took his hidden stand,
The evicke skipping from a rock) into the breast he smote,
And headlong fell'd him from his cliff. The forehead of the goat
Held out a wondrous goodly palm, that sixteen branches brought;
Of all which join'd, an useful bow a skilful bowyer wrought,
Which pick'd and polish'd, both the ends he hid with horns of gold.
And this bow, bent, he close laid down, and bad his soldiers hold
Their shields before him, lest the Greeks, discerning him, should rise
In tumults ere the Spartan king could be his arrow's prise.
Mean space, with all his care he choos'd, and from his quiver drew,
An arrow, feather'd best for flight and yet that never flew,
Strong headed, and most apt to pierce; then took he up his bow,
And nock'd his shaft, the ground whence all their future grief did grow.

When, praying to his God the Sun, that was in Lycia bred,
And king of archers, promising that he the blood would shed
Of full an hundred first-fall'n lambs, all offer'd to his name,
When to Zelia's sacred walls from rescu'd Troy he came,
He took his arrow by the nock, and to his bended breast [1]
The oxy sinew close he drew, ev'n till the pile did rest
Upon the bosom of the bow; and as that savage prise
His strength constrain'd into an orb, as if the wind did rise
The coming of it made a noise, the sinew-forgéd string
Did give a mighty twang, and forth the eager shaft did sing,
Affecting speediness of flight, amongst the Achive throng.
Nor were the blesséd Heav'nly Pow'rs unmindful of thy wrong,
O Menelaus, but, in chief, Jove's seed: the Pillager,
Stood close before, and slack'd the force the arrow did confer,
With as much care and little hurt, as doth a mother use,
And keep off from her babe, when sleep doth through his pow'rs diffuse
His golden humour, and th' assaults of rude and busy flies
She still checks with her careful hand; for so the shaft she plies
That on the buttons made of gold, which made his girdle fast,
And where his curets double were, the fall of it she plac'd.
And thus much proof she put it to: the buckle made of gold;
The belt it fast'ned, bravely wrought; his curets' double fold;
And last, the charméd plate he wore, which help'd him more than all,
And, 'gainst all darts and shafts bestow'd, was to his life a wall;
So, through all these, the upper skin the head did only race;
Yet forth the blood flow'd, which did much his royal person grace,
And show'd upon his ivory skin, as doth a purple dye
Laid, by a dame of Caïra, or lovely Mæony,
On ivory, wrought in ornaments to deck the cheeks of horse;
Which in her marriage room must lie; whose beauties have such force
That they are wish'd of many knights, but are such precious things,
That they are kept for horse that draw the chariots of kings,
Which horse, so deck'd, the charioteer esteems a grace to him;
Like these, in grace, the blood upon thy solid thighs did swim,
O Menelaus, down by calves and ankles to the ground.
For nothing decks a soldier so, as doth an honour'd wound.
Yet, fearing he had far'd much worse, the hair stood up on end
On Agamemnon, when he saw so much black blood descend.
And stiff'ned with the like dismay was Menelaus too,
But seeing th' arrow's stale without, and that the head did go
No further than it might be seen, he call'd his spirits again;
Which Agamemnon marking not but thinking he was slain,
He grip'd his brother by the hand, and sigh'd as he would break,
Which sigh the whole host took from him, who thus at last did speak:
"O dearest brother, is't for this, that thy death must be wrought,
Wrought I this truce? For this has thou the single combat fought
For all the army of the Greeks? For this hath Ilion sworn,
And trod all faith beneath their feet? Yet all this hath not worn

The right we challeng'd out of force; this cannot render vain
Our stricken right hands, sacred wine, nor all our off'rings slain;
For though Olympius be not quick in making good our ill,
He will be sure as he is slow, and sharplier prove his will.
Their own hands shall be ministers of those plagues they despise,
Which shall their wives and children reach, and all their progenies.
For both in mind and soul I know, that there shall come a day
When Ilion, Priam, all his pow'r, shall quite be worn away,
When heav'n-inhabiting Jove shall shake his fiery shield at all,
For this one mischief. This, I know, the world cannot recall.
But be all this, all my grief still for thee will be the same,
Dear brother. If thy life must here put out his royal flame,
I shall to sandy Argos turn with infamy my face;
And all the Greeks will call for home; old Priam and his race
Will flame in glory; Helena untouch'd be still their prey;
And thy bones in our enemies' earth our curséd fates shall lay;
Thy sepulchre be trodden down; the pride of Troy desire
Insulting on it, 'Thus, O thus, let Agamemnon's ire
In all his acts be expiate, as now he carries home
His idle army, empty ships, and leaves here overcome
Good Menelaus.' When this rave breaks in their bated breath,
Then let the broad earth swallow me, and take me quick to death."
"Nor shall this ever chance," said he, "and therefore be of cheer,
Lest all the army, led by you, your passions put in fear.
The arrow fell in no such place a death could enter at,
My girdle, curets doubled here, and my most trusted plate,
Objected all 'twixt me and death, the shaft scarce piercing one."
"Good brother," said the king, "I wish it were no further gone,
For then our best in med'cines skilled shall ope and search the wound,
Applying balms to ease thy pains, and soon restore thee sound."
This said, divine Talthybiús he call'd, and bad him haste
Machaon (Æsculapius' son, who most of men was grac'd
With physic's sov'reign remedies) to come and lend his hand
To Menelaus, shot by one well-skill'd in the command
Of bow and arrows, one of Troy, or of the Lycian aid,
Who much hath glorified our foe, and us as much dismay'd.
He heard, and hasted instantly, and cast his eyes about
The thickest squadrons of the Greeks, to find Machaon out.
He found him standing guarded well with well-arm'd men of Thrace;
With whom he quickly join'd, and said: "Man of Apollo's race,
Haste, for the king of men commands, to see a wound impress'd
In Menelaus, great in arms, by one instructed best
In th' art of archery, of Troy, or of the Lycian bands,
That them with much renown adorns, us with dishonour brands."
Machaon much was mov'd with this, who with the herald flew
From troop to troop alongst the host; and soon they came in view
Of hurt Atrides, circled round with all the Grecian kings;
Who all gave way, and straight he draws the shaft, which forth he brings

Without the forks; the girdle then, plate, curets, off he plucks,
And views the wound; when first from it the clotter'd blood he sucks,
Then med'cines, wondrously compos'd, the skilful leech applied,
Which loving Chiron taught his sire, he from his sire had tried.
While these were thus employ'd to ease the Atrean martialist,
The Trojans arm'd, and charg'd the Greeks; the Greeks arm and resist.
Then not asleep, nor maz'd with fear, nor shifting off the blows,
You could behold the king of men, but in full speed he goes
To set a glorious fight on foot; and he examples this,
With toiling, like the worst, on foot; who therefore did dismiss
His brass-arm'd chariot, and his steeds, with Ptolemëus' son,
Son of Piraides, their guide, the good Eurymedon;
"Yet," said the king, "attend with them, lest weariness should seize
My limbs, surcharg'd with ord'ring troops so thick and vast as these."
Eurymedon then rein'd his horse, that trotted neighing by;
The king a footman, and so scours the squadrons orderly.
Those of his swiftly-mounted Greeks, that in their arms were fit,
Those he put on with cheerful words, and bad them not remit
The least spark of their forward spirits, because the Trojans durst
Take these abhorr'd advantages, but let them do their worst;
For they might be assur'd that Jove would patronise no lies,
And that who, with the breach of truce, would hurt their enemies,
With vultures should be torn themselves; that they should raze their town,
Their wives, and children at their breast, led vassals to their own.
But such as he beheld hang of from that increasing fight,
Such would he bitterly rebuke, and with disgrace excite:
"Base Argives, blush ye not to stand as made for butts to darts?
Why are ye thus discomfited, like hinds that have no hearts,
Who, wearied with a long-run field, are instantly emboss'd,
Stand still, and in their beastly breasts is all their courage lost?
And so stand you strook with amaze, nor dare to strike a stroke.
Would ye the foe should nearer yet your dastard spleens provoke,
Ev'n where on Neptune's foamy shore our navies lie in sight,
To see if Jove will hold your hands, and teach ye how to fight?"
Thus he, commanding, rang'd the host, and, passing many a band,
He came to the Cretensian troops, where all did arméd stand
About the martial Idomen; who bravely stood before
In vanguard of his troops, and match'd for strength a savage boar;
Meriones, his charioteer, the rearguard bringing on.
Which seen to Atreus' son, to him it was a sight alone,
And Idomen's confirméd mind with these kind words he seeks:
"O Idomen! I ever lov'd thy self past all the Greeks,
In war, or any work of peace, at table, ev'rywhere;
For when the best of Greece besides mix ever, at our cheer,
My good old ardent wine with small, and our inferior mates
Drink ev'n that mix'd wine measur'd too, thou drink'st, without those rates,
Our old wine neat, and evermore thy bowl stands full like mine,
To drink still when and what thou wilt. Then rouse that heart of thine,

And, whatsoever heretofore thou hast assum'd to be,
This day be greater." To the king in this sort answer'd he:
"Atrides, what I ever seem'd, the same at ev'ry part
This day shall show me at the full, and I will fit thy heart.
But thou shouldst rather cheer the rest, and tell them they in right
Of all good war must offer blows, and should begin the fight,
(Since Troy first brake the holy truce) and not endure these braves.
To take wrong first, and then be dar'd to the revenge it craves;
Assuring them that Troy in fate must have the worst at last,
Since first, and 'gainst a truce, they hurt, where they should have embrac'd."
This comfort and advice did fit Atrides' heart indeed
Who still through new-rais'd swarms of men held his laborious speed,
And came where both th' Ajaces stood; whom like the last he found
Arm'd, casqu'd, and ready for the fight. Behind them, hid the ground
A cloud of foot, that seem'd to smoke. And as a goatherd spies,
On some hill's top, out of the sea a rainy vapour rise,
Driv'n by the breath of Zephyrus which, though far off he rest,
Comes on as black as pitch, and brings a tempest in his breast,
Whereat he frighted, drives his herds apace into a den;
So dark'ning earth with darts and shields show'd these with all their men.
This sight with like joy fir'd the king, who thus let forth the flame
In crying out to both the dukes: "O you of equal name,
I must not cheer, nay, I disclaim all my command of you,
Yourselves command with such free minds, and make your soldiers show
As you nor I led, but themselves. O would our father Jove,
Minerva, and the God of Light, would all our bodies move
With such brave spirits as breathe in you, then Priam's lofty town
Should soon be taken by our hands, for ever overthrown!"
Then held he on to other troops, and Nestor next beheld,
The subtle Pylian orator, range up and down the field
Embattelling his men at arms, and stirring all to blows,
Points ev'ry legion out his chief, and ev'ry chief he shows
The forms and discipline of war, yet his commanders were
All expert, and renownéd men. Great Pelagon was there,
Alastor, manly Chromius, and Hæmon worth a throne,
Arid Bias that could armies lead. With these he first put on
His horse troops with their chariots; his foot (of which he choos'd
Many, the best and ablest men, and which he ever us'd
As rampire to his gen'ral pow'r) he in the rear dispos'd.
The slothful, and the least of spirit, he in the midst inclos'd,
That, such as wanted noble wills, base need might force to stand.
His horse troops, that the vanguard had, he strictly did command
To ride their horses temp'rately, to keep their ranks, and shun
Confusion, lest their horsemanship and courage made them run
(Too much presum'd on) much too far, and, charging so alone,
Engage themselves in th' enemy's strength, where many fight with one.
"Who his own chariot leaves to range, let him not freely go,
But straight unhorse him with a lance; for 'tis much better so.

And with this discipline," said he, "this form, these minds, this trust,
Our ancestors have walls and towns laid level with the dust."
Thus prompt, and long inur'd to arms, this old man did exhort;
And this Atrides likewise took in wondrous cheerful sort,
And said: "O father, would to heav'n, that as thy mind remains
In wonted vigour, so thy knees could undergo our pains!
But age, that all men overcomes, hath made his prise on thee;
Yet still I wish that some young man, grown old in mind, might be
Put in proportion with thy years, and thy mind, young in age,
Be fitly answer'd with his youth; that still where conflicts rage,
And young men us'd to thirst for fame, thy brave exampling hand
Might double our young Grecian spirits, and grace our whole command."
The old knight answer'd: "I myself could wish, O Atreus' son,
I were as young as when I slew brave Ereuthalion,
But Gods at all times give not all their gifts to mortal men.
If then I had the strength of youth, I miss'd the counsels then
That years now give me; and now years want that main strength of youth;
Yet still my mind retains her strength (as you now said the sooth)
And would be where that strength is us'd, affording counsel sage
To stir youth's minds up; 'tis the grace and office of our age;
Let younger sinews, men sprung up whole ages after me,
And such as have strength, use it, and as strong in honour be."
The king, all this while comforted, arriv'd next where he found
Well-rode Menestheus (Peteus' son) stand still, inviron'd round
With his well-train'd Athenian troops, and next to him he spied
The wise Ulysses, deedless too, and all his bands beside
Of strong Cephalians; for as yet th' alarm had not been heard
In all their quarters, Greece and Troy were then so newly stirr'd,
And then first mov'd, as they conceiv'd; and they so look'd about
To see both hosts give proof of that they yet had cause to doubt.
Atrides seeing them stand so still, and spend their eyes at gaze,
Began to chide: "And why," said he, "dissolv'd thus in amaze,
Thou son of Peteus, Jove-nurs'd king, and thou in wicked sleight
A cunning soldier, stand ye off? Expect ye that the fight
Should be by other men begun? 'Tis fit the foremost band
Should show you there; you first should front who first lifts up his hand.
First you can hear, when I invite the princes to a feast,
When first, most friendly, and at will, ye eat and drink the best,
Yet in the fight, most willingly, ten troops ye can behold
Take place before ye." Ithacus at this his brows did fold,
And said: "How hath thy violent tongue broke through thy set of teeth,
To say that we are slack in fight, and to the field of death
Look others should enforce our way, when we were busied then,
Ev'n when thou spak'st, against the foe to cheer and lead our men?
But thy eyes shall be witnesses, if it content thy will,
And that (as thou pretend'st) these cares do so affect thee still,
The father of Telemachus (whom I esteem so dear,
And to whom, as a legacy, I'll leave my deeds done here)

Ev'n with the foremost band of Troy hath his encounter dar'd,
And therefore are thy speeches vain, and had been better spar'd."
He, smiling, since he saw him mov'd, recall'd his words, and said:
"Most generous Laertes' son, most wise of all our aid,
I neither do accuse thy worth, more than thyself may hold
Fit, (that inferiors think not much, being slack, to be controll'd)
Nor take I on me thy command; for well I know thy mind
Knows how sweet gentle counsels are, and that thou stand'st inclin'd,
As I myself, for all our good. On then; if now we spake
What hath displeas'd, another time we full amends will make;
And Gods grant that thy virtue ere may prove so free and brave,
That my reproofs may still be vain, and thy deservings grave."
Thus parted they; and forth he went, when he did leaning find,
Against his chariot, near his horse, him with the mighty mind,
Great Diomedes, Tydeus' son, and Sthenelus, the seed
Of Capaneius; whom the king seeing likewise out of deed,
Thus cried he out on Diomed: "O me! In what a fear
The wise great warrior, Tydeus' son, stands gazing ev'rywhere
For others to begin the fight! It was not Tydeus' use
To be so daunted, whom his spirit would evermore produce
Before the foremost of his friends in these affairs of fright,
As they report that have beheld him labour in a fight.
For me, I never knew the man, nor in his presence came,
But excellent, above the rest, he was in gen'ral fame;
And one renown'd exploit of his, I am assur'd, is true.
He came to the Mycenian court, without arms, and did sue,
At godlike Polynices' hands, to have some worthy aid
To their designs that 'gainst the walls of sacred Thebes were laid.
He was great Polynices' guest, and nobly entertain'd,
And of the kind Mycenian state what he requested gain'd,
In mere consent; but when they should the same in act approve,
By some sinister prodigies, held out to them by Jove,
They were discourag'd. Thence he went, and safely had his pass
Back to Asopus' flood, renown'd for bulrushes and grass.
Yet, once more, their ambassador, the Grecian peers address
Lord Tydeus to Eteocles; to whom being giv'n access,
He found him feasting with a crew of Cadmeans in his hall;
Amongst whom, though an enemy, and only one to all;
To all yet he his challenge made at ev'ry martial feat,
And eas'ly foil'd all, since with him Minerva was so great.
The rank-rode Cadmeans, much incens'd with their so foul disgrace,
Lodg'd ambuscadoes for their foe, in some well-chosen place
By which he was to make return. Twice five-and-twenty men,
And two of them great captains too, the ambush did contain.
The names of those two men of rule were Mæon, Hæmon's son,
And Lycophontes, Keep-field call'd, the heir of Autophon,
By all men honour'd like the Gods; yet these and all their friends
Were sent to hell by Tydeus' hand, and had untimely ends.

He trusting to the aid of Gods, reveal'd by augury,
Obeying which, one chief he sav'd, and did his life apply
To be the heavy messenger of all the others' deaths;
And that sad message, with his life, to Mæon he bequeaths.
So brave a knight was Tydeüs of whom a son is sprung,
Inferior far in martial deeds, though higher in his tongue."
All this Tydides silent heard, aw'd by the rev'rend king;
Which stung hot Sthenelus with wrath, who thus put forth his sting:
"Atrides, when thou know'st the truth, speak what thy knowledge is,
And do not lie so; for I know and I will brag in this,
That we are far more able men than both our fathers were.
We took the sev'n-fold ported Thebes, when yet we had not there
So great help as our fathers had; and fought beneath a wall,
Sacred to Mars, by help of Jove, and trusting to the fall
Of happy signs from other Gods, by whom we took the town
Untouch'd; our fathers perishing here by follies of their own;
And therefore never more compare our fathers' worth with ours."
Tydides frown'd at this, and said: "Suppress thine anger's pow'rs,
Good friend, and hear why I refrain'd. Thou seest I am not mov'd
Against our gen'ral, since he did but what his place behov'd,
Admonishing all Greeks to fight; for, if Troy prove our prise,
The honour and the joy is his; if here our ruin lies,
The shame and grief for that as much is his in greatest kinds.
As he then his charge, weigh we ours; which is our dauntless minds."
Thus, from his chariot, amply arm'd, he jump'd down to the ground;
The armour of the angry king so horribly did sound,
It might have made his bravest foe let fear take down his braves.
And as when with the west-wind flaws, the sea thrusts up her waves,
One after other, thick and high, upon the groaning shores,
First in herself loud, but oppos'd with banks and rocks she roars,
And, all her back in bristles set, spits ev'ry way her foam;
So, after Diomed, instantly the field was overcome
With thick impressions of the Greeks; and all the noise that grew
(Ord'ring and cheering up their men) from only leaders flew.
The rest went silently away, you could not hear a voice,
Nor would have thought, in all their breasts, they had one in their choice,
Their silence uttering their awe of them that them controll'd,
Which made each man keep right his arms, march, fight still where he should
The Trojans (like a sort of ewes, penn'd in a rich man's fold,
Close at his door, till all be milk'd, and never baaing hold
Hearing the bleating of their lambs) did all their wide host fill
With shouts and clamours, nor observ'd one voice, one baaing still,
But show'd mix'd tongues from many a land of men call'd to their aid.
Rude Mars had th' ordering of their spirits; of Greeks, the learned Maid
But Terror follow'd both the hosts, and Flight, and furious Strife
The sister, and the mate, of Mars, that spoil of human life;
And never is her rage at rest, at first she is but small,
Yet after, but a little fed, she grows so vast and tall

That, while her feet move here in earth, her forehead is in heav'n;
And this was she that made ev'n then both hosts so deadly giv'n.
Through ev'ry troop she stalk'd, and stirr'd rough sighs up as she went;
But when in one field both the foes her fury did content,
And both came under reach of darts, then darts and shields oppos'd
To darts and shields; strength answer'd strength; then swords and targets clos'd
With swords and targets; both with pikes; and then did tumult rise
Up to her height; then conqu'rors' boasts mix'd with the conquer'd's cries;
Earth flow'd with blood. And as from hills rainwaters headlong fall,
That all ways eat huge ruts, which, met in one bed, fill a vall
With such a confluence of streams, that on the mountain grounds
Far off, in frighted shepherds' ears, the bustling noise rebounds:
So grew their conflicts, and so show'd their scuffling to the ear,
With flight and clamour still commix'd, and all effects of fear.
And first renown'd Antilochus slew (fighting, in the face
Of all Achaia's foremost bands, with an undaunted grace)
Echepolus Thalysiades; he was an arméd man;
Whom on his hair-plum'd helmet's crest the dart first smote, then ran
Into his forehead, and there stuck; the steel pile making way
Quite through his skull; a hasty night shut up his latest day.
His fall was like a fight-rac'd tow'r; like which lying there dispread,
King Elephenor (who was son to Chalcodon, and led
The valiant Abants) covetous that he might first possess
His arms, laid hands upon his feet, and hal'd him from the press
Of darts and jav'lins hurl'd at him. The action of the king
When great-in-heart Agenor saw, he made his jav'lin sing
To th' others' labour; and along as he the trunk did wrest,
His side (at which he bore his shield) in bowing of his breast
Lay naked, and receiv'd the lance, that made him lose his hold
And life together; which, in hope of that he lost, he sold,
But for his sake the fight grew fierce, the Trojans and their foes
Like wolves on one another rush'd, and man for man it goes.
The next of name, that serv'd his fate, great Ajax Telamon
Preferr'd so sadly. He was heir to old Anthemion,
And deck'd with all the flow'r of youth; the fruit of which yet fled,
Before the honour'd nuptial torch could light him to his bed.
His name was Simoisius; for, some few years before,
His mother walking down the hill of Ida, by the shore
Of silver Simois, to see her parents' flocks, with them
She, feeling suddenly the pains of child-birth, by the stream
Of that bright river brought him forth; and so (of Simois)
They call'd him Simoisius. Sweet was that birth of his
To his kind parents, and his growth did all their care employ;
And yet those rites of piety, that should have been his joy
To pay their honour'd years again in as affectionate sort,
He could not graciously perform, his sweet life was so short,
Cut off with mighty Ajax' lance; for, as his spirit put on,
He strook him at his breast's right pap, quite through his shoulder-bone,

And in the dust of earth he fell, that was the fruitful soil
Of his friends' hopes; but where he sow'd he buried all his toil.
And as a poplar shot aloft, set by a river side,
In moist edge of a mighty fen, his head in curls implied,
But all his body plain and smooth, to which a wheel-wright puts
The sharp edge of his shining axe, and his soft timber cuts
From his in native root, in hope to hew out of his bole
The fell'ffs, or out-parts of a wheel, that compass in the whole,
To serve some goodly chariot; but, being big and sad,
And to be hal'd home through the bogs, the useful hope he had
Sticks there, and there the goodly plant lies with'ring out his grace:
So lay, by Jove-bred Ajax' hand, Anthemion's forward race,
Nor could through that vast fen of toils be drawn to serve the ends
Intended by his body's pow'rs, nor cheer his aged friends.
But now the gay-arm'd Antiphus, a son of Priam, threw
His lance at Ajax through the prease; which went by him, and flew
On Leucus, wise Ulysses' friend; his groin it smote, as fain
He would have drawn into his spoil the carcass of the slain,
By which he fell, and that by him; it vex'd Ulysses' heart,
Who thrust into the face of fight, well-arm'd at ev'ry part,
Came close, and look'd about to find an object worth his lance;
Which when the Trojans saw him shake, and he so near advance,
All shrunk; he threw, and forth it shin'd, nor fell but where it fell'd;
His friend's grief gave it angry pow'r, and deadly way it held
Upon Democoon, who was sprung of Priam's wanton force,
Came from Abydus, and was made the master of his horse.
Through both his temples strook the dart, the wood of one side shew'd,
The pile out of the other look'd, and so the earth he strew'd
With much sound of his weighty arms. Then back the foremost went;
Ev'n Hector yielded; then the Greeks gave worthy clamours vent,
Effecting then their first-dumb pow'rs; some drew the dead, and spoil'd,
Some follow'd, that, in open flight, Troy might confess it foil'd.
Apollo, angry at the sight, from top of Ilion cried:
"Turn head, ye well-rode peers of Troy, feed not the Grecians' pride,
They are not charm'd against your points, of steel, nor iron, fram'd;
Nor fights the fair-hair'd Thetis' son, but sits at fleet inflam'd."
So spake the dreadful God from Troy. The Greeks, Jove's noblest Seed
Encourag'd to keep on the chace; and, where fit spirit did need,
She gave it, marching in the midst. Then flew the fatal hour
Back on Diores, in return of Ilion's sun-burn'd pow'r;
Diores Amaryncides, whose right leg's ankle-bone,
And both the sinews, with a sharp and handful-charging stone
Pirus Imbrasides did break, that led the Thracian bands
And came from Ænos; down he fell, and up he held his hands
To his lov'd friends; his spirit wing'd to fly out of his breast
With which not satisfied, again Imbrasides address'd
His jav'lin at him, and so ripp'd his navel, that the wound,
As endlessly it shut his eyes, so, open'd, on the ground

It pour'd his entrails. As his foe went then suffic'd away,
Thoas Ætolius threw a dart, that did his pile convey,
Above his nipple, through his lungs; when, quitting his stern part,
He clos'd with him, and, from his breast first drawing out his dart,
His sword flew in, and by the midst it wip'd his belly out;
So took his life, but left his arms; his friends so flock'd about,
And thrust forth lances of such length before their slaughter'd king,
Which, though their foe were big and strong, and often brake the ring
Forg'd of their lances, yet (enforc'd) he left th' affected prise.
The Thracian and Epeian dukes, laid close with closéd eyes
By either other, drown'd in dust; and round about the plain,
All hid with slaughter'd carcasses, yet still did hotly reign
The martial planet; whose effects had any eye beheld,
Free and unwounded (and were led by Pallas through the field,
To keep off jav'lins, and suggest the least fault could be found)
He could not reprehend the fight, so many strew'd the ground.

[1] Virgil useth these verses.

THE END OF THE FOURTH BOOK.

THE ARGUMENT

King Diomed (by Pallas' spirit inspir'd
With will and pow'r) is for his acts admir'd,
Mere men, and men deriv'd from Deities,
And Deities themselves, he terrifies.
Adds wounds to terrors. His inflamed lance
Draws blood from Mars, and Venus. In a trance
He casts Æneas, with a weighty stone;
Apollo quickens him, and gets him gone.
Mars is recur'd by Pæon, but by Jove
Rebuk'd for authoring breach of human love.

ANOTHER ARGUMENT

In Epsilon, Heav'n's blood is shed
By sacred rage of Diomed.
Then Pallas breath'd in Tydeus' son; to render whom supreme
To all the Greeks, at all his parts, she cast a hotter beam
On his high mind, his body fill'd with much superior might,
And made his cómplete armour cast a far more cómplete light.
From his bright helm and shield did burn a most unwearied fire, [1]

Like rich Autumnus' golden lamp, whose brightness men admire
Past all the other host of stars, when, with his cheerful face
Fresh wash'd in lofty Ocean waves, he doth the skies enchase.
To let whose glory, lose no sight, still Pallas made him turn
Where tumult most express'd his pow'r, and where the fight did burn.
An honest and a wealthy man inhabited in Troy,
Dares, the priest of Mulciber, who two sons did enjoy,
Idæus, and bold Phegeüs, well-seen in ev'ry fight.
These (singled from their troops, and hors'd) assail'd Minerva's knight,
Who rang'd from fight to fight on foot. All hasting mutual charge,
And now drawn near, first Phegeus threw a jav'lin swift and large,
Whose head the king's left shoulder took, but did no harm at all;
Then rush'd he out a lance at him, that had no idle fall,
But in his breast stuck 'twixt the paps, and strook him from his horse.
Which stern sight when Idæus saw, distrustful of his force
To save his slaughter'd brother's spoil, it made him headlong leap
From his fair chariot, and leave all; yet had not 'scap'd the heap
Of heavy fun'ral, if the God, great President of fire,
Had not in sudden clouds of smoke and pity of his sire
To leave him utterly unheir'd, giv'n safe pass to his feet.
He gone, Tydides sent the horse and chariot to the fleet.
The Trojans seeing Dares' sons one slain, the other fled,
Were strook amaz'd. The blue-ey'd Maid (to grace her Diomed
In giving free way to his pow'r) made this so ruthful fact
A fit advantage to remove the War-god out of act,
Who rag'd so on the Ilion side. She grip'd his hand, and said:
"Mars, Mars, thou ruiner of men, that in the dust hast laid
So many cities, and with blood thy godhead dost distain,
Now shall we cease to show our breasts as passionate as men,
And leave the mixture of our hands, resigning Jove his right,
As Rector of the Gods, to give the glory of the fight
Where he affecteth, lest he force what he should freely yield?"
He held it fit, and went with her from the tumultuous field,
Who set him in an herby seat on broad Scamander's shore.
He gone, all Troy was gone with him, the Greeks drave all before.
And ev'ry leader slew a man; but first the king of men
Deserv'd the honour of his name, and led the slaughter then,
And slew a leader, one more huge than any man he led,
Great Odius, duke of Halizons; quite from his chariot's head
He strook him with a lance to earth, as first he flight address'd;
It took his forward-turnéd back, and look'd out of his breast;
His huge trunk sounded, and his arms did echo the resound.
Idomenæus to the death did noble Phæstus wound,
The son of Meon-Borus, that from cloddy Terna came;
Who, taking chariot, took his wound, and tumbled with the same
From his attempted seat: the lance through his right shoulder strook,
And horrid darkness strook through him; the spoil his soldiers took.
Atrides-Menelaus slew, as he before him fled,

Scamandrius, son of Strophius, that was a huntsman bred;
A skilful huntsman, for his skill Diana's self did teach,
And made him able with his dart infallibly to reach
All sorts of subtlest savages, which many a woody hill
Bred for him, and he much preserv'd, and all to show his skill.
Yet not the dart-delighting Queen taught him to shun this dart,
Nor all his hitting so far off, the mast'ry of his art;
His back receiv'd it, and he fell upon his breast withal;
His body's ruin, and his arms, so sounded in his fall,
That his affrighted horse flew off, and left him, like his life.
Meriones slew Phereclus, whom she that ne'er was wife,
Yet Goddess of good housewives, held in excellent respect
For knowing all the witty things that grace an architect,
And having pow'r to give it all the cunning use of hand.
Harmonides, his sire, built ships, and made him understand,
With all the practice it requir'd, the frame of all that skill.
He built all Alexander's ships, that author'd all the ill
Of all the Trojans and his own, because he did not know
The oracles advising Troy (for fear of overthrow)
To meddle with no sea affair, but live by tilling land.
This man Meriones surpris'd, and drave his deadly hand
Through his right hip; the lance's head ran through the región
About the bladder, underneath th' in-muscles and the bone;
He, sighing, bow'd his knees to death, and sacrific'd to earth.
Phylides stay'd Pedæus' flight, Antenor's bastard birth,
Whom virtuous Theano his wife, to please her husband, kept
As tenderly as those she lov'd. Phylides near him stept,
And in the fountain of the nerves did drench his fervent lance,
At his head's back-part; and so far the sharp head did advance,
It cleft the organ of his speech, and th' iron, cold as death,
He took betwixt his grinning teeth, and gave the air his breath.
Eurypylus, the much renown'd, and great Evemon's son,
Divine Hypsenor slew, begot by stout Dolopion,
And consecrate Scamander's priest; he had a God's regard
Amongst the people; his hard flight the Grecian follow'd hard,
Rush'd in so close, that with his sword he on his shoulder laid
A blow that his arm's brawn cut off; nor there his vigour stay'd,
But drave down, and from off his wrist it hew'd his holy hand
That gush'd out blood, and down it dropp'd upon the blushing sand;
Death, with his purple finger, shut, and violent fate, his eyes.
Thus fought these, but distinguish'd well. Tydides so implies
His fury that you could not know whose side had interest
In his free labours, Greece or Troy; but as a flood, increas'd
By violent and sudden show'rs, let down from hills, like hills
Melted in fury, swells and foams, and so he overfills
His natural channel; that besides both hedge and bridge resigns
To his rough confluence, far spread; and lusty flourishing vines
Drown'd in his outrage; Tydeus' son so overran the field,

Strew'd such as flourish'd in his way, and made whole squadrons yield,
When Pandarus, Lycaon's son, beheld his ruining hand,
With such resistless insolence, make lanes through ev'ry band,
He bent his gold-tipp'd bow of horn, and shot him rushing in,
At his right shoulder, where his arms were hollow; forth did spin
The blood, and down his curets ran; then Pandarus cried out:
"Rank-riding Trojans, now rush in. Now, now, I make no doubt:
Our bravest foe is mark'd for death; he cannot long sustain
My violent shaft, if Jove's fair Son did worthily constrain
My foot from Lycia." Thus he brav'd, and yet his violent shaft
Strook short with all his violence, Tydides' life was saft;
Who yet withdrew himself behind his chariot and steeds,
And call'd to Sthenelus: "Come, friend, my wounded shoulder needs
Thy hand to ease it of this shaft." He hasted from his seat
Before the coach, and drew the shaft; the purple wound did sweat,
And drown his shirt of mail in blood, and as it bled he pray'd:
"Hear me, of Jove-Ægiochus thou most unconquer'd Maid!
If ever in the cruel field thou has assistful stood
Or to my father, or myself, now love, and do me good.
Give him into my lance's reach, that thus hath giv'n a wound
To him thou guard'st, preventing me, and brags that never more
I shall behold the cheerful sun." Thus did the king implore.
The Goddess heard, came near, and took the weariness of fight
From all his nerves and lineaments, and made them fresh and light,
And said: "Be bold, O Diomed, in ev'ry combat shine,
The great shield-shaker Tydeus' strength (that knight, that sire of thine)
By my infusion breathes in thee; and from thy knowing mind
I have remov'd those erring mists that made it lately blind,
That thou may'st diff'rence Gods from men, and therefore use thy skill
Against the tempting Deities, if any have a will
To try if thou presum'st of that, as thine, that flows from them,
And so assum'st above thy right. "Where thou discern'st a beam
Of any other Heav'nly Pow'r than She that rules in love,
That calls thee to the change of blows, resist not, but remove;
But if that Goddess be so bold (since she first stirr'd this war)
Assault and mark her from the rest with some infámous scar."
The blue-eyed Goddess vanishéd, and he was seen again
Amongst the foremost, who before though he were prompt and fain
To fight against the Trojans' pow'rs, now, on his spirits were call'd
With thrice the vigour; lion-like, that hath been lately gall'd
By some bold shepherd in a field, where his curl'd flocks were laid,
Who took him as he leap'd the fold, not slain yet, but appaid
With greater spirit, comes again, and then the shepherd hides,
(The rather for the desolate place) and in his cot abides,
His flocks left guardless; which, amaz'd, shake and shrink up in heaps;
He, ruthless, freely takes his prey, and out again he leaps;
So sprightly, fierce, victorious, the great heroë flew
Upon the Trojans, and, at once, he two commanders slew,

Hypenor and Astynous; in one his lance he fix'd
Full at the nipple of his breast; the other smote betwixt
The neck and shoulder with his sword, which was so well laid on
It swept his arm and shoulder off. These left, he rush'd upon
Abas and Polyëidus, of old Eurydamas
The hapless sons; who could by dreams tell what would come to pass,
Yet, when his sons set forth to Troy, the old man could not read
By their dreams what would chance to them, for both were stricken dead
By great Tydides, After these, he takes into his rage
Xanthus and Thoön, Phænops' sons, born to him in his age;
The good old man ev'n pin'd with years, and one son more
To heir his goods; yet Diomed took both, and left him store
Of tears and sorrows in their steads, since he could never see
His sons leave those hot wars alive; so this the end must be
Of all his labours; what he heap'd, to make his issue great,
Authority heir'd, and with her seed fill'd his forgotten seat.
Then snatch'd he up two Priamists, that in one chariot stood,
Echemon, and fair Chromius. As feeding in a wood
Oxen or steers are, one of which a lion leaps upon,
Tears down, and wrings in two his neck; so, sternly, Tydeus' son
Threw from their chariot both these hopes of old Dardanides,
Then took their arms, and sent their horse to those that ride the seas,
Æneas, seeing the troops thus toss'd, brake through the heat of fight,
And all the whizzing of the darts, to find the Lycian knight,
Lycaon's son; whom having found, he thus bespake the peer;
"O Pandarus, where's now thy bow, thy deathful arrows where,
In which no one in all our host but gives the palm to thee,
Nor in the sun-lov'd Lycian greens, that breed our archery,
Lives any that exceeds thyself? Come, lift thy hands to Jove,
And send an arrow at this man, if but a man he prove,
That wins such god-like victories, and now affects our host
With so much sorrow, since so much of our best blood is lost
By his high valour. I have fear some God in him doth threat,
Incens'd for want of sacrifice; the wrath of God is great."
Lycaon's famous son replied: "Great counsellor of Troy,
This man, so excellent in arms, I think is Tydeus' joy;
I know him by his fi'ry shield, by his bright three-plum'd casque,
And by his horse; nor can I say, if or some God doth mask
In his appearance, or he be whom I nam'd Tydeus' son,
But without God the things he does for certain are not done.
Some great Immortal, that conveys his shoulders in a cloud,
Goes by and puts by ev'ry dart at his bold breast bestow'd,
Or lets it take with little hurt; for I myself let fly
A shaft that shot him through his arms, but had as good gone by,
Yet which I gloriously affirm'd had driv'n him down to hell.
Some God is angry, and with me; for far hence, where I dwell,
My horse and chariots idle stand, with which some other way
I might repair this shameful miss. Elev'n fair chariots stay

In old Lycaon's court, new made, new trimm'd to have been gone,
Curtain'd, and arrast under foot; two horse to ev'ry one,
That eat white barley and black oats, and do no good at all;
And these Lycaon (that well knew how these affairs would fall)
Charg'd, when I set down this design, I should command with here,
And gave me many lessons more, all which much better were
Than any I took forth myself. The reason I laid down
Was but the sparing of my horse, since in a siegéd town
I thought our horse-meat would be scant; when they were us'd to have
Their manger full; so I left them, and like a lackey slave
Am come to Ilion, confident in nothing but my bow
That nothing profits me. Two shafts I vainly did bestow
At two great princes, but of both my arrows neither slew,
Nor this, nor Atreus' younger son; a little blood I drew,
That serv'd but to incense them more. In an unhappy star
I therefore from my armoury have drawn those tools of war
That day, when, for great Hector's sake, to amiable Troy:
I came to lead the Trojan bands. But if I ever joy,
In safe return, my country's sight, my wife's, my lofty tow'rs,
Let any stranger take this head, if to the fi'ry Pow'rs
This bow, these shafts, in pieces burst, by these hands be not thrown;
Idle companions that they are to me and my renown."
Æneas said: "Use no such words; for, any other way
Than this, they shall not now be us'd. We first will both assay
This man with horse and chariot. Come then, ascend to me,
That thou may'st try our Trojan horse, how skill'd in field they be,
And in pursuing those that fly, or flying, being pursued,
How excellent they are of foot; and these, if Jove conclude
The 'scape of Tydeüs again, and grace him with our flight,
Shall serve to bring us safely off. Come, I'll be first shall fight,
Take thou these fair reins and this scourge; or, if thou wilt, fight thou,
And leave the horses' care to me." He answer'd: "I will now
Descend to fight, keep thou the reins, and guide thyself thy horse;
Who with their wonted manager will better wield the force
Of the impulsive chariot, if we be driv'n to fly,
Than with a stranger; under whom they will be much more shy,
And, fearing my voice, wishing thine, grow resty, nor go on
To bear us off, but leave engag'd for mighty Tydeus' son
Themselves and us. Then be thy part thy one-hoof'd horses' guide,
I'll make the fight, and with a dart receive his utmost pride."
With this the gorgeous chariot both, thus prepar'd, ascend
And make full way at Diomed; which noted by his friend,
"Mine own most-lovéd mind," said he, "two mighty men of war
I see come with a purpos'd charge; one's he that hits so far
With bow and shaft, Lycaon's son; the other fames the brood
Of great Anchises and the Queen that rules in amorous blood,
Æneas, excellent in arms. Come up, and use your steeds,
And look not war so in the face, lest that desire that feeds

Thy great mind be the bane of it." This did with anger sting
The blood of Diomed, to see his friend, that chid the king
Before the fight, and then preferr'd his ablesse and his mind
To all his ancestors in fight, now come so far behind;
Whom thus he answer'd: "Urge no flight, you cannot please me so;
Nor is it honest in my mind to fear a coming foe,
Or make a flight good, though with fight. My pow'rs are yet entire,
And scorn the help-tire of a horse. I will not blow the fire
Of their hot valours with my flight, but cast upon the blaze
This body borne upon my knees. I entertain amaze?
Minerva will not see that shame. And since they have begun,
They shall not both elect their ends; and he that 'scapes shall run,
Or stay and take the other's fate. And this I leave for thee;—
If amply-wise Athenia give both their lives to me,
Rein our horse to their chariot hard, and have a special heed
To seize upon Æneas' steeds, that we may change their breed,
And make a Grecian race of them that have been long of Troy.
For these are bred of those brave beasts which, for the lovely boy
That waits now on the cup of Jove, Jove, that far-seeing God,
Gave Tros the king in recompense; the best that ever trod
The sounding centre, underneath the morning and the sun.
Anchises stole the breed of them; for, where their sires did run,
He closely put his mares to them, and never made it known
To him that heir'd them, who was then the king Laomedon.
Six horses had he of that race, of which himself kept four,
And gave the other two his son; and these are they that scour
The field so bravely towards us, expert in charge and flight.
If these we have the pow'r to take, our prise is exquisite,
And our renown will far exceed." While these were talking thus,
The fir'd horse brought th' assailants near, and thus spake Pandarus:
"Most suff'ring-minded Tydeus' son, that hast of war the art,
My shaft, that strook thee, slew thee not, I now will prove a dart."
This said, he shook, and then he threw, a lance, aloft and large,
That in Tydides' curets stuck, quite driving through his targe;
Then bray'd he out so wild a voice that all the field might hear:
"Now have I reach'd thy root of life, and by thy death shall bear
Our praise's chief prise from the field." Tydides undismay'd
Replied: "Thou err'st, I am not touch'd; but more charge will be laid
To both your lives before you part; at least the life of one
Shall satiate the throat of Mars." This said, his lance was gone,
Minerva led it to his face, which at his eye ran in,
And, as he stoop'd, strook through his jaws, his tongue's root, and his chin.
Down from the chariot he fell, his gay arms shin'd and rung,
The swift horse trembled, and his soul for ever charm'd his tongue.
Æneas with his shield, and lance, leapt swiftly to his friend,
Afraid the Greeks would force his trunk; and that he did defend,
Bold as a lion of his strength; he hid him with his shield,
Shook round his lance, and horribly did threaten all the field

With death, if any durst make in. Tydides rais'd a stone
With his one hand, of wondrous weight, and pour'd it mainly on
The hip of Anchisiades, wherein the joint doth move
The thigh ('tis call'd the huckle-bone) which all in sherds it drove,
Brake both the nerves, and with the edge cut all the flesh away.
It stagger'd him upon his knees, and made th' heroë stay
His strook-blind temples on his hand, his elbow on the earth;
And there this prince of men had died, if She that gave him birth,
(Kiss'd by Anchises on the green, where his fair oxen fed)
Jove's loving daughter, instantly had not about him spread
Her soft embraces, and convey'd within her heav'nly veil
(Us'd as a rampire 'gainst all darts that did so hot assail)
Her dear-lov'd issue from the field, Then Sthenelus in haste,
Rememb'ring what his friend advis'd, from forth the prease made fast
His own horse to their chariot, and presently laid hand
Upon the lovely-coated horse Æneas did command.
Which bringing to the wond'nng Greeks, he did their guard commend
To his belov'd Deipylus, who was his inward friend,
And, of his equals, one to whom he had most honour shown,
That he might see them safe at fleet; then stept he to his own.
With which he cheerfully made in to Tydeus' mighty race,
He, mad with his great enemy's rape, was hot in desp'rate chace
Of her that made it, with his lance, arm'd less with steel than spite,
Well knowing her no Deity that had to do in fight,
Minerva his great patroness, nor, She that raceth towns,
Bellona, but a goddess weak, and foe to men's renowns.
Her, through a world of fight pursu'd, at last he overtook,
And, thrusting up his ruthless lance, her heav'nly veil he strook
(That ev'n the Graces wrought themselves, at her divine command)
Quite through, and hurt the tender back of her delicious hand.
The rude point piercing through her palm, forth flow'd th' immortal blood;
Blood, such as flows in blesséd Gods, that eat no human food,
Nor drink of our inflaming wine, and therefore bloodless are,
And call'd Immortals; out she cried, and could no longer bear
Her lov'd son; whom she cast from her, and in a sable cloud
Phœbus, receiving, hid him close from all the Grecian crowd,
Lest some of them should find his death. Away flew Venus then,
And after her cried Diomed: "Away, thou spoil of men,
Though sprung from all-preserving Jove, these hot encounters leave.
Is't not enough that silly dames thy sorc'ries should deceive,
Unless thou thrust into the war, and rob a soldier's right?
I think a few of these assaults will make thee fear the fight,
Wherever thou shalt hear it nam'd." She, sighing, went her way
Extremely griev'd, and with her griefs her beauties did decay,
And black her ivory body grew. Then from a dewy mist
Brake swift-foot Iris to her aid, from all the darts that hiss'd
At her quick rapture; and to Mars they took their plaintive course,
And found him on the fight's left hand, by him his speedy horse,

And huge lance, lying in a fog. The Queen of all things fair
Her lovéd brother, on her knees, besought, with instant pray'r,
His golden-riband-bound-man'd horse to lend her up to heav'n
For she was much griev'd with a wound a mortal man had giv'n,
Tydides, that 'gainst Jove himself durst now advance his arm.
He granted, and his chariot (perplex'd with her late harm)
She mounted, and her waggoness was She that paints the air.
The horse she rein'd, and with a scourge importun'd their repair,
That of themselves out-flew the wind, and quickly they ascend
Olympus, high seat of the Gods. Th' horse knew their journey's end,
Stood still, and from their chariot the windy-footed dame
Dissolv'd, and gave them heav'nly food; and to Dione came
Her wounded daughter, bent her knees. She kindly bade her stand,
With sweet embraces help'd her up, strok'd her with her soft hand,
Call'd kindly by her name, and ask'd: "What God hath been so rude,
Sweet daughter, to chastise thee thus, as if thou wert pursu'd
Ev'n to the act of some light sin, and deprehended so?
For otherwise, each close escape is in the great let go."
She answer'd: "Haughty Tydeus' son hath been so insolent,
Since, him whom most my heart esteems of all my lov'd descent,
I rescu'd from his bloody hand. Now battle is not giv'n
To any Trojans by the Greeks, but by the Greeks to heav'n."
She answer'd: "Daughter, think not much, though much it grieve thee; use
The patience, whereof many Gods examples may produce,
In many bitter ills receiv'd, as well that men sustain
By their inflictions as by men repaid to them again.
Mars suffer'd much more than thyself by Ephialtes' pow'r,
And Otus', Aloëus' sons; who in a brazen tow'r,
And in inextricable chains, cast that war-greedy God,
Where twice-six months and one he liv'd, and there the period
Of his sad life perhaps had clos'd, if his kind step-dame's eye,
Fair Erebæa, had not seen; who told it Mercury,
And he by stealth enfranchis'd him; though he could scarce enjoy
The benefit of franchisement, the chains did so destroy
His vital forces with their weight. So Juno suffer'd more
When, with a three-fork'd arrow's head, Amphitryo's son did gore
Her right breast, past all hope of cure. Pluto sustain'd no less
By that self man, and by a shaft of equal bitterness
Shot through his shoulder at hell gates; and there, amongst the dead,
Were he not deathless, he had died; but up to heav'n he fled,
Extremely tortur'd, for recure, which instantly he won
At Pæon's hand, with sov'reign balm; and this did Jove's great son,
Unblest, great-high-deed-daring man, that car'd not doing ill,
That with his bow durst wound the Gods! But, by Minerva's will,
Thy wound the foolish Diomed was so profane to give;
Not knowing he that fights with Heav'n hath never long to live,
And for this deed, he never shall have child about his knee
To call him father, coming home. Besides, hear this from me,

Strength-trusting man, though thou be strong, and art in strength a tow'r,
Take heed a stronger meet thee not, and that a woman's pow'r
Contains not that superior strength, and lest that woman be
Adrastus' daughter, and thy wife, the wise Ægiale;
When, from this hour not far, she wakes, ev'n sighing with desire
To kindle our revenge on thee, with her enamouring fire,
In choosing her some fresh young friend, and so drown all thy fame,
Won here in war, in her court-piece, and in an opener shame."
This said, with both her hands she cleans'd the tender back and palm
Of all the sacred blood they lost; and, never using balm,
The pain ceas'd, and the wound was cur'd of this kind Queen of love.
Juno and Pallas, seeing this, assay'd to anger Jove,
And quit his late-made mirth with them, about the loving Dame,
With some sharp jest, in like sort, built upon her present shame.
Gray-ey'd Athenia began, and ask'd the Thunderer,
If, nothing moving him to wrath, she boldly might prefer,
What she conceiv'd, to his conceit; and, staying no reply,
She bade him view the Cyprian fruit he lov'd so tenderly,
Whom she thought hurt, and by this means;—intending to suborn
Some other lady of the Greeks (whom lovely veils adorn)
To gratify some other friend of her much-lovéd Troy,
As she embrac'd and stirr'd her blood to the Venerean joy,
The golden clasp, those Grecian dames upon their girdles wear,
Took hold of her delicious hand, and hurt it, she had fear.
The Thund'rer smil'd, and call'd to him love's golden Arbitress,
And told her those rough works of war were not for her access;
She should be making marriages, embracings, kisses, charms,
Stern Mars and Pallas had the charge of those affairs in arms.
While these thus talk'd, Tydides' rage still thirsted to achieve
His prise upon Anchises' son, though well he did perceive
The Sun himself protected him; but his desires (inflam'd
With that great Trojan prince's blood, and arms so highly fam'd)
Not that great God did reverence. Thrice rush'd he rudely on,
And thrice, betwixt his darts and death, the Sun's bright target shone;
But when upon the fourth assault, much like a spirit, he flew,
The far-off-working Deity exceeding wrathful grew,
And ask'd him: "What! Not yield to gods? Thy equals learn to know.
The race of Gods is far above men creeping here below."
This drave him to some small retreat; he would not tempt more near
The wrath of him that strook so far; whose pow'r had now set clear
Æneas from the stormy field within the holy place
Of Pergamus, where, to the hope of his so sov'reign grace,
A goodly temple was advanc'd; in whose large inmost part
He left him, and to his supply inclin'd his mother's heart,
Latona, and the dart-pleas'd Queen; who cur'd, and made him strong.
The silver-bow'd fair God then threw in the tumultuous throng
An image, that in stature, look, and arms, he did create
Like Venus' son; for which the Greeks and Trojans made debate,

Laid loud strokes on their ox-hide shields, and bucklers eas'ly borne;
Which error Phœbus pleas'd to urge on Mars himself in scorn:
"Mars, Mars," said he, "thou plague of men, smear'd with the dust and blood
Of humans, and their ruin'd walls, yet thinks thy Godhead good
To fright this fury from the field, who next will fight with Jove?
First in a bold approach he hurt, the moist palm of thy love,
And next, as if he did affect to have a Deity's pow'r,
He held out his assault on me." This said, the lofty tow'r
Of Pergamus he made his seat; and Mars did now excite
The Trojan forces, in the form of him that led to fight
The Thracian troops, swift Acamas. "O Priam's sons," said he,
"How long the slaughter of your men can ye sustain to see?
Ev'n till they brave you at your gates? Ye suffer beaten down
Æneas, great Anchises' son, whose prowess we renown
As much as Hector's; fetch him off from this contentious prease."
With this, the strength and spirits of all his courage did increase;
And yet Sarpedon seconds him, with this particular taunt
Of noble Hector: "Hector, where is thy unthankful vaunt,
And that huge strength on which it built, that thou, and thy allies,
With all thy brothers (without aid of us or our supplies,
And troubling not a citizen) the city safe would hold?
In all which friends' and brothers' helps I see not, nor am told
Of anyone of their exploits, but (all held in dismay
Of Diomed, like a sort of dogs, that at a lion bay,
And entertain no spirit to pinch) we, your assistants here,
Fight for the town as you help'd us; and I, an aiding peer,
No citizen, ev'n out of care, that doth become a man
For men and children's liberties, add all the aid I can;
Not out of my particular cause; far hence my profit grows,
For far hence Asian Lycia lies, where gulfy Xanthus flows,
And where my lov'd wife, infant son, and treasure nothing scant,
I left behind me, which I see those men would have that want,
And therefore they that have would keep. Yet I, as I would lose
Their sure fruition, cheer my troops, and with their lives propose
Mine own life, both to gen'ral fight, and to particular cope
With this great soldier; though, I say, I entertain no hope
To have such gettings as the Greeks, nor fear to lose like Troy.
Yet thou, ev'n Hector, deedless stand'st, and car'st not to employ
Thy town-born friends, to bid them stand, to fight and save their wives,
Lest as a fowler casts his nets upon the silly lives
Of birds of all sorts, so the foe your walls and houses hales,
One with another, on all heads; or such as 'scape their falls,
He made the prey and prise of them (as willing overthrown)
That hope not for you with their force; and so this brave-built town
Will prove a chaos. That deserves in thee so hot a care,
As should consume thy days and nights, to hearten and prepare
Th' assistant princes; pray their minds to bear their far-brought toils;
To give them worth with worthy fight; in victories and foils

Still to be equal; and thyself, exampling them in all,
Need no reproofs nor spurs. All this in thy free choice should fall."
This stung great Hector's heart; and yet, as ev'ry gen'rous mind
Should silent bear a just reproof, and show what good they find
In worthy counsels, by their ends put into present deeds,
Not stomach nor be vainly sham'd; so Hector's spirit proceeds,
And from his chariot, wholly arm'd, he jump'd upon the sand,
On foot so toiling through the host, a dart in either hand,
And all hands turn'd against the Greeks. The Greeks despis'd their worst,
And, thick'ning their instructed pow'rs, expected all they durst.
Then with the feet of horse and foot, the dust in clouds did rise.
And as, in sacred floors of barns, upon corn-winnow'rs flies
The chaff, driv'n with an opposite wind, when yellow Ceres dites,
Which all the diters' feet, legs, arms, their heads and shoulders whites;
So look'd the Grecians gray with dust, that strook the solid heav'n,
Rais'd from returning chariots, and troops together driv'n.
Each side stood to their labours firm. Fierce Mars flew through the air,
And gather'd darkness from the fight, and, with his best affair,
Obey'd the pleasure of the Sun, that wears the golden sword
Who bade'him raise the spirits of Troy, when Pallas ceas'd t' afford
Her helping office to the Greeks; and then his own hands wrought,
Which, from his fane's rich chancel, cur'd, the true Æneas brought,
And plac'd him by his peers in field; who did with joy admire
To see him both alive and safe, and all his pow'rs entire
Yet stood not sifting how it chanc'd; another sort of task,
Then stirring th' idle sieve of news, did all their forces ask,
Inflam'd by Phœbus, harmful Mars, and Eris eag'rer far.
The Greeks had none to hearten them; their hearts rose with the war;
But chiefly Diomed, Ithacus, and both th' Ajaces us'd
Stirring examples and good words; their own fames had infus'd
Spirit enough into their bloods, to make them neither fear
The Trojans' force, nor Fate itself, but still expecting were,
When most was done, what would be more; their ground they still made good,
And in their silence, and set pow'rs, like fair still clouds, they stood,
With which Jove crowns the tops of hills, in any quiet day,
When Boreas and the ruder winds (that use to drive away
Air's dusky vapours, being loose, in many a whistling gale)
Are pleasingly bound up, and calm, and not a breath exhale;
So firmly stood the Greeks, nor fled for all the Ilion's aid.
Atrides yet coasts through the troops, confirming men so staid:
"O friends," said he, "hold up your minds; strength is but strength of will;
Rev'rence each other's good in fight and shame at things done ill.
"There soldiers show an honest shame, and love of honour lives,
That ranks men with the first in fight, death fewer liveries gives
Than life, or than where Fame's neglect makes cowards fight at length.
Flight neither doth the body grace, nor shows the mind hath strength."
He said, and swiftly through the troops a mortal lance did send,
That reft a standard-bearer's life, renown'd Æneas' friend,

Deïcoon Pergasides, whom all the Trojans lov'd
As he were one of Priam's sons, his mind was so approv'd
In always fighting with the first. The lance his target took,
Which could not interrupt the blow, that through it clearly strook,
And in his belly's rim was sheath'd, beneath his girdle-stead.
He sounded falling, and his arms with him resounded, dead.
Then fell two princes of the Greeks by great Æneas' ire,
Diocleus' sons (Orsilochus and Crethon), whose kind sire
In bravely-builded Phæra dwelt, rich, and of sacred blood.
He was descended lineally from great Alphæus' flood,
That broadly flows through Pyles' fields; Alphæus did beget
Orsilochus, who in the rule of many men was set;
And that Orsilochus begat the rich Diocleüs;
Diocleus sire to Crethon was, and this Orsilochus.
Both these; arriv'd at man's estate, with both th' Atrides went,
To honour them in th' Ilion wars; and both were one day sent,
To death as well as Troy, for death hid both in one black hour.
As two young lions (with their dam, sustain'd but to devour)
Bred on the tops of some steep hill, and in the gloomy deep
Of an inaccessible wood, rush out, and prey on sheep,
Steers, oxen, and destroy men's stalls, so long that they come short,
And by the owner's steel are slain; in such unhappy sort
Fell these beneath Æneas' pow'r. When Menelaus view'd
Like two tall fir-trees these two fall, their timeless falls he rued,
And to the first fight, where they lay, a vengeful force he took;
His arms beat back the sun in flames, a dreadful lance he shook;
Mars put the fury in his mind, that by Æneas' hands,
Who was to make the slaughter good, he might have strew'd the sands.
Antilochus, old Nestor's son, observing he was bent
To urge a combat of such odds, and knowing, the event
Being ill on his part, all their pains (alone sustain'd for him)
Err'd from their end, made after hard, and took them in the trim
Of an encounter. Both their hands and darts advanc'd, and shook,
And both pitch'd in full stand of charge; when suddenly the look
Of Anchisiades took note of Nestor's valiant son,
In full charge too; which, two to one, made Venus' issue shun
The hot adventure, though he were a soldier well-approv'd.
Then drew they off their slaughter'd friends; who giv'n to their belov'd,
They turn'd where fight show'd deadliest hate; and there mix'd with the dead
Pylæmen, that the targeteers of Paphlagonia led,
A man like Mars; and with him fell good Mydon that did guide
His chariot, Atymnus' son. The prince Pylæmen died
By Menelaus; Nestor's joy slew Mydon; one before
The other in the chariot. Atrides' lance did gore
Pylæmen's shoulder, in the blade. Antilochus did force
A mighty stone up from the earth, and, as he turn'd his horse,
Strook Mydon's elbow in the midst; the reins of ivory
Fell from his hands into the dust; Antilochus let fly

His sword withal, and, rushing in, a blow so deadly laid
Upon his temples, that he groan'd, tumbled to earth, and stay'd
A mighty while preposterously (because the dust was deep)
Upon his neck and shoulders there, ev'n till his foe took keep
Of his pris'd horse, and made them stir; and then he prostrate fell.
His horse Antilochus took home. When Hector had heard tell,
Amongst the uproar, of their deaths, he laid out all his voice,
And ran upon the Greeks. Behind came many men of choice,
Before him march'd great Mars himself match'd with his female mate,
The dread Bellona. She brought on, to fight for mutual fate,
A tumult that was wild and mad. He shook a horrid lance,
And now led Hector, and anon behind would make the chance.
This sight when great Tydides saw, his hair stood up on end;
And him, whom all the skill and pow'r of arms did late attend,
Now like a man in counsel poor, that, travelling, goes amiss,
And having pass'd a boundless plain, not knowing where he is,
Comes on the sudden where he sees a river rough, and raves
With his own billows ravishéd into the king of waves,
Murmurs with foam, and frights him back; so he, amaz'd, retir'd,
And thus would make good his amaze: "O friends, we all admir'd
Great Hector, as one of himself, well-darting, bold in war,
When some God guards him still from death, and makes him dare so far.
Now Mars himself, form'd like a man, is present in his rage,
And therefore, whatsoever cause importunes you to wage
War with these Trojans, never strive, but gently take your rod,
Lest in your bosoms, for a man, ye ever find a God."
As Greece retir'd, the pow'r of Troy did much more forward prease,
And Hector two brave men of war sent to the fields of peace;
Menesthes, and Anchialus; one chariot bare them both.
Their falls made Ajax Telamon ruthful of heart, and wroth
Who lighten'd out a lance that smote Amphius Selages,
That dwelt in Pæsos, rich in lands, and did huge goods possess,
But Fate, to Priam and his sons, conducted his supply.
The jav'lin on his girdle strook, and piercéd mortally
His belly's lower part; he fell: his arms had looks so trim,
That Ajax needs would prove their spoil; the Trojans pour'd on him
Whole storms of lances, large, and sharp, of which a number stuck
In his rough shield; yet from the slain he did his jav'lin pluck,
But could not from his shoulders force the arms he did affect,
The Trojans with such drifts of darts the body did protect;
And wisely Telamonius fear'd their valorous defence,
So many, and so strong of hand, stood in with such expense
Of deadly prowess; who repell'd, though big, strong, bold, he were,
The famous Ajax, and their friend did from his rapture bear.
Thus this place fill'd with strength of fight; in th' army's other prease,
Tlepolemus, a tall big man, the son of Hercules,
A cruel destiny inspir'd, with strong desire to prove
Encounter with Sarpedon's strength, the son of cloudy Jove;

Who, coming on to that stern end, had chosen him his foe.
Thus Jove's great nephew, and his son, 'gainst one another go.
Tlepolemus, to make his end more worth the will of fate,
Began as if he had her pow'r, and show'd the mortal state
Of too much confidence in man, with this superfluous brave:
"Sarpedon, what necessity or needless humour drave
Thy form to these wars, which in heart I know thou dost abhor,
A man not seen in deeds of arms, a Lycian counsellor?
They lie that call thee son to Jove, since Jove bred none so late;
The men of elder times were they, that his high pow'r begat,
Such men as had Herculean force. My father Hercules
Was Jove's true issue; he was bold; his deeds did well express
They sprung out of a lion's heart. He whilome came to Troy,
(For horse that Jupiter gave Tros, for Ganymed, his boy)
With six ships only, and few men, and tore the city down,
Left all her broad ways desolate, and made the horse his own.
For thee, thy mind is ill dispos'd, thy body's pow'rs are poor,
And therefore are thy troops so weak; the soldier evermore
Follows the temper of his chief; and thou pull'st down a side.
But say thou art the son of Jove, and hast thy means supplied
With forces fitting his descent, the pow'rs that I compel
Shall throw thee hence, and make thy head run ope the gates of hell."
Jove's Lycian issue answer'd him: "Tlepolemus, 'tis true
Thy father holy Ilion in that sort overthrew;
Th' injustice of the king was cause, that, where thy father had
Us'd good deservings to his state, he quitted him with bad.
Hesione, the joy and grace of king Laomedon,
Thy father rescu'd from a whale, and gave to Telamon
In honour'd nuptials (Telamon, from whom your strongest Greek
Boasts to have issu'd) and this grace might well expect the like;
Yet he gave taunts for thanks, and kept, against his oath, his horse,
And therefore both thy father's strength, and justice, might enforce
The wreak he took on Troy; but this and thy cause differ far.
Sons seldom heir their fathers' worths. Thou canst not make his war.
What thou assum'st for him, is mine, to be on thee impos'd."
With this, he threw an ashen dart; and then Tlepolemus los'd
Another from his glorious hand. Both at one instant flew,
Both strook, both wounded. From his neck Sarpedon's jav'lin drew
The life blood of Tlepolemus; full in the midst it fell;
And what he threaten'd, th' other gave, that darkness, and that hell.
Sarpedon's left thigh took the lance; it pierc'd the solid bone,
And with his raging head ran through; but Jove preserv'd his son.
The dart yet vex'd him bitterly, which should have been pull'd out,
But none consider'd then so much, so thick came on the rout,
And fill'd each hand so full of cause to ply his own defence;
'Twas held enough, both fall'n that both were nobly carried thence
Ulysses knew th' events of both, and took it much to heart
That his friend's enemy should 'scape; and in a twofold part

His thoughts contended, if he should pursue Sarpedon's life,
Or take his friend's wreak on his men. Fate did conclude this strife,
By whom 'twas otherwise decreed than that Ulysses' steel
Should end Sarpedon. In this doubt Minerva took the wheel
From fickle Chance, and made his mind resolve to right his friend
With that blood he could surest draw. Then did Revenge extend
Her full pow'r on the multitude; then did he never miss;
Alastor, Halius, Chromius, Noemon, Prytanis,
Alcander, and a number more, he slew, and more had slain,
If Hector had not understood; whose pow'r made in amain,
And strook fear through the Grecian troops, but to Sarpedon gave
Hope of full rescue, who thus cried: "O Hector! Help and save
My body from the spoil of Greece, that to your lovéd town
My friends may see me borne, and then let earth possess her own
In this soil, for whose sake I left my country's; for no day
Shall ever show me that again, nor to my wife display,
And young hope of my name, the joy of my much thirsted sight;
All which I left for Troy, for them let Troy then do this right."
To all this Hector gives no word, but greedily he strives
With all speed to repel the Greeks, and shed in floods their lives,
And left Sarpedon; but what face soever he put on
Of following the common cause, he left this prince alone
For his particular grudge, because, so late, he was so plain
In his reproof before the host, and that did he retain;
However, for example sake, he would not show it then,
And for his shame too, since 'twas just. But good Sarpedon's men
Ventur'd themselves, and forc'd him off, and set him underneath
The goodly beech of Jupiter, where now they did unsheath
The ashen lance; strong Pelagon, his friend, most lov'd, most true,
Enforc'd it from his maiméd thigh; with which his spirit flew,
And darkness over-flew his eyes; yet with a gentle gale,
That round about the dying prince cool Boreas did exhale,
He was reviv'd, recomforted, that else had griev'd and died.
All this time flight drave to the fleet the Argives, who applied
No weapon 'gainst the proud pursuit, nor ever turn'd a head,
They knew so well that Mars pursu'd, and dreadful Hector led.
Then who was first, who last, whose lives the iron Mars did seize,
And Priam's Hector? Helenus, surnam'd Œnopides;
Good Teuthras; and Orestes, skill'd in managing of horse;
Bold Œnomaus; and a man renown'd for martial force,
Trechus, the great Ætolian chief; Oresbius, that did wear
The gaudy mitre, studied wealth extremely, and dwelt near
Th' Atlantic lake Cephisides, in Hyla, by whose seat
The good men of Bœotia dwelt. This slaughter grew so great,
It flew to heav'n; Saturnia discern'd it, and cried out
To Pallas: "O unworthy sight! To see a field so fought,
And break our words to Sparta's king, that Ilion should be rac'd,
And he return reveng'd; when thus we see his Greeks disgrac'd,

And bear the harmful rage of Mars! Come, let us use our care,
That we dishonour not our pow'rs." Minerva was as yare
As she at the despite of Troy. Her golden-bridled steeds
Then Saturn's daughter brought abroad; and Hebe, she proceeds
T' address her chariot; instantly she gives it either wheel,
Beam'd with eight spokes of sounding brass; the axle-tree was steel;
The fell'ffs incorruptible gold, their upper bands of brass,
Their matter most unvalued, their work of wondrous grace;
The naves, in which the spokes were driv'n, were all with silver bound;
The chariot's seat two hoops of gold and silver strengthen'd round,
Edg'd with a gold and silver fringe; the beam, that look'd before,
Was massy silver; on whose top, gears all of gold it wore,
And golden poitrils. Juno mounts, and her hot horses rein'd,
That thirsted for contentión, and still of peace complain'd.
Minerva wrapt her in the robe, that curiously she wove,
With glorious colours, as she sate on th' azure floor of Jove,
And wore the arms that he puts on, bent to the tearful field.
About her broad-spread shoulders hung his huge and horrid shield,
Fring'd round with ever-fighting snakes; through it was drawn to life
The miseries and deaths of fight; in it frown'd bloody Strife,
In it shin'd sacred Fortitude, in it fell Púrsuit flew,
In it the monster Gorgon's head, in which held out to view
Were all the dire ostents of Jove; on her big head she plac'd
His four-plum'd glitt'ring casque of gold, so admirably vast
It would an hundred garrisons of soldiers comprehend.
Then to her shining chariot her vig'rous feet ascend;
And in her violent hand she takes his grave, huge, solid lance,
With which the conquests of her wrath she useth to advance,
And overturn whole fields of men, to show she was the Seed
Of him that thunders. Then heav'n's Queen, to urge her horses' speed,
Takes up the scourge, and forth they fly. The ample gates of heav'n
Rung, and flew open of themselves; the charge whereof is giv'n,
With all Olympus, and the sky, to the distinguish'd Hours,
That clear, or hide it all in clouds, or pour it down in show'rs.
This way their scourge-obeying horse made haste, and soon they won
The top of all the topful heav'ns, where aged Saturn's son
Sat sever'd from the other Gods; then stay'd the white-arm'd Queen
Her steeds, and ask'd of Jove, if Mars did not incense his spleen
With his foul deeds, in ruining so many and so great
In the command and grace of Greece, and in so rude a heat?
At which, she said, Apollo laugh'd, and Venus, who still sue
To that mad God, for violence that never justice knew;
For whose impiety, she ask'd, if, with his wishéd love,
Herself might free the field of him? He bade her rather move
Athenia to the charge she sought, who us'd of old to be
The bane of Mars, and had as well the gift of spoil as he.
This grace she slack'd not, but her horse scourg'd, that in nature flew
Betwixt the cope of stars and earth; and how far at a view

A man into the purple sea may from a hill descry,
So far a high-neighing horse of heav'n at ev'ry jump would fly. [2]
Arriv'd at Troy, where, broke in curls, the two floods mix their force,
Scamander and bright Simois, Saturnia stay'd her horse,
Took them from chariot, and a cloud of mighty depth diffus'd
About them; and the verdant banks of Simois produc'd
In nature what they eat in heav'n. Then both the Goddesses [3]
March'd, like a pair of tim'rous doves, in hasting their access
To th' Argive succour. Being arriv'd, where both the most and best
Were heap'd together (showing all, like lions at a feast
Of new-slain carcasses, or boars, beyond encounter strong)
There found they Diomed; and there, 'midst all th' admiring throng,
Saturnia put on Stentor's shape, that had a brazen voice,
And spake as loud as fifty men; like whom she made a noise,
And chid the Argives: "O ye Greeks, in name and outward rite
But princes only, not in act, what scandal, what despite,
Use ye to honour! All the time the great Æacides
Was conversant in arms, your foes durst not a foot address
Without their ports, so much they fear'd his lance that all controll'd,
And now they outray to your fleet." This did with shame make bold
The gen'ral spirit and pow'r of Greece: when, with particular note
Of their disgrace, Athenia made Tydeus' issue hot.
She found him at his chariot, refreshing of his wound
Inflicted by slain Pandarus; his sweat did so abound,
It much annoy'd him, underneath the broad belt of his shield;
With which, and tiréd with his toil, his soul could hardly yield
His body motion. With his hand he lifted up the belt,
And wip'd away that clotter'd blood the fervent wound did melt.
Minerva lean'd against his horse, and near their withers laid
Her sacred hand, then spake to him: "Believe me, Diomed,
Tydeus exampled not himself in thee his son; not great,
But yet he was a soldier; a man of so much heat,
That in his ambassy for Thebes, when I forbad his mind
To be too vent'rous, and when feasts his heart might have declin'd,
With which they welcom'd him, he made a challenge to the best,
And foil'd the best; I gave him aid, because the rust of rest,
That would have seiz'd another mind, he suffer'd not, but us'd
The trial I made like a man, and their soft feasts refus'd.
Yet, when I set thee on, thou faint'st; I guard thee, charge, exhort
That, I abetting thee, thou shouldst be to the Greeks a fort,
And a dismay to Ilion, yet thou obey'st in nought,
Afraid, or slothful, or else both; henceforth renounce all thought
That ever thou wert Tydeus' son." He answer'd her: "I know
Thou art Jove's daughter, and, for that, in all just duty owe
Thy speeches rev'rence, yet affirm ingeniously that fear
Doth neither hold me spiritless, nor sloth. I only bear
Thy charge in zealous memory, that I should never war
With any blesséd Deity, unless (exceeding far

The limits of her rule) the Queen, that governs chamber sport,
Should press to field; and her thy will enjoin'd my lance to hurt.
But, He whose pow'r hath right in arms, I knew in person here,
Besides the Cyprian Deity; and therefore did forbear,
And here have gather'd in retreat these other Greeks you see,
With note and rev'rence of your charge." "My dearest mind," said she,
"What then was fit is chang'd. 'Tis true, Mars hath just rule in war,
But just war; otherwise he raves, not fights. He's alter'd far.
He vow'd to Juno, and myself, that his aid should be us'd
Against the Trojans, whom it guards; and therein he abus'd
His rule in arms, infring'd his word, and made his war unjust.
He is inconstant, impious, mad. Resolve then; firmly trust
My aid of thee against his worst, or any Deity;
Add scourge to thy free horse, charge home; he fights perfidiously."
This said; as that brave king, her knight, with his horse-guiding friend,
Were set before the chariot, for sign he should descend,
That she might serve for waggoness, she pluck'd the wagg'ner back,
And up into his seat she mounts; the beechen tree did crack
Beneath the burthen; and good cause, it bore so huge a thing,
A Goddess so replete with pow'r, and such a puissant king.
She snatch'd the scourge up and the reins, and shut her heav'nly look
In Hell's vast helm from Mars's eyes; and full career she took
At him, who then had newly slain the mighty Periphas,
Renown'd son to Ochesius, and far the strongest was
Of all th' Ætolians; to whose spoil the bloody God was run.
But when this man-plague saw the approach of god-like Tydeus' son,
He let his mighty Periphas lie, and in full charge he ran
At Diomed; and he at him. Both near; the God began,
And, thirsty of his blood, he throws a brazen lance that bears
Full on the breast of Diomed, above the reins and gears;
But Pallas took it on her hand, and strook the eager lance
Beneath the chariot. Then the knight of Pallas doth advance,
And cast a jav'lin off at Mars, Minerva sent it on,
That, where his arming girdle gilt, his belly graz'd upon,
Just at the rim, and ranch'd the flesh; the lance again he got,
But left the wound, that stung him so, he laid out such a throat
As if nine or ten thousand men had bray'd out all their breaths
In one confusion, having felt as many sudden deaths.
The roar made both the hosts amaz'd. Up flew the God to heav'n;
And with him was through all the air as black a tincture driv'n
To Diomed's eyes, as when the earth half-choked with smoking heat
Of gloomy clouds, that stifle men, and pitchy tempests threat,
Usher'd with horrid gusts of wind; with such black vapours plum'd,
Mars flew t' Olympus, and broad heav'n, and there his place resum'd.
Sadly he went and sat by Jove, show'd his immortal blood,
That from a mortal-man-made wound pour'd such an impious flood,
And weeping pour'd out these complaints: "O Father, storms't thou not
To see us take these wrongs from men? Extreme griefs we have got

Ev'n by our own deep councils, held for gratifying them;
And thou, our council's president, conclud'st in this extreme
Of fighting ever; being rul'd by one that thou hast bred;
One never well, but doing ill; a girl so full of head
That, though all other Gods obey, her mad moods must command,
By thy indulgence, nor by word, nor any touch of hand,
Correcting her; thy reason is, she is a spark of thee,
And therefore she may kindle rage in men 'gainst Gods, and she
May make men hurt Gods, and those Gods that are besides thy seed.
First in the palm's hit Cyprides; then runs the impious deed
On my hurt person; and, could life give way to death in me,
Or had my feet not fetched me off, heaps of mortality
Had kept me consort." Jupiter, with a contracted brow,
Thus answered Mars: "Thou many minds, inconstant changeling thou,
Sit not complaining thus by me, whom most of all the Gods,
Inhabiting the starry hill, I hate; no periods
Being set to thy contentions, brawls, fights, and pitching fields;
Just of thy mother Juno's moods, stiff-neck'd, and never yields,
Though I correct her still, and chide, nor can forbear offence,
Though to her son; this wound I know tastes of her insolence;
But I will prove more natural; thou shalt be cur'd, because
Thou com'st of me, but hadst thou been so cross to sacred laws,
Being born to any other God, thou had'st been thrown from heav'n
Long since, as low as Tartarus, beneath the giants driv'n."
This said, he gave his wound in charge to Pæon, who applied
Such sov'reign med'cines, that as soon the pain was qualified,
And he recur'd; as nourishing milk, when runnet is put in,
Runs all in heaps of tough thick curd, though in his nature thin,
Ev'n so soon his wound's parted sides ran close in his recure;
For he, all deathless, could not long the parts of death endure,
Then Hebe bath'd, and put on him fresh garments, and he sate
Exulting by his sire again, in top of all his state.
So, having, from the spoils of men, made his desir'd remove,
Juno and Pallas re-ascend the starry court of Jove.

[1] This simile likewise Virgil learns of him.

[2] How far a heavenly horse took at one reach or stroke in galloping or running; wherein Homer's mind is far from being expressed in his interpreters, all taking it for how far Deities were borne from the earth, when instantly they came down to earth: τόσσον ἐπιθρώσκουσι, etc. tantun uno saltu conficiunt, vel, tantum subsultim progrediuntur, deorum altizoni equi, etc. uno being understood, and the horse's swiftness highly expressed. The sense, otherwise, is senseless and contradictory.

[3] Ἀμβροσίην is the original word, which Scaliger taxeth very learnedly, asking how the horse came by it on those banks, when the text tells him Simois produced it; being willing to express by hyperbole the delicacy of that soil. If not, I hope the Deities could ever command it.

THE END OF THE FIFTH BOOK.

THE SIXTH BOOK OF HOMER'S ILIADS

THE ARGUMENT

The Gods now leaving an indiff'rent field,
The Greeks prevail, the slaughter'd Trojans yield.
Hector, by Helenus' advice, retires
In haste to Troy, and Hecuba desires
To pray Minerva to remove from fight
The son of Tydeus, her affected knight,
And vow to her, for favour of such price,
Twelve oxen should be slain in sacrifice.
In mean space Glaucus and Tydides meet;
And either other with remembrance greet
Of old love 'twixt their fathers, which inclines
Their hearts to friendship; who change arms for signs
Of a continu'd love for either's life.
Hector, in his return, meets with his wife,
And, taking in his arméd arms his son,
He prophesies the fall of Ilion.

ANOTHER ARGUMENT

In Zeta, Hector prophesies;
Prays for his son; wills sacrifice.
The stern fight freed of all the Gods, conquest with doubtful wings
Flew on their lances; ev'ry way the restless field she flings
Betwixt the floods of Simois and Xanthus, that confin'd
All their affairs of Ilion, and round about them shin'd.
The first that weigh'd down all the field, of one particular side,
Was Ajax, son of Telamon; who, like a bulwark, plied
The Greeks' protection, and of Troy the knotty orders brake,
Held out a light to all the rest, and showed them how to make
Way to their conquest, He did wound the strongest man of Thrace,
The tallest and the biggest set, Eussorian Acamas;
His lance fell on his casque's plum'd top, in stooping; the fell head
Drave through his forehead to his jaws; his eyes night shadowéd.
Tydides slew Teuthranides Axylus, that did dwell,
In fair Arisba's well-built tow'rs. He had of wealth a well,
And yet was kind and bountiful; he would a traveller pray
To be his guest, his friendly house stood in the broad highway,
In which he all sorts nobly us'd; yet none of them would stand
'Twixt him and death, but both himself, and he that had command
Of his fair horse, Calesius, fell lifeless on the ground.

Euryalus, Opheltius and Dresus dead did wound;
Nor ended there his fi'ry course, which he again begins,
And ran to it successfully, upon a pair of twins,
Æsepus, and bold Pedasus, whom good Bucolion
(That first call'd father, though base-born, renown'd Laomedon)
On Nais Abarbaræa got, a nymph that, as she fed
Her curléd flocks, Bucolion woo'd, and mix'd in love and bed.
Both these were spoiled of arms and life, by Mecistiades.
Then Polypœtes, for stern death, Astyalus did seize;
Ulysses slew Percosius; Teucer Aretaön;
Antilochus (old Nestor's joy) Ablerus; the great son
Of Atreüs, and king of men, Elatus, whose abode:
He held at upper Pedasus, where Satnius' river flowed;
The great heroë Leitus stay'd Phylacus in flight
From further life; Eurypylus, Melanthius reft of light.
The brother to the king of men, Adrestus took alive;
Whose horse, affrighted with the flight, their driver now did drive
Amongst the low-grown tam'risk trees, and at an arm of one
The chariot in the draught-tree brake; the horse brake loose, and run
The same way other flyers fled, contending all to town;
Himself close at the chariot wheel, upon his face was thrown,
And there lay flat, rolled up in dust. Atrides inwards drave;
And, holding at his breast his lance, Adrestus sought to save
His head by losing of his feet, and trusting to his knees;
On which the same parts of the king he hugs, and offers fees
Of worthy value for his life, and thus pleads their receipt:
"Take me alive, O Atreus' son, and take a worthy weight
Of brass, elab'rate iron, and gold. [1] A heap of precious things
Are in my father's riches hid, which, when your servant brings
News of my safety to his ears, he largely will divide
With your rare bounties." Atreus' son thought this the better side,
And meant to take it, being about to send him safe to fleet;
Which when, far off, his brother saw, he wing'd his royal feet,
And came in threat'ning, crying out: "O soft heart! What's the cause
Thou spar'st these men thus? Have not they observ'd these gentle laws
Of mild humanity to thee, with mighty argument
Why thou shouldst deal thus; in thy house, and with all precedent
Of honour'd guest-rites, entertain'd? Not one of them shall fly
A bitter end for it from heav'n, and much less, dotingly,
'Scape our revengeful fingers; all, ev'n th' infant in the womb,
Shall taste of what they merited, and have no other tomb
Than razéd Ilion; nor their race have more fruit than the dust."
This just cause turn'd his brother's mind, who violently thrust
The pris'ner from him; in whose guts the king of men impress'd
His ashen lance, which (pitching down his foot upon the breast
Of him that upwards fell) he drew; then Nestor spake to all:
"O friends, and household men of Mars, let not your púrsuit fall,
With those ye fell, for present spoil; nor, like the king of men,

Let any 'scape unfell'd; but on, dispatch them all, and then
Ye shall have time enough to spoil." This made so strong their chace,
That all the Trojans had been hous'd, and never turned a face,
Had not the Priamist Helenus, an augur most of name,
Will'd Hector and Æneas thus: "Hector! Anchises' fame!
Since on your shoulders, with good cause, the weighty burden lies
Of Troy and Lycia (being both of noblest faculties
For counsel, strength of hand, and apt to take chance at her best
In ev'ry turn she makes) stand fast, and suffer not the rest,
By any way search'd out for 'scape, to come within the ports,
Lest, fled into their wives' kind arms, they there be made the sports
Of the pursuing enemy. Exhort, and force your bands
To turn their faces; and, while we employ our ventur'd hands,
Though in a hard conditión, to make the other stay,
Hector, go thou to Ilion, and our queen-mother pray
To take the richest robe she hath; the same that's chiefly dear
To her court fancy; with which gem, assembling more to her
Of Troy's chief matrons, let all go, for fear of all our fates,
To Pallas' temple, take the key, unlock the leavy gates,
Enter, and reach the highest tow'r, where her Palladium stands,
And on it put the precious veil with pure and rev'rend hands,
And vow to her, besides the gift, a sacrificing stroke
Of twelve fat heifers-of-a-year, that never felt the yoke,
(Most answ'ring to her maiden state) if she will pity us,
Our town, our wives, our youngest joys, and him, that plagues them thus,
Take from the conflict, Diomed, that fury in a fight,
That true son of great Tydeús, that cunning lord of flight,
Whom I esteem the strongest Greek; for we have never fled
Achilles, that is prince of men, and whom a Goddess bred,
Like him; his fury flies so high, and all men's wraths commands."
Hector intends his brother's will, but first through all his bands
He made quick way, encouraging; and all, to fear afraid,
All turn'd their heads, and made Greece turn. Slaughter stood still dismay'd
On their parts, for they thought some God, fall'n from the vault of stars,
Was rush'd into the Ilions' aid, they made such dreadful wars.
Thus Hector, toiling in the waves, and thrusting back the flood
Of his ebb'd forces, thus takes leave: "So, so, now runs your blood
In his right current; forwards now, Trojans, and far-call'd friends!
Awhile hold out, till, for success to this your brave amends,
I haste to Ilion, and procure our counsellors and wives
To pray, and offer hecatombs, for their states in our lives."
Then fair-helm'd Hector turn'd to Troy, and, as he trode the field,
The black bull's hide, that at his back he wore about his shield,
In the extreme circumference, was with his gait so rock'd,
That, being large, it both at once his neck and ankles knock'd.
And now betwixt the hosts were met, Hippolochus' brave son,
Glaucus, who in his very look hope of some wonder won,
And little Tydeus' mighty heir; who seeing such a man

Offer the field, for usual blows, with wondrous words began:
"What art thou, strong'st of mortal men, that putt'st so far before,
Whom these fights never show'd mine eyes? They have been evermore
Sons of unhappy parents born, that came within the length
Of this Minerva-guided lance, and durst close with the strength
That she inspires in me. If heav'n be thy divine abode,
And thou a Deity thus inform'd, no more with any God
Will I change lances. The strong son of Dryus did not live
Long after such a conflict dar'd, who godlessly did drive
Nysæus' nurses through the hill made sacred to his name,
And called Nysseius; with a goad he punch'd each furious dame,
And made them ev'ry one cast down their green and leavy spears.
This th' homicide Lycurgus did; and those ungodly fears,
He put the froes in, seiz'd their God. Ev'n Bacchus he did drive
From his Nysseius; who was fain, with huge exclaims, to dive
Into the ocean. Thetis there in her bright bosom took
The flying Deity; who so fear'd Lycurgus' threats, he shook.
For which the freely-living Gods so highly were incens'd,
That Saturn's great Son strook him blind, and with his life dispens'd
But small time after; all because th' Immortals lov'd him not,
Nor lov'd him since he striv'd with them; and his end hath begot
Fear in my pow'rs to fight with heav'n. But, if the fruits of earth
Nourish thy body, and thy life be of our human birth,
Come near, that thou mayst soon arrive on that life-bounding shore,
To which I see thee hoise such sail." "Why dost thou so explore,"
Said Glaucus, "of what race I am, when like the race of leaves
The race of man is, that deserves no question; nor receives
My being any other breath? The wind in autumn strows
The earth with old leaves then the spring the woods with new endows;
And so death scatters men on earth, so life puts out again
Man's leavy issue. But my race, if, like the course of men,
Thou seek'st in more particular terms, 'tis this, to many known:
In midst of Argos, nurse of horse, there stands a walléd town,
Ephyré, where the mansion-house of Sisyphus did stand,
Of Sisyphus-Æölides, most wise of all the land.
Glaucus was son to him, and he begat Bellerophon,
Whose body heav'n indu'd with strength, and put a beauty on,
Exceeding lovely. Prætis yet his cause of love did hate,
And banish'd him the town; he might; he rul'd the Argive state.
The virtue of the one Jove plac'd beneath the other's pow'r,
His exile grew, since he denied to be the paramour
Of fair Anteia, Prætus' wife, who felt a raging fire
Of secret love to him; but he, whom wisdom did inspire
As well as prudence, (one of them advising him to shun
The danger of a princess' love, the other not to run
Within the danger of the Gods, the act being simply ill,)
Still entertaining thoughts divine, subdu'd the earthly still.
She, rul'd by neither of his wits, preferr'd her lust to both,

And, false to Prætus, would seem true, with this abhorr'd untroth:
'Prætus, or die thyself,' said she, 'or let Bellerophon die.
He urg'd dishonour to thy bed; which since I did deny,
He thought his violence should grant, and sought thy shame by force.'
The king, incens'd with her report, resolv'd upon her course,
But doubted how it should be run; he shunn'd his death direct,
(Holding a way so near not safe) and plotted the effect
By sending him with letters seal'd (that, open'd, touch his life) [2]
To Rhëuns king of Lycia, and father to his wife.
He went; and happily he went, the Gods walk'd all his way;
And being arriv'd in Lycia, where Xanthus doth display
The silver ensigns of his waves, the king of that broad land
Receiv'd him with a wondrous free and honourable hand.
Nine days he feasted him, and kill'd an ox in ev'ry day,
In thankful sacrifice to heav'n, for his fair guest; whose stay,
With rosy fingers, brought the world, the tenth well-welcom'd morn,
And then the king did move to see, the letters he had borne
From his lov'd son-in-law; which seen, he wrought thus their contents:
Chimæra, the invincible, he sent him to convince,
Sprung from no man, but mere divine; a lion's shape before,
Behind a dragon's, in the midst a goat's shagg'd form, she bore,
And flames of deadly fervency flew from her breath and eyes;
Yet her he slew; his confidence in sacred prodigies
Render'd him victor. Then he gave his second conquest way
Against the famous Solymi, when (he himself would say,
Reporting it) he enter'd on a passing vig'rous fight.
His third huge labour he approv'd against a woman's spite,
That fill'd a field of Amazons; he overcame them all.
Then set they on him sly Deceit, when Force had such a fall;
An ambush of the strongest men, that spacious Lycia bred,
Was lodg'd for him; whom he lodg'd sure, they never rais'd a head.
His deeds thus showing him deriv'd from some celestial race,
The king detain'd, and made amends, with doing him the grace
Of his fair daughter's princely gift; and with her, for a dow'r,
Gave half his kingdom; and to this, the Lycians on did pour
More than was giv'n to any king; a goodly planted field,
In some parts thick of groves and woods, the rest rich crops did yield,
This field the Lycians futurely (of future wand'rings there
And other errors of their prince, in the unhappy rear
Of his sad life) the Errant call'd, The princess brought him forth
Three children (whose ends griev'd him more, the more they were of worth)
Isander; and Hippolochus; and fair Laodomy,
With whom, ev'n Jupiter himself left heav'n itself, to lie,
And had by her the man at arms, Sarpedon, call'd divine,
The Gods then left him, lest a man should in their glories shine,
And set against him; for his son, Isandrus, in a strife
Against the valiant Solymi, Mars reft of light and life;
Laodamïa, being envied of all the Goddesses,

The golden-bridle-handling Queen, the maiden Patroness,
Slew with an arrow; and for this he wander'd evermore
Alone through his Aleian field, and fed upon the core
Of his sad bosom, flying all the loth'd consórts of men.
Yet had he one surviv'd to him, of those three childeren,
Hippolochus, the root of me; who sent me here with charge
That I should always bear me well, and my deserts enlarge
Beyond the vulgar, lest I sham'd my race, that far excell'd
All that Ephyra's famous tow'rs, or ample Lycia, held.
This is my stock, and this am I." This cheer'd Tydides' heart,
Who pitch'd his spear down, lean'd, and talk'd in this affectionate part:
"Certés, in thy great ancestor, and in mine own, thou art
A guest of mine, right ancient. King Oeneus twenty days
Detain'd, with feasts, Bellerophon, whom all the world did praise.
Betwixt whom mutual gifts were giv'n, My grandsire gave to thine
A girdle of Phœnician work, impurpl'd wondrous fine,
Thine gave a two-neck'd jug of gold, which, though I use not here,
Yet still it is my gem at home. But, if our fathers were
Familiar, or each other knew, I know not, since my sire
Left me a child, at siege of Thebes, where he left his life's fire.
But let us prove our grandsires' sons, and be each other's guests.
To Lycia when I come, do thou receive thy friend with feasts;
Peloponnesus, with the like, shall thy wish'd presence greet.
Mean space, shun we each other here, though in the press we meet.
There are enow of Troy beside, and men enow renown'd,
To right my pow'rs, whomever heav'n shall let my lance confound,
So are there of the Greeks for thee; kill who thou canst. And now,
For sign of amity 'twixt us, and that all these may know
We glory in th' hospitious rites our grandsires did commend,
Change we our arms before them all." From horse then both descend,
Join hands, give faith, and take; and then did Jupiter elate [3]
The mind of Glaucus, who, to show his rev'rence to the state
Of virtue in his grandsire's heart, and gratulate beside
The offer of so great a friend, exchang'd in that good pride,
Curets of gold for those of brass, that did on Diomed shine,
One of a hundred oxen's price, the other but of nine,
By this, had Hector reach'd the ports of Scæa, and the tow'rs.
About him flock'd the wives of Troy, the children, paramours,
Inquiring how their husbands did, their fathers, brothers, loves.
He stood not then to answer them, but said: "It now behoves
Ye should all go t' implore the aid of heav'n, in a distress
Of great effect, and imminent." Then hasted he access
To Priam's goodly builded court, which round about was run
With walking porches, galleries, to keep off rain and sun.
Within, of one side, on a rew, of sundry-colour'd stones,
Fifty fair lodgings were built out, for Priam's fifty sons,
And for as fair sort of their wives; and, in the opposite view,
Twelve lodgings of like stone, like height, were likewise built arew,

Where, with their fair and virtuous wives, twelve princes, sons in law
To honourable Priam, lay. And here met Hecuba,
The loving mother, her great son; and with her needs must be
The fairest of her female race, the bright Laodice.
The queen gript hard her Hector's hand, and said: "O worthiest son,
Why leav'st thou field? Is't not because the curséd nation
Afflict our countrymen and friends? They are their moans that move
Thy mind to come and lift thy hands, in his high tow'r, to Jove.
But stay a little, that myself may fetch our sweetest wine
To offer first to Jupiter, then that these joints of thine
May be refresh'd; for, woe is me, how thou art toil'd and spent!
Thou for our city's gen'ral state, thou for our friends far sent,
Must now the press of fight endure; now solitude, to call
Upon the name of Jupiter; thou only for us all.
But wine will something comfort thee; for to a man dismay'd
With careful spirits, or too much with labour overlaid,
Wine brings much rescue, strength'ning much the body and the mind."
The great helm-mover thus receiv'd the auth'ress of his kind:
"My royal mother, bring no wine; lest rather it impair
Than help my strength, and make my mind forgetful of th' affair
Committed to it; and (to pour it out in sacrifice)
I fear with unwash'd hands to serve the pure-liv'd Deities.
Nor is it lawful, thus imbru'd with blood and dust, to prove
The will of heav'n, or offer vows to cloud-compelling Jove.
I only come to use your pains (assembling other dames,
Matrons, and women honour'd most, with high and virtuous names)
With wine and odours, and a robe most ample, most of price,
And which is dearest in your love, to offer sacrifice
In Pallas' temple; and to put the precious robe ye bear.
On her Palladium; vowing all, twelve oxen-of-a-year,
Whose necks were never wrung with yoke, shall pay her grace their lives,
If she will pity our sieg'd town; pity ourselves, our wives;
Pity our children; and remove, from sacred Ilion,
The dreadful soldier Diomed. And, when yourselves are gone
About this work, myself will go, to call into the field,
If he will hear me, Helen's love; whom would the earth would yield)
And headlong take into her gulf, even quick before mine eyes;
For then my heart, I hope, would cast her load of miseries,
Borne for the plague he hath been born, and bred to the deface,
By great Olympius, of Troy, our sire, and all our race."
This said, grave Hecuba went home, and sent her maids about,
To bid the matrons. She herself descended, and search'd out,
Within a place that breath'd perfumes, the richest robe she had;
Which lay with many rich ones more, most curiously made
By women of Sidonia; which Paris brought from thence,
Sailing the broad sea, when he made that voyage of offence,
In which he brought home Helena. That robe, transferr'd so far,
(That was the undermost) she took; it glitter'd like a star;

And with it went she to the fane, with many ladies more;
Amongst whom fair-cheek'd Theano unlock'd the folded door;
Chaste Theano, Antenor's wife, and of Cissëus' race,
Sister to Hecuba, both born to that great king of Thrace.
Her th' Ilions made Minerva's priest; and her they follow'd all
Up to the temple's highest tow'r, where on their knees they fall,
Lift up their hands, and fill the fane with ladies' piteous cries.
Then lovely Theano took the veil, and with it she implies
The great Palladium, praying thus: "Goddess of most renown
In all the heav'n of Goddesses, great Guardian of our town,
Rev'rend Minerva, break the lance of Diomed, cease his grace,
Give him to fall in shameful flight, headlong, and on his face,
Before our ports of Ilion, that instantly we may,
Twelve unyok'd oxen-of-a-year, in this thy temple slay,
To thy sole honour; take their bloods, and banish our offence;
Accept Troy's zeal, her wives, and save her infants' innocence."
She pray'd, but Pallas would not grant. Mean space was Hector come
Where Alexander's lodgings were, that many a goodly room
Had built in them by architects, of Troy's most curious sort,
And were no lodgings, but a house; nor no house, but a court;
Or had all these contain'd in them; and all within a tow'r,
Next Hector's lodgings and the king's. The lov'd of heav'n's chief Pow'r,
Hector, here enter'd. In his hand a goodly lance he bore,
Ten cubits long; the brazen head went shining ill before,
Help'd with a burnish'd ring of gold. He found his brother then
Amongst the women, yet prepar'd to go amongst the men,
For in their chamber he was set, trimming his arms, his shield,
His curets, and was trying how his crookéd bow would yield
To his straight arms. Amongst her maids was set the Argive Queen,
Commanding them in choicest works. When Hector's eye had seen
His brother thus accompanied, and that he could not bear
The very touching of his arms but where the women were,
And when the time so needed men, right cunningly he chid.
That he might do it bitterly, his cowardice he hid,
That simply made him so retir'd, beneath an anger, feign'd
In him by Hector, for the hate the citizens sustain'd
Against him, for the foil he took in their cause; and again,
For all their gen'ral foils in his. So Hector seems to plain
Of his wrath to them, for their hate, and not his cowardice; [4]
As that were it that shelter'd him in his effeminacies,
And kept him, in that dang'rous time, from their fit aid in fight;
For which he chid thus: "Wretched man! So timeless is thy spite
That 'tis not honest; and their hate is just, 'gainst which it bends.
War burns about the town for thee; for thee our slaughter'd friends
Besiege Troy with their carcasses, on whose heaps our high walls
Are overlook'd by enemies; the sad sounds of their falls
Without, are echo'd with the cries of wives and babes within;
And all for thee; and yet for them thy honour cannot win

Head of thine anger. Thou shouldst need no spirit to stir up thine,
But thine should set the rest on fire, and with a rage divine
Chastise impartially the best, that impiously forbears.
Come forth, lest thy fair tow'rs and Troy be burn'd about thine ears."
Paris acknowledg'd, as before, all just that Hector spake,
Allowing justice, though it were for his injustice' sake;
And where his brother put a wrath upon him by his art,
He takes it, for his honour's sake, as sprung out of his heart,
And rather would have anger seem his fault than cowardice;
And thus he answer'd: "Since, with right, you join'd check with advice,
And I hear you, give equal ear: It is not any spleen
Against the town, as you conceive, that makes me so unseen,
But sorrow for it; which to ease, and by discourse digest
Within myself, I live so close; and yet, since men might wrest
My sad retreat, like you, my wife with her advice inclin'd
This my addression to the field; which was mine own free mind,
As well as th' instance of her words; for though the foil were mine,
Conquest brings forth her wreaths by turns. Stay then this haste of thine
But till I arm, and I am made a cónsort for thee straight;—
Or go, I'll overtake thy haste." Helen stood at receipt,
And took up all great Hector's pow'rs, t' attend her heavy words,
By which had Paris no reply. This vent her grief affords:
"Brother (if I may call you so, that had been better born
A dog, than such a horrid dame, as all men curse and scorn,
A mischief-maker, a man-plague) O would to God, the day,
That first gave light to me, had been a whirlwind in my way,
And borne me to some desert hill, or hid me in the rage
Of earth's most far-resounding seas, ere I should thus engage
The dear lives of so many friends! Yet since the Gods have been
Helpless foreseers of my plagues, they might have likewise seen
That he they put in yoke with me, to bear out their award,
Had been a man of much more spirit, and, or had nobler dar'd
To shield mine honour with this deed, or with his mind had known
Much better the upbraids of men, that so he might have shown
(More like a man) some sense of grief for both my shame and his.
But he is senseless, nor conceives what any manhood is,
Nor now, nor ever after will; and therefore hangs, I fear,
A plague above him. But come near, good brother; rest you here,
Who, of the world of men, stands charg'd with most unrest for me,
(Vile wretch) and for my lover's wrong; on whom a destiny
So bitter is impos'd by Jove, that all succeeding times
Will put, to our unended shames, in all men's mouths our crimes."
He answer'd: "Helen, do not seek to make me sit with thee;
I must not stay, though well I know thy honour'd love of me.
My mind calls forth to aid our friends, in whom my absence breeds
Longings to see me; for whose sakes, importune thou to deeds
This man by all means, that your care may make his own make hast,
And meet me in the open town, that all may see at last

He minds his lover. I myself will now go home, and see
My household, my dear wife, and son, that little hope of me;
For, sister, 'tis without my skill, if I shall evermore
Return, and see them, or to earth, her right in me, restore.
The Gods may stoop me by the Greeks." This said, he went to see
The virtuous princess, his true wife, white-arm'd Andromache.
She, with her infant son and maid, was climb'd the tow'r about
The sight of him that sought for her, weeping and crying out.
Hector, not finding her at home, was going forth; retir'd;
Stood in the gate; her woman call'd, and curiously inquir'd
Where she was gone; bad tell him true, if she were gone to see
His sisters, or his brothers' wives; or whether she should be
At temple with the other dames, t' implore Minerva's ruth.
Her woman answer'd: Since he ask'd, and urg'd so much the truth,
The truth was she was neither gone, to see his brothers' wives,
His sisters, nor t' implore the ruth of Pallas on their lives;
But she (advertis'd of the bane Troy suffer'd, and how vast
Conquest had made herself for Greece) like one distraught, made hast
To ample Ilion with her son, and nurse, and all the way
Mourn'd, and dissolv'd in tears for him. Then Hector made no stay,
But trod her path, and through the streets, magnificently built,
All the great city pass'd, and came where, seeing how blood was spilt,
Andromache might see him come: who made as he would pass
The ports without saluting her, not knowing where she was.
She, with his sight, made breathless haste, to meet him; she, whose grace
Brought him withal so great a dow'r; she that of all the race
Of king Aëtion only liv'd; Aëtion, whose house stood
Beneath the mountain Placius, environ'd with the wood
Of Theban Hypoplace, being court to the Cilician land.
She ran to Hector, and with her, tender of heart and hand,
Her son, borne in his nurse's arms; when, like a heav'nly sign,
Compact of many golden stars, the princely child did shine,
Whom Hector call'd Scamandrius, but whom the town did name
Astyanax, because his sire did only prop the same.
Hector, though grief bereft his speech, yet smil'd upon his joy.
Andromache cried out, mix'd hands, and to the strength of Troy
Thus wept forth her affectión: "O noblest in desire!
Thy mind, inflam'd with others' good, will set thyself on fire.
Nor pitiest thou thy son, nor wife, who must thy widow be,
If now thou issue; all the field will only run on thee.
Better my shoulders underwent the earth, than thy decease;
For then would earth bear joys no more; then comes the black increase
Of griefs (like Greeks on Ilion). Alas! What one survives
To be my refuge? One black day bereft sev'n brothers' lives,
By stern Achilles; by his hand my father breath'd his last,
His high-wall'd rich Cilician Thebes [5] sack'd by him, and laid wast;
The royal body yet he left unspoil'd; religion charm'd
That act of spoil; and all in fire he burn'd him cómplete arm'd;

Built over him a royal tomb; and to the monument
He left of him, th' Oreades (that are the high descent
Of Ægis-bearing Jupiter) another of their own
Did add to it, and set it round with elms; by which is shown,
In theirs, the barrenness of death; yet might it serve beside
To shelter the sad monument from all the ruffinous pride
Of storms and tempests, us'd to hurt things or that noble kind,
The short life yet my mother liv'd he sav'd, and serv'd his mind
With all the riches of the realm; which not enough esteem'd
He kept her pris'ner; whom small time, but much more wealth, redeem'd,
And she, in sylvan Hypoplace, Cilicia rul'd again,
But soon was over-rul'd by death; Diana's chaste disdain
Gave her a lance, and took her life. Yet, all these gone from me,
Thou amply render'st all; thy life makes still my father be,
My mother, brothers; and besides thou art my husband too,
Most lov'd, most worthy. Pity them, dear love, and do not go,
For thou gone, all these go again; pity our common joy,
Lest, of a father's patronage, the bulwark of all Troy,
Thou leav'st him a poor widow's charge. Stay, stay then, in this tow'r,
And call up to the wild fig-tree all thy retiréd pow'r;
For there the wall is easiest scal'd, and fittest for surprise,
And there, th' Ajaces, Idomen, th' Atrides, Diomed, thrice
Have both survey'd and made attempt; I know not if induc'd
By some wise augury, or the fact was naturally infus'd
Into their wits, or courages." To this, great Hector said:
"Be well assur'd, wife, all these things in my kind cares are weigh'd.
But what a shame, and fear, it is to think how Troy would scorn
(Both in her husbands, and her wives, whom long-train'd gowns adorn)
That I should cowardly fly off! The spirit I first did breath
Did never teach me that; much less, since the contempt of death
Was settled in me, and my mind knew what a worthy was,
Whose office is to lead in fight, and give no danger pass
Without improvement. In this fire must Hector's trial shine;
Here must his country, father, friends, be, in him, made divine.
And such a stormy day shall come (in mind and soul I know)
When sacred Troy shall shed her tow'rs, for tears of overthrow;
When Priam, all his birth and pow'r, shall in those tears be drown'd.
But neither Troy's posterity so much my soul doth wound,
Priam, nor Hecuba herself, nor all my brothers' woes,
(Who though so many, and so good, must all be food for foes)
As thy sad state; when some rude Greek shall lead thee weeping hence,
These free days clouded, and a night of captive violence
Loading thy temples, out of which thine eyes must never see,
But spin the Greek wives' webs of task, and their fetch water be
To Argos, from Messeides, or clear Hyperia's spring; [6]
Which howsoever thou abhorr'st, Fate's such a shrewish thing
She will be mistress; whose curs'd hands, when they shall crush out cries
From thy oppressions (being beheld by other enemies)

Thus they will nourish thy extremes: 'This dame was Hector's wife,
A man that, at the wars of Troy, did breathe the worthiest life
Of all their army.' This again will rub thy fruitful wounds,
To miss the man that to thy bands could give such narrow bounds.
But that day shall not wound mine eyes; the solid heap of night
Shall interpose, and stop mine ears against thy plaints, and plight."
This said, he reach'd to take his son; who, of his arms afraid,
And then the horse-hair plume, with which he was so overlaid,
Nodded so horribly, he cling'd back to his nurse, and cried.
Laughter affected his great sire, who doff'd, and laid aside
His fearful helm, that on the earth cast round about it light;
Then took and kiss'd his loving son, and (balancing his weight
In dancing him) these loving vows to living Jove he us'd
And all the other bench of Gods: "O you that have infus'd
Soul to this infant, now set down this blessing on his star;—
Let his renown be clear as mine; equal his strength in war;
And make his reign so strong in Troy, that years to come may yield
His facts this fame, when, rich in spoils, he leaves the conquer'd field
Sown with his slaughters: 'These high deeds exceed his father's worth.'
And let this echo'd praise supply the comforts to come forth
Of his kind mother with my life." This said, th' heroic sire
Gave him his mother; whose fair eyes fresh streams of love's salt fire
Billow'd on her soft cheeks, to hear the last of Hector's speech,
In which his vows compris'd the sum of all he did beseech
In her wish'd comfort. So she took into her od'rous breast
Her husband's gift; who, mov'd to see her heart so much oppress'd,
He dried her tears, and thus desir'd: "Afflict me not, dear wife,
With these vain griefs. He doth not live, that can disjoin my life
And this firm bosom, but my fate; and fate, whose wings can fly?
Noble, ignoble, fate controls. Once born, the best must die,
Go home, and set thy housewif'ry on these extremes of thought;
And drive war from them with thy maids; keep them from doing nought.
These will be nothing; leave the cares of war to men, and me
In whom, of all the Ilion race, they take their high'st degree."
On went his helm; his princess home, half cold with kindly fears;
When ev'ry fear turn'd back her looks, and ev'ry look shed tears.
Foe-slaught'ring Hector's house soon reach'd, her many women there
Wept all to see her: in his life great Hector's fun'rals were;
Never look'd any eye of theirs to see their lord safe home,
'Scap'd from the gripes and pow'rs of Greece. And now was Paris come
From his high tow'rs; who made no stay, when once he had put on
His richest armour, but flew forth; the flints he trod upon
Sparkled with lustre of his arms; his long-ebb'd spirits now flow'd
The higher for their lower ebb. And as a fair steed, proud [7]
With full-giv'n mangers, long tied up, and now, his head stall broke,
He breaks from stable, runs the field, and with an ample stroke
Measures the centre, neighs, and lifts aloft his wanton head,
About his shoulders shakes his crest, and where he hath been fed,

Or in some calm flood wash'd, or, stung with his high plight, he flies
Amongst his females, strength put forth, his beauty beautifies,
And, like life's mirror, bears his gait; so Paris from the tow'r
Of lofty Pergamus came forth; he show'd a sun-like pow'r
In carriage of his goodly parts, address'd now to the strife;
And found his noble brother near the place he left his wife.
Him thus respected he salutes: "Right worthy, I have fear
That your so serious haste to field, my stay hath made forbear,
And that I come not as you wish." He answer'd: "Honour'd man,
Be confident, for not myself, nor any others, can
Reprove in thee the work of fight, at least, not any such
As is an equal judge of things; for thou hast strength as much
As serves to execute a mind very important, but
Thy strength too readily flies off, enough will is not put
To thy ability. My heart is in my mind's strife sad,
When Troy (out of her much distress, she and her friends have had
By thy procurement) doth deprave thy noblesse in mine ears.
But come, hereafter we shall calm these hard conceits of theirs,
When, from their ports the foe expuls'd, high Jove to them hath giv'n
Wish'd peace, and us free sacrifice to all the Powers of heav'n."

[1] This Virgil imitates.

[2] *Bellerophontis literæ. Ad Eras.* This long speech many critics tax as untimely, being, as they take it, in the heat of fight; Hier. Vidas, a late observer, being eagerest against Homer. Whose ignorance in this I cannot but note, and prove to you; for, besides the authority and office of a poet, to vary and quicken his poem with these episodes, sometimes beyond the leisure of their actions, the critic notes not how far his forerunner prevents his worst as far; and sets down his speech at the sudden and strange turning of the Trojan field, set on a little before by Hector; and that so fiercely, it made an admiring stand among the Grecians, and therein gave fit time for these great captains to utter their admirations, the whole field in that part being to stand like their commanders. And then how full of decorum this gallant show and speech was to sound understandings, I leave only to such, and let our critics go cavil.

[3] Φρένας ἐξέλετο Ζεύς, *Mentem ademit Jup.*, the text hath it; which only I alter of all Homer's original, since Plutarch against the Stoics excuses this supposed folly in Glaucus. Spondanus likewise encouraging my alterations, which I use for the loved and simple nobility of the free exchange in Glaucus, contrary to others that, for the supposed folly in Glaucus, turned his change into a proverb, χρύσεα χαλχείων, golden for brazen.

[4] Hector dissembles the cowardice he finds in Paris turning it, as if he chid him for his anger at the Trojans for hating him, being conquered by Menelaus, when it is for his effeminacy. Which is all paraphrastical in my translation.

[5] Thebes, a most rich city of Cilicia.

[6] The names of two fountains: of which one in Thessaly, the other near Argos, or, according to others, in Peloponnesus or Lacedæmon.

[7] *His simile, high and expressive; which Virgil almost word for word hath translated, Æn. xi. (v. 492).*

THE END OF THE SIXTH BOOK.

THE SEVENTH BOOK OF HOMER'S ILIADS [1]

THE ARGUMENT

Hector, by Helenus' advice, doth seek
Advent'rous combat on the boldest Greek,
Nine Greeks stand up, acceptants ev'ry one,
But lot selects strong Ajax Telamon.
Both, with high honour, stand th' important fight,
Till heralds part them by approached night.
Lastly, they grave the dead. The Greeks erect
A mighty wall, their navy to protect;
Which angers Neptune. Jove, by hapless signs,
In depth of night, succeeding woes divines.

ANOTHER ARGUMENT

In Eta, Priam's strongest son
Combats with Ajax Telamon.
This said, brave Hector through the Troy's bane-bringing knight;
Made issue to th' insatiate field, resolv'd to fervent fight.
And as the Weather-wielder sends to seamen prosp'rous gales,
When with their sallow polish'd oars, long lifted from their falls,
Their wearied arms, dissolv'd with toil, can scarce strike one stroke more;
Like those sweet winds appear'd these lords, to Trojans tir'd before.
Then fell they to the works of death. By Paris' valour fell
King Arëithous' hapless son, that did in Arna dwell,
Menesthius, whose renownéd sire a club did ever bear,
And of Phylomedusa gat, that had her eyes so clear,
This slaughter'd issue. Hector's dart strook Eionëus dead;
Beneath his good steel casque it pierc'd, above his gorget-stead.
Glaucus, Hippolochus's son, that led the Lycian crew,
Iphinous-Dexiades with sudden jav'lin slew,
As he was mounting to his horse; his shoulders took the spear,
And ere he sate, in tumbling, down, his powers dissolvéd were.
When gray-ey'd Pallas had perceiv'd the Greeks so fall in fight,
From high Olympus' top she stoop'd, and did on Ilion light.
Apollo, to encounter her, to Pergamus did fly,
From whence he, looking to the field, wish'd Trojans' victory.
At Jove's broad beech these Godheads met; and first Jove's son objects;
"Why, burning in contention thus, do thy extreme affects

Conduct thee from our peaceful hill? Is it to oversway
The doubtful victory of fight, and give the Greeks the day?
Thou never pitiest perishing Troy. Yet now let me persuade,
That this day no more mortal wounds may either side invade.
Hereafter, till the end of Troy, they shall apply the fight,
Since your immortal wills resolve to overturn it quite."
Pallas replied: "It likes me well; for this came I from heav'n;
But to make either armies cease, what order shall be giv'n?"
He said: "We will direct the spirit, that burns in Hector's breast,
To challenge any Greek to wounds, with single pow'rs impress'd;
Which Greeks, admiring, will accept, and make some one stand out
So stout a challenge to receive, with a defence as stout."
It is confirm'd; and Helenus (king Priam's lovéd seed)
By augury discern'd th' event that these two pow'rs decreed,
And greeting Hector ask'd him this: "Wilt thou be once advis'd?
I am thy brother, and thy life with mine is ev'nly prized.
Command the rest of Troy and Greece; to cease this public fight,
And, what Greek bears the greatest mind, to single strokes excite.
I promise thee that yet thy soul shall not descend to fates;
So heard I thy survival cast, by the celestial States."
Hector with glad allowance gave his brother's counsel ear,
And, fronting both the hosts, advanc'd just in the midst his spear.
The Trojans instantly surcease; the Greeks Atrides stay'd.
The God that bears the silver bow, and war's triumphant Maid,
On Jove's beech like two vultures sat, pleas'd to behold both parts
Flow in to hear, so sternly arm'd with huge shields, helms, and darts.
And such fresh horror as you see, driv'n through the wrinkled waves
By rising Zephyr, under whom the sea grows black, and raves;
Such did the hasty gath'ring troops' of both hosts make to hear;
Whose tumult settled, 'twixt them both, thus spake the challenger:
"Hear, Trojans, and ye well-arm'd Greeks, what my strong mind, diffus'd
Through all my spirits, commands me speak: Saturnius hath not us'd
His promis'd favour for our truce, but, studying both our ills,
Will never cease, till Mars, by you, his rav'nous stomach fills.
With ruin'd Troy, or we consume your mighty sea-borne fleet.
Since then the gen'ral peers of Greece in reach of one voice meet,
Amongst you all, whose breast includes the most impulsive mind,
Let him stand forth as combatant, by all the rest design'd.
Before whom thus I call high Jove, to witness of our strife:—
If he with home-thrust iron can reach th' exposure of my life,
Spoiling my arms, let him at will convey them to his tent,
But let my body be return'd, that Troy's two-sex'd descent
May waste it in the fun'ral pile. If I can slaughter him,
Apollo honouring me so much, I'll spoil his conquer'd limb,
And bear his arms to Ilion, where in Apollo's shrine
I'll hang them, as my trophies due; his body I'll resign
To be disposed by his friends in flamy funerals,
And honour'd with erected tomb, where Hellespontus falls

Into Ægæum, and doth reach ev'n to your naval road,
That, when our beings in the earth shall hide their period,
Survivors, sailing the black sea, may thus his name renew:
'This is his monument whose blood long since did fates imbrue,
Whom, passing far in fortitude illustrate Hector slew.'
This shall posterity report, and my fame never die."
This said, dumb silence seiz'd them all; they shaméd to deny,
And fear'd to undertake. At last did Menelaus speak,
Check'd their remissness, and so sigh'd, as if his heart would break:
"Ah me! But only threat'ning Greeks, not worthy Grecian names! [2]
This more and more, not to be borne, makes grow our huge defames,
If Hector's honourable proof be entertain'd by none.
But you are earth and water all, which, symboliz'd in one,
Have fram'd your faint unfi'ry spirits; ye sit without your hearts,
Grossly inglorious; but myself will use acceptive darts,
And arm against him, though you think I arm 'gainst too much odds;
But conquest's garlands hang aloft, amongst th' Immortal Gods."
He arm'd, and gladly would have fought; but Menelaus, then,
By Hector's far more strength, thy soul had fled th' abodes of men,
Had not the kings of Greece stood up, and thy attempt restrain'd;
And ev'n the king of men himself, that in such compass reign'd,
Who took him by the bold right hand, and sternly pluck'd him back:
"Mad brother, 'tis no work for thee, thou seek'st thy wilful wrack!
Contain, though it despite thee much, nor for this strife engage
Thy person with a man more strong, and whom all fear t' enrage;
Yea whom Æacides himself, in men-renowning war,
Makes doubt t' encounter, whose huge strength surpasseth thine by far.
Sit thou then by thy regiment; some other Greek will rise
(Though he be dreadless, and no war will his desires suffice,
That makes this challenge to our strength) our valours to avow;
To whom, if he can 'scape with life, he will be glad to bow."
This drew his brother from his will, who yielded, knowing it true,
And his glad soldiers took his arms; when Nestor did pursue
The same reproof he set on foot, and thus supplied his turn:
"What huge indignity is this! How will our country mourn!
Old Peleus that good king will weep, that worthy counsellor,
That trumpet of the Myrmidons, who much did ask me for
All men of name that went to Troy; with joy he did inquire
Their valour and their towardness, and I made him admire;
But, that ye all fear Hector now, if his grave ears shall hear,
How will he lift his hands to heav'n, and pray that death may bear
His grieved soul into the deep! O would to heav'n's great King, [3]
Minerva, and the God of light, that now my youthful spring
Did flourish in my willing veins, as when at Phæa's tow'rs
About the streams of Jardanus, my gather'd Pylean pow'rs,
And dart-employ'd Arcadians, fought, near raging Celadon!
Amongst whom, first of all, stood forth great Ereuthalion,
Who th' arms of Arëithoús wore, brave Arëithoús,

And, since he still fought with a club, surnam'd Clavigerus,
All men, and fair-girt ladies both, for honour call'd him so.
He fought not with a keep-off spear, or with a far-shot bow,
But, with a massy club of iron, he broke through arméd bands.
And yet Lycurgus was his death, but not with force of hands;
With sleight (encount'ring in a lane, where his club wanted sway)
He thrust him through his spacious waist; who fell, and upwards lay,
In death not bowing his face to earth; his arms he did despoil,
Which iron Mars bestow'd on him; and those, in Mars's toil,
Lycurgus ever after wore; but when he agéd grew,
Enforc'd to keep his peaceful house, their use he did renew
On mighty Ereuthalion's limbs, his soldier, lovéd well;
And, with these arms he challeng'd all, that did in arms excel;
All shook, and stood dismay'd, none durst his adverse champion make.
Yet this same forward mind of mine, of choice, would undertake
To fight with all his confidence; though youngest enemy
Of all the army we conduct, yet I fought with him, I,
Minerva made me so renown'd, and that most tall strong peer
I slew; his big bulk lay on earth, extended here and there,
As it were covetous to spread the centre ev'rywhere.
O that my youth were now as fresh, and all my pow'rs as sound,
Soon should bold Hector be impugn'd! Yet you that most are crown'd
With fortitude of all our host, ev'n you methinks are slow,
Not free, and set on fire with lust, t' encounter such a foe."
With this, nine royal princes rose. Atrides for the first;
Then Diomed; th' Ajaces then, that did th' encounter thirst;
King Idomen and his consórts; Mars-like Meriones;
Evemon's son, Eurypylus: and Andrǽmonides,
Whom all the Grecians Thoas call'd, sprung of Andrǽmon's blood;
And wise Ulysses; ev'ry one, propos'd for combat, stood.
Again Gerenius Nestor spake: "Let lots be drawn by all;
His hand shall help the well-arm'd Greeks, on whom the lot doth fall,
And to his wish shall he be help'd, if he escape with life
The harmful danger-breathing fit of his advent'rous strife."
Each mark'd his lot, and cast it into Agamemnon's casque.
The soldiers pray'd, held up their hands, and this of Jove did ask,
With eyes advanc'd to heav'n: "O Jove, so lead the herald's hand,
That Ajax, or great Tydeus' son, may our wish'd champion stand,
Or else the king himself that rules the rich Mycenian land."
This said, old Nestor mix'd the lots. The foremost lot survey'd
With Ajax Telamon was sign'd, as all the soldiers pray'd;
One of the heralds drew it forth, who brought and show'd it round,
Beginning at the right hand first, to all the most renown'd.
None knowing it, ev'ry man denied; but when he forth did pass
To him which mark'd and cast it in; which famous Ajax was,
He stretch'd his hand, and into it the herald put the lot,
Who, viewing it, th' inscription knew; the duke deniéd not,
But joyfully acknowledg'd it, and threw it at his feet,

And said: "O friends, the lot is mine, which to my soul is sweet;
For now I hope my fame shall rise, in noble Hector's fall.
But, whilst I arm myself, do you on great Saturnius call,
But silently, or to yourselves, that not a Trojan hear;
Or openly, If you think good, since none alive we fear.
None with a will, if I will not, can my bold pow'rs affright,
At least for plain fierce swing of strength, or want of skill in fight;
For I will well prove that my birth; and breed, in Salamine
Was not all consecrate to meat, or mere effects of wine."
This said, the well-giv'n soldiers pray'd; up went to heav'n their eyne:
"O Jove, that Ida dost protect, most happy, most divine,
Send victory to Ajax' side; fame; grace his goodly limb;
Or (if thy love bless Hector's life, and thou hast care of him.)
Bestow on both like pow'r, like fame." This said, in bright arms, shone
The good strong Ajax; who, when all his war attire was on,
March'd like the hugely-figur'd Mars, when angry Jupiter
With strength, on people proud of strength, sends him forth to infer
Wreakful contention, and comes on with presence full of fear;
So th' Achive rampire, Telamon, did 'twixt the hosts appear;
Smil'd; yet of terrible aspéct; on earth, with ample pace,
He boldly stalk'd, and shook aloft his dart with deadly grace.
It did the Grecians good to see; but heartquakes shook the joints
Of all the Trojans, Hector's self felt thoughts, with horrid points,
Tempt his bold bosom; but he now must make no counterflight,
Nor, with his honour, now refuse, that had provok'd the fight.
Ajax came near; and, like a tow'r, his shield his bosom barr'd,
The right side brass, and sev'n ox-hides within it quilted hard; [4]
Old Tychius, the best currier; that did in Hyla dwell,
Did frame it for exceeding proof, and wrought it wondrous well.
With this stood he to Hector close, and with this brave began:
"Now, Hector, thou shalt clearly know, thus meeting man to man,
What other leaders arm our host, besides great Thetis' son,
Who with his hardy lion's heart hath armies overrun;
But he lies at our crook'd-stern'd fleet, a rival with our king
In height of spirit; yet to Troy he many knights did bring,
Coequal with Æacides, all able to sustain
All thy bold challenge can import. Begin then, words are vain,"
The helm-grac'd Hector answer'd him: "Renownéd Telamon,
Prince of the soldiers came from Greece, assay not me, like one
Young and immartial, with great words, as to an Amazon dame;
I have the habit of all fights, and know the bloody frame
Of ev'ry slaughter; I well know the ready right hand charge,
I know the left, and ev'ry sway of my secureful targe;
I triumph in the cruelty of fixéd combat fight,
And manage horse to all designs; I think then with good right
I may be confident as far as this my challenge goes,
Without being taxéd' with a vaunt, borne out with empty shows.
But, being a soldier so renown'd, I will not work on thee

With least advantage of that skill I know doth strengthen me,
And so, with privity of sleight, win that for which I strive,
But at thy best, ev'n open strength, if my endeavours thrive."
Thus sent he his long jav'lin forth. It strook his foe's huge shield
Near to the upper skirt of brass, which was the eighth it held.
Six folds th' untamed dart strook through, and in the sev'nth tough hide
The point was check'd. Then Ajax threw; his angry lance did glide
Quite through his bright orbicular targe, his curace, shirt of mail,
And did his manly stomach's mouth with dang'rous taint assail;
But, in the bowing of himself, black death too short did strike.
Then both, to pluck their jav'lins forth, encounter'd, lion-like,
Whose bloody violence is, increas'd by that raw food they eat,
Or boars whose strength wild nourishment doth make so wondrous great.
Again Priamides did wound in midst his shield of brass,
Yet pierc'd not through the upper plate, the head reflected was.
But Ajax, following his lance, smote through his target quite,
And stay'd bold Hector rushing in; the lance held way outright,
And hurt his neck; out gush'd the blood. Yet Hector ceas'd not so,
But in his strong hand took a flint, as he did backwards go,
Black, sharp, and big, laid in the field; the sev'nfold targe it smit
Full on the boss, and round about the brass did ring with it.
But Ajax a far greater stone lift-up, and (wreathing round,
With all his body laid to it) he sent it forth to wound,
And gave unmeasur'd force to it; the round stone broke within
His rundled target; his lov'd knees to languish did begin;
And he lean'd, stretch'd out on his shield; but Phœbus rais'd him straight.
Then had they laid on wounds with swords, in use of closer fight,
Unless the heralds (messengers of Gods and godlike men)
The one of Troy, the other Greece, had held betwixt them then
Imperial sceptres; when the one, Idæus, grave and wise,
Said to them: "Now no more, my sons; the Sov'reign of the skies
Doth love you both; both soldiers are, all witness with good right;
But now night lays her mace on earth; 'tis good t' obey the night."
"Idæus," Telamon replied, "to Hector speak, not me;
He that call'd all our Achive peers to station-fight, 'twas he;
If he first cease, I gladly yield." Great Hector then began:
"Ajax, since Jove, to thy big form, made thee so strong a man,
And gave thee skill to use thy strength, so much, that for thy spear
Thou art most excellent of Greece, now let us fight forbear.
Hereafter we shall war again, till Jove our herald be,
And grace with conquest which he will. Heav'n yields to night, and we.
Go thou and comfort all thy fleet, all friends and men of thine,
As I in Troy my favourers, who in the fane divine
Have offer'd orisons for me; and come, let us impart
Some ensigns of our strife, to show each other's suppled heart,
That men of Troy and Greece may say, Thus their high quarrel ends.
Those that, encount'ring, were such foes, are now, being sep'rate, friends,"
He gave a sword, whose handle was with silver studs through driv'n, [5]

Scabbard and all, with hangers rich. By Telamon was giv'n
A fair well-glosséd purple waist. Thus Hector went to Troy,
And after him a multitude, fill'd with his safety's joy,
Despairing he could ever 'scape the puissant fortitude
And unimpeachéd Ajax' hands. The Greeks like joy renew'd
For their reputed victory, and brought him to the king;
Who to the great Saturnides preferr'd an offering,
An ox that fed on five fair springs; they flay'd and quarter'd him, [6]
And then, in pieces cut, on spits they roasted ev'ry limb;
Which neatly dress'd, they drew it off. Work done, they fell to feast;
All had enough; but Telamon, the king fed past the rest
With good large pieces of the chine. Thus thirst and hunger stay'd,
Nestor, whose counsels late were best, vows new, and first he said:
"Atrides, and my other lords, a sort of Greeks are dead,
Whose black blood, near Scamander's stream, inhuman Mars hath shed;
Their souls to hell descended are. It fits thee then, our king,
To make our soldiers cease from war; and, by the day's first spring,
Let us ourselves, assembled all, the bodies bear to fire,
With mules and oxen near our fleet, that, when we home retire,
Each man may carry to the sons, of fathers slaughter'd here,
Their honour'd bones. One tomb for all, for ever, let us rear,
Circling the pile without the field; at which we will erect
Walls, and a rav'lin, that may safe our fleet and us protect.
And in them let us fashion gates, solid, and barr'd about,
Through which our horse, and chariots, may well get in and out.
Without all, let us dig a dike, so deep it may avail
Our forces 'gainst the charge of horse, and foot, that come t' assail.
And thus th' attempts, that I see swell, in Troy's proud heart, shall fail."
The kings do his advice approve. So Troy doth court convent
At Priam's gate, in th' Ilion tow'r, fearful and turbulent.
Amongst all, wise Antenor spake: "Trojans, and Dardan friends,
And peers assistants, give good ear to what my care commends
To your consents, for all our good. Resolve, let us restore
The Argive Helen, with her wealth, to him she had before.
We now defend but broken faiths. If, therefore, ye refuse,
No good event can I expect of all the wars, we use."
He ceas'd; and Alexander spake; husband to the Argive queen:
"Antenor, to mine ears thy words harsh and ungracious been.
Thou canst use better if thou wilt: but, if these truly fit
Thy serious thoughts, the Gods with age have reft thy graver wit,
To warlike Trojans I will speak: I clearly do deny
To yield my wife, but all her wealth I render willingly,
Whatever I from Argos brought, and vow to make it more,
Which I have ready in my house, if peace I may restore."
Priam, surnam'd Dardanides, godlike; in counsels grave;
In his son's favour well-advis'd, this resolution gave:
"My royal friends of ev'ry state, there is sufficient done,
For this late council we have call'd, in th' offer of my son.

Now then let all take needful food, then let the watch be set,
And ev'ry court of guard held strong; so, when the morn doth wet
The high-rais'd battlements of Troy, Idæus shall be sent
To th' Argive fleet, and Atreus' sons, t' unfold my son's intent,
From whose fact our contention springs; and, if they will, obtain
Respite from heat of fight, till fire consume our soldiers slain;
And after, our most fatal war let us importune still,
Till Jove the conquest have dispos'd to his unconquer'd will."
All heard, and did obey the king; and, in their quarters, all,
That were to set the watch that night, did to their suppers fall.
Idæus in the morning went, and th' Achive peers did find
In council at Atrides' ship; his audience was assign'd;
And, in the midst of all the kings, the vocal herald said:
"Atrides! My renownéd king, and other kings, his aid,
Propose by me, in their commands, the offers Paris makes,
From whose joy all our woes proceed. He princely undertakes
That all the wealth he brought from Greece (would he had died before!)
He will, with other added wealth, for your amends restore
But famous Menelaus' wife he still means to enjoy,
Though he be urg'd the contrary, by all the peers of Troy.
And this besides I have in charge, that, if it please you all,
They wish both sides may cease from war, that rites of funeral
May on their bodies be perform'd, that ill, the fields lie slain;
And after, to the will of Fate, renew the fight again."
All silence held at first; at last Tydides made reply:
"Let no man take the wealth, or dame; for now a child's weak eye
May see the imminent black end of Priam's empery."
This sentence, quick and briefly giv'n, the Greeks did all admire.
Then said, the king: "Herald, thou hear'st the voice entire
Of all our peers, to answer thee, for that of Priam's son.
But, for our burning of the dead, by all means I am won
To satisfy thy king therein, without the slend'rest gain
Made of their spoiléd carcasses; but freely, being slain,
They shall be all consum'd with fire. To which I cite
High thund'ring Jove; that is the king of Juno's delight."
With this, he held his sceptre up, to all the sky-thron'd Pow'rs;
And grave Idæus did return to sacred Ilion's tow'rs,
Where Ilians, and Dardanians, did still their counsels ply,
Expecting his return. He came, and told his legacy.
All, whirlwind-like, assembled then, some bodies to transport,
Some to hew trees. On th' other part, the Argives did exhort
Their soldiers to the same affairs. Then, did the new fir'd sun
Smite the broad fields, ascending heav'n, and th' ocean smooth did run;
When Greece and Troy mix'd in such peace, you scarce could either know.
Then wash'd they off their blood and dust, and did warm tears bestow
Upon the slaughter'd, and in cars convey'd them from the field.
Priam commanded none should mourn, but in still silence yield
Their honour'd carcasses to fire, and only grieve in heart.

All burn'd; to Troy Troy's friends retire, to fleet the Grecian part.
Yet doubtful night obscur'd the earth, the day did not appear,
When round about the fun'ral pile, the Grecians gather'd were.
The pile they circled with a tomb, and by it rais'd a wall,
High tow'rs, to guard the fleet and them; and in the midst of all
They built strong gates, through which the horse and chariots passage had;
Without the rampire a broad dike, long and profound, they made,
On which they pallisadoes pitch'd; and thus the Grecians wrought.
Their huge works in so little time were to perfection brought,
That all Gods, by the Lightner set, the frame thereof admir'd;
'Mongst whom the Earthquake-making God, this of their king inquir'd:
"Father of Gods, will any man, of all earth's grassy sphere,
Ask any of the Gods' consents to any actions there,
If thou wilt see the shag-hair'd Greeks, with headstrong labours frame
So huge a work, and not to us due off'rings first enflame?
As far as white Aurora's dews are sprinkled through the air,
Fame will renown the hands of Greece, for this divine affair;
Men will forget the sacred work, the Sun and I did raise
For king Laomedon (bright Troy) and this will bear the praise."
Jove was extremely mov'd with him, and said: "What words are these,
Thou mighty Shaker of the earth, thou Lord of all the seas?
Some other God, of far less pow'r, might hold conceits, dismay'd
With this rare Grecian stratagem, and thou rest well apaid; [7]
For it will glorify thy name, as far as light extends;
Since, when these Greeks shall see again their native soil and friends,
The bulwark batter'd, thou mayst quite devour it with thy waves,
And cover, with thy fruitless sands, this fatal shore of graves;
That, what their fi'ry industries have so divinely wrought
In raising it, in razing it thy pow'r will prove it nought."
Thus spake the Gods among themselves. Set was the fervent sun;
And now the great work of the Greeks was absolutely done.
Then slew they oxen in their tents, and strength with food reviv'd,
When out of Lemnos a great fleet of od'rous wine arrived,
Sent by Eunëus, Jason's son, born of Hypsipyle.
The fleet contain'd a thousand tun, which must transported be
To Atreus' sons, as he gave charge, whose merchandise it was.
The Greeks bought wine for shining steel, and some for sounding brass,
Some for ox-hides, for oxen some, and some for prisoners.
A sumptuous banquet was prepar'd; and all that night the peers
And fair-hair'd Greeks consum'd in feast. So Trojans, and their aid.
And all the night Jove thunder'd loud; pale fear all thoughts dismay'd.
While they were gluttonous in earth, Jove wrought their banes in heav'n.
They pour'd full cups upon the ground, and were to off'rings driv'n
Instead of quaffings; and to drink, none durst attempt, before
In solemn sacrifice they did almighty Jove adore.
Then to their rests they all repair'd; bold zeal their fear bereav'd;
And sudden sleep's refreshing gift, securely they receiv'd.

[1] *These next four books have not my last hand; and because the rest (for a time) will be sufficient to employ your censures, suspend them of these. Spare not the other.*

[2] *O verè Phrygiæ, neque enim Phryges; saith his imitator.*

[3] *O si præteritos referat mihi Jupiter annos Qualis eram, etc.*

[4] *Hine illud: Dominus clypei septemplicis Ajax.*

[5] *Hector gives Ajax a sword; Ajax, Hector a girdle. Both which gifts were afterwards cause of both their deaths.*

[6] *Virgil imit.*

[7] *The fortification that in the twelfth book is razed.*

THE END OF THE SEVENTH BOOK.

THE ARGUMENT

When Jove to all the Gods had giv'n command,
That none to either host should helpful stand,
To Ida he descends; and sees from thence
Juno and Pallas haste the Greeks' defence;
Whose purpose, his command, by Iris given,
Doth intervent. Then came the silent even,
When Hector charg'd fires should consume the night,
Lest Greeks in darkness took suspected flight.

ANOTHER ARGUMENT

In Theta, Gods a Council have.
Troy's conquest. Glorious Hector's brave.
The cheerful Lady of the light, deck'd in her saffron robe,
Dispers'd her beams through ev'ry part of this enflow'red globe,
When thund'ring Jove a Court of Gods assembled by his will
In top of all the topful heights, that crown th' Olympian hill.
He spake, and all the Gods gave ear: "Hear how I stand inclin'd,
That God nor Goddess may attempt t' infringe my sov'reign mind,
But all give suffrage that with speed I may these discords end.
What God soever I shall find endeavour to defend
Or Troy or Greece, with wounds to heav'n he, sham'd, shall reascend;
Or, taking with him his offence, I'll cast him down as deep
As Tartarus, the brood of night, where Barathrum doth steep [1]

Torment, in his profoundest sinks, where is the floor of brass,
And gates of iron; the place, for depth, as far doth hell surpass,
As heav'n, for height, exceeds the earth; then shall he know from thence
How much my pow'r, past all the Gods, hath sov'reign eminence.
Endanger it the whiles and see. Let down our golden chain,
And at it let all Deities their utmost strengths constrain
To draw me to the earth from heav'n; you never shall prevail,
Though, with your most contention, ye dare my state assail,
But when my will shall be dispos'd, to draw you all to me,
Ev'n with the earth itself, and seas, ye shall enforced be;
Then will I to Olympus' top our virtuous engine bind,
And by it ev'rything shall hang, by my command inclin'd.
So much I am supreme to Gods, to men supreme as much."
The Gods sat silent, and admir'd, his dreadful speech was such.
At last his blue-ey'd daughter spake: "O great Saturnides!
O father, O heav'n's highest king, well know we the excess
Of thy great pow'r, compar'd with all; yet the bold Greeks' estate
We needs must mourn, since they must fall beneath so hard a fate;
For, if thy grave command enjoin, we will abstain from fight.
But to afford them such advice, as may relieve their plight,
We will, with thy consent, be bold; that all may not sustain
The fearful burthen of thy wrath, and with their shames be slain."
He smil'd, and said: "Be confident, thou art belov'd of me;
I speak not this with serious thoughts, but will be kind to thee."
This said, his brass-hoof'd wingéd horse he did to chariot bind,
Whose crests were fring'd with manes of gold; and golden garments shin'd
On his rich shoulders; in his hand he took a golden scourge,
Divinely fashion'd, and with blows their willing speed did urge
Mid way betwixt the earth and heav'n. To Ida: then he came,
Abounding in delicious springs, and nurse of beasts untame,
Where, on the mountain Gargarus, men did a fane erect
To his high name, and altars sweet; and there his horse he check'd,
Dissolv'd them from his chariot, and in a cloud of jet
He cover'd them, and on the top took his triumphant seat,
Beholding Priam's famous town, and all the fleet of Greece.
The Greeks took breakfast speedily, and arm'd at ev'ry piece.
So Trojans; who though fewer far, yet all to fight took arms,
Dire need enforc'd them to avert their wives' and children's harms.
All gates flew open; all the host did issue, foot and horse,
In mighty tumult; straight one place adjoin'd each adverse force.
Then shields with shields met, darts with darts, strength against strength oppos'd;
The boss-pik'd targets were thrust on, and thunder'd as they clos'd
In mighty tumult; groan for groan, and breath for breath did breathe,
Of men then slain, and to be slain; earth flow'd with fruits of death.
While the fair morning's beauty held, and day increas'd in height,
Their jav'lins mutually made death transport an equal freight,
But when the hot meridian point, bright Phœbus did ascend,
Then Jove his golden balances did equally extend,

And, of long-rest-conferring death, put in two bitter fates
For Troy and Greece; he held the midst; the day of final dates
Fell on the Greeks; the Greeks' hard lot sunk to the flow'ry ground,
The Trojans' leapt as high as heav'n. Then did the claps resound
Of his fierce thunder; lightning leapt amongst each Grecian troop;
The sight amaz'd them; pallid fear made boldest stomachs stoop,
Then Idomen durst not abide, Atrides went his way,
And both th' Ajaces; Nestor yet, against his will did stay,
That grave protector of the Greeks, for Paris with a dart
Enrag'd one of his chariot horse; he smote the upper part
Of all his skull, ev'n where the hair, that made his foretop, sprung.
The hurt was deadly, and the pain so sore the courser stung,
(Pierc'd to the brain) he stamp'd and plung'd. One on another bears,
Entangled round about the beam; then Nestor cut the gears
With his new-drawn authentic sword. Meanwhile the fi'ry horse
Of Hector brake into the press, with their bold ruler's force;
Then good old Nestor had been slain, had Diomed not espy'd,
Who to Ulysses, as he fled, importunately cried:
"Thou that in counsels dost abound, O Laertiades,
Why fly'st thou? Why thus, coward-like, shunn'st thou the honour'd prease?
Take heed thy back take not a dart. Stay, let us both intend
To drive this cruel enemy, from our dear agéd friend."
He spake, but wary Ithacus would find no patient ear,
But fled forthright, ev'n to the fleet. Yet, though he single were,
Brave Diomed mix'd amongst the fight, and stood before the steeds
Of old Neleides, whose estate thus kingly he areeds:
"O father, with these youths in fight, thou art unequal plac'd,
Thy willing sinews are unknit, grave age pursues thee fast,
And thy unruly horse are slow; my chariot therefore use,
And try how ready Trojan horse, can fly him that pursues,
Pursue the flier, and ev'ry way perform the varied fight;
I forc'd them from Anchises' son, well skill'd in cause of flight.
Then let my squire lead hence thy horse; mine thou shalt guard, whilst I,
By thee advanc'd, assay the fight, that Hector's self may try
If my lance dote with the defects, that fail best minds in age,
Or finds the palsy in my hands, that doth thy life engage."
This noble Nestor did accept, and Diomed's two friends,
Eurymedon that valour loves, and Sthenelus, ascends
Old Nestor's coach. Of Diomed's horse Nestor the charge sustains,
And Tydeus' son took place of fight. Neleides held the reins,
And scourg'd the horse, who swiftly ran direct in Hector's face;
Whom fierce Tydides bravely charg'd, but, he turn'd from the chace,
His jav'lin Eniopeus smit, mighty Thebæus' son,
And was great Hector's charioteer; it through his breast did run,
Near to his pap; he fell to earth, back flew his frighted horse,
His strength and soul were both dissolv'd. Hector had deep remorse
Of his mishap; yet left he him, and for another sought;
Nor long his steeds did want a guide, for straight good fortune brought

Bold Archeptolemus, whose life did from Iphitis spring;
He made him take the reins and mount. Then souls were set on wing;
Then high exploits were undergone; then Trojans in their walls
Had been infolded like meek lambs, had Jove wink'd at their falls,
Who hurl'd his horrid thunder forth, and made pale lightnings fly.
Into the earth, before the horse that Nestor did apply.
A dreadful flash burnt through the air, that savour'd sulphur-like,
Which down before the chariot the dazzled horse did strike.
The fair reins fell from Nestor's hand, who did in fear entreat
Renown'd Tydides into flight to turn his fury's heat:
"For know'st thou not," said he, "our aid is not supplied from Jove?
This day he will give fame to Troy, which when it fits his love
We shall enjoy. Let no man tempt his unresisted will,
Though he exceed in gifts of strength; for he exceeds him still."
"Father," replied the king, "'tis true; but both my heart and soul
Are most extremely griev'd to think how Hector will control
My valour with his vaunts in Troy, that I was terror-sick
With his approach; which when he boasts, let earth devour me quick."
"Ah! warlike Tydeus' son," said he, "what needless words are these?
Though Hector should report thee faint, and amorous of thy ease,
The Trojans, nor the Trojan wives, would never give him trust,
Whose youthful husbands thy free hand hath smother'd so in dust."
This said, he turn'd his one-hoof'd horse to flight, and troop did take,
When Hector and his men, with shouts, did greedy púrsuit make,
And pour'd on darts that made air sigh. Then Hector did exclaim:
"O Tydeus' son, the kings of Greece do most renown thy name
With highest place, feasts, and full cups; who now will do thee shame;
Thou shalt be like a woman us'd, and they will say: 'Depart,
Immartial minion, since to stand Hector thou hadst no heart.'
Nor canst thou scale our turrets' tops, nor lead the wives to fleet
Of valiant men; that wife-like fear'st my adverse charge to meet."
This two ways mov'd him,—still to fly, or turn his horse and fight.
Thrice thrust he forward to assault, and ev'ry time the fright
Of Jove's fell thunder drave him back, which he propos'd for sign
(To show the change of victory) Trojans should victors shine.
Then Hector comforted his men: "All my advent'rous friends,
Be men, and, of your famous strength, think of the honour'd ends.
I know benevolent Jupiter, did by his beck profess
Conquest and high renown to me, and to the Greeks distress.
O fools, to raise such silly forts, not worth the least account,
Nor able to resist our force! With ease our horse may mount,
Quite over all their hollow dike. But, when their fleet I reach,
Let Memory to all the world a famous bonfire teach,
For I will all their ships inflame, with whose infestive smoke,
Fear-shrunk, and hidden near their keels, the conquer'd Greeks shall choke."
Then cherish'd he his famous horse: "O Xanthus, now," said he,
"And thou Podargus, Æthon too, and Lampus, dear to me,
Make me some worthy recompense, for so much choice of meat,

Giv'n you by fair Andromache; bread of the purest wheat,
And with it, for your drink, mix'd wine, to make ye wishéd cheer,
Still serving you before myself, her husband young and dear.
Pursue, and use your swiftest speed, that we may take for prise
The shield of old Neleides, which fame lifts to the skies,
Ev'n to the handles telling it to be of massy gold.
And from the shoulders let us take, of Diomed the bold,
The royal curace Vulcan wrought, with art so exquisite,
These if we make our sacred spoil, I doubt not, but this night,
Ev'n to their navy to enforce the Greeks unturnéd flight."
This Juno took in high disdain, and made Olympus shake
As she but stirr'd within her throne, and thus to Neptune spake:
"O Neptune, what a spite is this! Thou God so huge in pow'r,
Afflicts it not thy honour'd heart, to see rude spoil devour
These Greeks that have in Helice, and Aege, offer'd thee
So many and such wealthy gifts? Let them the victors be.
If we, that are the aids of Greece, would beat home these of Troy,
And hinder broad-ey'd Jove's proud will, it would abate his joy."
He, angry, told her she was rash, and he would not be one
Of all the rest, should: strive with Jove, whose pow'r was match'd by none.
Whiles they conferr'd thus, all the space the trench contain'd before
(From that part of the fort that flank'd the navy-anchoring shore)
Was filled with horse and targeteers, who there for refuge came,
By Mars-swift Hector's pow'r engaged; Jove gave his strength the fame;
And he with spoilful fire had burn'd the fleet, if Juno's grace
Had not inspir'd the king himself, to run from place to place,
And stir up ev'ry soldier's pow'r, to some illustrious deed.
First visiting their leaders' tents, his ample purple weed
He wore, to show all who he was, and did his station take
At wise Ulysses' sable barks, that did the battle make
Of all the fleet; from whence his speech might with more ease be driv'n
To Ajax' and Achilles' ships, to whose chief charge were giv'n
The vantguard and the rearguard both, both for their force of hand,
And trusty bosoms. There arriv'd, thus urg'd he to withstand
Th' insulting Trojans: "O what shame, ye empty-hearted lords,
Is this to your admiréd forms! Where are your glorious words,
In Lemnos vaunting you the best of all the Grecian host?
'We are the strongest men,' ye said, 'we will command the most,
Eating most flesh of high-horn'd beeves, and drinking cups full crown'd,
And ev'ry man a hundred foes, two hundred, will confound;
Now all our strength, dar'd to our worst; one Hector cannot tame,'
Who presently with horrid fire, will all our fleet inflame.
O Father Jove, hath ever yet thy most unsuffer'd hand
Afflicted, with such spoil of souls, the king of any land,
And taken so much fame from him? when I did never fail,
(Since under most unhappy stars; this fleet was under sail)
Thy glorious altars, I protest, but, above all the Gods,
Have burnt fat thighs of beeves to thee, and pray'd to raze th' abodes

Of rape-defending Ilions. Yet grant, almighty Jove,
One favour;—that we may at least with life from hence remove,
Not under such inglorious hands, the hands of death employ;
And, where Troy should be stoop'd by Greece, let Greece fall under Troy."
To this ev'n weeping king did Jove remorseful audience give,
And shook great heav'n to him, for sign his men and he should live.
Then quickly cast he off his hawk, the eagle prince of air,
That perfects his unspotted vows; who seiz'd in her repair
A sucking hind calf, which she truss'd in her enforcive seres,
And by Jove's altar let it fall, amongst th' amazéd peers,
Where the religious Achive kings, with sacrifice did please
The author of all oracles, divine Saturnides.
Now, when they knew the bird of Jove, they turn'd courageous head.
When none, though many kings put on; could make his vaunt, he led
Tydides to renew'd assault, or issu'd first the dike,
Or first did fight; but, far the first, stone dead his lance did strike
Arm'd Agelaus, by descent surnam'd Phradmonides;
He turn'd his ready horse to flight, and Diomed's lance did seize
His back betwixt his shoulder-blades, and look'd out at his breast;
He fell, and his arms rang his fall. Th' Atrides next address'd
Themselves to fight; th' Ajaces next, with vehement strength endued;
Idomenëus and his friend, stout Merion, next pursued;
And after these Eurypylus, Evemon's honour'd race;
The ninth, with backward-wreathéd bow, had little Teucer place,
He still fought under Ajax' shield, who sometimes held it by,
And then he look'd his object out, and let his arrow fly,
And, whomsoever in the press he wounded; him he slew,
Then under Ajax' sev'n-fold shield, he presently withdrew.
He far'd like an unhappy child, that doth to mother run
For succour, when he knows full well, he some shrewd turn hath done.
What Trojans then were to their deaths, by Teucer's shafts impress'd?
Hapless Orsilochus was first, Ormenus, Ophelest,
Dæter, and hardy Chromius, and Lycophon divine,
And Amopaon that did spring from Polyæmon's line,
And Menalippus; all, on heaps, he tumbled to the ground.
The king rejoic'd to see his shafts the Phrygian ranks confound,
Who straight came near, and spake to him: "O Teucer, lovely man,
Strike still so sure, and be a grace to ev'ry Grecian,
And to thy father Telamon, who took thee kindly home
(Although not by his wife his son) and gave thee foster room,
Ev'n from thy childhood; then to him, though far from hence remov'd,
Make good fame reach; and to thyself, I vow what shall be prov'd:
If he that dreadful Ægis bears, and Pallas, grant to me
Th' expugnance of well-builded Troy; I first will honour thee
Next to myself with some rich gift, and put it in thy hand:
A three-foot vessel, that, for grace, in sacred fanes doth stand;
Or two horse and a chariot; or else a lovely dame
That may ascend on bed with thee, and amplify thy name."

Teucer right nobly answer'd him: "Why, most illustrate king,
I being thus forward of myself, dost thou, adjoin a sting?
Without which, all the pow'r I have, I cease not to employ,
For, from the place where we repuls'd the Trojans towards Troy,
I all the purple field have strew'd, with, one or other slain.
Eight shafts I shot, with long steel heads, of which not one in vain,
All were in youthful bodies fix'd, well skill'd in war's constraint;
Yet this wild dog; with all my aim, I have no pow'r to taint."
This said, another arrow forth, from his stiff string he sent,
At Hector, whom he long'd to wound; but still amiss it went.
His shaft smit fair Gorgythion, of Priam's princely race,
Who in Æpina was brought forth, a famous town in Thrace,
By Castianira, that, for form, was like celestial breed;
And, as a crimson poppy flow'r, surchargéd with his seed,
And vernal humours falling thick, declines his heavy brow,
So, of one side, his helmet's weight his fainting head did bow.
Yet Teucer would, another shaft at Hector's life dispose,
So fain he such a mark would hit, but still beside it goes;
Apollo did avert the shaft; but Hector's charioteer,
Bold Archeptolemus, he smit, as he was rushing near
To make the fight; to earth he fell, his swift horse back did fly,
And there were both his strength and soul exil'd eternally.
Huge grief, for Hector's slaughter'd friend, pinch'd-in his mighty mind,
Yet was he forc'd to leave him there, and his void place resign'd
To his sad brother, that was by, Cebriones; whose ear
Receiving Hector's charge, he straight the weighty reins did bear;
And Hector from his shining coach, with horrid voice, leap'd on,
To wreak his friend on Teucer's hand; and up he took a stone,
With which he at the archer ran; who from his quiver drew
A sharp-pil'd shaft, and nock'd it sure; but in great Hector flew
With such fell speed, that; in his draught, he his right shoulder strook
Where,'twixt his neck and breast, the joint his native closure took.
The wound was wondrous full of death, his, string in sunder flees,
His numméd hand fell strengthless down, and he upon his knees.
Ajax neglected not to aid his brother thus depress'd,
But came and saft him with his shield; and two more friends, address'd
To be his aid, took him to fleet, Mecisteus, Echius' son,
And gay Alastor. Teucer sigh'd, for all his service done.
Then did Olympius, with fresh strength, the Trojan pow'rs revive,
Who, to their trenches once again, the troubled Greeks did drive.
Hector brought terror with his strength, and ever fought before.
As when some highly stomach'd hound, that hunts a sylvan boar,
Or kingly lion, loves the haunch, and pincheth oft behind,
Bold of his feet, and still observes the game to turn inclin'd,
Not utterly dissolv'd in flight; so Hector did pursue,
And whosoever was the last, he ever did subdue,
They fled, but, when they had their dike, and palisadoes, pass'd,
(A number of them put to sword) at ships they stay'd at last.

Then mutual exhortations flew, then, all with hands and eyes
Advanc'd to, all the Gods, their plagues wrung from them open cries.
Hector, with his four rich-man'd horse, assaulting always rode,
The eyes of Gorgon burnt in him, and war's vermilion God.
The Goddess that all Goddesses, for snowy arms, out-shin'd,
Thus spake to Pallas, to the Greeks with gracious ruth inclin'd:
"O Pallas, what a grief is this! Is all our succour past
To these our perishing Grecian friends? At least withheld at last,
Ev'n now, when one man's violence must make them perish all,
In satisfaction of a fate so full of funeral?
Hector Priamides now raves, no more to be endur'd.
That hath already on the Greeks so many harms inur'd."
The azure Goddess answer'd her: "This man had surely found
His fortitude and life dissolv'd, ev'n on his father's ground,
By Grecian valour, if my sire, infested with ill moods,
Did not so dote on these of Troy, too jealous of their bloods,
And ever an unjust repulse stands to my willing pow'rs,
Little rememb'ring what I did, in all the desp'rate hours
Of his affected Hercules; I ever rescu'd him,
In labours of Eurystheüs, untouch'd in life or limb,
When he, heav'n knows, with drownéd eyes look'd up for help to heav'n,
Which ever, at command of Jove, was by my suppliance giv'n,
But had my wisdom reach'd so far, to, know of this event,
When to the solid-ported depths of hell his son was sent,
To hale out hateful Pluto's dog from darksome Erebus,
He had not 'scap'd the streams of Styx, so deep and dangerous.
Yet Jove hates me, and shows his love in doing Thetis' will,
That kiss'd his knees, and strok'd his chin, pray'd, and importun'd till,
That he would honour with his aid her city-razing son,
Displeas'd Achilles; and for him our friends are thus undone.
But time shall come again, when he, to do his friends some aid,
Will call me his Glaucopides, his sweet and blue-eyed Maid.
Then harness thou thy horse for me, that his bright palace gates
I soon may enter, arming me, to order these debates;
And I will try if Priam's son will still maintain his cheer,
When in the crimson paths of war, I dreadfully appear;
For some proud Trojans shall be sure to nourish dogs and fowls,
And pave the shore with fat and flesh, depriv'd of lives and souls."
Juno prepar'd her horse, whose manes ribands of gold enlac'd.
Pallas her party-colour'd robe on her bright shoulders cast,
Divinely wrought with her own hands, in th' entry of her sire.
Then put she on her ample breast her under-arming tire,
And on it her celestial arms. The chariot straight she takes,
With her huge heavy violent lance, with which she slaughter makes
Of armies fatal to her wrath. Saturnia whipp'd horse,
And heav'n-gates, guarded by the Hours, op'd by their proper force.
Through which they flew. Whom when Jove saw (set near the Idalian springs)
Highly, displeas'd, he Iris call'd, that hath the golden wings,

And said: "Fly, Iris, turn them back, let them not come at me,
Our meetings, sev'rally dispos'd, will nothing gracious be.
Beneath their o'erthrown chariot I'll shiver their proud steeds,
Hurl down themselves, their waggon break, and, for their stubborn deeds,
In ten whole years they shall not heal the wounds I will impress
With horrid thunder; that my maid may know when to address
Arms 'gainst her father. For my wife, she doth not so offend.
'Tis but her use to interrupt whatever I intend."
Iris, with this, left Ida's hills, and up t' Olympus flew,
Met near heav'n-gates the Goddesses, and thus their haste withdrew:
"What course intend you? Why are you wrapp'd with your fancies' storm?
Jove likes not ye should aid the Greeks, but threats, and will perform,
To crush in pieces your swift horse beneath their glorious yokes,
Hurl down yourselves, your chariot break, and, those impoison'd strokes
His wounding thunder shall imprint in your celestial parts,
In ten full springs ye shall not cure; that She that tames proud hearts
(Thyself, Minerva) may be taught to know for what, and when,
Thou dost against thy father fight; for sometimes childeren
May with discretion plant themselves against their fathers' wills,
But not, where humours only rule, in works beyond their skills.
For Juno; she offends him not, nor vexeth him so much,
For 'tis her use to cross his will, her impudence is such,
The habit of offence in this she only doth contract,
And so grieves or incenseth less, though ne'er the less her fact.
But thou most griev'st him, doggéd dame, whom he rebukes in time,
Lest silence should pervert thy will, and pride too highly climb
In thy bold bosom, desp'rate girl, if seriously thou dare
Lift thy unwieldy lance 'gainst Jove, as thy pretences are."
She left them, and Saturnia said: "Ah me! Thou seed of Jove,
By my advice we will no more unfit convention move
With Jupiter, for mortal men; of whom, let this man die,
And that man live, whoever he pursues with destiny;
And let him, plotting all events, dispose of either host,
As he thinks fittest for them both, and may become us most."
Thus turn'd she back, and to the Hours her rich-man'd horse resign'd,
Who them t' immortal mangers bound; the chariot they inclin'd
Beneath the crystal walls of heav'n; and they in golden thrones
Consorted other Deities, replete with passións,
Jove, in his bright-wheel'd chariot, his fi'ry horse now, beats
Up to Olympus, and aspir'd the Gods' eternal seats.
Great Neptune loos'd his horse, his car upon the altar plac'd,
And heav'nly-linen coverings did round about it cast.
The Far-seer us'd his throne of gold. The vast Olympus shook
Beneath his feet. His wife, and maid, apart places took,
Nor any word afforded him. He knew their thoughts, and said:
"Why do you thus torment yourselves? You need not sit dismay'd
With the long labours you have us'd in your victorious fight,
Destroying Trojans, 'gainst whose lives you heap such high despite.

Ye should have held your glorious course; for, be assur'd, as far
As all my pow'rs, by all means urg'd, could have sustain'd the war,
Not all the host of Deities should have retir'd my hand
From vow'd inflictions on the Greeks, much less you two withstand.
But you, before you saw the fight, much less the slaughter there,
Had all your goodly lineaments possess'd with shaking fear,
And never had your chariot borne their charge to heav'n again,
But thunder should have smit you both, had you one Trojan slain."
Both Goddesses let fall their chins upon their ivory breasts,
Set next to Jove, contriving still afflicted Troy's unrests.
Pallas for anger could not speak; Saturnia, contrary,
Could not for anger hold her peace, but made this bold reply:
"Not-to-be-suff'red Jupiter, what need'st thou still enforce
Thy matchless pow'r? We know it well; but we must yield remorse
To them that yield us sacrifice. Nor need'st thou thus deride
Our kind obedience, nor our griefs, but bear our pow'rs applied
To just protection of the Greeks, that anger tomb not all
In Troy's foul gulf of perjury, and let them stand should fall."
"Grieve not," said Jove, "at all done yet; for, if thy fair eyes please
This next red morning they shall see the great Saturnides
Bring more destruction to the Greeks; and Hector shall not cease,
Till he have rouséd from the fleet swift-foot Æacides,
In that day, when before their ships, for his Patroclus slain,
The Greeks in great distress shall fight; for so the Fates ordain.
I weigh not thy displeaséd spleen, though to th' extremest bounds
Of earth and seas it carry thee, where endless night confounds
Japet, and my dejected Sire, who sit so far beneath,
They never see the flying sun, nor hear the winds that breath,
Near to profoundest Tartarus. Nor, thither if thou went,
Would I take pity of thy moods, since none more impudent."
To this she nothing did reply. And now Sol's glorious light
Fell to the sea, and to the land drew up the drowsy night.
The Trojans griev'd at Phœbus' fall, which all the Greeks desir'd,
And sable night, so often wish'd, to earth's firm throne aspir'd.
Hector (intending to consult) near to the gulfy flood,
Far from the fleet, led to a place, pure and exempt from blood,
The Trojans' forces. From their horse all lighted, and did hear
Th' oration Jove-lov'd Hector made; who held a goodly spear,
Elev'n full cubits long, the head was brass, and did reflect
A wanton light before him still, it round about was deck'd
With strong hoops of new-burnish'd gold. On this he lean'd, and said:
"Hear me, my worthy friends of Troy, and you our honour'd aid.
A little since, I had conceit we should have made retreat,
By light of the inflaméd fleet, with all the Greeks' escheat,
But darkness hath prevented us; and saft, with special grace,
These Achives and their shore-hal'd fleet. Let us then render place
To sacred Night, our suppers dress, and from our chariot free
Our fair-man'd horse, and meat them well. Then let there convoy'd be,

From forth the city presently, oxen and well-fed sheep,
Sweet wine, and bread; and fell much wood, that all night we may keep
Plenty of fires, ev'n till the light bring forth the lovely morn,
And let their brightness glaze the skies, that night may not suborn
The Greeks' escape, if they for flight the sea's broad back would take;
At least they may not part with ease, but, as retreat they make,
Each man may bear a wound with him, to cure when he comes home,
Made with a shaft or sharp'ned spear; and others fear to come,
With charge of lamentable war, 'gainst soldiers bred in Troy.
Then let our heralds through the town their offices employ
To warn the youth, yet short of war, and time-white fathers, past,
That in our god-built tow'rs they see strong courts of guard be plac'd,
About the walls; and let out dames, yet flourishing in years,
That, having beauties to keep pure, are most inclin'd to fears
(Since darkness in distressful times more dreadful is than light)
Make lofty fires in ev'ry house; and thus, the dang'rous night,
Held with strong watch, if th' enemy have ambuscadoes laid
Near to our walls (and therefore seem in flight the more dismay'd,
Intending a surprise, while we are all without the town)
They ev'ry way shall be impugn'd, to, ev'ry man's renown.
Perform all this, brave Trojan friends. What now I have to say
Is all express'd; the cheerful morn shall other things display.
It is my glory (putting trust in Jove, and other Gods)
That I shall now expulse these dogs Fates sent to our abodes,
Who bring ostents of destiny, and black their threat'ning fleet.
But this night let us hold strong guards; to-morrow we will meet
(With fierce-made war) before their ships, and I'll make known to all
If strong Tydides from their ships can drive me to their wall,
Or I can pierce him with my sword, and force his bloody spoil.
The wishéd morn shall show his pow'r, if he can shun his foil
I running on him with my lance. I think; when day ascends,
He shall lie wounded with the first, and by him many friends.
O that I were as sure to live immortal, and sustain
No frailties with increasing years, but evermore remain
Ador'd like Pallas, or the Sun, as all doubts die in me
That heav'n's next light shall be the last the Greeks shall ever see!"
This speech all Trojans did applaud; who from their traces los'd
Their sweating horse, which sev'rally with headstalls they repos'd,
And fast'ned by their chariots; when others brought from town
Fat sheep and oxen, instantly, bread, wine; and hewéd down
Huge store of wood. The winds transferr'd into the friendly sky
Their supper's savour; to the which they sat delightfully,
And spent all night in open field; fires round about them shin'd.
As when about the silver moon, when air is free from wind,
And stars shine clear, to whose sweet beams, high prospects, and the brows
Of all steep hills and pinnacles, thrust up themselves for shows,
And ev'n the lowly valleys joy to glitter in their sight,
When the unmeasur'd firmament bursts to disclose her light,

And all the signs in heav'n are seen, that glad the shepherd's heart;
So many fires disclos'd their beams, made by the Trojan part,
Before the face of Ilion, and her bright turrets show'd.
A thousand courts of guard kept fires, and ev'ry guard allow'd
Fifty stout men, by whom their horse ate oats and hard white corn,
And all did wishfully expect the silver-thronéd morn.

[1] Virgil maketh this likewise his place, adding, Bis patet in præceps tantum, tenditque sub umbras, etc.

THE END OF THE EIGHTH BOOK.

THE NINTH BOOK OF HOMER'S ILIADS

THE ARGUMENT

To Agamemnon, urging hopeless flight,
Stand Diomed, and Nestor, opposite.
By Nestor's counsel, legates are dismiss'd
To Thetis' son; who still denies t' assist.

ANOTHER ARGUMENT

Iota sings the Ambassy,
And great Achilles' stern reply.
So held the Trojans sleepless guard; the Greeks to flight were giv'n,
The feeble consort of cold fear, strangely infus'd from heav'n;
Grief, not to be endur'd, did wound all Greeks of greatest worth.
And as two lateral-sited winds, the west wind and the north,
Meet at the Thracian sea's black breast, join in a sudden blore,
Tumble together the dark waves, and pour upon the shore
A mighty deal of froth and weed, with which men manure ground;
So Jove, and Troy did drive the Greeks, and all their minds confound.
But Agamemnon most of all was tortur'd at his heart,
Who to the voiceful heralds went, and bade them cite, apart,
Each Grecian leader sev'rally, not openly proclaim.
In which he labour'd with the first; and all together came.
They sadly sate. The king arose, and pour'd out tears as fast
As from a lofty rock a spring doth his black waters cast,
And, deeply sighing, thus bespake the Achives: "O my friends,
Princes, and leaders of the Greeks, heav'n's adverse King extends
His wrath, with too much detriment, to my so just design,
Since he hath often promis'd me, and bound it with the sign
Of his bent forehead, that this Troy our vengeful hands should race,
And safe return; yet, now engag'd, he plagues us with disgrace,
When all our trust to him hath drawn so much blood from our friends.

My glory, nor my brother's wreak, were the proposéd ends,
For which he drew you to these toils, but your whole countries' shame,
Which had been huge to bear the rape of so divine a dame,
Made in despite of our revenge. And yet not that had mov'd
Our pow'rs to these designs, if Jove had not our drifts approv'd;
Which since we see he did for blood, 'tis desp'rate fight in us
To strive with him; then let us fly; 'tis flight he urgeth thus."
Long time still silence held them all; at last did Diomed rise:
"Atrides, I am first must cross thy indiscreet advice, [1]
As may become me, being a king, in this our martial court.
Be not displeas'd then; for thyself didst broadly misreport
In open field my fortitude, and call'd me faint and weak,
Yet I was silent, knowing the time, loth any rites to break
That appertain'd thy public rule, yet all the Greeks knew well,
Of ev'ry age, thou didst me wrong. As thou then didst refell
My valour first of all the host, as of a man dismay'd;
So now, with fit occasion giv'n, I first blame thee afraid.
Inconstant Saturn's son hath giv'n inconstant spirits to thee,
And, with a sceptre over all, an eminent degree;
But with a sceptre's sov'reign grace, the chief pow'r, fortitude,
(To bridle thee) he thought not best thy breast should be endu'd.
Unhappy king, think'st thou the Greeks are such a silly sort,
And so excessive impotent, as thy weak words import?
If thy mind move thee to be gone, the way is open, go;
Mycenian ships enow ride near, that brought thee to this woe;
The rest of Greece will stay, nor stir till Troy be overcome
With full eversion; or if not, but (doters of their home)
Will put on wings to fly with thee. Myself and Sthenelus
Will fight till (trusting favouring Jove) we bring home Troy with us."
This all applauded, and admir'd the spirit of Diomed;
When Nestor, rising from the rest, his speech thus seconded:
"Tydides, thou art, questionless, our strongest Greek in war,
And gravest in thy counsels too, of all that equal are
In place with thee, and stand on strength; nor is there any one
Can blame, or contradict thy speech; and yet thou hast not gone
So far, but we must further go. Thou'rt young, and well mightst be
My youngest son, though still I yield thy words had high degree
Of wisdom in them to our king, since well they did become
Their right in question, and refute inglorious going home.
But I (well known thy senior far) will speak, and handle all
Yet to propose, which none shall check; no, not our general.
A hater of society, unjust, and wild, is he
That loves intestine war, being stuff'd with manless cruelty.
And therefore in persuading peace, and home-flight, we the less
May blame our gen'ral, as one loth to wrap in more distress
His lovéd soldiers. But because they bravely are resolv'd
To cast lives after toils, before they part in shame involv'd,
Provide we for our honour'd stay; obey black night, and fall

Now to our suppers; then appoint our guards without the wall,
And in the bottom of the dike; which guard I wish may stand
Of our brave youth. And, Atreus' son, since thou art in command
Before our other kings, be first in thy command's effect.
It well becomes thee; since 'tis both what all thy peers expect,
And in the royal right of things is no impair to thee.
Nor shall it stand with less than right, that they invited be
To supper by thee; all thy tents are amply stor'd with wine,
Brought daily in Greek ships from Thrace; and to this grace of thine
All necessaries thou hast fit, and store of men to wait;
And, many meeting there, thou may'st hear ev'ry man's conceit,
And take the best. It much concerns all Greeks to use advice
Of gravest nature, since so near our ships our enemies
Have lighted such a sort of fires, with which what man is joy'd?
Look, how all bear themselves this night; so live, or be destroy'd."
All heard, and follow'd his advice. There was appointed then
Sev'n captains of the watch, who forth did march with all their men.
The first was famous Thrasymed, adviceful Nestor's son;
Ascalaphus; and Ialmen; and mighty Merion;
Alphareus; and Deipyrus; and lovely Lycomed,
Old Creon's joy. These sev'n bold lords an hundred soldiers led,
In ev'ry sever'd company, and ev'ry man his pike,
Some placéd on the rampire's top, and some amidst the dike.
All fires made, and their suppers took. Atrides to his tent
Invited all the peers of Greece, and food sufficient
Appos'd before them, and the peers appos'd their hands to it.
Hunger and thirst being quickly quench'd, to counsel still they sit.
And first spake Nestor, who they thought of late advis'd so well,
A father grave, and rightly wise, who thus his tale did tell:
"Most high Atrides, since in thee I have intent to end,
From thee will I begin my speech, to whom Jove doth commend
The empire of so many men, and puts into thy hand
A sceptre, and establish'd laws, that thou mayst well command,
And counsel all men under thee. It therefore doth behove
Thyself to speak most, since of all thy speeches most will move;
And yet to hear, as well as speak; and then perform as well
A free just counsel; in thee still must stick what others tell.
For me, what in my judgment stands the most convenient
I will advise, and am assur'd advice more competent
Shall not be giv'n; the gen'ral proof, that hath before been made
Of what I speak, confirms me still, and now may well persuade,
Because I could not then, yet ought, when thou, most royal king,
Ev'n from the tent, Achilles' love didst violently bring,
Against my counsel, urging thee by all means to relent;
But you, obeying your high mind, would venture the event,
Dishonouring our ablest Greek, a man th' Immortals grace.
Again yet let's deliberate, to make him now embrace
Affection to our gen'ral good, and bring his force to field;

Both which kind words and pleasing gifts must make his virtues yield."
"O father," answeréd the king, "my wrongs thou tell'st me right.
Mine own offence mine own tongue grants. One man must stand in fight
For our whole army; him I wrong'd; him Jove loves from his heart,
He shows it in thus honouring him; who, living thus apart,
Proves us but number, for his want makes all our weakness seen.
Yet after my confess'd offence, soothing my hum'rous spleen,
I'll sweeten his affects again with presents infinite,
Which, to prove my firm intent, I'll openly recite:
Sev'n sacred tripods free from fire; ten talents of fine gold;
Twenty bright cauldrons; twelve young horse, well-shap'd, and well-controll'd,
And victors too, for they have won the prize at many a race,
That man should not be poor that had but what their wingéd pace
Hath added to my treasury, nor feel sweet gold's defect.
Sev'n Lesbian ladies he shall have, that were the most select,
And in their needles rarely skill'd, whom, when he took the town
Of famous Lesbos, I did choose; who won the chief renown
For beauty from their whole fair sex; amongst whom I'll resign
Fair Brisis, and I deeply swear (for any fact of mine
That may discourage her receipt) she is untouch'd, and rests
As he resign'd her. To these gifts (if Jove to our requests
Vouchsafe performance, and afford the work, for which we wait,
Of winning Troy) with brass and gold he shall his navy freight;
And, ent'ring when we be at spoil, that princely hand of his
Shall choose him twenty Trojan dames, excepting Tyndaris,
The fairest Pergamus enfolds; and, if we make retreat
To Argos, call'd of all the world the Navel, or chief seat,
He shall become my son-in-law, and I will honour him
Ev'n as Orestes, my sole son, that cloth in honours swim.
Three daughters in my well-built court unmarried are, and fair;
Laodice, Chrysothemis that hath the golden hair,
And Iphianassa; of all three the worthiest let him take
All-jointureless to Peleus' court; I will her jointure make,
And that so great as never yet did any maid prefer,
Sev'n cities right magnificent, I will bestow on her;
Enope, and Cardamyle, Mira for herbs renown'd,
The fair Æpea, Pedasus that doth with grapes abound,
Anthæa girded with green meads, Phera surnam'd Divine;
All whose bright turrets on the sea, in sandy Pylos, shine.
Th' inhabitants in flocks and herds are wondrous confluent,
Who like a God will honour him, and him with gifts present,
And to his throne will contribute what tribute he will rate.
All this I gladly will perform, to pacify his hate.
Let him be mild and tractable; 'tis for the God of ghosts
To be unrul'd, implacable, and seek the blood of hosts,
Whom therefore men do much abhor; then let him yield to me,
I am his greater, being a king, and more in years than he
"Brave king," said Nestor, "these rich gifts must make him needs relent,

Choose then fit legates instantly to greet him at his tent,
But stay; admit my choice of them, and let them straight be gone.
Jove-lovéd Phœnix shall be chief, then Ajax Telamon,
And prince Ulysses; and on them let these two heralds wait,
Grave Odius and Eurybates, Come, lords, take water straight,
Make pure your hand, and with sweet words appease Achilles' mind,
Which we will pray the king of Gods may gently make inclin'd."
All lik'd his speech; and on their hands the heralds water shed,
The youths crown'd cups of sacred wine to all distributed.
But having sacrific'd, and drunk to ev'ry man's content,
With many notes by Nestor giv'n, the legates forward went.
With courtship in fit gestures us'd he did prepare them well,
But most Ulysses, for his grace did not so much excel.
Such rites beseem ambassadors; and Nestor urgéd these,
That their most honours might reflect enrag'd Æacides.
They went along the shore, and pray'd the God, that earth doth bind
In brackish chains, they might not fail, but bow his mighty mind.
The quarter of the Myrmidons they reach'd, and found him set
Delighted with his solemn harp, which curiously was fret
With works conceited, through the verge; the bawdrick that embrac'd
His lofty neck was silver twist; this, when his hand laid waste
Aëtion's city, he did choose as his especial prise,
And, loving sacred music well, made it his exercise.
To it he sung the glorious deeds of great heroës dead,
And his true mind, that practice fail'd, sweet contemplation fed.
With him alone, and opposite, all silent sat his friend,
Attentive, and beholding him, who now his song did end.
Th' ambassadors did forwards press, renown'd Ulysses led,
And stood in view. Their sudden sight his admiration bred,
Who with his harp and all arose; so did Menœtius' son
When he beheld them. Their receipt Achilles thus begun:
"Health to my lords! Right welcome men, assure yourselves you be,
Though some necessity, I know, doth make you visit me,
Incens'd with just cause 'gainst the Greeks." This said, a sev'ral seat
With purple cushions he set forth, and did their ease intreat,
And said: "Now, friend, our greatest bowl, with wine unmix'd and neat,
Appose these lords, and of the depth let every man make proof,
These are my best esteeméd friends, and underneath my roof."
Patroclus did his dear friend's will; and he that did desire
To cheer the lords, come faint from fight, set on a blazing fire
A great brass pot, and into it a chine of mutton put,
And fat goat's flesh. Automedon held, while he pieces cut,
To roast and boil, right cunningly; then of a well-fed swine
A huge fat shoulder he cuts out, and spits it wondrous fine.
His good friend made a goodly fire; of which the force once past,
He laid the spit low, near the coals, to make it brown at last,
Then sprinkled it with sacred salt, and took it from the racks.
This roasted and on dresser set, his friend Patroclus takes

Bread in fair baskets; which set on, Achilles brought the meat,
And to divinest Ithacus took his opposéd seat
Upon the bench. Then did he will his friend to sacrifice,
Who cast sweet incense in the fire to all the Deities.
Thus fell they to their ready food. Hunger and thirst allay'd,
Ajax to Phœnix made a sign, as if too long they stay'd
Before they told their legacy. Ulysses saw him wink,
And, filling the great bowl with wine, did to Achilles drink:
"Health to Achilles! But our plights stand not in need of meat,
Who late supp'd at Atrides' tent, though for thy love we eat
Of many things, whereof a part would make a cómplete feast.
Nor can we joy in these kind rites, that have our hearts oppress'd,
O prince, with fear of utter spoil. 'Tis made a question now,
If we can save our fleet or not, unless thyself endow
Thy pow'rs with wonted fortitude. Now Troy and her consórts,
Bold of thy want, have pitch'd their tents close to our fleet and forts,
And made a firmament of fires; and now no more, they say,
Will they be prison'd in their walls, but force their violent way
Ev'n to our ships; and Jove himself hath with his lightnings show'd
Their bold adventures happy signs; and Hector grows so proud
Of his huge strength, borne out by Jove, that fearfully he raves,
Presuming neither men nor Gods can interrupt his braves.
Wild rage invades him, and he prays that soon the sacred Morn
Would light his fury; boasting then our streamers shall be torn,
And all our naval ornaments fall by his conqu'ring stroke,
Our ships shall burn, and we ourselves lie stifled in the smoke.
And I am seriously afraid, Heav'n will perform his threats,
And that 'tis fatal to us all, far from our native seats,
To perish in victorious Troy. But rise, though it be late,
Deliver the afflicted Greeks from Troy's tumultuous hate;
It will hereafter be thy grief, when no strength can suffice
To remedy th' effected threats of our calamities.
Consider these affairs in time, while thou mayst use thy pow'r.
And have the grace to turn from Greece fate's unrecover'd hour.
O friend, thou know'st thy royal sire forewarn'd what should be done,
That day he sent thee from his court to honour Atreus' son:
'My son,' said he, 'the victory let Jove and Pallas use
At their high pleasures, but do thou no honour'd means refuse
That may advance her. In fit bounds contain thy mighty mind,
Nor let the knowledge of thy strength be factiously inclin'd,
Contriving mischiefs. Be to fame and gen'ral good profess'd.
The more will all sorts honour thee. Benignity is best.'
Thus charg'd thy sire, which thou forgett'st. Yet now those thoughts appease,
That torture thy great spirit with wrath; which if thou wilt surcease,
The king will merit it with gifts; and, if thou wilt give ear,
I'll tell how much he offers thee yet thou sitt'st angry here:
Sev'n tripods that no fire must touch; twice-ten pans, fit for flame;
Ten talents of fine gold; twelve horse that ever overcame,

And brought huge prises from the field, with swiftness of their feet,
That man should bear no poor account, nor want gold's quick'ning sweet,
That had but what he won with them; sev'n worthiest Lesbian dames,
Renown'd for skill in housewif'ry, and bear the sov'reign fames
For beauty from their gen'ral sex, which, at thy overthrow
Of well-built Lesbos, he did choose; and these he will bestow,
And with these her he took from thee, whom, by his state, since then,
He swears he touch'd not, as fair dames use to be touch'd by men.
All these are ready for thee now. And, if at length we take,
By helps of Gods, this wealthy town, thy ships shall burthen make
Of gold and brass at thy desires, when we the spoil divide;
And twenty beauteous Trojan dames thou shalt select beside,
Next Helen, the most beautiful; and, when return'd we be
To Argos, be his son-in-law, for he will honour thee
Like his Orestes, his sole son, maintained in height of bliss.
Three daughters beautify his court, the fair Chrysothemis,
Laodice, and Iphianesse; of all the fairest take
To Peleus' thy grave father's court, and never jointure make;
He will the jointure make himself, so great, as never sire
Gave to his daughter's nuptials. Sev'n cities left entire;
Cardamyle, and Enope, and Hira full of flow'rs,
Anthæa for sweet meadows prais'd, and Phera deck'd with tow'rs,
The bright Epea, Pedasus that doth God Bacchus please;
All, on the sandy Pylos' soil, are seated near the seas;
Th' inhabitants in droves and flocks exceeding wealthy be,
Who, like a God, with worthy gifts will gladly honour thee,
And tribute of especial rate to thy high sceptre pay.
All this he freely will perform, thy anger to allay.
But if thy hate to him be more than his gifts may repress,
Yet pity all the other Greeks, in such extreme distress,
Who with religion honour thee; and to their desp'rate ill
Thou shalt triumphant glory bring; and Hector thou may'st kill,
When pride makes him encounter thee, fill'd with a baneful sprite,
Who vaunts our whole fleet brought not one, equal to him in fight."
Swift-foot Æacides replied: "Divine Laertes' son,
'Tis requisite I should be short, and show what place hath won
Thy serious speech, affirming nought but what you shall approve
Establish'd in my settled heart, that in the rest I move
No murmur nor exceptión; for, like hell mouth I loath,
Who holds not in his words and thoughts one indistinguish'd troth.
What fits the freeness of my mind, my speech shall make display'd.
Nor Atreus' son, nor all the Greeks, shall win me to their aid,
Their suit is wretchedly enforc'd, to free their own despairs,
And my life never shall be hir'd with thankless desp'rate pray'rs;
For never had I benefit, that ever foil'd the foe;
Ev'n share hath he that keeps his tent, and he to field doth go,
With equal honour cowards die, and men most valiant,
The much performer, and the man that can of nothing vaunt.

No overplus I ever found, when, with my mind's most strife
To do them good, to dang'rous fight I have expos'd my life.
But ev'n as to unfeather'd birds the careful dam brings meat,
Which when she hath bestow'd, herself hath nothing left to eat;
So, when my broken sleeps have drawn the nights t' extremest length,
And ended many bloody days with still-employéd strength,
To guard their weakness, and preserve their wives' contents infract,
I have been robb'd before their eyes: Twelve cities I have sack'd
Assail'd by sea, elev'n by land, while this siege held at Troy;
And of all these, what was most dear, and most might crown the joy
Of Agamemnon, he enjoy'd, who here behind remain'd:
Which when he took, a few he gave, and many things retain'd,
Other to optimates and kings he gave, who hold them fast,
Yet mine he forceth; only I sit with my loss disgrac'd.
But so he gain a lovely dame, to be his bed's delight,
It is enough; for what cause else do Greeks and Trojans fight?
Why brought he hither such an host? Was it not for a dame?
For fair-hair'd Helen? And doth love alone the hearts inflame
Of the Atrides to their wives, of all the men that move?
Ev'ry discreet and honest mind cares for his private love,
As much as they; as I myself lov'd Brisis as my life,
Although my captive, and had will to take her for my wife.
Whom since he forc'd, preventing me, in vain he shall prolong
Hopes to appease me that know well the deepness of my wrong.
But, good Ulysses, with thyself, and all you other kings,
Let him take stomach to repel Troy's fi'ry threatenings.
Much hath he done without my help, built him a goodly fort,
Cut a dike by it, pitch'd with pales, broad and of deep import;
And cannot all these helps repress this kill-man Hector's fright?
When I was arm'd among the Greeks, he would not offer fight
Without the shadow of his walls; but to the Scæan ports,
Or to the holy beach of Jove, come back'd with his consorts;
Where once he stood my charge alone, and hardly made retreat,
And to make new proof of our pow'rs, the doubt is not so great.
To-morrow then, with sacrifice perform'd t' imperial Jove
And all the Gods, I'll launch my fleet, and all my men remove;
Which (if thou wilt use so thy sight, or think'st it worth respect)
In forehead of the morn, thine eyes shall see, with sails erect
Amidst the fishy Hellespont, help'd with laborious oars.
And, if the Sea-god send free sail, the fruitful Phthian shores
Within three days we shall attain, where I have store of prise
Left, when with prejudice I came to these indignities.
There have I gold as well as here, and store of ruddy brass,
Dames slender, elegantly girt, and steel as bright as glass.
These will I take as I retire, as shares I firmly save,
Though Agamemnon be so base to take the gifts he gave.
Tell him all this, and openly, I on your honours charge,
That others may take shame to hear his lusts command so large,

And, if there yet remain a man he hopeth to deceive
(Being dyed in endless impudence) that man may learn to leave
His trust and empire. But alas, though, like a wolf he be,
Shameless and rude, he durst not take my prise, and look on me.
I never will partake his works, nor counsels, as before,
He once deceiv'd and injur'd me, and he shall never more
Tye my affections with his words. Enough is the increase
Of one success in his deceits; which let him joy in peace,
And bear it to a wretched end. Wise Jove hath reft his brain
To bring him plagues, and these his gifts I, as my foes, disdain.
Ev'n in the numbness of calm death I will revengeful be,
Though ten or twenty times so much he would bestow on me,
All he hath here, or any where, or Orchomen contains,
To which men bring their wealth for strength, or all the store remains
In circuit of Egyptian Thebes, where much hid treasure lies,
Whose walls contain an hundred ports, of so admir'd a size
Two hundred soldiers may a-front with horse and chariots pass.
Nor, would he amplify all this like sand, or dust, or grass,
Should he reclaim me, till this wreak pay'd me for all the pains
That with his contumely burn'd, like poison, in my veins.
Nor shall his daughter be my wife, although she might contend
With golden Venus for her form, or if she did transcend
Blue-ey'd Minerva for her works; let him a Greek select
Fit for her, and a greater king. For if the Gods protect
My safety to my father's court, he shall choose me a wife.
Many fair Achive princesses of unimpeachéd life
In Helle and in Phthia live, whose sires do cities hold,
Of whom I can have whom I will. And, more an hundred fold
My true mind in my country likes to take a lawful wife
Than in another nation; and there delight my life
With those goods that my father got, much rather than die here.
Not all the wealth of well-built Troy, possess'd when peace was there,
All that Apollo's marble fane in stony Pythos holds,
I value equal with the life that my free breast enfolds.
Sheep, oxen, tripods, crest-deck'd horse, though lost, may come again,
But when the white guard of our teeth no longer can contain
Our human soul, away it flies, and, once gone, never more
To her frail mansion any man can her lost pow'rs restore.
And therefore since my mother-queen, fam'd for her silver feet,
Told me two fates about my death in my direction meet:
The one, that, if I here remain t' assist our victory,
My safe return shall never live, my fame shall never die;
If my return obtain success, much of my fame decays,
But death shall linger his approach, and I live many days,
This being reveal'd, 'twere foolish pride, t' abridge my life for praise.
Then with myself, I will advise, others to hoise their sail,
For, 'gainst the height of Ilion, you never shall prevail,
Jove with his hand protecteth it, and makes the soldiers bold.

This tell the kings in ev'ry part, for so grave legates should,
That they may better counsels use, to save their fleet and friends
By their own valours; since this course, drown'd in my anger, ends.
Phœnix may in my tent repose, and in the morn steer course
For Phthia, if he think it good; if not, I'll use no force."
All wonder'd at his stern reply; and Phœnix, full of fears
His words would be more weak than just, supplied their wants with tears.
"If thy return incline thee thus, Peleus' renownéd joy,
And thou wilt let our ships be burn'd with harmful fire of Troy,
Since thou art angry, O my son, how shall I after be
Alone in these extremes of death, relinquishéd by thee?
I, whom thy royal father sent as ord'rer of thy force,
When to Atrides from his court he left thee for this course,
Yet young, and when in skill of arms thou didst not so abound,
Nor hadst the habit of discourse, that makes men so renown'd.
In all which I was set by him, t' instruct thee as my son,
That thou might'st speak, when speech was fit, and do, when deeds were done,
Not sit as dumb, for want of words, idle, for skill to move,
I would not then be left by thee, dear son, begot in love,
No, not if God would promise me, to raze the prints of time
Carv'd in my bosom and my brows, and grace me with the prime
Of manly youth, as when at first I left sweet Helle's shore
Deck'd with fair dames, and fled the grudge my angry father bore;
Who was the fair Amyntor call'd, surnam'd Ormenides,
And for a fair-hair'd harlot's sake, that his affects could please,
Contemn'd my mother, his true wife, who ceaseless urgéd me
To use his harlot Clytia, and still would clasp my knee
To do her will, that so my sire might turn his love to hate
Of that lewd dame, converting it to comfort her estate.
At last I was content to prove to do my mother good,
And reconcile my father's love; who straight suspicious stood,
Pursuing me with many a curse, and to the Furies pray'd
No dame might love, nor bring me seed. The Deities obey'd
That govern hell; infernal Jove, and stern Persephone.
Then durst I in no longer date with my stern father be.
Yet did my friends, and near allies, inclose me with desires
Not to depart; kill'd sheep, boars, beeves; roast them at solemn fires;
And from my father's tuns we drunk exceeding store of wine.
Nine nights they guarded me by turns, their fires did ceaseless shine,
One in the porch of his strong hall, and in the portal one,
Before my chamber; but when day beneath the tenth night shone,
I brake my chamber's thick-fram'd doors, and through the hall's guard pass'd,
Unseen of any man or maid. Through Greece then, rich and vast,
I fled to Phthia, nurse of sheep, and came to Peleus' court;
Who entertain'd me heartily, and in as gracious sort
As any sire his only son, born when his strength is spent,
And bless'd with great possessions to leave to his descent.
He made me rich, and to my charge did much command commend.

I dwelt in th' utmost region rich Phthia doth extend,
And govern'd the Dolopians, and made thee what thou art,
O thou that like the Gods art fram'd. Since, dearest to my heart,
I us'd thee so, thou lov'dst none else; nor anywhere wouldst eat,
Till I had crown'd my knee with thee, and carv'd thee tend'rest meat,
And giv'n thee wine so much, for love, that, in thy infancy
(Which still discretion must protect, and a continual eye)
My bosom lovingly sustain'd the wine thine could not bear.
Then, now my strength needs thine as much, be mine to thee as dear,
Much have I suffer'd for thy love, much labour'd, wishéd much,
Thinking, since I must have no heir (the Gods' decrees are such)
I would adopt thyself my heir. To thee my heart did give
What any sire could give his son. In thee I hop'd to live.
O mitigate thy mighty spirits. It fits not one that moves
The hearts of all, to live unmov'd, and succour hates for loves.
The Gods themselves are flexible; whose virtues, honours, pow'rs,
Are more than thine, yet they will bend their breasts as we bend ours.
Perfumes, benign devotions, savours of off'rings burn'd,
And holy rites, the engines are with which their hearts are turn'd,
By men that pray to them, whose faith their sins have falsified.
For Pray'rs are daughters of great Jove, lame, wrinkled, ruddy-ey'd,
And ever following injury, who, strong and sound of feet,
Flies through the world, afflicting men. Believing Prayers yet,
To all that love that Seed of Jove, the certain blessing get
To have Jove hear, and help them too; but if he shall refuse,
And stand inflexible to them, they fly to Jove, and use
Their pow'rs against him, that the wrongs he doth to them may fall
On his own head, and pay those pains whose cure he fails to call.
Then, great Achilles, honour thou this sacred Seed of Jove,
And yield to them, since other men of greatest minds they move.
If Agamemnon would not give the self-same gifts he vows,
But offer other afterwards, and in his still-bent brows
Entomb his honour and his word, I would not thus exhort,
With wrath appeas'd, thy aid to Greece, though plagu'd in heaviest sort;
But much he presently will give, and after yield the rest.
T' assure which he hath sent to thee the men thou lovest best,
And most renown'd of all the host, that they might soften thee.
Then let not both their pains and pray'rs lost and despiséd be,
Before which none could reprehend the tumult of thy heart,
But now to rest inexpiate were much too rude a part.
Of ancient worthies we have heard, when they were more displeas'd,
To their high fames, with gifts and pray'rs they have been still appeas'd.
For instance, I remember well a fact perform'd of old,
Which to you all, my friends, I'll tell: The Curets wars did hold
With the well-fought Ætolians, where mutual lives had end
About the city Calydon. Th' Ætolians did defend
Their flourishing country, which to spoil the Curets did contend.
Diana with-the-golden-throne, with Oeneus much incens'd,

Since with his plenteous land's first fruits she was not reverenc'd,
(Yet other Gods, with hecatombs, had feasts, and she alone,
Great Jove's bright daughter, left unserv'd, or by oblivion,
Or undue knowledge of her dues) much hurt in heart she swore;
And she, enrag'd, excited much, she sent a sylvan boar
From their green groves, with wounding tusks; who usually did spoil
King Oeneus' fields, his lofty woods laid prostrate on the soil,
Rent by the roots trees fresh, adorn'd with fragrant apple flow'rs.
Which Meleager (Oeneus' son) slew, with assembl'd pow'rs
Of hunters, and of fiercest hounds, from many cities brought;
For such he was that with few lives his death could not be bought,
Heaps of dead humans, by his rage, the fun'ral piles applied.
Yet, slain at last, the Goddess stirr'd about his head, and hide,
A wondrous tumult, and a war betwixt the Curets wrought
And brave Ætolians. All the while fierce Meleager fought,
Ill-far'd the Curets; near the walls none durst advance his crest,
Though they were many. But when wrath inflam'd his haughty breast
(Which oft the firm mind of the wise with passion doth infest)
Since 'twixt his mother-queen and him arose a deadly strife,
He left the court, and privately liv'd with his lawful wife,
Fair Cleopatra, female birth of bright Marpessa's pain,
And of Ideus; who of all terrestrial men did reign,
At that time, king of fortitude, and for Marpessa's sake,
'Gainst wanton Phœbus, king of flames; his bow in hand did take,
Since he had ravish'd her, his joy; whom her friends after gave
The surname of Alcyone, because they could not save
Their daughter from Alcyone's fate. In Cleopatra's arms
Lay Meleager, feeding on his anger, for the harms
His mother pray'd might fall on him; who, for her brother slain
By Meleager, griev'd, and pray'd the Gods to wreak her pain
With all the horror could be pour'd upon her furious birth.
Still knock'd she with her impious hands the many-feeding earth,
To urge stern Pluto and his Queen t' incline their vengeful ears,
Fell on her knees, and all her breast dew'd with her fi'ry tears,
To make them massacre her son, whose wrath enrag'd her thus.
Erinnys, wand'ring through the air, heard, out of Erebus,
Pray'rs fit for her unpleaséd mind. Yet Meleager lay
Obscur'd in fury. Then the bruit of the tumultuous fray
Rung through the turrets as they scal'd; then came th' Ætolian peers
To Meleager with low suits, to rise and free their fears;
Then sent they the chief priests of Gods, with offer'd gifts t' atone
His diff'ring fury, bade him choose, in sweet-soil'd Calydon,
Of the most fat and yieldy soil, what with an hundred steers
Might in a hundred days be plough'd, half that rich vintage bears,
And half of naked earth to plough; yet yielded not his ire.
Then to his lofty chamber-door, ascends his royal sire
With ruthful plaints, shook the strong bars; then came his sisters' cries;
His mother then; and all intreat;—yet still more stiff he lies;—

His friends, most rev'rend, most esteem'd; yet none impression took,
Till the high turrets where he lay, and his strong chamber, shook
With the invading enemy, who now forced dreadful way
Along the city. Then his wife, in pitifil dismay,
Besought him, weeping; telling him the miseries sustain'd
By all the citizens, whose town the enemy had gain'd;
Men slaughter'd; children bondslaves made; sweet ladies forc'd with lust;
Fires climbing tow'rs, and turning them to heaps of fruitless dust.
These dangers soften'd his steel heart. Up the stout prince arose,
Indu'd his body with rich arms, and freed th' Ætolian's woes,
His smother'd anger giving air; which gifts did not assuage,
But his own peril. And because he did not disengage
Their lives for gifts, their gifts he lost. But for my sake, dear friend,
Be not thou bent to see our plights to these extremes descend,
Ere thou assist us; be not so by thy ill angel turn'd
From thine own honour. It were shame to see our navy burn'd,
And then come with thy timeless aid. For offer'd presents, come,
And all the Greeks will honour thee, as of celestial room.
But if without these gifts thou fight, forc'd by thy private woe,
Thou wilt be nothing so renown'd, though thou repel the foe."
Achilles answer'd the last part of this oration thus:
"Phœnix, renown'd and reverend, the honours urg'd on us
We need not, Jove doth honour me, and to my safety sees,
And will, whiles I retain a spirit, or can command my knees.
Then do not thou with tears and woes impassion my affects,
Becoming gracious to my foe. Nor fits it the respects
Of thy vow'd love to honour him that hath dishonour'd me,
Lest such loose kindness lose his heart that yet is firm to thee.
It were thy praise to hurt with me the hurter of my state,
Since half my honour and my realm thou mayst participate.
Let these lords then return th' event, and do thou here repose,
And, when dark sleep breaks with the day, our counsels shall disclose
The course of our return or stay." This said, he with his eye
Made to his friend a covert sign, to hasten instantly
A good soft bed, that the old prince, soon as the peers were gone,
Might take his rest; when, soldier-like, brave Ajax Telamon
Spake to Ulysses, as with thought Achilles was not worth
The high direction of his speech, that stood so sternly forth
Unmov'd with th' other orators, and spake, not to appease
Pelides' wrath, but to depart. His arguments were these:
"High-issu'd Laertiades, let us insist no more
On his persuasion. I perceive the world would end before
Our speeches end in this affair. We must with utmost haste
Return his answer, though but bad. The peers are elsewhere plac'd,
And will not rise till we return. Great Thetis' son hath stor'd
Proud wrath within him, as his wealth, and will not be implor'd,
Rude that he is, nor his friends' love respects, do what they can,
Wherein past all, we honour'd him. O unremorseful man!

Another for his brother slain, another for his son,
Accepts of satisfaction; and he the deed hath done
Lives in belov'd society long after his amends,
To which his foe's high heart, for gifts, with patience condescends;
But thee a wild and cruel spirit the Gods for plague have giv'n,
And for one girl, of whose fair sex we come to offer sev'n,
The most exempt for excellence, and many a better prise.
Then put a sweet mind in thy breast, respect thy own allies,
Though others make thee not remiss. A multitude we are,
Sprung of thy royal family, and our supremest care
Is to be most familiar, and hold most love with thee
Of all the Greeks, how great an host soever here there be."
He answer'd: "Noble Telamon, prince of our soldiers here,
Out of thy heart I know thou speak'st, and as thou hold'st me dear;
But still as often as I think, how rudely I was us'd,
And, like a stranger, for all rites, fit for our good, refus'd
My heart doth swell against the man, that durst be so profane
To violate his sacred place; not for my private bane,
But since wrack'd virtue's gen'ral laws he shameless did infringe;
For whose sake I will loose the reins, and give mine anger swinge,
Without my wisdom's least impeach. He is a fool, and base,
That pities vice-plagu'd minds, when pain, not love of right, gives place.
And therefore tell your king, my lords, my just wrath will not care
For all his cares, before my tents and navy chargéd are
By warlike Hector, making way through flocks of Grecian lives,
Enlighten'd by their naval fire; but when his rage arrives
About my tent, and sable bark, I doubt not but to shield
Them and myself, and make him fly the there strong-bounded field."
This said, each one but kiss'd the cup, and to the ships retir'd;
Ulysses first. Patroclus then the men and maids requir'd
To make grave Phœnix' bed with speed, and see he nothing lacks.
They straight obey'd, and thereon laid the subtile fruit of flax,
And warm sheep-fells for covering; and there the old man slept,
Attending till the golden Morn her usual station kept.
Achilles lay in th' inner room of his tent richly wrought,
And that fair lady by his side, that he from Lesbos brought,
Bright Diomeda, Phorbas' seed. Patroclus did embrace
The beauteous Iphis, giv'n to him, when his bold friend did race
The lofty Scyrus that was kept in Enyeius' hold.
Now at the tent of Atreus' son, each man with cups of gold
Receiv'd th' ambassadors return'd. All cluster'd near to know
What news they brought; which first the king would have Ulysses show:
"Say, most praiseworthy Ithacus, the Grecians' great renown,
Will he defend us? Or not yet will his proud stomach down?"
Ulysses made reply: "Not yet will he appeaséd be,
But grows more wrathful, prizing light thy offer'd gifts and thee,
And wills thee to consult with us, and take some other course
To save our army and our fleet, and says, 'with all his force,

The morn shall light him on his way to Phthia's wishéd soil,
For never shall high-seated Troy be sack'd with all our toil,
Jove holds his hand 'twixt us and it, the soldiers gather heart.'
Thus he replies, which Ajax here can equally impart,
And both these heralds. Phœnix stays, for so was his desire,
To go with him, if he thought good; if not, he might retire."
All wonder'd he should be so stern; at last bold Diomed spake:
"Would God, Atrides, thy request were yet to undertake,
And all thy gifts unoffer'd him! He's proud enough beside,
But this ambassage thou hast sent will make him burst with pride.
But let us suffer him to stay, or go, at his desire,
Fight when his stomach serves him best, or when Jove shall inspire.
Meanwhile, our watch being strongly held, let us a little rest
After our food; strength lives by both, and virtue is their guest.
Then when the rosy-finger'd Morn holds out her silver light,
Bring forth thy host, encourage all, and be thou first in fight."
The kings admir'd the fortitude, that so divinely mov'd
The skilful horseman Diomed, and his advice approv'd.
Then with their nightly sacrifice each took his sev'ral tent,
Where all receiv'd the sov'reign gifts soft Somnus did present.

[1] Diomed takes fit time to answer his wrong done by Agamemnon in the fourth book.

THE END OF THE NINTH BOOK.

THE TENTH BOOK OF HOMER'S ILIADS

THE ARGUMENT

Th' Atrides, watching, wake the other peers,
And (in the fort, consulting of their fears)
Two kings they send, most stout, and honour'd most,
For royal scouts, into the Trojan host;
Who meeting Dolon, Hector's bribéd spy,
Take him, and learn how all the quarters lie.
He told them, in the Thracian regiment
Of rich king Rhesus, and his royal tent,
Striving for safety; but they end his strife,
And rid poor Dolon of a dang'rous life,
Then with digressive wiles they use their force
On Rhesus' life, and take his snowy horse.

ANOTHER ARGUMENT

Kappa the night exploits applies:

Rhesus' and Dolons tragedies.

The other princes at their ships soft-finger'd sleep did bind,
But not the Gen'ral; Somnus' silks bound not his labouring mind
That turn'd, and return'd, many thoughts. And as quick lightnings fly, [l]
From well-deck'd Juno's sovereign, out of the thicken'd sky,
Preparing some exceeding rain, or hail, the fruit of cold,
Or down-like snow that suddenly makes all the fields look old,
Or opes the gulfy mouth of war with his ensulphur'd hand,
In dazzling flashes pour'd from clouds, on any punish'd land;
So from Atrides' troubled heart, through his dark sorrows, flew
Redoubled sighs; his entrails shook, as often as his view
Admir'd the multitude of fires, that gilt the Phrygian shade,
And heard the sounds of fifes, and shawms, and tumults soldiers made.
But when he saw his fleet and host kneel to his care and love,
He rent his hair up by the roots as sacrifice to Jove,
Burnt in his fi'ry sighs, still breath'd out of his royal heart,
And first thought good to Nestor's care his sorrows to impart,
To try if royal diligence, with his approv'd advice,
Might fashion counsels to prevent their threaten'd miseries.
So up he rose, attir'd himself, and to his strong feet tied
Rich shoes, and cast upon his back a ruddy lion's hide,
So ample it his ankles reach'd, then took his royal spear.
Like him was Menelaus pierc'd with an industrious fear,
Nor sat sweet slumber on his eyes, lest bitter fates should quite
The Greeks' high favours, that for him resolv'd such endless fight.
And first a freckled panther's hide hid his broad back athwart;
His head his brazen helm did arm; his able hand his dart;
Then made he all his haste to raise his brother's head as rare,
That he who most excell'd in rule might help t' effect his care.
He found him, at his ship's crook'd stern, adorning him with arms;
Who joy'd to see his brother's spirits awak'd without alarms,
Well weighing th' importance of the time. And first the younger spake:
"Why, brother, are ye arming thus? Is it to undertake
The sending of some vent'rous Greek, t' explore the foe's intent?
Alas! I greatly fear, not one will give that work consent,
Expos'd alone to all the fears that flow in gloomy night.
He that doth this must know death well, in which ends ev'ry fright."
"Brother," said he, "in these affairs we both must use advice,
Jove is against us, and accepts great Hector's sacrifice.
For I have never seen, nor heard, in one day, and by one,
So many high attempts well urg'd, as Hector's pow'r hath done
Against the hapless sons of Greece: being chiefly dear to Jove,
And without cause, being neither fruit of any Goddess' love,
Nor helpful God; and yet I fear the deepness of his hand,
Ere it be ras'd out of our thoughts, will many years withstand.
But, brother, hie thee to thy ships, and Idomen's disease
With warlike Ajax; I will haste to grave Neleides,
Exhorting him to rise, and give the sacred watch command,

For they will specially embrace incitement at his hand,
And now his son their captain is, and Idomen's good friend,
Bold Merion, to whose discharge we did that charge commend."
"Command'st thou then," his brother ask'd, "that I shall tarry here
Attending thy resolv'd approach, or else the message bear,
And quickly make return to thee?" He answer'd: "Rather stay,
Lest otherwise we fail to meet, for many a diff'rent way
Lies through our labyrinthian host. Speak ever as you go,
Command strong watch, from sire to son urge all t' observe the foe,
Familiarly, and with their praise, exciting ev'ry eye,
Not with unseason'd violence of proud authority.
We must our patience exercise, and work ourselves with them,
Jove in our births combin'd such care to either's diadem."
Thus he dismiss'd him, knowing well his charge before he went.
Himself to Nestor, whom he found in bed within his tent,
By him his damask curets hung, his shield, a pair of darts,
His shining casque, his arming waist; in these he led the hearts
Of his apt soldiers to sharp war, not yielding to his years.
He quickly started from his bed, when to his watchful ears
Untimely feet told some approach; he took his lance in hand,
And spake to him: "Ho, what art thou that walk'st at midnight? Stand.
Is any wanting at the guards? Or lack'st thou any peer?
Speak, come not silent towards me; say, what intend'st thou here?"
He answer'd: "O Neleides, grave honour of our host,
'Tis Agamemnon thou mayst know, whom Jove afflicteth most
Of all the wretched men that live, and will, whilst any breath
Gives motion to my toiléd limbs, and pears me up from death.
I walk the round thus, since sweet sleep cannot inclose mine eyes,
Nor shut those organs care breaks ope for our calamities.
My fear is vehement for the Greeks; my heart, the fount of heat,
With his extreme affects made cold, without my breast doth beat;
And therefore are my sinews strook with trembling; ev'ry part
Of what my friends may feel hath act in my dispenséd heart.
But, if thou think'st of any course may to our good redound,
(Since neither thou thyself canst sleep) come, walk with me the round;
In way whereof we may confer, and look to ev'ry guard,
Lest watching long, and weariness with labouring so hard,
Drown their oppresséd memories of what they have in charge.
The liberty we give the foe, alas, is over large,
Their camp is almost mix'd with ours, and we have forth no spies
To learn their drifts; who may perchance this night intend surprise."
Grave Nestor answer'd: "Worthy king, let good hearts bear our ill.
Jove is not bound to perfect all this busy Hector's will;
But I am confidently giv'n, his thoughts are much dismay'd
With fear, lest our distress incite Achilles to our aid,
And therefore will not tempt his fate, nor ours, with further pride.
But I will gladly follow thee, and stir up more beside;
Tydides, famous for his lance; Ulysses; Telamon;

And bold Phylëus' valiant heir. Or else, if anyone
Would haste to call king Idomen, and Ajax, since their sail
Lie so remov'd, with much good speed, it might our haste avail.
But, though he be our honour'd friend, thy brother I will blame,
Not fearing if I anger thee. It is his utter shame
He should commit all pains to thee, that should himself employ,
Past all our princes, in the care, and cure, of our annoy,
And be so far from needing spurs to these his due respects,
He should apply our spirits himself, with pray'rs and urg'd affects.
Necessity (a law to laws, and not to be endur'd)
Makes proof of all his faculties, not sound if not inur'd."
"Good father," said the king, "sometimes you know I have desir'd
You would improve his negligence, too oft to ease retir'd.
Nor is it for defect of spirit, or compass of his brain,
But with observing my estate, he thinks, he should abstain
Till I commanded, knowing my place; unwilling to assume,
For being my brother, anything might prove he did presume.
But now he rose before me far, and came t' avoid delays,
And I have sent him for the men yourself desir'd to raise.
Come, we shall find them at the guards we plac'd before the fort,
For thither my direction was they should with speed resort."
"Why now," said Nestor, "none will grudge, nor his just rule withstand.
Examples make excitements strong, and sweeten a command."
Thus put he on his arming truss, fair shoes upon his feet,
About him a mandilion, that did with buttons meet,
Of purple, large, and full of folds, curl'd with a warmful nap,
A garment that 'gainst cold in nights did soldiers use to wrap;
Then took he his strong lance in hand, made sharp with proved steel,
And went along the Grecian fleet. First at Ulysses' keel
He call'd, to break the silken fumes that did his senses bind.
The voice through th' organs of his ears straight rung about his mind.
Forth came Ulysses, asking him: "Why stir ye thus so late?
Sustain we such enforcive cause?" He answered, "Our estate
Doth force this perturbation; vouchsafe it, worthy friend,
And come, let us excite one more, to counsel of some end
To our extremes, by fight, or flight." He back, and took his shield,
And both took course to Diomed. They found him laid in field,
Far from his tent; his armour by; about him was dispread
A ring of soldiers, ev'ry man his shield beneath his head;
His spear fix'd by him as he slept, the great end in the ground,
The point, that bristled the dark earth, cast a reflection round
Like palid lightnings thrown from Jove; thus this heroë lay,
And under him a big ox-hide; his royal head had stay
On arras hangings, rolléd up; whereon he slept so fast,
That Nestor stirr'd him with his foot, and chid to see him cast
In such deep sleep in such deep woes, and ask'd him why he spent
All night in sleep, or did not hear the Trojans near his tent,
Their camp drawn close upon their dike, small space 'twixt foes and foes?

He, starting up, said, "Strange old man, that never tak'st repose,
Thou art too patient of our toil. Have we not men more young,
To be employ'd from king to king? Thine age hath too much wrong."
"Said like a king," replied the sire, "for I have sons renown'd,
And there are many other men, might go this toilsome round;
But, you must see, imperious Need hath all at her command.
Now on the eager razor's edge, for life or death, we stand [2]
Then go (thou art the younger man) and if thou love my ease,
Call swift-foot Ajax up thyself, and young Phyleides."
This said, he on his shoulders cast a yellow lion's hide,
Big, and reach'd earth; then took his spear, and Nestor's will applied,
Rais'd the heroes, brought them both. All met; the round they went,
And found not any captain there asleep or negligent,
But waking, and in arms, gave ear to ev'ry lowest sound.
And as keen dogs keep sheep in cotes, or folds of hurdles bound,
And grin at ev'ry breach of air, envious of all that moves,
Still list'ning when the rav'nous beast stalks through the hilly groves,
Then men and dogs stand on their guards, and mighty tumults make,
Sleep wanting weight to close one wink; so did the captains wake,
That kept the watch the whole sad night, all with intentive ear
Converted to the enemies' tents, that they might timely hear
If they were stirring to surprise; which Nestor joy'd to see.
"Why so, dear sons, maintain your watch, sleep not a wink," said he,
"Rather than make your fames the scorn of Trojan perjury."
This said, he foremost passed the dike, the others seconded,
Ev'n all the kings that had been call'd to council from the bed,
And with them went Meriones, and Nestor's famous son;
For both were call'd by all the kings to consultation.
Beyond the dike they choos'd a place, near as they could from blood,
Where yet appear'd the falls of some, and whence, the crimson flood
Of Grecian lives being pour'd on earth by Hector's furious chace,
He made retreat, when night repour'd grim darkness in his face.
There sat they down, and Nestor spake: "O friends, remains not one
That will rely on his bold mind, and view the camp, alone,
Of the proud Trojans, to approve if any straggling mate
He can surprise near th' utmost tents, or learn the brief estate
Of their intentions for the time, and mix like one of them
With their outguards, expiscating if the renown'd extreme
They force on us will serve their turns, with glory to retire,
Or still encamp thus far from Troy? This may he well inquire,
And make a brave retreat untouch'd; and this would win him fame
Of all men canopied with heav'n, and ev'ry man of name,
In all this host shall honour him with an enriching meed,
A black ewe and her sucking lamb (rewards that now exceed
All other best possessions, in all men's choice requests)
And still be bidden by our kings to kind and royal feasts."
All rev'renc'd one another's worth; and none would silence break,
Lest worst should take best place of speech; at last did Diomed speak:

"Nestor, thou ask'st if no man here have heart so well inclin'd
To work this stratagem on Troy? Yes, I have such a mind.
Yet, if some other prince would join, more probable will be
The strengthen'd hope of our exploit. Two may together see
(One going before another still) sly danger ev'ry way;
One spirit upon another works, and takes with firmer stay
The benefit of all his pow'rs; for though one knew his course,
Yet might he well distrust himself, which the other might enforce."
This offer ev'ry man assum'd, all would with Diomed go;
The two Ajaces, Merion, and Menelaus too;
But Nestor's son enforc'd it much; and hardy Ithacus,
Who had to ev'ry vent'rous deed a mind as venturous.
Amongst all these thus spake the king: "Tydides, most belov'd,
Choose thy associate worthily; a man the most approv'd
For use and strength in these extremes. Many thou seest stand forth;
But choose not thou by height of place, but by regard of worth,
Lest with thy nice respect of right to any man's degree,
Thou wrong'st thy venture, choosing one least fit to join with thee,
Although perhaps a greater king." This spake he with suspect
That Diomed, for honour's sake, his brother would select.
Then said Tydides: "Since thou giv'st my judgment leave to choose,
How can it so much truth forget Ulysses to refuse,
That bears a mind so most exempt, and vig'rous in th' effect
Of all high labours, and a man Pallas doth most respect?
We shall return through burning fire, if I with him combine,
He sets strength in so true a course, with counsels so divine."
Ulysses, loth to be esteem'd a lover of his praise,
With such exceptions humbled him as did him higher raise,
And said: "Tydides, praise me not more than free truth will bear,
Nor yet impair me; they are Greeks that give judicial ear.
But come, the morning hastes, the stars are forward in their course,
Two parts of night are past, the third is left t' employ our force."
Now borrow'd they for haste some arms. Bold Thrasymedes lent
Advent'rous Diomed his sword (his own was at his tent),
His shield, and helm tough and well-tann'd, without or plume or crest,
And call'd a murrion, archers' heads it uséd to invest.
Meriones lent Ithacus his quiver and his bow,
His helmet fashion'd of a hide; the workman did bestow
Much labour in it, quilting it with bow-strings, and, without
With snowy tusks of white-mouth'd boars 'twas arméd round about
Right cunningly, and in the midst an arming cap was plac'd,
That with the fix'd ends of the tusks his head might not be ras'd.
This, long since, by Autolycus was brought from Eleon,
When he laid waste Amyntor's house, that was Ormenus' son:
In Scandia, to Cytherius, surnam'd Amphidamas,
Autolycus did give this helm; he, when he feasted was
By honour'd Molus, gave it him, as present of a guest;
Molus to his son Merion did make it his bequest.

With this Ulysses arm'd his head; and thus they, both address'd,
Took leave of all the other kings. To them a glad ostent,
As they were ent'ring on their way, Minerva did present,
A hernshaw consecrate to her, which they could ill discern
Through sable night, but, by her clange, they knew it was a hern.
Ulysses joy'd, and thus invok'd: "Hear me, great Seed of Jove,
That ever dost my labours grace with presence of thy love,
And all my motions dost attend! Still love me, sacred Dame,
Especially in this exploit, and so protect our fame
We both may safely make retreat, and thriftily employ
Our boldness in some great affair baneful to them of Troy."
Then pray'd illustrate Diomed: "Vouchsafe me likewise ear,
O thou unconquer'd Queen of arms! Be with thy favours near,
As, to my royal father's steps, thou went'st a bounteous guide,
When th' Achives and the peers of Thebes he would have pacified,
Sent as the Greeks' ambassador, and left them at the flood
Of great Æsopus; whose retreat thou mad'st to swim in blood
Of his enambush'd enemies; and, if thou so protect
My bold endeavours, to thy name an heifer most select,
That never yet was tam'd with yoke, broad-fronted, one year old,
I'll burn in zealous sacrifice, and set the horns in gold."
The Goddess heard; and both the kings their dreadless passage bore
Through slaughter, slaughter'd carcassed, arms, and discolour'd gore,
Nor Hector let his princes sleep, but all to council call'd,
And ask'd, "What one is here will vow, and keep it unappall'd,
To have a gift fit for his deed, a chariot and two horse,
That pass for speed the rest of Greece? What one dares take this course,
For his renown, besides his gifts, to mix amongst the foe,
And learn if still they hold their guards, or with this overthrow
Determine flight, as being too weak to hold us longer war?"
All silent stood; at last stood forth one Dolon, that did dare
This dang'rous work, Eumedes' heir, a herald much renown'd.
This Dolon did in gold and brass exceedingly abound,
But in his form was quite deform'd, yet passing swift to run;
Amongst five sisters, he was left Eumedes' only son.
And he told Hector, his free heart would undertake t' explore
The Greeks' intentions, "but," said he, "thou shalt be sworn before,
By this thy sceptre, that the horse of great Æacides,
And his strong chariot bound with brass, thou wilt (before all these)
Resign me as my valour's prise; and so I rest unmov'd
To be thy spy, and not return before I have approv'd
(By vent'ring to Atrides' ship, where their consults are held)
If they resolve still to resist, or fly as quite expell'd."
He put his sceptre in his hand, and call'd the thunder's God,
Saturnia's husband, to his oath, those horse should not be rode
By any other man than he, but he for ever joy
(To his renown) their services, for his good done to Troy.
Thus swore he, and forswore himself, yet made base Dolon bold;

Who on his shoulders hung his bow, and did about him fold
A white wolf's hide, and with a helm of weasels' skins did arm
His weasel's head, then took his dart, and never turn'd to harm
The Greeks with their related drifts; but being past the troops
Of horse and foot, he promptly runs, and as he runs he stoops
To undermine Achilles' horse. Ulysses straight did see,
And said to Diomed: "This man makes footing towards thee,
Out of the tents. I know not well, if he be us'd as spy
Bent to our fleet, or come to rob the slaughter'd enemy.
But let us suffer him to come a little further on,
And then pursue him. If it chance, that we be overgone
By his more swiftness, urge him still to run upon our fleet,
And (lest he 'scape us to the town) still let thy jav'lin meet
With all his offers of retreat." Thus stepp'd they from the plain
Amongst the slaughter'd carcasses. Dolon came on amain,
Suspecting nothing; but once past, as far as mules outdraw
Oxen at plough, being both put on, neither admitted law,
To plough a deep-soil'd furrow forth, so far was Dolon past.
Then they pursu'd, which he perceiv'd, and stay'd his speedless haste,
Subtly supposing Hector sent to countermand his spy;
But, in a jav'lin's throw or less, he knew them enemy.
Then laid he on his nimble knees, and they pursu'd like wind.
As when a brace of greyhounds are laid in with hare and hind,
Close-mouth'd and skill'd to make the best of their industrious course,
Serve either's turn, and, set on hard, lose neither ground nor force;
So constantly did Tydeus' son, and his town-razing peer,
Pursue this spy, still turning him, as he was winding near
His covert, till he almost mix'd with their out-courts of guard.
Then Pallas prompted Diomed, lest his due worth's reward
Should be impair'd if any man did vaunt he first did sheath
His sword in him, and he be call'd but second in his death.
Then spake he, threat'ning with his lance: "Or stay, or this comes on,
And long thou canst not run before thou be by death outgone."
This said, he threw his jav'lin forth; which missed as Diomed would,
Above his right arm making way, the pile stuck in the mould.
He stay'd and trembled, and his teeth did chatter in his head.
They came in blowing, seiz'd him fast; he, weeping, offeréd
A wealthy ransom for his life, and told them he had brass,
Much gold, and iron, that fit for use in many labours was,
From whose rich heaps his father would a wondrous portion give,
If, at the great Achaian fleet, he heard his son did live.
Ulysses bad him cheer his heart. "Think not of death," said he,
"But tell us true, why runn'st thou forth, when others sleeping be?
Is it to spoil the carcasses? Or art thou choicely sent
T' explore our drifts? Or of thyself seek'st thou some wish'd event?"
He trembling answer'd: "Much reward did Hector's oath propose,
And urg'd me, much against my will, t' endeavour to disclose
If you determin'd still to stay, or bent your course for flight,

As all dismay'd with your late foil, and wearied with the fight.
For which exploit, Pelides' horse and chariot he did swear,
I only ever should enjoy." Ulysses smil'd to hear
So base a swain have any hope so high a prise t' aspire,
And said, his labours did affect a great and precious hire,
And that the horse Pelides rein'd no mortal hand could use
But he himself, whose matchless life a Goddess did produce.
"But tell us, and report but truth, where left'st thou Hector now?
Where are his arms? His famous horse? On whom doth he bestow
The watch's charge? Where sleep the kings? Intend they still to lie
Thus near encamp'd, or turn suffic'd with their late victory?"
"All this," said he, "I'll tell most true. At Ilus' monument
Hector with all our princes sits, t' advise of this event;
Who choose that place remov'd to shun the rude confuséd sounds
The common soldiers throw about. But, for our watch, and rounds,
Whereof, brave lord, thou mak'st demand, none orderly we keep.
The Trojans, that have roofs to save, only abandon sleep,
And privately without command each other they exhort
To make prevention of the worst; and in this slender sort
Is watch and guard maintain'd with us. Th' auxiliary bands
Sleep soundly, and commit their cares into the Trojans' hands,
For they have neither wives with them, nor children to protect;
The less they need to care, the more they succour dull neglect."
"But tell me," said wise Ithacus, "are all these foreign pow'rs
Appointed quarters by themselves, or else commix'd with yours?"
"And this," said Dolon, "too, my lords, I'll seriously unfold.
The Pæons with the crookéd bows, and Cares, quarters hold
Next to the sea, the Leleges, and Caucons, join'd with them,
And brave Pelasgians. Thymber's mead, remov'd more from the stream,
Is quarter to the Lycians, the lofty Mysian force,
The Phrygians and Meonians, that fight with arméd horse.
But what need these particulars? If ye intend surprise
Of any in our Trojan camps, the Thracian quarter lies
Utmost of all, and uncommix'd with Trojan regiments,
That keep the voluntary watch. New pitch'd are all their tents.
King Rhesus, Eioneus' son, commands them, who hath steeds
More white than snow, huge, and well-shap'd, their fi'ry pace exceeds
The winds in swiftness; these I saw; his chariot is with gold
And pallid silver richly fram'd, and wondrous to behold;
His great and golden armour is not fit a man should wear,
But for immortal shoulders fram'd. Come then, and quickly bear
Your happy prisn'er to your fleet; or leave him here fast bound,
Till your well-urg'd and rich return prove my relation sound."
Tydides dreadfully replied: "Think not of passage thus,
Though of right acceptable news thou hast advértis'd us,
Our hands are holds more strict than so; and should we set the free
For offer'd ransom, for this 'scape thou still wouldst scouting be
About our ships, or do us scathe in plain opposéd arms,

But, if I take thy life, no way can we repent thy harms."
With this, as Dolon reach'd his hand to use a suppliant's part,
And stroke the beard of Diomed, he strook his neck athwart
With his forc'd sword, and both the nerves he did in sunder wound,
And suddenly his head, deceiv'd, fell speaking on the ground.
His weasel's helm they took, his bow, his wolf's skin, and his lance,
Which to Minerva Ithacus did zealously advance,
With lifted arm into the air; and to her thus he spake:
"Goddess, triumph in thine own spoils; to thee we first will make
Our invocations, of all pow'rs thron'd on th' Olympian hill;
Now to the Thracians, and their horse, and beds, conduct us still."
With this, he hung them up aloft upon a tamrick bough
As eyeful trophies, and the sprigs that did about it grow
He proinéd from the leafy arms, to make it easier view'd
When they should hastily retire, and be perhaps pursu'd,
Forth went they through black blood and arms, and presently aspir'd
The guardless Thracian regiment, fast bound with sleep, and tir'd;
Their arms lay by, and triple ranks they, as they slept, did keep,
As they should watch and guard their king, who, in a fatal sleep,
Lay in the midst; their chariot horse, as they coach-fellows were,
Fed by them; and the famous steeds, that did their gen'ral bear,
Stood next him, to the hinder part of his rich chariot tied.
Ulysses saw them first, and said, "Tydides, I have spied
The horse that Dolon, whom we slew, assur'd us we should see.
Now use thy strength; now idle arms are most unfit for thee;
Prise thou the horse; or kill the guard, and leave the horse to me."
Minerva, with the azure eyes, breath'd strength into her king,
Who filled the tent with mixéd death. The souls, he set on wing,
Issu'd in groans, and made air swell into her stormy flood.
Horror and slaughter had one pow'r, the earth did blush with blood.
As when a hungry lion flies, with purpose to devour,
On flocks unkept, and on their lives doth freely use his pow'r;
So Tydeus' son assail'd the foe; twelve souls before him flew;
Ulysses waited on his sword, and ever as he slew,
He drew them by their strengthless heels out of the horses' sight.
That, when he was to lead them forth, they should not with affright
Boggle, nor snore, in treading on the bloody carcasses;
For being new come, they were unus'd to such stern sights as these.
Through four ranks now did Diomed the king himself attain,
Who, snoring in his sweetest sleep, was like his soldiers slain.
An ill dream by Minerva sent that night stood by his head,
Which was Oenides' royal, unconquer'd Diomed.
Meanwhile Ulysses loos'd his horse, took all their reins in hand,
And led them forth; but Tydeus' son did in contention stand
With his great mind to do some deed of more audacity;
If he should take the chariot, where his rich arms did lie,
And draw it by the beam away, or bear it on his back,
Or if, of more dull Thracian lives, he should their bosoms sack.

In this contention with himself, Minerva did suggest
And bade him think of his retreat; lest from their tempted rest
Some other God should stir the foe, and send him back dismay'd.
He knew the voice, took horse, and fled. The Trojan's heav'nly aid,
Apollo with the silver how, stood no blind sentinel
To their secure and drowsy host, but did discover well
Minerva following Diomed; and, angry with his act,
The mighty host of Ilion he enter'd, and awak'd
The cousin-german of the king, a counsellor of Thrace,
Hippocoon; who when he rose, and saw the desert place,
Where Rhesus' horse did use to stand, and th' other dismal harms,
Men struggling with the pangs of death, he shriek'd out thick alarms,
Call'd "Rhesus! Rhesus!" but in vain; then still, "Arm! Arm!" he cried.
The noise and tumult was extreme on every startled side
Of Troy's huge host; from whence in throngs all gather'd, and admir'd
Who could perform such harmful facts, and yet be safe retir'd,
Now, coming where they slew the scout, Ulysses stay'd the steeds,
Tydides lighted, and the spoils, hung on the tamrick reeds,
He took and gave to Ithacus, and up he got again.
Then flew they joyful to their fleet. Nestor did first attain
The sounds the horse-hoofs strook through air, and said: "My royal peers!
Do I but dote, or say I true? Methinks about mine ears
The sounds of running horses beat. O would to God they were
Our friends thus soon return'd with spoils! But I have hearty fear,
Lest this high tumult of the foe doth their distress intend."
He scarce had spoke, when they were come. Both did from horse descend.
All, with embraces and sweet words, to heav'n their worth did raise.
Then Nestor spake: "Great Ithacus, ev'n heap'd with Grecian praise,
How have you made these horse your prise? Pierc'd you the dang'rous host,
Where such gems stand? Or did some God your high attempts accost,
And honour'd you with this reward? Why, they be like the rays
The sun effuseth. I have mix'd with Trojans all my days;
And now, I hope you will not say, I always lie aboard,
Though an old soldier I confess; yet did all Troy afford
Never the like to any sense that ever I possess'd.
But some good God, no doubt, hath met, and your high valours bless'd,
For He that shadows heav'n with clouds loves both as his delights,
And She that supples earth with blood cannot forbear your sights."
Ulysses answer'd: "Honour'd sire, the willing Gods can give
Horse much more worth than these men yield, since in more pow'r they live.
These horse are of the Thracian breed; their king, Tydides slew,
And twelve of his most trusted guard; and of that meaner crew
A scout for thirteenth man we kill'd, whom Hector sent to spy
The whole estate of our designs, if bent to fight or fly."
Thus, follow'd with whole troops of friends, they with applauses pass'd
The spacious dike, and in the tent of Diomed they plac'd
The horse without contention, as his deserving's meed,
Which, with his other horse set up, on yellow wheat did feed.

Poor Dolon's spoils Ulysses had; who shrin'd them on his stern,
As trophies vow'd to her that sent the good-aboding hern.
Then enter'd they the mere main sea, to cleanse their honour'd sweat
From off their feet, their thighs and necks; and, when their vehement heat
Was calm'd, and their swoln hearts refresh'd, more curious baths they us'd,
Where od'rous and dissolving oils, they through their limbs diffus'd.
Then, taking breakfast, a big bowl, fill'd with the purest wine,
They offer'd to the Maiden Queen, that hath the azure eyne.

[1] *These are the lightnings before snow, etc. that Scaliger's Criticus so unworthily taxeth; citing the place falsely, as in the third book's annotations, etc.*

[2] Ἐπὶ ξυροῦ ἵσταται ἀκμῆς. *This went into a proverb, used by Theocritus, in Dioscuris, out of Homer.*

THE END OF THE TENTH BOOK.

THE ELEVENTH BOOK OF HOMER'S ILIADS

THE ARGUMENT

Atrides and his other peers of name
Lead forth their men; whom Eris oath enflame.
Hector (by Iris' charge) takes deedless breath,
Whiles Agamemnon plies the work of death,
Who with the first bears his imperial head.
Himself, Ulysses, and King Diomed,
Eurypylus, and Æsculapius' son,
(Enforc'd with wounds) the furious skirmish shun.
Which martial sight when great Achilles views,
A little his desire of fight renews;
And forth he sends his friend, to bring him word
From old Neleides, what wounded lord
He in his chariot from the skirmish brought;
Which was Machaon. Nestor then besought
He would persuade his friend to wreak their harms,
Or come himself, deck'd in his dreadful arms.

ANOTHER ARGUMENT

Lambda presents the General,
In fight the worthiest man of all,
Aurora out of restful bed did from bright Tithon rise,
To bring each deathless Essence light, and use to mortal eyes;
When Jove sent Eris to the Greeks, sustaining in her hand
Stern signs of her designs for war. She took her horrid stand

Upon Ulysses' huge black bark, that did at anchor ride
Amidst the fleet, from whence her sounds might ring on ev'ry side,
Both to the tents of Telamon, and th' author of their smarts,
Who held, for fortitude and force, the navy's utmost parts.
The red-ey'd Goddess, seated there, thunder'd the Orthian song,
High, and with horror, through the ears of all the Grecian throng,
Her verse with spirits invincible did all their breasts inspire,
Blew out all darkness from their limbs, and set their hearts on fire;
And presently was bitter war more sweet a thousand times,
Than any choice in hollow keels to greet their native climes.
Atrides summon'd all to arms, to arms himself dispos'd,
First on his legs he put bright greaves, with silver buttons clos'd;
Then with rich curace arm'd his breast, which Cinyras bestow'd
To gratify his royal guest; for ev'n to Cyprus flowed
Th' unbounded fame of those designs the Greeks propos'd for Troy,
And therefore gave he him those arms, and wish'd his purpose joy.
Ten rows of azure mix'd with black, twelve golden like the sun,
Twice-ten of tin, in beaten paths, did through this armour run.
Three serpents to the gorget crept, that like three rainbows shin'd,
Such as by Jove are fix'd in clouds, when wonders are divin'd.
About his shoulders hung his sword, whereof the hollow hilt
Was fashion'd all with shining bars, exceeding richly gilt;
The scabbard was of silver plate, with golden hangers grac'd.
Then he took up his weighty shield, that round about him cast
Defensive shadows; ten bright zones of gold-affecting brass
Were driv'n about it; and of tin, as full of gloss as glass,
Swell'd twenty bosses out of it; in centre of them all
One of black metal had engrav'n, full of extreme appall,
An ugly Gorgon, compasséd with Terror and with Fear.
At it a silver bawdrick hung, with which he us'd to bear,
Wound on his arm, his ample shield; and in it there was wov'n
An azure dragon, curl'd in folds, from whose one neck was clov'n
Three heads contorted in an orb. Then plac'd he on his head
His four-plum'd casque; and in his hands two darts he managéd,
Arm'd with bright steel that blaz'd to heav'n. Then Juno, and the Maid
That conquers empires, trumpets serv'd to summon out their aid
In honour of the General, and on a sable cloud,
To bring them furious to the field, sat thund'ring out aloud.
Then all enjoin'd their charioteers, to rank their chariot horse
Close to the dike. Forth march'd the foot, whose front they did r'enforce
With some horse troops. The battle then was all of charioteers,
Lin'd with light horse. But Jupiter disturb'd this form with fears,
And from air's upper region bid bloody vapours rain,
For sad ostent much noble life should ere their times be slain.
The Trojan host at Ilus' tomb was in battalia led
By Hector and Polydamas, and old Anchises' seed
Who god-like was esteem'd in Troy, by grave Antenor's race
Divine Agenor, Polybus, unmarried Acamas

Proportion'd like the States of heav'n. In front of all the field,
Troy's great Priamides did bear his all-ways-equal shield,
Still plying th' ord'ring of his pow'r. And as amids the sky
We sometimes see an ominous star blaze clear and dreadfully,
Then run his golden head in clouds, and straight appear again;
So Hector otherwhiles did grace the vaunt-guard, shining plain,
Then in the rear-guard hid himself, and labour'd ev'rywhere
To order and encourage all; his armour was so clear,
And he applied each place so fast, that, like a lightning thrown
Out of the shield of Jupiter, in ev'ry eye he shone.
And as upon a rich man's crop of barley or of wheat,
Oppos'd for swiftness at their work, a sort of reaper's sweat,
Bear down the furrows speedily, and thick their handfuls fall;
So at the joining of the hosts ran slaughter through them all,
None stoop'd to any fainting thought of foul inglorious flight,
But equal bore they up their heads, and far'd like wolves in fight.
Stern Eris, with such weeping sights, rejoic'd to feed her eyes,
Who only show'd herself in field, of all the Deities;
The other in Olympus' tops sat silent, and repined
That Jove to do the Trojans grace should bear so fix'd a mind.
He car'd not, but, enthron'd apart, triumphant sat in sway
Of his free pow'r, and from his seat took pleasure to display
The city so adorn'd with tow'rs, the sea with vessels fill'd,
The splendour of refulgent arms, the killer and the kill'd.
As long as bright Aurora rul'd, and sacred day increas'd,
So long their darts made mutual wounds, and neither had the best;
But when, in hill-environ'd vales, the timber-feller takes
A sharp set stomach to his meat, and dinner ready makes,
His sinews fainting, and his spirits become surcharg'd and dull,
Time of accustom'd ease arriv'd, his hands with labour full,
Then by their valours Greeks brake through the Trojan ranks, and cheer'd
Their gen'ral squadrons through the host; then first of all appear'd
The person of the king himself; and then the Trojans lost
Bianor by his royal charge, a leader in the host.
Who being slain, his charioteer, Oïleus, did alight,
And stood in skirmish with the king; the king did deadly smite
His forehead with his eager lance, and through his helm it ran,
Enforcing passage to his brain, quite through the harden'd pan,
His brain mix'd with his clotter'd blood, his body strew'd the ground.
There left he them, and presently he other objects found;
Isus and Antiphus, two sons King Priam did beget,
One lawful, th' other wantonly. Both in one chariot met
Their royal foe; the baser born, Isus, was charioteer,
And famous Antiphus did fight; both which king Peleus' heir,
Whilome in Ida keeping flocks, did deprehend and bind
With pliant osiers, and, for price, them to their sire resign'd.
Atrides, with his well-aim'd lance, smote Isus on the breast
Above the nipple; and his sword a mortal wound impress'd

Beneath the ear of Antiphus; down from their horse they fell.
The king had seen the youths before, and now did know them well,
Rememb'ring them the prisoners of swift Æacides,
Who brought them to the sable fleet from Ida's foody leas.
And as a lion having found the furrow of a hind,
Where she hath calv'd two little twins, at will and ease doth grind
Their joints snatch'd in his solid jaws, and crusheth into mist
Their tender lives; their dam, though near, not able to resist,
But shook with vehement fear herself, flies through the oaken chace
From that fell savage, drown'd in sweat, and seeks some covert place;
So when with most unmatched strength the Grecian Gen'ral bent
'Gainst these two princes, none durst aid their native king's descent,
But fled themselves before the Greeks. And where these two were slain,
Pisander and Hippolochus (not able to restrain
Their headstrong horse, the silken reins being from their hands let fall)
Were brought by their unruly guides before the General.
Antimachus begat them both, Antimachus that took
Rich gifts, and gold, of Helen's love, and would by no means brook
Just restitution should be made of Menelaus' wealth,
Bereft him, with his ravish'd queen, by Alexander's stealth.
Atrides, lion-like, did charge his sons, who on their knees
Fell from their chariot, and besought regard to their degrees,
Who, being Antimachus's sons, their father would afford
A worthy ransom for their lives, who in his house did hoard
Much hidden treasure, brass, and gold, and steel, wrought wondrous choice.
Thus wept they, using smoothing terms, and heard this rugged voice
Breath'd from the unrelenting king: "If you be of the breed
Of stout Antimachus, that stay'd the honourable deed
The other peers of Ilion in council had decreed,
To render Helen and her wealth; and would have basely slain
My brother and wise Ithacus, ambassadors t' attain
The most due motion; now receive wreak for his shameful part."
This said, in poor Pisander's breast he fix'd his wreakful dart,
Who upward spread th' oppresséd earth; his brother crouch'd for dread,
And, as he lay, the angry king cut off his arms and head,
And let him like a football lie for ev'ry man to spurn.
Then to th' extremest heat of fight he did his valour turn,
And led a multitude of Greeks, where foot did foot subdue,
Horse slaughter'd horse, Need feather'd flight, the batter'd centre flew
In clouds of dust about their ears, raised from the horses' hooves,
That beat a thunder out of earth as horrible as Jove's.
The king, persuading speedy chace, gave his persuasions way
With his own valour, slaught'ring still. As in a stormy day
In thick-set woods a rav'nous fire wraps in his fierce repair
The shaken trees, and by the roots doth toss them into air;
Ev'n so beneath Atrides' sword flew up Troy's flying heels,
Their horse drew empty chariots, and sought their thund'ring wheels
Some fresh directors through the field, where least the pursuit drives.

Thick fell the Trojans, much more sweet to vultures than their wives.
Then Jove drew Hector from the darts, from dust, from death and blood,
And from the tumult. Still the king firm to the púrsuit stood,
Till at old Ilus' monument, in midst of all the field,
They reach'd the wild fig-tree, and long'd to make their town their shield.
Yet there they rested not; the king still cried, 'Pursue! Pursue!'
And all his unreprovéd hands did blood and dust imbrue.
But when they came to Scæa's ports, and to the beech of Jove,
There made they stand; there ev'ry eye, fixed on each other, strove
Who should outlook his mate amaz'd; through all the field they fled.
And as a lion, when the night becomes most deaf and dead,
Invades ox-herds, affrighting all, that he of one may wreak
His dreadful hunger, and his neck he first of all doth break,
Then laps his blood and entrails up; so Agamemnon plied
The manage of the Trojan chace, and still the last man died,
The other fled, a number fell by his imperial hand,
Some grovelling downwards from their horse, some upwards strew'd the sand.
High was the fury of his lance. But, having beat them close
Beneath their walls, the both worlds' Sire did now again repose
On fountain-flowing Ida's tops, being newly slid from heav'n,
And held a lightning in his hand; from thence this charge was giv'n
To Iris with the golden wings: "Thaumantia, fly," said he,
"And tell Troy's Hector, that as long as he enrag'd shall see
The soldier-loving Atreus' son amongst the foremost fight,
Depopulating troops of men, so long he must excite
Some other to resist the foe, and he no arms advance;
But when he wounded takes his horse, attain'd with shaft or lance,
Then will I fill his arm with death, ev'n till he reach the fleet,
And peaceful night treads busy day beneath her sacred feet."
The wind-foot swift Thaumantia obey'd, and us'd her wings
To famous Ilion, from the mount enchas'd with silver springs,
And found in his bright chariot the hardy Trojan knight,
To whom she spake the words of Jove, and vanish'd from his sight.
He leapt upon the sounding earth, and shook his lengthful dart,
And ev'rywhere he breath'd exhorts, and stirr'd up ev'ry heart.
A dreadful fight he set on foot. His soldiers straight turn'd head.
The Greeks stood firm. In both the hosts, the field was perfected.
But Agamemnon, foremost still, did all his side exceed,
And would not be the first in name unless the first in deed.
Now sing, fair Presidents of verse, that in the heav'ns embow'r,
Who first encounter'd with the king, of all the adverse pow'r.
Iphidamas, Antenor's son, ample and bigly set,
Brought up in pasture-springing Thrace, that doth soft sheep beget,
In grave Cisseus' noble house, that was his mother's sire,
Fair Theano; and when his breast was heighten'd with the fire
Of gaysome youth, his grandsire gave his daughter to his love.
Who straight his bridal-chamber left. Fame with affection strove,
And made him furnish twelve fair ships, to lend fair Troy his hand.

His ships he in Percope left, and came to Troy by land.
And now he tried the fame of Greece, encount'ring with the king,
Who threw his royal lance and miss'd. Iphidamas did fling,
And strook him on the arming waist, beneath his coat of brass,
Which forc'd him stay upon his arm, so violent it was,
Yet pierc'd it not his well-wrought zone, but when the lazy head
Tried hardness with his silver waist, it turn'd again like lead.
He follow'd, grasping the ground end, but with a lion's wile
That wrests away a hunter's staff, he caught it by the pile,
And pluck'd it from the caster's hand, whom with his sword he strook
Beneath the ear, and with his wound his timeless death he took.
He fell and slept an iron sleep; wretched young man, he died,
Far from his newly-married wife, in aid of foreign pride,
And saw no pleasure of his love; yet was her jointure great,
An hundred oxen gave he her, and vow'd in his retreat
Two thousand head of sheep and goats, of which he store did leave.
Much gave he of his love's first-fruits, and nothing did receive.
When Coon (one that for his form might feast an amorous eye,
And elder brother of the slain) beheld this tragedy,
Deep sorrow sat upon his eyes, and (standing laterally,
And to the Gen'ral undiscern'd) his jav'lin he let fly,
That 'twixt his elbow and his wrist transfix'd his armless arm;
The bright head shin'd on th' other side. The unexpected harm
Impress'd some horror in the king; yet so he ceas'd not fight,
But rush'd on Coon with his lance, who made what haste he might,
Seizing his slaughter'd brother's foot, to draw him from the field,
And call'd the ablest to his aid, when under his round shield
The king's brass jav'lin, as he drew, did strike him helpless dead;
Who made Iphidamas the block, and cut off Coon's head.
Thus under great Atrides' arm Antenor's issue thriv'd,
And, to suffice precisest fate, to Pluto's mansion div'd.
He with his lance, sword, mighty stones, pour'd his heroic wreak
On other squadrons of the foe, whiles yet warm blood did break
Through his cleft veins; but when the wound was quite exhaust and crude,
The eager anguish did approve his princely fortitude.
As when most sharp and bitter pangs distract a labouring dame,
Which the divine Ilithyæ, that rule the painful frame
Of human child-birth, pour on her; th' Ilithyæ that are
The daughters of Saturnia; with whose extreme repair
The woman in her travail strives to take the worst it gives,
With thought it must be, 'tis love's fruit, the end for which she lives,
The mean to make herself new born, what comforts will redound;
So Agamemnon did sustain the torment of his wound.
Then took he chariot, and to fleet bad haste his charioteer,
But first pour'd out his highest voice to purchase ev'ry ear:
"Princes and leaders of the Greeks, brave friends, now from our fleet
Do you expel this boist'rous sway. Jove will not let me meet
Illustrate Hector, nor give leave that I shall end the day

In fight against the Ilion pow'r; my wound is in my way."
This said, his ready charioteer did scourge his spriteful horse,
That freely to the sable fleet perform'd their fi'ry course.
To bear their wounded sovereign apart the martial thrust,
Sprinkling their pow'rful breasts with foam, and snowing on the dust.
When Hector heard of his retreat, thus he for fame contends:
"Trojans, Dardanians, Lycians, all my close-fighting friends,
Think what it is to be renown'd, be soldiers all of name,
Our strongest enemy is gone, Jove vows to do us fame,
Then in the Grecian faces drive your one-hoof'd violent steeds,
And far above their best be best, and glorify your deeds."
Thus as a dog-giv'n hunter sets upon a brace of boars
His white-tooth'd hounds, puffs, shouts, breathes terms, and on his emprese pours
All his wild art to make them pinch; so Hector urg'd his host
To charge the Greeks, and, he himself most bold and active most,
He brake into the heat of fight, as when a tempest raves,
Stoops from the clouds, and all on heaps doth cuff the purple waves.
Who then was first, and last, he kill'd, when Jove did grace his deed?
Assæus, and Autonous, Opys, and Clytus' seed
Prince Dolops, and the honour'd sire of sweet Euryalus
Opheltes, Agelaus next, and strong Hipponous,
Orus, Æsymnus, all of name. The common soldiers fell,
As when the hollow flood of air in Zephyr's cheeks doth swell,
And sparseth all the gather'd clouds white Notus' pow'r did draw,
Wraps waves in waves, hurls up the froth beat with a vehement flaw;
So were the common soldiers wrack'd in troops by Hector's hand.
Then ruin had enforc'd such works as no Greeks could withstand,
Then in their fleet they had been hous'd, had not Laertes' son
Stirr'd up the spirit of Diomed, with this impression:
"Tydides, what do we sustain, forgetting what we are?
Stand by me, dearest in my love. 'Twere horrible impair
For our two valours to endure a customary flight,
To leave our navy still engag'd, and but by fits to fight."
He answer'd: "I am bent to stay, and anything sustain;
But our delight to prove us men will prove but short and vain,
For Jove makes Trojans instruments, and virtually then
Wields arms himself. Our cross affairs are not 'twixt men and men."
This said, Thymbræus with his lance he tumbled from his horse,
Near his left nipple wounding him. Ulysses did enforce
Fair Molion, minion to this king that Diomed subdu'd.
Both sent they thence till they return'd, who now the king pursu'd
And furrow'd through the thicken'd troops. As when two chaséd boars
Turn head 'gainst kennels of bold hounds, and race way through their gores;
So, turn'd from flight, the forward kings show'd Trojans backward death.
Nor fled the Greeks, but by their wills, to get great Hector breath.
Then took they horse and chariot from two bold city foes,
Merops Percosius' mighty sons. Their father could disclose,
Beyond all men, hid auguries, and would not give consent

To their egression to these wars, yet wilfully they went,
For Fates, that order sable death, enforc'd their tragedies.
Tydides slew them with his lance, and made their arms his prise.
Hypirochus, and Hippodus, Ulysses reft of light.
But Jove, that out of Ida look'd, then equalis'd the fight,
A Grecian for a Trojan then paid tribute to the Fates.
Yet royal Diomed slew one, ev'n in those even debates,
That was of name more than the rest, Pæon's renownéd son,
The prince Agastrophus; his lance into his hip did run;
His squire detain'd his horse apart, that hinder'd him to fly,
Which he repented at his heart, yet did his feet apply
His 'scape with all the speed they had alongst the foremost bands,
And there his lovéd life dissolv'd. This Hector understands,
And rush'd with clamour on the king, right soundly seconded
With troops of Trojans. Which perceiv'd by famous Diomed,
The deep conceit of Jove's high will stiffen'd his royal hair,
Who spake to near-fought Ithacus: "The fate of this affair
Is bent to us. Come let us stand, and bound his violence."
Thus threw he his long jav'lin forth, which smote his head's defence
Full on the top, yet pierc'd no skin; brass took repulse with brass;
His helm (with three folds made, and sharp) the gift of Phœbus was.
The blow made Hector take the troop, sunk him upon his hand,
And strook him blind. The king pursu'd before the foremost band
His dart's recov'ry, which he found laid on the purple plain;
By which time Hector was reviv'd, and, taking horse again,
Was far commix'd within his strength, and fled his darksome grave.
He follow'd with his thirsty lance, and this elusive brave:
"Once more be thankful to thy heels, proud dog, for thy escape.
Mischief sat near thy bosom now; and now another rape
Hath thy Apollo made of thee, to whom thou well mayst pray,
When through the singing of our darts thou find'st such guarded way.
But I shall meet with thee at length, and bring thy latest hour,
If with like favour any God be fautour of my pow'r.
Meanwhile some other shall repay, what I suspect in thee."
This said, he set the wretched soul of Pæon's issue free,
Whom his late wound not fully slew. But Priam's amorous birth
Against Tydides bent his bow, hid with a hill of earth,
Part of the ruinated tomb for honour'd Ilus built,
And as the curace of the slain, engrav'n and richly gilt,
Tydides from his breast had spoil'd, and from his shoulders raft
His target and his solid helm, he shot, and his keen shaft
(That never flew from him in vain) did nail unto the ground
The king's right foot; the spleenful knight laugh'd sweetly at the wound,
Crept from his covert, and triumph'd: "Now art thou maim'd," said he,
"And would to God my happy hand had so much honour'd me
To have infix'd it in thy breast, as deep as in thy foot,
Ev'n to th' expulsure of thy soul! Then blest had been my shoot
Of all the Trojans; who had then breath'd from their long unrests.

Who fear thee, as the braying goats abhor the king of beasts."
Undaunted Diomed replied: "You braver with your bow,
You slick-hair'd lover, you that hunt and fleer at wenches so,
Durst thou but stand in arms with me, thy silly archery
Would give thee little cause to vaunt. As little suffer I
In this same tall exploit of thine, perform'd when thou wert hid,
As if a woman, or a child that knew not what it did,
Had touch'd my foot. A coward's steel hath never any edge.
But mine, t' assure it sharp, still lays dead carcasses in pledge;
Touch it, it renders lifeless straight, it strikes the fingers' ends
Of hapless widows in their cheeks, and children blind of friends.
The subject of it makes earth red, and air with sighs inflames,
And leaves limbs more embrac'd with birds than with enamour'd dames."
Lance-fam'd Ulysses now came in, and stept before the king,
Kneel'd opposite, and drew the shaft. The eager pain did sting
Through all his body. Straight he took his royal chariot there,
And with direction to the fleet did charge his charioteer.
Now was Ulysses desolate, fear made no friend remain,
He thus spake to his mighty mind: "What doth my state sustain?
If I should fly this odds in fear, that thus comes clust'ring on,
'Twere high dishonour; yet 'twere worse, to be surpris'd alone.
'Tis Jove that drives the rest to fight; but that's a faint excuse.
Why do I tempt my mind so much? Pale cowards fight refuse.
He that affects renown in war must like a rock be fix'd,
Wound, or be wounded. Valour's truth puts no respect betwixt."
In this contention with himself, in flew the shady bands
Of targeteers, who sieg'd him round with mischief-fill'd hands.
As when a crew of gallants watch the wild muse of a boar,
Their dogs put after in full cry, he rusheth on before,
Whets, with his lather-making jaws, his crookéd tusks for blood,
And, holding firm his usual haunts, breaks through the deepen'd wood,
They charging, though his hot approach be never so abhorr'd;
So, to assail the Jove-lov'd Greek, the Ilians did accord,
And he made through them. First he hurt, upon his shoulder blade,
Deiops, a blameless man at arms; then sent to endless shade
Thoon and Eunomus; and strook the strong Chersidamas,
As from his chariot he leap'd down, beneath his targe of brass;
Who fell, and crawl'd upon the earth with his sustaining palms,
And left the fight. Nor yet his lance left dealing martial alms,
But Socus' brother by both sides, young Carops, did impress.
Then princely Socus to his aid made brotherly access,
And, coming near, spake in his charge: "O great Laertes' son,
Insatiate in sly stratagems, and labours never done,
This hour, or thou shalt boast to kill the two Hippasides
And prise their arms, or fall thyself in my resolv'd access."
This said, he threw quite through his shield his fell and well-driv'n lance,
Which held way through his curaces, and on his ribs did glance,
Plowing the flesh alongst his sides; but Pallas did repel

All inward passage to his life. Ulysses, knowing well
The wound undeadly (setting back his foot to form his stand)
Thus spake to Socus: "O thou wretch, thy death is in this hand,
That stay'st my victory on Troy, and where thy charge was made
In doubtful terms (or this or that) this shall thy life invade."
This frighted Socus to retreat, and, in his faint reverse,
The lance betwixt his shoulders fell, and through his breast did perse,
Down fell he sounding, and the king thus play'd with his mis-ease:
"O Socus, you that make by birth the two Hippasides,
Now may your house and you perceive death can outfly the flyer.
Ah wretch! thou canst not 'scape my vows. Old Hippasus thy sire,
Nor thy well-honour'd mother's hands, in both which lies thy worth,
Shall close thy wretched eyes in death, but vultures dig them forth,
And hide them with their darksome wings; but when Ulysses dies,
Divinest Greeks shall tomb my corse with all their obsequies."
Now from his body and his shield the violent lance he drew,
That princely Socus had infix'd; which drawn, a crimson dew
Fell from his bosom on the earth; the wound did dare him sore.
And when the furious Trojans saw Ulysses' forcéd gore,
Encouraging themselves in gross, all his destruction vow'd.
Then he retir'd, and summon'd aid. Thrice shouted he aloud,
As did denote a man engag'd. Thrice Menelaus' ear
Observ'd his aid-suggesting voice, and Ajax being near,
He told him of Ulysses' shouts, as if he were enclos'd
From all assistance, and advis'd their aids might be dispos'd
Against the ring that circled him, lest, charg'd with troops alone,
(Though valiant) he might be oppress'd, whom Greece so built upon.
He led, and Ajax seconded. They found their Jove-lov'd king
Circled with foes. As when a den of bloody lucerns cling
About a goodly-palméd hart, hurt with a hunter's bow,
Whose 'scape his nimble feet enforce, whilst his warm blood doth flow,
And his light knees have pow'r to move; but, master'd of his wound,
Emboss'd within a shady hill, the lucerns charge him round,
And tear his flesh; when instantly fortune sends in the pow'rs
Of some stern lion, with whose sight they fly, and he devours;
So charged the Ilians Ithacus, many and mighty men.
But then made Menelaus in, and horrid Ajax then,
Bearing a target like a tow'r, close was his violent stand,
And every way the foe dispers'd, when, by the royal hand,
Kind Menelaus led away the hurt Laertes' son,
Till his fair squire had brought his horse. Victorious Telamon
Still plied the foe, and put to sword a young Priamides,
Doryclus, Priam's bastard son; then did his lance impress
Pandocus, and strong Pirasus, Lysander and Palertes.
As when a torrent from the hills, swoln with Saturnian show'rs,
Falls on the fields, bears blasted oaks, and wither'd rosin flow'rs,
Loose weeds, and all disperséd filth, into the ocean's force;
So matchless Ajax beat the field, and slaughter'd men and horse.

Yet had not Hector heard of this, who fought on the left wing
Of all the host, near those sweet herbs Scamander's flood doth spring,
Where many foreheads trod the ground, and where the skirmish burn'd
Near Nestor and king Idomen, where Hector over turn'd
The Grecian squadrons, authoring high service with his lance,
And skilful manage of his horse. Nor yet the discrepance
He made in death betwixt the hosts had made the Greeks retire,
If fair-hair'd Helen's second spouse had not repress'd the fire
Of bold Machaon's fortitude, who with a three-fork'd head
In his right shoulder wounded him. Then had the Grecians dread.
Lest, in his strength declin'd, the foe should slaughter their hurt friend.
Then Crete's king urg'd Neleides his chariot to ascend,
And getting near him, take him in, and bear him to their tents.
A surgeon is to be preferr'd, with physic ornaments,
Before a multitude; his life gives hurt lives native bounds,
With sweet inspersion of fit balms, and perfect search of wounds.
Thus spake the royal Idomen. Neleides obey'd,
And to his chariot presently the wounded Greek convey'd,
The son of Æsculapius, the great physician.
To fleet they flew. Cebriones perceiv'd the slaughter done
By Ajax on the other troops, and spake to Hector thus:
"Whiles we encounter Grecians here, stern Telamonius
Is yonder raging, turning up in heaps our horse and men;
I know him by his spacious shield. Let us turn chariot then,
Where, both of horse and foot, the fight most hotly is propos'd,
In mutual slaughters. Hark, their throats from cries are never clos'd."
This said, with his shrill scourge he strook the horse, that fast ensu'd
Stung with his lashes, tossing shields, and carcasses imbru'd.
The chariot tree was drown'd in blood, and th' arches by the seat
Disperpled from the horses' hoofs, and from the wheel bands beat.
Great Hector long'd to break the ranks, and startle their close fight,
Who horribly amaz'd the Greeks, and plied their sudden fright
With busy weapons, ever wing'd; his lance, sword, weighty stones.
Yet charg'd he other leader's hands, not dreadful Telamon's;
With whom he wisely shunn'd foul blows. But Jove (that weighs above
All human pow'rs) to Ajax' breast divine repressions drove,
And made him shun who shunn'd himself; he ceas'd from fight amaz'd,
Cast on his back his sev'n-fold shield, and round about him gaz'd
Like one turn'd wild, look'd on himself in his distract retreat,
Knee before knee did scarcely move. As when from herds of neat,
Whole threaves of boors and mongrels chase a lion skulking near,
Loth he should taint the well-prized fat of any stall-fed steer,
Consuming all the night in watch, he, greedy of his prey,
Oft thrusting on is oft thrust off, so thick the jav'lins play
On his bold charges, and so hot the burning fire-brands shine,
Which he (though horrible) abhors, about his glowing eyne,
And early his great heart retires; so Ajax from the foe,
For fear their fleet should be inflam'd, 'gainst his swoln heart did go.

As when a dull mill ass comes near a goodly field of corn,
Kept from the birds by children's cries, the boys are overborne
By his insensible approach, and simply he will eat;
About whom many wands are broke, and still the children beat,
And still the self-providing ass doth with their weakness bear,
Not stirring till his paunch be full, and scarcely then will steer;
So the huge son of Telamon amongst the Trojans far'd,
Bore show'rs of darts upon his shield, yet scorn'd to fly as scar'd,
And so kept softly on his way; nor would he mend his pace
For all their violent pursuits, that still did arm the chace
With singing lances. But, at last, when their cur-like presumes
More urg'd the more forborne, his spirits did rarify their fumes,
And he revok'd his active strength, turn'd head, and did repell
The horse-troops that were new made in, 'twixt whom the fight grew fell;
And by degrees he stole retreat, yet with such puissant stay
That none could pass him to the fleet. In both the armies' sway
He stood, and from strong hands receiv'd sharp jav'lins on his shield,
Where many stuck, thrown on before, many fell short in field,
Ere the white body they could reach, and stuck, as telling how
They purpos'd to have pierc'd his flesh. His peril piercéd now
The eyes of prince Eurypylus, Evemon's famous son,
Who came close on, and with his dart strook duke Apisaon,
Whose surname was Phausiades, ev'n to the concrete blood
That makes the liver; on the earth, out gush'd his vital flood.
Eurypylus made in, and eas'd his shoulders of his arms;
Which Paris seeing, he drew his bow, and wreak'd in part the harms
Of his good friend Phausiades, his arrow he let fly
That smote Eurypylus, and brake in his attainted thigh;
Then took he troop to shun black death, and to the flyers cried:
"Princes, and leaders of the Greeks, stand, and repulse the tide
Of this our honour-wracking chace. Ajax is drown'd in darts,
I fear past 'scape; turn, honour'd friends, help out his vent'rous parts."
Thus spake the wounded Greek; the sound cast on their backs their shields,
And rais'd their darts; to whose relief Ajax his person wields.
Then stood he firmly with his friends, retiring their retire.
And thus both hosts indiff'rent join'd, the fight grew hot as fire.
Now had Neleides' sweating steeds brought him, and his hurt friend,
Amongst their fleet. Æacides, that wishly did intend,
Standing astern his tall-neck'd ship, how deep the skirmish drew
Amongst the Greeks, and with what ruth the insecution grew,
Saw Nestor bring Machaon hurt, and from within did call
His friend Patroclus; who, like Mars in form celestial,
Came forth with first sound of his voice, first spring of his decay,
And ask'd his princely friend's desire. "Dear friend," said he, "this day
I doubt not will enforce the Greeks, to swarm about my knees;
I see unsuffer'd need employ'd in their extremities.
Go, sweet Patroclus, and inquire of old Neleides
Whom he brought wounded from the fight; by his back parts I guess

It is Machaon, but his face I could not well descry,
They pass'd me in such earnest speed." Patroclus presently
Obey'd his friend, and ran to know. They now descended were,
And Nestor's squire, Eurymedon, the horses did ungear;
Themselves stood near th' extremest shore, to let the gentle air
Dry up their sweat; then to the tent where Hecamed the fair
Set chairs, and for the wounded prince a potion did prepare.
This Hecamed, by war's hard fate, fell to old Nestor's share,
When Thetis' son sack'd Tenedos; she was the princely seed
Of worthy king Arsinous, and by the Greeks decreed
The prise of Nestor, since all men in counsel he surpass'd.
First, a fair table she appos'd, of which the feet were grac'd
With bluish metal mix'd with black; and on the same she put
A brass fruit-dish, in which she serv'd a wholesome onion cut
For pittance to the potion, and honey newly wrought,
And bread, the fruit of sacred meal. Then to the board she brought
A right fair cup with gold studs driv'n, which Nestor did transfer
From Pylos; on whose swelling sides four handles fixéd were,
And upon ev'ry handle sat a pair of doves of gold,
Some billing, and some pecking meat; two gilt feet did uphold
The antique body; and withal so weighty was the cup
That, being propos'd brimful of wine, one scarce could lift it up,
Yet Nestor drunk in it with ease, spite of his years' respect.
In this the goddess-like fair dame a potion did confect
With good old wine of Pramnius, and scrap'd into the wine
Cheese made of goat's milk, and on it spers'd flour exceeding fine.
In this sort for the wounded lord the potion she prepar'd,
And bad him drink. For company, with him old Nestor shar'd.
Thus physically quench'd they thirst, and then their spirits reviv'd
With pleasant conference. And now Patroclus, being arriv'd,
Made stay at th' entry of the tent. Old Nestor, seeing it,
Rose, and receiv'd him by the hand, and fain would have him sit.
He set that courtesy aside, excusing it with haste,
Since his much-to-be-rev'renced friend sent him to know who past,
Wounded with him in chariot, so swiftly through the shore;
"Whom now," said he, "I see and know, and now can stay no more;
You know, good father, our great friend is apt to take offence,
Whose fi'ry temper will inflame sometimes with innocence."
He answer'd: "When will Peleus' son some royal pity show
On his thus wounded countrymen? Ah! is he yet to know
How much affliction tires our host? How our especial aid,
Tainted with lances, at their tents are miserably laid?
Ulysses, Diomed, our king, Eurypylus, Machaon,
All hurt, and all our worthiest friends; yet no compassion
Can supple thy friend's friendless breast! Doth he reserve his eye
Till our fleet burn, and we ourselves one after other die?
Alas, my forces are not now as in my younger life.
Oh would to God I had that strength I uséd in the strife

Betwixt us and the Elians, for oxen to be driv'n,
When Itymonius' lofty soul was by my valour giv'n
As sacrifice to destiny, Hypirochus' strong son,
That dwelt in Elis, and fought first in our contention!
We forag'd, as proclaiméd foes, a wondrous wealthy boot,
And he, in rescue of his herds, fell breathless at my foot.
All the dorp boors with terror fled. Our prey was rich and great;
Twice five and twenty flocks of sheep; as many herds of neat;
As many goats, and nasty swine; an hundred fifty mares,
All sorrel, most with sucking foals. And these soon-monied wares
We drave into Neleius' town, fair Pylos, all by night.
My father's heart was glad to see so much good fortune quite
The forward mind of his young son, that us'd my youth in deeds,
And would not smother it in moods. Now drew the Sun's bright steeds
Light from the hills; our heralds now accited all that were
Endamag'd by the Elians; our princes did appear;
Our boot was parted; many men th' Epeians much did owe,
That, being our neighbours, they did spoil; afflictions did so flow
On us poor Pylians, though but few. In brake great Hercules
To our sad confines of late years, and wholly did suppress
Our hapless princes. Twice-six Sons renown'd Neleius bred,
Only myself am left of all, the rest subdu'd and dead.
And this was it that made so proud the base Epeian bands,
On their near neighbours, being oppress'd, to lay injurious hands.
A herd of oxen for himself, a mighty flock of sheep,
My sire selected, and made choice of shepherds for their keep;
And from the gen'ral spoil he cull'd three hundred of the best.
The Elians ought him infinite, most plagu'd of all the rest.
Four wager-winning horse he lost, and chariots intervented,
Being led to an appointed race; the prize that was presented
Was a religious three-foot urn; Augeas was the king
That did detain them, and dismiss'd their keeper sorrowing
For his lov'd charge lost with foul words. Then both for words and deeds
My sire being worthily incens'd, thus justly he proceeds
To satisfaction, in first choice of all our wealthy prize;
And, as he shar'd much, much he left his subjects to suffice,
That none might be oppress'd with pow'r, or want his portion due.
Thus for the public good we shar'd. Then we to temples drew
Our cómplete city, and to heav'n we thankful rites did burn
For our rich conquest. The third day ensuing our return
The Elians flew on us in heaps; their gen'ral leaders were
The two Moliones, two boys, untrainéd in the fear
Of horrid war, or use of strength. A certain city shines
Upon a lofty prominent, and in th' extreme confines
Of sandy Pylos, seated where Alpheus' flood doth run,
And call'd Thryessa; this they sieg'd, and gladly would have won,
But, having pass'd through all our fields, Minerva as our spy
Fell from Olympus in the night, and arm'd us instantly;

Nor muster'd she unwilling men, nor unprepar'd for force.
My sire yet would not let me arm, but hid away my horse,
Esteeming me no soldier yet; yet shin'd I nothing less
Amongst our gallants, though on foot; Minerva's mightiness
Led me to fight, and made me bear a soldier's worthy name.
There is a flood falls into sea, and his crook'd course doth frame
Close to Arena, and is call'd bright Minyæus' stream.
There made we halt, and there the sun cast many a glorious beam
On our bright armours, horse and foot insea'd together there.
Then march'd we on. By fi'ry noon we saw the sacred clear
Of great Alpheus, where to Jove we did fair sacrifice;
And to the azure God, that rules the under-liquid skies,
We offer'd up a solemn bull; a bull t' Alpheus' name;
And to the blue-ey'd Maid we burn'd a heifer never tame.
Now was it night; we supp'd and slept, about the flood, in arms.
The foe laid hard siege to our town, and shook it with alarms,
But, for prevention of their spleens, a mighty work of war
Appear'd behind them; for as soon as Phœbus' fi'ry car
Cast night's foul darkness from his wheels (invoking rev'rend Jove,
And the unconquer'd Maid his birth) we did th' event approve,
And gave them battle. First of all, I slew (the army saw)
The mighty soldier Mulius, Augeas' son-in-law,
And spoil'd him of his one hoof'd horse; his eldest daughter was
Bright Agamede, that for skill in simples did surpass,
And knew as many kind of drugs, as earth's broad centre bred.
Him charg'd I with my brass-arm'd lance, the dust receiv'd him dead.
I, leaping to his chariot, amongst the foremost press'd,
And the great-hearted Elians fled frighted, seeing their best
And loftiest soldier taken down, the gen'ral of their horse.
I follow'd like a black whirlwind, and did for prize enforce
Full fifty chariots, ev'ry one furnish'd with two arm'd men,
Who ate the earth, slain with my lance. And I had slaughter'd then
The two young boys, Moliones, if their world-circling sire,
Great Neptune, had not saft their lives, and cover'd their retire
With unpierc'd clouds. Then Jove bestow'd a haughty victory
Upon us Pylians; for so long we did the chace apply,
Slaught'ring and making spoil of arms, till sweet Buprasius' soil,
Alesius, and Olenia, were fam'd with our recoil;
For there Minerva turn'd our pow'r, and there the last I slew
As, when our battle join'd, the first. The Pylians then withdrew
To Pylas from Buprasius. Of all th' Immortals then,
They most thank'd Jove for victory; Nestor the most of men.
Such was I ever, if I were employ'd with other peers,
And I had honour of my youth, which dies not in my years.
And great Achilles only joys hability of act
In his brave prime, and doth not deign t' impart it where 'tis lack'd.
No doubt he will extremely mourn, long after that black hour
Wherein our ruin shall be brought, and rue his ruthless pow'r,

O friend! my memory revives the charge Menœtius gave
Thy towardness, when thou sett'st forth, to keep out of the grave
Our wounded honour. I myself and wise Ulysses were
Within the room, where ev'ry word then spoken we did hear,
For we were come to Peleus' court, as we did must'ring pass
Through rich Achaia, where thy sire, Menœtius, was,
Thyself and great Æacides, when Peleüs the king
To thunder-loving Jove did burn an ox for offering,
In his court-yard. A cup of gold, crown'd with red wine, he held
On th' holy incensory pour'd. You, when the ox was fell'd,
Were dressing his divided limbs; we in the portal stood.
Achilles seeing us come so near, his honourable blood
Was strook with a respective shame, rose, took us by the hands,
Brought us both in, and made us sit, and us'd his kind commands
For seemly hospitable rites, which quickly were appos'd.
Then, after needfulness of food, I first of all disclos'd
The royal cause of our repair; mov'd you and your great friend
To consort our renown'd designs; both straight did condescend.
Your fathers knew it, gave consent, and grave instruction
To both your valours. Peleus charg'd his most unequall'd son
To govern his victorious strength, and shine past all the rest
In honour, as in mere main force. Then were thy partings blest
With dear advices from thy sire; 'My lovéd son,' said he,
'Achilles, by his grace of birth, superior is to thee,
And for his force more excellent, yet thou more ripe in years;
Then with sound counsels, age's fruits, employ his honour'd years,
Command and overrule his moods; his nature will obey
In any charge discreetly giv'n, that doth his good assay.'
"Thus charg'd thy sire, which thou forgett'st. Yet now at last approve,
With forcéd reference of these, th' attraction of his love;
Who knows if sacred influence may bless thy good intent,
And enter with thy gracious words, ev'n to his full consent?
The admonition of a friend is sweet and vehement.
If any oracle he shun, or if his mother-queen
Hath brought him some instinct from Jove, that fortifies his spleen,
Let him resign command to thee of all his Myrmidons,
And yield by that means some repulse to our confusions,
Adorning thee in his bright arms, that his resembled form
May haply make thee thought himself, and calm this hostile storm;
That so a little we may ease our overchargéd hands,
Draw some breath, not expire it all. The foe but faintly stands
Beneath his labours; and your charge being fierce, and freshly giv'n,
They eas'ly from our tents and fleet may to their walls be driv'n."
This mov'd the good Patroclus' mind; who made his utmost haste
T' inform his friend; and as the fleet of Ithacus he past,
(At which their markets were dispos'd, councils, and martial courts,
And where to th' altars of the Gods they made divine resorts)
He met renown'd Eurypylus, Evemon's noble son,

Halting, his thigh hurt with a shaft, the liquid sweat did run
Down from his shoulders and his brows, and from his raging wound
Forth flow'd his melancholy blood, yet still his mind was sound.
His sight in kind Patroclus' breast to sacred pity turn'd,
And (nothing more immartial for true ruth) thus he mourn'd:
"Ah wretched progeny of Greece, princes, dejected kings,
Was it your fates to nourish beasts, and serve the outcast wings
Of savage vultures here in Troy? Tell me, Evemon's fame,
Do yet the Greeks withstand his force, whom yet no force can tame?
Or are they hopeless thrown to death by his resistless lance?"
"Divine Patroclus," he replied, "no more can Greece advance
Defensive weapons, but to fleet they headlong must retire,
For those that to this hour have held our fleet from hostile fire,
And are the bulwarks of our host, lie wounded at their tents,
And Troy's unvanquishable pow'r, still as it toils augments.
But take me to thy black-stern'd ship, save me, and from my thigh
Cut out this arrow, and the blood, that is ingor'd and dry,
Wash with warm water from the wound; then gentle salves apply,
Which thou know'st best, thy princely friend hath taught thee surgery,
Whom, of all Centaurs the most just, Chiron did institute.
Thus to thy honourable hands my ease I prosecute,
Since our physicians cannot help. Machaon at his tent
Needs a physician himself, being leech and patient;
And Podalirius, in the field, the sharp conflict sustains."
Strong Menœtiades replied: "How shall I ease thy pains?
What shall we do, Eurypylus? I am to use all haste,
To signify to Thetis' son occurrents that have past,
At Nestor's honourable suit. But be that work achiev'd
When this is done, I will not leave thy torments unrelieved."
This said, athwart his back he cast, beneath his breast, his arm,
And nobly help'd him to his tent. His servants, seeing his harm,
Dispread ox-hides upon the earth, whereon Machaon lay.
Patroclus cut out the sharp shaft, and clearly wash'd away
With lukewarm water the black blood; then 'twixt his hands he bruis'd
A sharp and mitigatory root; which when he had infus'd
Into the green, well-cleansed, wound, the pains he felt before
Were well, and instantly allay'd; the wound did bleed no more.

THE END OF THE ELEVENTH BOOK.

THE TWELFTH BOOK OF HOMER'S ILIADS

THE ARGUMENT

The Trojans at the trench their pow'rs engage,
Though greeted by a bird of bad presage.

In five parts they divide their pow'r to scale,
And Prince Sarpedon forceth down the pale.
Great Hector from the ports tears out a stone,
And with so dead a strength he sets it gone
At those broad gates the Grecians made to guard
Their tents and ships, that, broken, and unbarr'd,
They yield way to his pow'r; when all contend
To reach the ships; which all at last ascend.

ANOTHER ARGUMENT

MY works the Trojans all the grace,
And doth the Grecian fort deface.
Patroclus thus employ'd in cure of hurt Eurypylus,
Both hosts are all for other wounds doubly contentious,
One always labouring to expel, the other to invade.
Nor could the broad dike of the Greeks, or that strong wall they made
To guard their fleet, be long unras'd; because it was not rais'd
By grave direction of the Gods, nor were their Deities prais'd
(When they begun) with hecatombs, that then they might be sure
(Their strength being season'd well with heav'n's) it should have force t' endure,
And so, the safeguard of their fleet, and all their treasure there,
Infallibly had been confirm'd; when, now, their bulwarks were
Not only without pow'r of check to their assaulting foe
(Ev'n now, as soon as they were built) but apt to overthrow;
Such as, in very little time, shall bury all their sight
And thought that ever they were made. As long as the despite
Of great Æacides held up, and Hector went not down,
And that by those two means stood safe king Priam's sacred town,
So long their rampire had some use, though now it gave some way;
But when Troy's best men suffer'd fate, and many Greeks did pay;
Dear for their suff'rance, then the rest home to their country turn'd,
The tenth year of their wars at Troy, and Troy was sack'd and burn'd.
And then the Gods fell to their fort; then they their pow'rs employ
To ruin their work, and left less of that than they of Troy.
Neptune and Phœbus tumbled down, from the Idalian hills,
An inundation of all floods, that thence the broad sea fills
On their huge rampire; in one glut, all these together roar'd,
Rhesus, Heptaporus, Rhodius, Scamander the ador'd,
Caresus, Simois, Grenicus, Æsepus; of them all
Apollo open'd the rough mouths, and made their lusty fall
Ravish the dusty champian, where many a helm and shield,
And half-god race of men, were strew'd. And, that all these might yield
Full tribute to the heav'nly work, Neptune and Phœbus won
Jove to unburthen the black wombs of clouds, fill'd by the sun,
And pour them into all their streams, that quickly they might send
The huge wall swimming to the sea. Nine days their lights did spend

To nights in tempests; and when all their utmost depth had made,
Jove, Phœbus, Neptune, all came down, and all in state did wade
To ruin of that impious fort. Great Neptune went before,
Wrought with his trident, and the stones, trunks, roots of trees, he tore
Out of the rampire, toss'd them all into the Hellespont,
Ev'n all the proud toil of the Greeks, with which they durst confront
The to-be shunnéd Deities, and not a stone remain'd
Of all their huge foundations, all with the earth were plain'd.
Which done, again the Gods turn'd back the silver-flowing floods
By that vast channel, through whose vaults they pour'd abroad their broods,
And cover'd all the ample shore again with dusty sand.
And this the end was of that wall, where now so many a hand
Was emptiéd of stones and darts, contending to invade;
Where Clamour spent so high a throat; and where he fell blows made
The new-built wooden turrets groan. And here the Greeks were pent,
Tam'd with the iron whip of Jove, that terrors vehement
Shook over them by Hector's hand, who was in ev'ry thought
The terror-master of the field, and like a whirlwind fought,
As fresh as in his morn's first charge. And as a savage boar,
Or lion, hunted long, at last, with hounds' and hunters' store
Is compass'd round; they charge him close, and stand (as in a tow'r
They had inchas'd him) pouring on of darts an iron show'r;
His glorious heart yet nought appall'd, and forcing forth his way,
Here overthrows a troop, and there a running ring doth stay
His utter passage; when, again, that stay he overthrows,
And then the whole field frees his rage; so Hector wearies blows,
Runs out his charge upon the fort, and all his force would force
To pass the dike; which, being so deep, they could not get their horse
To venture on, but trample, snore, and on the very brink
To neigh with spirit, yet still stand off. Nor would a human think
The passage safe; or, if it were, 'twas less safe for retreat;
The dike being ev'rywhere so deep, and, where 'twas least deep, set
With stakes exceeding thick, sharp, strong, that horse could never pass,
Much less their chariots after them; yet for the foot there was
Some hopeful service, which they wish'd. Polydamas then spake:
"Hector, and all our friends of Troy, we indiscreetly make
Offer of passage with our horse; ye see the stakes, the wall,
Impossible for horse to take; nor can men fight at all,
The place being strait, and much more apt to let us take our bane
Than give the enemy. And yet, if Jove decree the wane
Of Grecian glory utterly, and so bereave their hearts
That we may freely charge them thus, and then will take our parts,
I would with all speed wish th' assault, that ugly shame might shed
(Thus far from home) these Grecians' bloods. But, if they once turn head
And sally on us from their fleet, when in so deep a dike
We shall lie struggling, not a man of all our host is like
To live and carry back the news. And therefore be it thus:
Here leave we horse kept by our men, and all on foot let us

Hold close together, and attend the grace of Hector's guide,
And then they shall not bear our charge, our conquest shall be dyed
In their lives' purples." This advice pleas'd Hector, for 'twas sound;
Who first obey'd it, and full-arm'd betook him to the ground.
And then all left their chariots when he was seen to lead,
Rushing about him, and gave up each chariot and steed
To their directors to be kept, in all procinct of war,
There, and on that side of the dike. And thus the rest prepare
Their onset: In five regiments they all their pow'r divide,
Each regiment allow'd three chiefs. Of all which ev'n the pride
Serv'd in great Hector's regiment; for all were set on fire
(Their passage beaten through the wall) with hazardous desire
That they might once but fight at fleet. With Hector captains were
Polydamas, and Cebriones, who was his charioteer;
But Hector found that place a worse. Chiefs of the second band
Were Paris and Alcathous, Agenor. The command
The third strong phalanx had, was giv'n to th' augur Helenus,
Deiphobus, that god-like man, and mighty Asius,
Ev'n Asius Hyrtacides, that from Arisba rode
The huge bay horse, and had his house where river Selleës flow'd.
The fourth charge good Æneas led, and with him were combin'd
Archelochus, and Acamas, Antenor's dearest kind,
And excellent at ev'ry fight. The fifth brave company
Sarpedon had to charge, who choos'd, for his command's supply,
Asteropseus great in arms, and Glaucus; for both these
Were best of all men but himself, but he was fellowless.
Thus fitted with their well-wrought shields, down the steep dike they go,
And (thirsty of the wall's assault) believe in overthrow,
Not doubting but with headlong falls to tumble down the Greeks
From their black navy. In which trust, all on; and no man seeks
To cross Polydamas' advice with any other course,
But Asius Hyrtacides, who (proud of his bay horse)
Would not forsake them, nor his man, that was their manager,
(Fool that he was) but all to fleet, and little knew how near
An ill death sat him, and a sure, and that he never more
Must look on lofty Ilion; but looks, and all, before,
Put on th' all-cov'ring mist of fate, that then did hang upon
The lance of great Deucalides; he fatally rush'd on
The left hand way, by which the Greeks, with horse and chariot,
Came usually from field to fleet; close to the gates he got,
Which both unbarr'd and ope he found, that so the easier might
An entry be for any friend that was behind in flight;
Yet not much easier for a foe, because there was a guard
Maintain'd upon it, past his thought; who still put for it hard,
Eagerly shouting; and with him were five more friends of name,
That would not leave him, though none else would hunt that way for fame
(In their free choice) but he himself. Orestes, Iamenus,
And Acamas Asiades, Thoon, Oenomaus,

Were those that follow'd Asius. Within the gates they found
Two eminently valorous, that from the race renown'd
Of the right valiant Lapithes deriv'd their high descent;
Fierce Leontëus was the one, like Mars in detriment. [1]
The other mighty Polypæt, the great Pirithous' son.
These stood within the lofty gates, and nothing more did shun
The charge of Asius and his friends, than two high hill-bred oaks,
Well-rooted in the binding earth, obey the airy strokes
Of wind and weather, standing firm 'gainst ev'ry season's spite.
Yet they pour on continued shouts, and bear their shields upright;
When in the mean space Polypæt and Leonteus cheer'd
Their soldiers to the fleet's defence. But when the rest had heard
The Trojans in attempt to scale, clamour and flight did flow
Amongst the Grecians; and then, the rest dismay'd, these two
Met Asius ent'ring, thrust him back, and fought before their doors.
Nor far'd they then like oaks that stood, but as a brace of boars,
Couch'd in their own bred hill, that hear a sort of hunter's shout,
And hounds in hot trail coming on, then from their dens break out,
Traverse their force, and suffer not, in wildness of their way,
About them any plant to stand, but thickets off'ring stay
Break through, and rend up by the roots, whet gnashes into air,
Which Tumult fills with shouts, hounds, horns, and all the hot affair
Beats at their bosoms; so their arms rung with assailing blows,
And so they stirr'd them in repulse, right well assur'd that those
Who were within, and on the wall, would add their parts, who knew
They now fought for their tents, fleet, lives, and fame, and therefore threw
Stones from the walls and tow'rs, as thick as when a drift wind shakes
Black clouds in pieces, and plucks snow, in great and plumy flakes,
From their soft bosoms, till the ground be wholly cloth'd in white;
So earth was hid with stones and darts, darts from the Trojan fight,
Stones from the Greeks, that on the helms and bossy Trojan shields
Kept such a rapping, it amaz'd great Asius, who now yields
Sighs, beats his thighs, and in a rage his fault to Jove applies:
"O Jove," said he, "now clear thou show'st thou art a friend to lies,
Pretending, in the flight of Greece, the making of it good,
To all their ruins, which I thought could never be withstood;
Yet they, as yellow wasps, or bees (that having made their nest [2]
The grasping cranny of a hill) when for a hunter's feast
Hunters come hot and hungry in, and dig for honey-combs,
Then fly upon them, strike and sting, and from their hollow homes
Will not be beaten, but defend their labour's fruit, and brood;
No more will these be from their port, but either lose their blood
(Although but two against all us) or be our pris'ners made."
All this, to do his action grace, could not firm Jove persuade,
Who for the gen'ral counsel stood, and 'gainst his singular brave,
Bestow'd on Hector that day's fame. Yet he and these behave
Themselves thus nobly at this port; but how at other ports,
And all alongst the stony wall, sole force, 'gainst force and forts,

Rag'd in contention 'twixt both hosts, it were no easy thing,
Had I the bosom of a God, to tune to life and sing.
The Trojans fought not of themselves, a fire from heav'n was thrown
That ran amongst them, through the wall, mere added to their own.
The Greeks held not their own; weak Grief went with her wither'd hand,
And dipp'd it deeply in their spirits, since they could not command
Their forces to abide the field, whom harsh Necessity,
To save those ships should bring them home, and their good fort's supply,
Drave to th' expulsive fight they made; and this might stoop them more
Than Need itself could elevate, for ev'n Gods did deplore
Their dire estates, and all the Gods that were their aids in war,
Who, though they could not clear their plights, yet were their friends thus far,
Still to uphold the better sort; for then did Polypæt pass
A lance at Damasus, whose helm was made with cheeks of brass,
Yet had not proof enough, the pile drave through it and his skull.
His brain in blood drown'd, and the man, so late so spiritfull,
Fell now quite spiritless to earth. So emptied he the veins
Of Pylon, and Ormenus' lives. And then Leonteüs gains
The life's end of Hippomachus, Antimachus's son;
His lance fell at his girdle-stead, and with his end begun
Another end. Leonteüs left him, and through the prease
(His keen sword drawn) ran desp'rately upon Antiphates,
And lifeless tumbled him to earth. Nor could all these lives quench
His fi'ry spirit, that his flame in Menon's blood did drench,
And rag'd up ev'n to Iamen's, and young Orestes' life;
All heap'd together made their peace in that red field of strife.
Whose-fair arms while the victors spoil'd, the youth of Ilion
(Of which there serv'd the most and best) still boldly built upon
The wisdom of Polydamas, and Hector's matchless strength,
And follow'd, fill'd with wondrous spirit, with wish and hope at length,
The Greeks' wall won, to fire their fleet. But, having pass'd the dike,
And willing now to pass the wall, this prodigy did strike
Their hearts with some delib'rate stay: A high-flown eagle soar'd
On their troops' left hand, and sustain'd a dragon, all engor'd,
In her strong seres, of wondrous size, and yet had no such check
In life and spirit but still she fought, and turning back her neck
So stung the eagle's gorge, that down she cast her fervent prey
Amongst the multitude, and took upon the winds her way,
Crying with anguish. When they saw a branded serpent sprawl
So full amongst them from above, and from Jove's fowl let fall,
They took it an ostent from him, stood frighted, and their cause
Polydamas thought just, and spake: "Hector, you know, applause
Of humour hath been far from me; nor fits it, or in war,
Or in affairs of court, a man employ'd in public care
To blanch things further than their truth, or flatter any pow'r;
And therefore for that simple course your strength has oft been sour
To me in councils; yet again, what shows in my thoughts best,
I must discover. Let us cease, and make their flight our rest

For this day's honour, and not now attempt the Grecian fleet,
For this, I fear, will be th' event, the prodigy doth meet
So full with our affair in hand. As this high-flying fowl
Upon the left wing of our host, implying our control,
Hover'd above us, and did truss within her golden seres
A serpent so embru'd and big, which yet, in all her fears,
Kept life and fervent spirit to fight, and wrought her own release,
Nor did the eagle's eyry feed; so though we thus far prease
Upon the Grecians, and perhaps may overrun their wall,
Our high minds aiming at their fleet, and that we much appall
Their trusséd spirits; yet are they so serpent-like dispos'd
That they will fight, though in our seres, and will at length be los'd
With all our outcries, and the life of many a Trojan breast
Shall with the eagle fly, before we carry to our nest
Them, or their navy." Thus expounds the augur this ostent,
Whose depth he knows, and these should fear. Hector, with count'nance bent,
Thus answer'd him: "Polydamus, your depth in augury
I like not, and know passing well thou dost not satisfy
Thyself in this opinion; or if thou think'st it true,
Thy thoughts the Gods blind, to advise, and urge that as our due,
That breaks our duties, and to Jove, whose vow and sign to me
Is pass'd directly for our speed; yet light-wing'd birds must be,
By thy advice, our oracles, whose feathers little stay
My serious actions. What care I, if this, or th' other, way
Their wild wings sway them; if the right, on which the sun doth rise,
Or, to the left hand, where he sets? 'Tis Jove's high counsel flys
With those wings that shall bear up us; Jove's, that both earth and heav'n,
Both men and Gods, sustains and rules. One augury is giv'n
To order all men, best of all; Fight for thy country's right.
But why fear'st thou our further charge? For though the dang'rous fight
Strew all men here about the fleet, yet thou need'st never fear
To bear their fates; thy wary heart will never trust thee where
An enemy's look is; and yet fight, for, if thou dar'st abstain,
Or whisper into any ear an abstinence so vain
As thou advisest, never fear that any foe shall take
Thy life from thee, for 'tis this lance." This said, all forwards make,
Himself the first; yet before him exulting Clamour flew,
And thunder-loving Jupiter from lofty Ida blew
A storm that usher'd their assault, and made them charge like him.
It drave directly on the fleet a dust so fierce and dim
That it amaz'd the Grecians, but was a grace divine
To Hector and his following troops, who wholly did incline
To him, being now in grace with Jove, and so put boldly on
To raze the rampire; in whose height they fiercely set upon
The parapets, and pull'd them down, raz'd ev'ry foremost fight,
And all the buttresses of stone, that held their tow'rs upright,
They tore away with crows of iron, and hop'd to ruin all.
The Greeks yet stood, and still repair'd the fore-fights of their wall

With hides of oxen, and from thence, they pour'd down stones in show'rs
Upon the underminer's heads. Within the foremost tow'rs
Both the Ajaces had command, who answer'd ev'ry part,
Th' assaulters, and their soldiers, repress'd, and put in heart;
Repairing valour as their wall; spake some fair, some reprov'd,
Whoever made not good his place; and thus they all sorts mov'd:
"O countrymen, now need in aid would have excess be spent,
The excellent must be admir'd, the meanest excellent,
The worst do well. In changing war all should not be alike,
Nor any idle; which to know fits all, lest Hector strike
Your minds with frights, as ears with threats. Forward be all your hands,
Urge one another. This doubt down, that now betwixt us stands,
Jove will go with us to their walls." To this effect aloud
Spake both the princes; and as high, with this, th' expulsion flow'd.
And as in winter time, when Jove his cold sharp jav'lins throws
Amongst us mortals, and is moved to white earth with his snows,
The winds asleep, he freely pours, till highest prominents,
Hill tops, low meadows, and the fields that crown with most contents
The toils of men, seaports, and shores, are hid, and ev'ry place,
But floods, that snow's fair tender flakes, as their own brood, embrace;
So both sides cover'd earth with stones, so both for life contend,
To show their sharpness; through the wall uproar stood up an end.
Nor had great Hector and his friends the rampire overrun,
If heav'n's great Counsellor, high Jove, had not inflam'd his son
Sarpedon (like the forest's king when he on oxen flies)
Against the Grecians; his round targe he to his arm applies,
Brass-leav'd without, and all within thick ox-hides quilted hard,
The verge nail'd round with rods of gold; and, with two darts prepar'd,
He leads his people. As ye see a mountain-lion fare,
Long kept from prey, in forcing which, his high mind makes him dare
Assault upon the whole full fold, though guarded never so
With well-arm'd men, and eager dogs; away he will not go,
But venture on, and either snatch a prey, or be a prey;
So far'd divine Sarpedon's mind, resolv'd to force his way
Through all the fore-fights, and the wall; yet since he did not see
Others as great as he in name, as great in mind as he,
He spake to Glaucus: [3] "Glaucus, say, why are we honour'd more
Than other men of Lycia, in place; with greater store
Of meats and cups; with goodlier roofs; delightsome gardens; walks;
More lands and better; so much wealth, that court and country talks
Of us and our possessions, and ev'ry way we go,
Gaze on us as we were their Gods? This where we dwell is so;
The shores of Xanthus ring of this; and shall we not exceed
As much in merit as in noise? Come, be we great in deed
As well as look; shine not in gold, but in the flames of fight;
That so our neat-arm'd Lycians may say: 'See, these are right
Our kings, our rulers; these deserve to eat and drink the best;
These govern not ingloriously; these, thus exceed the rest,

Do more than they command to do.' O friend, if keeping back
Would keep back age from us, and death, and that we might not wrack
In this life's human sea at all, but that deferring now
We shunn'd death ever, nor would I half this vain valour show,
Nor glorify a folly so, to wish thee to advance;
But since we must go, though not here, and that, besides the chance
Propos'd now, there are infinite fates of other sort in death,
Which, neither to be fled nor 'scaped, a man must sink beneath,
Come, try we, if this sort be ours, and either render thus
Glory to others, or make them resign the like to us."
This motion Glaucus shifted not, but without words obey'd.
Foreright went both, a mighty troop of Lycians followéd.
Which by Menestheus observ'd, his hair stood up on end,
For, at the tow'r where he had charge, he saw Calamity bend
Her horrid brows in their approach. He threw his looks about
The whole fights near, to see what chief might help the mis'ry out
Of his poor soldiers, and beheld where both th' Ajaces fought,
And Teucer newly come from fleet; whom it would profit nought
To call, since tumult on their helms, shields, and upon the ports,
Laid such loud claps; for ev'ry way, defences of all sorts
Were adding, as Troy took away; and Clamour flew so high
Her wings strook heav'n, and drown'd all voice. The two dukes yet so nigh
And at the offer of assault, he to th' Ajaces sent
Thoos the herald with this charge: "Run to the regiment
Of both th' Ajaces, and call both, for both were better here,
Since here will slaughter, instantly, be more enforc'd than there.
The Lycian captains this way make, who in the fights of stand
Have often show'd much excellence. Yet if laborious hand
Be there more needful than I hope, at least afford us some,
Let Ajax Telamonius and th' archer Teucer come."
The herald hasted, and arriv'd; and both th' Ajaces told,
That Peteus' noble son desir'd their little labour would
Employ himself in succouring him. Both their supplies were best,
Since death assail'd his quarter most; for on it fiercely press'd
The well-prov'd mighty Lycian chiefs. Yet if the service there
Allow'd not both, he pray'd that one part of his charge would bear,
And that was Ajax Telamon, with whom he wish'd would come
The archer Teucer. Telamon left instantly his room
To strong Lycomedes, and will'd Ajax Oiliades
With him to make up his supply, and fill with courages
The Grecian hearts till his return; which should he instantly
When he had well reliev'd his friend. With this the company
Of Teucer he took to his aid; Teucer, that did descend
(As Ajax did) from Telamon. With these two did attend
Pandion, that bore Teucer's bow. When to Menestheus' tow'r
They came, alongst the wall, they found him, and his hearten'd pow'r,
Toiling in making strong their fort. The Lycian princes set
Black whirlwind-like, with both their pow'rs, upon the parapet.

Ajax, and all, resisted them. Clamour amongst them rose.
The slaughter Ajax led; who first the last dear sight did close
Of strong Epicles, that was friend to Jove's great Lycian son.
Amongst the high munition heap, a mighty marble stone
Lay highest, near the pinnacle, a stone of such a paise
That one of this time's strongest men with both hands could not raise,
Yet this did Ajax rouse and throw, and all in sherds did drive
Epicles' four-topp'd casque and skull; who (as ye see one dive
In some deep river) left his height; life left his bones withal.
Teucer shot Glaucus, rushing up yet higher on the wall,
Where naked he discern'd his arm, and made him steal retreat
From that hot service, lest some Greek, with an insulting threat,
Beholding it, might fright the rest. Sarpedon much was griev'd
At Glaucus parting, yet fought on, and his great heart reliev'd
A little with Alcmaon's blood, surnam'd Thestorides,
Whose life he hurl'd out with his lance; which following through the prease
He drew from him. Down from the tow'r Alcmaon dead it strook;
His fair arms ringing out his death. Then fierce Sarpedon took
In his strong hand the battlement, and down he tore it quite,
The wall stripp'd naked, and broad way for entry and full fight
He made the many. Against him Ajax and Teucer made;
Teucer the rich belt on his breast did with a shaft invade;
But Jupiter averted death, who would not see his son
Die at the tails of th' Achive ships. Ajax did fetch his run,
And, with his lance, strook through the targe of that brave Lycian king;
Yet kept he it from further pass, nor did it anything
Dismay his mind, although his men stood off from that high way
His valour made them, which he kept, and hop'd that stormy day
Should ever make his glory clear. His men's fault thus he blam'd:
"O Lycians, why are your hot spirits so quickly disinflam'd?
Suppose me ablest of you all, 'tis hard for me alone
To ruin such a wall as this, and make confusion
Way to their navy. Lend your hands. What many can dispatch,
One cannot think. The noble work of many hath no match."
The wise king's just rebuke did strike a rev'rence to his will
Through all his soldiers; all stood in, and 'gainst all th' Achives still
Made strong their squadrons, insomuch, that to the adverse side,
The work show'd mighty, and the wall, when 'twas within descried,
No easy service; yet the Greeks could neither free their wall
Of these brave Lycians, that held firm the place they first did scale;
Nor could the Lycians from their fort the sturdy Grecians drive,
Nor reach their fleet. But as two men about the limits strive
Of land that toucheth in a field, their measures in their hands,
They mete their parts out curiously, and either stiffly stands
That so far is his right in law, both hugely set on fire
About a passing-little ground; so, greedily aspire
Both these foes to their sev'ral ends, and all exhaust their most
About the very battlements (for yet no more was lost). [4]

With sword and fire they vex'd for them their targes hugely round,
With ox-hides lin'd, and bucklers light; and many a ghastly wound
The stern steel gave for that one prize; whereof though some receiv'd
Their portions on their naked backs, yet others were bereav'd
Of brave lives, face-turn'd, through their shields; tow'rs, bulwarks, ev'rywhere
Were freckled with the blood of men. Nor yet the Greeks did bear
Base back-turn'd faces; nor their foes would therefore be out-fac'd.
But as a spinster poor and just, ye sometimes see, straight-lac'd
About the weighing of her web, who, careful, having charge
For which she would provide some means, is loth to be too large
In giving or in taking weight, but ever with her hand
Is doing with the weights and wool, till both in just paise stand; [5]
So ev'nly stood it with these foes, till Jove to Hector gave
The turning of the scales; who first against the rampire drave,
And spake so loud that all might hear: "O stand not at the pale,
Brave Trojan friends, but mend your hands; up, and break through the wall,
And make a bonfire of their fleet." All heard, and all in heaps
Got scaling-ladders, and aloft. In mean space, Hector leaps
Upon the port, from whose out-part he tore a massy stone,
Thick downwards, upward edg'd; it was so huge an one
That two vast yeomen of most strength, such as these times beget, [6]
Could not from earth lift to a cart, yet he did brandish it
Alone, Saturnius made it light; and swinging it as nought,
He came before the planky gates, that all for strength were wrought,
And kept the port; two-fold they were, and with two rafters barr'd,
High, and strong-lock'd; he rais'd the stone, bent to the hurl so hard,
And made it with so main a strength, that all the gates did crack,
The rafters left them, and the folds one from another brake,
The hinges piecemeal flew, and through the fervent little rock
Thunder'd a passage; with his weight th' inwall his breast did knock,
And in rush'd Hector, fierce and grim as any stormy night;
His brass arms round about his breast reflected terrible light;
Each arm held-up held each a dart; his presence call'd up all
The dreadful spirits his being held, that to the threaten'd wall
None but the Gods might check his way; his eyes were furnaces;
And thus he look'd back, call'd in all. All fir'd their courages,
And in they flow'd. The Grecians fled, their fleet now and their freight
Ask'd all their rescue. Greece went down; Tumult was at his height.

[1] Such maketh Virgil Pandaras and Bitias.

[2] Apta ad rem comparatio.

[3] Sarpedon's speech to Glaucus, neither equalled by any (in this kind) of all that have written.

[4] Admiranda et penè inimitabilis comparatio (saith Spond.); and
yet in the explication of it, he thinks all superfluous but three
words, ὀλίγῳ ἐνὶ χώρῳ, exiguo in loco, leaving out other words

more expressive, with his old rule, uno pede, etc.

[5] A simile superior to the other, in which, comparing mightiest things with meanest, and the meanest illustrating the mightiest, both meeting in one end of this life's preservation and credit, our Homer is beyond comparison and admiration.

[6] Δύ ἀνέρε δήμου, Duo viri plebei.

THE END OF THE TWELFTH BOOK.

THE ARGUMENT

Neptune (in pity of the Greeks' hard plight)
Like Calchas, both th' Ajaces doth excite,
And others, to repel the charging foe.
Idomenëus bravely doth bestow
His kingly forces, and doth sacrifice
Othryonëus to the Destinies,
With divers others. Fair Deiphobus,
And his prophetic brother Helenus,
Are wounded. But the great Priamides.
Gath'ring his forces, heartens their address
Against the enemy; and then the field
A mighty death on either side doth yield.

ANOTHER ARGUMENT

The Greeks, with Troy's bold pow'r dismay'd,
Are cheer'd by Neptune's secret aid.
Jove helping Hector, and his host, thus close Achive fleet,
He let them then their own strengths try, and season there their sweet
With ceaseless toils and grievances; for now he turn'd his face,
Look'd down, and view'd the far-off land of well-rode men in Thrace,
Of the renown'd milk-nourish'd men, the Hippemolgians,
Long-liv'd, most just, and innocent, and close-fought Mysians.
Nor turn'd he any more to Troy his ever-shining eyes,
Because he thought not any one, of all the Deities,
When his care left th' indiff'rent field, would aid on either side.
But this security in Jove the great Sea-Rector spied,
Who sat aloft on th' utmost top of shady Samothrace,
And view'd the fight. His chosen seat stood in so brave a place,
That Priam's city, th' Achive ships, all Ida, did appear

To his full view; who from the sea was therefore seated there.
He took much ruth to see the Greeks by Troy sustain such ill,
And, mightily incens'd with Jove, stoop'd straight from that steep hill,
That shook as he flew off, so hard his parting press'd the height.
The woods, and all the great hills near, trembled beneath the weight
Of his immortal moving feet. Three steps he only took,
Before he far-off Ægas reach'd, but, with the fourth, it shook
With his dread entry. In the depth of those seas he did hold
His bright and glorious palace, built of never-rusting gold;
And there arriv'd, he put in coach his brazen-footed steeds,
All golden-maned, and pac'd with wings; and all in golden weeds
He cloth'd himself. The golden scourge, most elegantly done,
He took, and mounted to his seat; and then the God begun
To drive his chariot through the waves. From whirlpits ev'ry way
The whales exulted under him, and knew their king; the sea
For joy did open; and, his horse so swift and lightly flew,
The under axletree of brass no drop of water drew;
And thus these deathless coursers brought their king to th' Achive ships.
'Twixt th' Imber cliffs and Tenedos, a certain cavern creeps
Into the deep sea's gulfy breast, and there th' Earth-shaker stay'd
His forward steeds, took them from coach, and heav'nly fodder laid
In reach before them; their brass hoves he girt with gyves of gold,
Not to be broken, nor dissolved, to make them firmly hold
A fit attendance on their king; who went to th' Achive host,
Which, like to tempests or wild flames, the clust'ring Trojans tost,
Insatiably valorous, in Hector's like command,
High sounding, and resounding, shouts; for hope cheer'd ev'ry hand,
To make the Greek fleet now their prise, and all the Greeks destroy.
But Neptune, circler of the earth, with fresh heart did employ
The Grecian hands. In strength of voice and body he did take
Calchas' resemblance, and, of all, th' Ajaces first bespake,
Who of themselves were free enough: "Ajaces, you alone
Sustain the common good of Greece, in ever putting on
The memory of fortitude, and flying shameful flight.
Elsewhere the desp'rate hands of Troy could give me no affright,
The brave Greeks have withstood their worst; but this our mighty wall
Being thus transcended by their pow'r, grave fear doth much appall
My careful spirits, lest we feel some fatal mischief here,
Where Hector, raging like a flame, doth in his charge appear,
And boasts himself the best God's son. Be you conceited so,
And fire so, more than human spirits, that God may seem to do
In your deeds, and, with such thoughts cheer'd, others to such exhort,
And such resistance; these great minds will in as great a sort
Strengthen your bodies, and force check to all great Hector's charge,
Though ne'er so spirit-like, and though Jove still, past himself, enlarge
His sacred actions." Thus he touched, with his fork'd sceptre's point,
The breasts of both; fill'd both their spirits, and made up ev'ry joint
With pow'r responsive; when, hawk-like, swift, and set sharp to fly,

That fiercely stooping from a rock, inaccessible and high,
Cuts through a field, and sets a fowl (not being of her kind)
Hard, and gets ground still; Neptune so left these two, either's mind
Beyond themselves rais'd. Of both which, Oïleus first discern'd
The masking Deity, and said: "Ajax, some God hath warn'd
Our pow'rs to fight, and save our fleet. He put on him the hue
Of th' augur Calchas. By his pace, in leaving us, I knew,
Without all question, 'twas a God; the Gods are eas'ly known;
And in my tender breast I feel a greater spirit blown,
To execute affairs of fight; I find my hands so free
To all high motion, and my feet seem feather'd under me,"
This Telamonius thus receiv'd: "So, to my thoughts, my hands
Burn with desire to toss my lance; each foot beneath me stands
Bare on bright fire, to use his speed; my heart is rais'd so high
That to encounter Hector's self, I long insatiately."
While these thus talk'd, as overjoy'd with study for the fight,
(Which God had stirr'd up in their spirits) the same God did excite
The Greeks that were behind at fleet, refreshing their free hearts
And joints, being ev'n dissolv'd with toil; and (seeing the desp'rate parts
Play'd by the Trojans past their wall) grief strook them, and their eyes
Sweat tears from under their sad lids, their instant destinies
Never supposing they could 'scape. But Neptune, stepping in,
With ease stirr'd up the able troops, and did at first begin
With Teucer, and Peneleüs, th' heroe Leitus,
Deipyrus, Meriones, and young Antilochus,
All éxpert in the deeds of arms: "O youths of Greece," said he,
"What change is this? In your brave fight, I only look'd to see
Our fleet's whole safety; and, if you neglect the harmful field,
Now shines the day when Greece to Troy must all her honours yield.
O grief! So great a miracle, and horrible to sight,
As now I see, I never thought could have profan'd the light!
The Trojans brave us at our ships, that have been heretofore
Like faint and fearful deer in woods, distracted evermore
With ev'ry sound, and yet 'scape not, but prove the torn up fare
Of lynces, wolves, and lëopards, as never born to war.
Nor durst these Trojans at first siege, in any least degree,
Expect your strength, or stand one shock of Grecian chivalry;
Yet now, far from their walls, they dare fight at our fleet maintain,
All by our Gen'ral's cowardice, that doth infect his men
Who, still at odds with him, for that will needs themselves neglect,
And suffer slaughter in their ships. Suppose there was defect
(Beyond all question) in our king, to wrong Æacides,
And he, for his particular wreak, from all assistance cease;
We must not cease t' assist ourselves. Forgive our Gen'ral then,
And quickly too. Apt to forgive are all good-minded men.
Yet you, quite void of their good minds, give good, in you quite lost,
For ill in others, though ye be the worthiest of your host.
As old as I am, I would scorn, to fight with one that flies,

Or leaves the fight as you do now. The Gen'ral slothful lies,
And you, though slothful too, maintain with him a fight of spleen.
Out, out, I hate ye from my heart. Ye rotten-minded men,
In this ye add an ill that's worse than all your sloth's dislikes.
But as I know to all your hearts my reprehension strikes,
So thither let just shame strike too; for while you stand still here
A mighty fight swarms at your fleet, great Hector rageth there,
Hath burst the long bar and the gates." Thus Neptune rous'd these men,
And round about th' Ajaces did their phalanxes maintain
Their station firm; whom Mars himself, had he amongst them gone,
Could not disparage, nor Jove's Maid that sets men fiercer on;
For now the best were chosen out, and they receiv'd th' advance
Of Hector and his men so full, that lance was lin'd with lance,
Shields thicken'd with opposéd shields, targets to targets nail'd,
Helms stuck to helms, and man to man grew, they so close assail'd,
Plum'd casques were hang'd in either's plumes, all join'd so close their stands,
Their lances stood, thrust out so thick by such all-daring hands,
All bent their firm breasts to the point, and made sad fight their joy
Of both. Troy all in heaps strook first, and Hector first of Troy.
And as a round piece of a rock, which with a winter's flood
Is from his top torn, when a show'r, pour'd from a bursten cloud,
Hath broke the natural bond it held within the rough steep rock,
And, jumping, it flies down the woods, resounding ev'ry shock,
And on, uncheck'd, it headlong leaps, till in a plain it stay,
And then, though never so impell'd, it stirs not any way;
So Hector hereto throated threats, to go to sea in blood,
And reach the Grecian ships and tents, without being once withstood.
But when he fell into the strengths the Grecians did maintain,
And that they fought upon the square, he stood as fetter'd then;
And so the adverse sons of Greece laid on with swords and darts,
Whose both ends hurt, that they repell'd his worst; and he converts
His threats, by all means, to retreats; yet made as he retir'd,
Only t' encourage those behind; and thus those men inspir'd:
"Trojans! Dardanians! Lycians! All warlike friends, stand close;
The Greeks can never bear me long, though tow'r-like they oppose.
This lance, be sure, will be their spoil; if ev'n the best of Gods,
High thund'ring Juno's husband, stirs my spirit with true abodes,"
With this all strengths and minds he mov'd; but young Deiphobus,
Old Priam's son, amongst them all was chiefly virtuous,
He bore before him his round shield, tripp'd lightly through the prease,
At all parts cover'd with his shield; and him Meriones
Charg'd with a glitt'ring dart, that took his bull-hide orby shield,
Yet pierc'd it not, but in the top itself did piecemeal yield,
Deiphobus thrust forth his targe, and fear'd the broken ends
Of strong Meriones's lance, who now turn'd to his friends;
The great heroë scorning much by such a chance to part
With lance and conquest, forth he went to fetch another dart,
Left at his tent. The rest fought on, the clamour heighten'd there

Was most unmeasur'd. Teucer first did flesh the massacre,
And slew a goodly man at arms, the soldier Imbrius,
The son of Mentor, rich in horse; he dwelt at Pedasus
Before the sons of Greece sieg'd Troy; from whence he married
Medesicaste, one that sprung of Priam's bastard-bed;
But when the Greek ships, double-oar'd, arriv'd at Ilion,
To Ilion he return'd, and prov'd beyond comparison
Amongst the Trojans; he was lodg'd with Priam, who held dear
His natural sons no more than him; yet him, beneath the ear,
The son of Telamon attain'd, and drew his lance. He fell,
As when an ash on some hill's top (itself topp'd wondrous well)
The steel hews down, and he presents his young leaves to the soil;
So fell he, and his fair arms groan'd, which Teucer long'd to spoil,
And in he ran; and Hector in, who sent a shining lance
At Teucer, who, beholding it, slipp'd by, and gave it chance
On Actor's son, Amphimachus, whose breast it strook; and in
Flew Hector, at his sounding fall, with full intent to win
The tempting helmet from his head; but Ajax with a dart
Reach'd Hector at his rushing in, yet touch'd not any part
About his body; it was hid quite through with horrid brass;
The boss yet of his targe it took, whose firm stuff stay'd the pass,
And he turn'd safe from both the trunks; both which the Grecians bore
From off the field. Amphimachus Menestheus did restore,
And Stichius, to th' Achaian strength. Th' Ajaces (that were pleas'd
Still most with most hot services) on Trojan Imbrius seiz'd.
And as from sharply-bitten hounds, a brace of lions force
A new-slain goat, and through the woods bear in their jaws the corse
Aloft, lift up into the air; so, up into the skies,
Bore both th' Ajaces Imbrius, and made his arms their prise.
Yet, not content, Oïliades, enrag'd to see there dead
His much-belov'd Amphimachus, he hew'd off Imbrius' head;
Which, swinging round, bowl-like he toss'd amongst the Trojan prease,
And full at Hector's feet it fell. Amphimachus' decease,
Being nephew to the God of waves, much vex'd the Deity's mind,
And to the ships and tents he march'd, yet more to make inclin'd
The Grecians to the Trojan bane. In hasting to which end,
Idomenëus met with him, returning from a friend,
Whose ham late hurt, his men brought off; and having giv'n command
To his physicians for his cure, much fir'd to put his hand
To Troy's repulse, he left his tent. Him (like Andremon's son,
Prince Thoas, that in Pleuron rul'd, and lofty Calydon,
Th' Ætolian pow'rs, and like a God was of his subjects lov'd)
Neptune encounter'd, and but thus his forward spirit mov'd:
"Idomenëus, prince of Crete! O whither now are fled
Those threats in thee, with which the rest the Trojans menacéd?"
"O Thoas," he replied, "no one of all our host stands now
In any question of reproof, as I am let to know,
And why is my intelligence false? We all know how to fight,

And, (fear disanimating none) all do our knowledge right.
Nor can our harms accuse our sloth, not one from work we miss.
The great God only works our ill, whose pleasure now it is
That, far from home, in hostile fields, and with inglorious fate,
Some Greeks should perish. But do thou, O Thoas, that of late
Hast prov'd a soldier, and was wont, where thou hast sloth beheld,
To chide it, and exhort to pains, now hate to be repell'd,
And set on all men." He replied, "I would to heav'n, that he,
Whoever this day doth abstain from battle willingly,
May never turn his face from Troy, but here become the prey
And scorn of dogs! Come then, take arms, and let our kind assay
Join both our forces. Though but two, yet, being both combin'd,
The work of many single hands we may perform. We find,
That virtue co-augmented thrives in men of little mind,
But we have singly match'd the great." Thus said, the God again,
With all his conflicts, visited the vent'rous flight of men.
The king turn'd to his tent; rich arms put on his breast, and took
Two darts in hand, and forth he flew. His haste on made him look
Much like a fi'ry meteor, with which Jove's sulph'ry hand
Opes heav'n, and hurls about the air bright flashes, showing aland
Abodes that ever run before tempest and plagues to men:
So, in his swift pace, show'd his arms. He was encounter'd then
By his good friend Meriones yet near his tent; to whom
Thus spake the pow'r of Idomen: "What reason makes thee come,
Thou son of Molus, my most lov'd, thus leaving fight alone?
Is't for some wound? The jav'lin's head, still sticking in the bone,
Desir'st thou ease of? Bring'st thou news? Or what is it that brings
Thy presence hither? Be assur'd, my spirit needs no stings
To this hot conflict. Of myself thou seest I come, and loth,
For any tent's love, to deserve the hateful taint of sloth."
He answer'd: Only for a dart, he that retreat did make,
(Were any left him at his tent) for, that he had, he brake
On proud Deiphobus's shield. "Is one dart all?" said he,
"Take one and twenty, if thou like, for in my tent they be;
They stand there shining by the walls. I took them as my prise
From those false Trojans I have slain. And this is not the guise
Of one that loves his tent, or fights afar off with his foe,
But since I love fight, therefore doth my martial star bestow,
Besides those darts, helms, targets boss'd, and corslets bright as day."
"So I," said Merion, "at my tent, and sable bark, may say,
I many Trojan spoils retain, but now not near they be,
To serve me for my present use; and therefore ask I thee.
Not that I lack a fortitude to store me with my own,
For ever in the foremost fights, that render men renown,
I fight, when any fight doth stir. And this perhaps may well
Be hid to others, but thou know'st, and I to thee appeal."
"I know," replied the king, "how much thou weigh'st in ev'ry worth,
What need'st thou therefore utter this? If we should now choose forth

The worthiest men for ambushes, in all our fleet and host,
(For ambushes are services that try men's virtues most,
Since there the fearful and the firm will, as they are, appear,
The fearful alt'ring still his hue, and rests not anywhere,
Nor is his spirit capable of th' ambush constancy,
But riseth, changeth still his place, and croucheth curiously
On his bent haunches; half his height scarce seen above the ground,
For fear to be seen, yet must see; his heart, with many a bound,
Off'ring to leap out of his breast, and, ever fearing death,
The coldness of it makes him gnash, and half shakes out his teeth;
Where men of valour neither fear, nor ever change their looks,
From lodging th' ambush till it rise, but, since there must be strokes,
Wish to be quickly in their midst) thy strength and hand in these
Who should reprove? For if, far off, or fighting in the prease,
Thou shouldst be wounded, I am sure the dart that gave the wound
Should not be drawn out of thy back, or make thy neck the ground,
But meet thy belly, or thy breast, in thrusting further yet
When thou art furthest, till the first, and before him, thou get.
But on; like children let not us stand bragging thus, but do;
Lest some hear, and past measure chide, that we stand still and woo.
Go, choose a better dart, and make Mars yield a better chance."
This said, Mars-swift Meriones, with haste, a brazen lance
Took from his tent, and overtook, most careful of the wars,
Idomenëus, And such two, in field, as harmful Mars,
And Terror, his belovéd son, that without terror fights,
And is of such strength that in war the frighter he affrights,
When, out of Thrace, they both take arms against th' Ephyran bands,
Or 'gainst the great-soul'd Phlegians, nor favour their own hands,
But give the grace to others still; in such sort to the fight,
March'd these two managers of men, in armours full of light.
And first spake Merion: "On which part, son of Deucalion,
Serves thy mind to invade the fight? Is't best to set upon
The Trojans, in our battle's aid, the right or left-hand wing,
For all parts I suppose employ'd?" To this the Cretan king
Thus answer'd: "In our navy's midst are others that assist;
The two Ajaces; Teucer too, with shafts the expertest
Of all the Grecians, and, though small, is great in fights of stand;
And these (though huge he be of strength) will serve to fill the hand
Of Hector's self, that Priamist, that studier for blows.
It shall be call'd a deed of height for him (even suff'ring throes
For knocks still) to outlabour them, and, bett'ring their tough hands,
Enflame our fleet. If Jove himself cast not his fire-brands
Amongst our navy, that affair no man can bring to field.
Great Ajax Telamonius to none alive will yield
That yields to death, and whose life takes Ceres' nutritions,
That can be cut with any iron, or pash'd with mighty stones;
Not to Æacides himself he yields for combats set,
Though clear he must give place for pace and free swing of his feet.

Since then, the battle (being our place of most care) is made good
By his high valour, let our aid see all pow'rs be withstood
That charge the left wing, and to that let us direct our course,
Where quickly feel we this hot foe, or make him feel our force."
This order'd, swift Meriones went, and forewent his king,
Till both arriv'd where one enjoin'd. When, in the Greeks' left wing,
The Trojans saw the Cretan king, like fire in fortitude,
And his attendant, in bright arms so gloriously indu'd,
Both cheering the sinister troops, all at the king address'd,
And so the skirmish at their sterns on both parts were increas'd,
That, as from hollow bustling winds engender'd storms arise,
When dust doth chiefly clog the ways which up into the skies
The wanton tempest ravisheth, begetting night of day;
So came together both the foes, both lusted to assay,
And work with quick steel either's death. Man's fierce corruptress, Fight,
Set up her bristles in the field with lances long and light,
Which thick fell foul on either's face. The splendour of the steel,
In new-scour'd curets, radiant casques, and burnish'd shields, did seel
Th' assailer's eyes up. He sustain'd a huge spirit, that was glad
To see that labour, or in soul that stood not stricken sad.
Thus these two disagreeing Gods, old Saturn's mighty sons,
Afflicted these heroic men with huge oppressións.
Jove honouring Æacides (to let the Greeks still try
Their want without him) would bestow, yet still, the victory
On Hector, and the Trojan pow'r; yet for Æacides,
And honour of his mother-queen, great Goddess of the seas,
He would not let proud Ilion see the Grecians quite destroy'd,
And therefore from the hoary deep he suffered so employ'd
Great Neptune in the Grecian aid; who griev'd for them, and storm'd
Extremely at his brother Jove. Yet both one Goddess form'd,
And one soil bred, but Jupiter precedence took in birth,
And had more knowledge; for which cause, the other came not forth [1]
Of his wet kingdom, but with care of not being seen t' excite
The Grecian host, and like a man appear'd, and made the fight.
So these Gods made men's valours great, but equall'd them with war
As harmful as their hearts were good; and stretch'd those chains as far
On both sides as their limbs could bear, in which they were involv'd
Past breach, or loosing, that their knees might therefore be dissolv'd.
Then, though a half-grey man he were, Crete's sov'reign did excite
The Greeks to blows, and flew upon the Trojans, ev'n to flight;
For he, in sight of all the host, Othryonëus slew,
That from Cabesus, with the fame of those wars, thither drew
His new-come forces, and requir'd, without respect of dow'r,
Cassandra, fair'st of Priam's race; assuring with his pow'r
A mighty labour, to expell, in their despite, from Troy
The sons of Greece. The king did vow, that done, he should enjoy
His goodliest daughter. He (in trust of that fair purchase) fought;
And at him threw the Cretan king a lance, that singled out

This great assumer, whom it strook just in his navel-stead.
His brazen curets helping nought, resign'd him to the dead.
Then did the conqueror exclaim, and thus insulted then:
"Othryonëus, I will praise, beyond all mortal men,
Thy living virtues, if thou wilt now perfect the brave vow
Thou mad'st to Priam, for the wife he promis'd to bestow.
And where he should have kept his word, there we assure thee here,
To give thee for thy princely wife the fairest and most dear
Of our great Gen'ral's female race, which from his Argive hall
We all will wait upon to Troy, if, with our aids, and all,
Thou wilt but raze this well-built town. Come, therefore, follow me,
That in our ships we may conclude this royal match with thee.
I'll be no jot worse than my word." With that he took his feet,
And dragg'd him through the fervent fight; in which did Asius meet
The victor, to inflict revenge. He came on foot before
His horse, that on his shoulders breath'd; so closely evermore
His coachman led them to his lord; who held a huge desire
To strike the king, but he strook first, and underneath his chin,
At his throat's height, through th' other side, his eager lance drave in;
And down he bustled like an oak, a poplar, or a pine,
Hewn down for shipwood, and so lay. His fall did so decline
The spirit of his charioteer, that, lest he should incense
The victor to impair his spoil, he durst not drive from thence
His horse and chariot; and so pleas'd, with that respective part,
Antilochus, that for his fear he reach'd him with a dart
About his belly's midst, and down his sad corse fell beneath
The richly built chariot, there labouring out his breath.
The horse Antilochus took off; when, griev'd for this event,
Deiphobus drew passing near, and at the victor sent
A shining jav'lin; which he saw, and shunn'd, with gath'ring round
His body in his all-round shield, at whose top, with a sound,
It overflew; yet, seizing there, it did not idly fly
from him that wing'd it, his strong hand still drave it mortally
On Prince Hypsenor; it did pierce his liver, underneath
The veins it passeth; his shrunk knees submitted him to death.
And then did lov'd Deiphobus miraculously vaunt:
"Now Asius lies not unreveng'd, nor doth his spirit want
The joy I wish it, though it be now ent'ring the strong gate
Of mighty Pluto, since this hand hath sent him down a mate."
This glory in him griev'd the Greeks, and chiefly the great mind
Of martial Antilochus, who though to grief inclin'd,
He left not yet his friend, but ran and hid him with his shield;
And to him came two lovely friends, that freed him from the field,
Mecisteus, son of Echius, and the right nobly born
Alastor, bearing him to fleet, and did extremely mourn.
Idomenëus sunk not yet, but held his nerves entire,
His mind much less deficient, being fed with firm desire
To hide more Trojans in dim night, or sink himself in guard

Of his lov'd countrymen. And then Alcathous prepar'd
Work for his valour, off'ring fate his own destructión.
A great heroë, and had grace to be the lovéd son
Of Æsyetes, son-in-law to prince Æneas' sire,
Hippodamia marrying; who most enflam'd the fire
Of her dear parents' love, and took precedence in her birth
Of all their daughters, and as much exceeded in her worth
(For beauty answer'd with her mind, and both with housewif'ry)
All the fair beauty of young dames that us'd her company,
And therefore, being the worthiest dame, the worthiest man did wed
Of ample Troy. Him Neptune stoop'd beneath the royal force
Of Idomen, his sparkling eyes deluding, and the course
Of his illustrious lineaments so out of nature bound,
That back nor forward he could stir, but, as he grew to ground,
Stood like a pillar, or high tree, and neither mov'd, nor fear'd;
When straight the royal Cretan's dart in his mid breast appear'd,
It brake the curets, that were proof to ev'ry other dart,
Yet now they cleft and rung; the lance stuck shaking in his heart;
His heart with panting made it shake; but Mars did now remit
The greatness of it, and the king, now quitting the brag fit
Of glory in Deiphobus, thus terribly exclaim'd:
"Deiphobus, now may we think that we are ev'nly fam'd,
That three for one have sent to Dis. But come, change blows with me,
Thy vaunts for him thou slew'st were vain. Come, wretch, that thou may'st see
What issue Jove hath. Jove begot Minos, the strength of Crete;
Minos begot Deucalion; Deucalion did beget
Me Idomen, now Creta's king, that here my ships have brought
To bring thyself, thy father, friends, all Ilion's pomp, to nought."
Deiphobus at two ways stood, in doubt to call some one,
With some retreat, to be his aid, or try the chance alone.
At last, the first seem'd best to him, and back he went to call
Anchises' son to friend, who stood in troop the last of all,
Where still he serv'd; which made him still incense against the king,
That, being amongst his best their peer, he grac'd not anything
His wrong'd deserts. Deiphobus spake to him, standing near:
"Æneas, prince of Troians, if any touch appear
Of glory in thee, thou must now assist thy sister's lord,
And one that to thy tend'rest youth did careful guard afford,
Alcathous, whom Creta's king hath chiefly slain to thee,
His right most challenging thy band. Come, therefore, follow me."
This much excited his good mind, and set his heart on fire
Against the Cretan, who child-like dissolv'd not in his ire,
But stood him firm. As when in hills a strength relying boar,
Alone, and hearing hunters come, whom tumult flies before,
Up-thrusts his bristles, whets his tusks, sets fire on his red eyes,
And in his brave prepar'd repulse doth dogs and men despise;
So stood the famous-for-his-lance, nor shunn'd the coming charge
That resolute Æneas brought. Yet, since the odds was large,

He call'd with good right to his aid war-skill'd Ascalaphus,
Aphareüs, Meriones, the strong Deipyrus,
And Nestor's honourable son: "Come near, my friends," said he,
"And add your aids to me alone. Fear taints me worthily,
Though firm I stand, and show it not. Æneas great in fight,
And one that bears youth in his flow'r, that bears the greatest might,
Comes on with aim direct at me. Had I his youthful limb
To bear my mind, he should yield fame, or I would yield it him."
This said, all held, in many souls, one ready helpful mind,
Clapp'd shields and shoulders, and stood close. Æneas, not inclin'd
With more presumption than the king, call'd aid as well as he,
Divine Agenor, Helen's love, who follow'd instantly,
And all their forces following them; as after bellwethers
The whole flocks follow to their drink, which sight the shepherd cheers.
Nor was Æneas' joy less mov'd to see such troops attend
His honour'd person; and all these fought close about his friend;
But two of them, past all the rest, had strong desire to shed
The blood of either; Idomen, and Cytherea's seed.
Æneas first bestow'd his lance, which th' other seeing shunn'd,
And that, thrown from an idle hand, stuck trembling in the ground.
But Idomen's, discharg'd at him, had no such vain success,
Which Œnomaus' entrails found, in which it did impress
His sharp pile to his fall; his palms tore his returning earth.
Idomenëus straight stepp'd in, and pluck'd his jav'lin forth,
But could not spoil his goodly arms, they press'd him so with darts.
And now the long toil of the fight had spent his vig'rous parts,
And made them less apt to avoid the foe that should advance,
Or, when himself advanc'd again, to run and fetch his lance,
And therefore in stiff fights of stand he spent the cruel day.
When, coming softly from the slain, Deiphobus gave way
To his bright jav'lin at the king, whom he could never brook;
But then he lost his envy too. His lance yet deadly took
Ascalaphus, the son of Mars; quite through his shoulder flew
The violent head, and down he fell. Nor yet by all means knew
Wide-throated Mars his son was fall'n, but in Olympus' top
Sat canopied with golden clouds; Jove's counsel had shut up
Both him and all the other Gods from that time's equal task,
Which now, about Ascalaphus, strife set. His shining casque
Deiphobus had forc'd from him, but instantly leap'd in
Mars-swift Meriones, and strook, with his long javelin,
The right arm of Deiphobus, which made his hand let fall
The sharp-topp'd helmet; the press'd earth resounding there withal.
When, vulture-like, Meriones rush'd in again and drew,
From out the low part of his arm his jav'lin, and then flew
Back to his friends. Deiphobus, faint with the blood's excess
Fall'n from his wound, was carefully convey'd out of the press
By his kind brother by both sides, Polites, till they gat
His horse and chariot that were still set fit for his retreat,

And bore him now to Ilion. The rest fought fiercely on,
And set a mighty fight on foot. When next, Anchises' son
Aphareus Caletorides, that ran upon him, strook
Just in the throat with his keen lance; and straight his head forsook
His upright carriage; and his shield, his helm, and all, with him
Fell to the earth; where ruinous death made prise of ev'ry limb.
Antilochus, discov'ring well that Thoon's heart took check,
Let fly, and cut the hollow vein, that runs up to his neck,
Along his back part, quite in twain; down in the dust he fell,
Upwards, and, with extended hands, bade all the world farewell.
Antilochus rush'd nimbly in, and, looking round, made prise
Of his fair arms; in which affair his round-set enemies
Let fly their lances, thundering on his advanced targe,
But could not get his flesh. The God that shakes the earth took charge
Of Nestor's son and kept him safe; who never was away,
But still amongst the thickest foes his busy lance did play,
Observing ever when he might, far off, or near, offend;
And watching Asius' son, in prease he spied him, and did send,
Close coming on, a dart at him, that smote in midst his shield,
In which the sharp head of the lance the blue-hair'd God made yield,
Not pleas'd to yield his pupil's life; in whose shield half the dart
Stuck like a truncheon burn'd with fire; on earth lay th' other part.
He, seeing no better end of all, retir'd in fear of worse
But him Meriones pursu'd; and his lance found full course
To th' other's life. It wounded him betwixt the privy parts
And navel, where, to wretched men that war's most violent smarts
Must undergo, wounds chiefly vex. His dart Meriones
Pursu'd, and Adamas so striv'd with it, and his misease,
As doth a bullock puff and storm, whom in disdainéd bands
The upland herdsmen strive to cast; so, fall'n beneath the hands
Of his stern foe, Asiades did struggle, pant, and rave.
But no long time; for when the lance was pluck'd out, up he gave
His tortur'd soul. Then Troy's turn came; when with a Thracian sword
The temples of Deipyrus did Helenus afford
So huge a blow, it strook all light out of his cloudy eyes,
And cleft his helmet; which a Greek, there fighting, made his prise,
It fell so full beneath his feet. Atrides griev'd to see
That sight, and, threat'ning, shook a lance at Helenus, and he
A bow half drew at him; at once out flew both shaft and lance.
The shaft Atrides' curets strook; and far away did glance.
Atrides' dart of Helenus the thrust out bow-hand strook,
And, through the hand, stuck in the bow. Agenor's hand did pluck
From forth the nailéd prisoner the jav'lin quickly out;
And fairly, with a little wool, enwrapping round about
The wounded hand, within a scarf he bore it, which his squire
Had ready for him. Yet the wound would needs he should retire.
Pisander, to revenge his hurt, right on the king ran he.
A bloody fate suggested him to let him run on thee,

O Menelaus, that he might, by thee, in dang'rous war
Be done to death. Both coming on, Atrides' lance did err.
Pisander strook Atrides' shield, that brake at point the dart
Not running through; yet he rejoic'd as playing a victor's part.
Atrides, drawing his fair sword, upon Pisander flew;
Pisander, from beneath his shield, his goodly weapon drew,
Two-edg'd, with right sharp steel, and long, the handle olive-tree,
Well-polish'd; and to blows they go. Upon the top strook he
Atrides' horse-hair'd-feather'd helm; Atrides on his brow,
Above th' extreme part of his nose, laid such a heavy blow
That all the bones crash'd under it, and out his eyes did drop
Before his feet in bloody dust; he after, and shrunk up
His dying body, which the foot of his triumphing foe
Open'd, and stood upon his breast, and off his arms did go,
This insultation us'd the while: "At length forsake our fleet,
Thus ye false Trojans, to whom war never enough is sweet.
Nor want ye more impieties, with which ye have abus'd
Me, ye bold dogs, that your chief friends so honourably us'd.
Nor fear you hospitable Jove, that lets such thunders go.
But build upon't, he will unbuild your tow'rs that clamber so,
For ravishing my goods, and wife, in flow'r of all her years,
And without cause; nay, when that fair and lib'ral hand of hers
Had us'd you so most lovingly. And now again ye would
Cast fire into our fleet, and kill our princes if ye could.
Go to, one day you will be curb'd, though never so ye thirst
Rude war, by war. O father Jove, they say thou art the first
In wisdom of all Gods and men, yet all this comes from thee,
And still thou gratifiest these men, how lewd so e'er they be,
Though never they be cloy'd with sins, nor can be satiate,
As good men should, with this vile war. Satiety of state,
Satiety of sleep and love, satiety of ease,
Of music, dancing, can find place; yet harsh war still must please
Past all these pleasures, ev'n past these. They will be cloy'd with these
Before their war joys. Never war gives Troy satieties."
This said, the bloody arms were oft; and to his soldiers thrown,
He mixing in first fight again. And then Harpalion,
Kind king Pylæmen's son, gave charge; who to those wars of Troy
His lovéd father followéd, nor ever did enjoy
His country's sight again. He strook the targe of Atreus' son
Full in the midst; his jav'lin's steel yet had no pow'r to run
The target through; nor had himself the heart to fetch his lance,
But took him to his strength, and cast on ev'ry side a glance,
Lest any his dear sides should dart. But Merion, as he fled,
Sent after him a brazen lance, that ran his eager head
Through his right hip, and all along the bladder's región
Beneath the bone; it settled him, and set his spirit gone
Amongst the hands of his best friends; and like a worm he lay
Stretch'd on the earth, which his black blood imbru'd, and flow'd away.

His corse the Paphlagonians did sadly wait upon,
Repos'd in his rich chariot, to sacred Ilion;
The king his father following, dissolv'd in kindly tears,
And no wreak sought for his slain son. But, at his slaughterers
Incenséd Paris spent a lance, since he had been a guest
To many Paphlagonians; and through the prease it press'd.
There was a certain augur's son, that did for wealth excell,
And yet was honest; he was born, and did at Corinth dwell;
Who, though he knew his harmful fate, would needs his ship ascend.
His father, Polyidus, oft would tell him that his end
Would either seize him at his house, upon a sharp disease,
Or else among the Grecian ships by Trojans slain. Both these
Together he desir'd to shun; but the disease, at last,
And ling'ring death in it, he left, and war's quick stroke embrac'd.
The lance betwixt his ear and cheek ran in, and drave the mind
Of both those bitter fortunes out. Night strook his whole pow'rs blind.
Thus fought they, like the spirit of fire; nor Jove-lov'd Hector knew
How in the fleet's left wing the Greeks his down-put soldiers slew
Almost to victory; the God that shakes the earth so well
Help'd with his own strength, and the Greeks so fiercely did impel.
Yet Hector made the first place good, where both the ports and wall
(The thick rank of the Greek shields broke) he enter'd, and did skall,
Where on the gray sea's shore were drawn (the wall being there but slight)
Protesilaus' ships, and those of Ajax, where the fight
Of men and horse were sharpest set. There the Bœotian bands,
Long-rob'd Iaons, Locrians, and, brave men of their hands,
The Phthian and Epeian troops did spritefully assail
The god-like Hector rushing in; and yet could not prevail
To his repulse, though choicest men of Athens there made head;
Amongst whom was Menestheus chief, whom Phidias followéd,
Stichius and Bias, huge in strength. Th' Epeian troops were led
By Meges' and Phylides' cares, Amphion, Dracius.
Before the Phthians Medon march'd, and Meneptolemus;
And these, with the Bœotian pow'rs, bore up the fleet's defence.
Oïleus by his brother's side stood close, and would not thence
For any moment of that time. But, as through fallow fields
Black oxen draw a well-join'd plough, and either ev'nly yields
His thrifty labour, all heads couch'd so close to earth they plow
The fallow with their horns, till out the sweat begins to flow,
The stretch'd yokes crack, and yet at last the furrow forth is driven;
So toughly stood these to their task, and made their work as even.
But Ajax Telamonius had many helpful men
That, when sweat ran about his knees, and labour flow'd, would then
Help bear his mighty sev'n-fold shield; when swift Oïliades
The Locrians left, and would not make those murth'rous fights of prease,
Because they wore no bright steel casques, nor bristled plumes for show,
Round shields, nor darts of solid ash, but with the trusty bow,
And jacks well-quilted with soft wool, they came to Troy, and were,

In their fit place, as confident as those that fought so near,
And reach'd their foes so thick with shafts, that these were they that brake
The Trojan orders first; and then, the brave arm'd men did make
Good work with their close fights before. Behind whom, having shot,
The Locrians hid still; and their foes all thought of fight forgot
With shows of those far-striking shafts, their eyes were troubled so.
And then, assur'dly, from the ships, and tents, th' insulting foe
Had miserably fled to Troy, had not Polydamas
Thus spake to Hector: "Hector, still impossible 'tis to pass
Good counsel upon you. But say some God prefers thy deeds,
In counsels wouldst thou pass us too? In all things none exceeds.
To some God gives the pow'r of war, to some the sleight to dance,
To some the art of instruments, some doth for voice advance;
And that far-seeing God grants some the wisdom of the mind,
Which no man can keep to himself, that, though but few can find,
Doth profit many, that preserves the public weal and state,
And that, who hath, he best can prize. But, for me, I'll relate
Only my censure what's our best. The very crown of war
Doth burn about thee; yet our men, when they have reach'd thus far,
Suppose their valours crown'd, and cease. A few still stir their feet,
And so a few with many fight, sperst thinly through the fleet.
Retire then, leave speech to the rout, and all thy princes call,
That, here, in counsels of most weight, we may resolve of all,
If having likelihood to believe that God will conquest give,
We shall charge through; or with this grace, make our retreat, and live.
For, I must needs affirm, I fear, the debt of yesterday
(Since war is such a God of change) the Grecians now will pay.
And since th' insatiate man of war remains at fleet, if there
We tempt his safety, no hour more his hot soul can forbear."
This sound stuff Hector lik'd, approv'd, jump'd from his chariot,
And said: "Polydamas make good this place, and suffer not
One prince to pass it; I myself will there go, where you see
Those friends in skirmish, and return (when they have heard from me
Command that your advice obeys) with utmost speed." This said,
With day-bright arms, white plume, white scarf, his goodly limbs array'd,
He parted from them, like a hill, removing, all of snow,
And to the Trojan peers and chiefs he flew, to let them know
The counsel of Polydamas. All turn'd, and did rejoice,
To haste to Panthus' gentle son, being call'd by Hector's voice;
Who, through the forefights making way, look'd for Deiphobus,
King Helenus, Asiades, Hyrtasian Asius,
Of whom, some were not to be found unhurt, or undeceas'd,
Some only hurt, and gone from field. As further he address'd,
He found within the fight's left wing the fair-hair'd Helen's love
By all means moving men to blows; which could by no means move
Hector's forbearance, his friends' miss so put his pow'rs in storm,
But thus in wonted terms he chid: "You with the finest form,
Impostor, woman's man! where are, in your care mark'd, all these,

Deiphobus, King Helenus, Asius Hyrtacides,
Othryonëus Acamas? Now haughty Ilion
Shakes to his lowest groundwork. Now just ruin falls upon
Thy head past rescue." He replied: "Hector, why chid'st thou now,
When I am guiltless? Other times, there are for ease, I know,
Than these, for she that brought thee forth, not utterly left me
Without some portion of thy spirit, to make me brother thee.
But since thou first brought'st in thy force, to this our naval fight,
I and my friends have ceaseless fought, to do thy service right.
But all those friends thou seek'st are slain; excepting Helenus,
Who parted wounded in his hand, and so Deiphobus;
Jove yet averted death from them. And now lead thou as far
As thy great heart affects, all we will second any war
That thou endurest; and I hope, my own strength is not lost;
Though least, I'll fight it to his best; nor further fights the most."
This calm'd hot Hector's spleen; and both turn'd where they saw the face
Of war most fierce, and that was where their friends made good the place
About renown'd Polydamas, and god-like Polypæt,
Palmus, Ascanius, Morus that Hippotion did beget,
And from Ascania's wealthy fields but ev'n the day before
Arriv'd at Troy, that with their aid they kindly might restore
Some kindness they receiv'd from thence. And in fierce fight with these,
Phalces and tall Orthæus stood, and bold Cebriones.
And then the doubt that in advice Polydamas disclos'd,
To fight or fly, Jove took away, and all to fight dispos'd.
And as the floods of troubled air to pitchy storms increase
That after thunder sweeps the fields, and ravish up the seas,
Encount'ring with abhorréd roars, when the engrosséd waves
Boil into foam, and endlessly one after other raves;
So rank'd and guarded th' Ilians march'd; some now, more now, and then
More upon more, in shining steel; now captains, then their men.
And Hector, like man-killing Mars, advanc'd before them all,
His huge round target before him, through thicken'd, like a wall.
With hides well-couch'd with store of brass; and on his temples shin'd
His bright helm, on which danc'd his plume; and in this horrid kind,
(All hid within his world-like shield) he ev'ry troop assay'd
For entry, that in his despite stood firm and undismay'd.
Which when he saw, and kept more off, Ajax came stalking then,
And thus provok'd him: "O good man, why fright'st thou thus our men?
Come nearer. Not art's want in war makes us thus navy-bound,
But Jove's direct scourge; his arm'd hand makes our hands give you ground.
Yet thou hop'st, of thyself, our spoil. But we have likewise hands
To hold our own, as you to spoil; and ere thy countermands
Stand good against our ransack'd fleet, your hugely-peopled town
Our hands shall take in, and her tow'rs from all their heights pull down.
And I must tell thee, time draws on, when, flying, thou shalt cry
To Jove and all the Gods to make thy fair-man'd horses fly
More swift than falcons, that their hoofs may rouse the dust, and bear

Thy body, hid, to Ilion." This said, his bold words were
Confirm'd as soon as spoke. Jove's bird, the high-flown eagle, took
The right hand of their host; whose wings high acclamations strook
From forth the glad breasts of the Greeks. Then Hector made reply:
"Vain-spoken man, and glorious, what hast thou said? Would I
As surely were the son of Jove, and of great Juno born,
Adorn'd like Pallas, and the God that lifts to earth the morn,
As this day shall bring harmful light to all your host, and thou,
If thou dar'st stand this lance, the earth before the ships shalt strow,
Thy bosom torn up, and the dogs, with all the fowl of Troy,
Be satiate with thy fat and flesh." This said, with shouting joy
His first troops follow'd, and the last their shouts with shouts repell'd.
Greece answer'd all, nor could her spirits from all show rest conceal'd.
And to so infinite a height all acclamations strove,
They reach'd the splendours stuck about the unreach'd throne of Jove.

[1] The empire of Jove exceeded Neptune's (saith Plut. upon this place) because he was more ancient, and excellent in knowledge and wisdom; and upon this verse, viz. ἀλλὰ Ζεὺς πρότερος, etc., sets down this his most worthy to be noted opinion: viz. I think also that the blessedness of eternal life, which God enjoys is this: that by any past time He forgets not notions presently apprehended; for otherwise, the knowledge and understanding of things taken away, immortality should not be life, but time, etc. (Plut. de Iside et Osiride).

THE END OF THE THIRTEENTH BOOK.

THE ARGUMENT

Atrides, to behold the skirmish, brings
Old Nestor, and the other wounded kings.
Juno (receiving of the Cyprian dame
Her Ceston, whence her sweet enticements came)
Descends to Somnus, and gets him to bind
The pow'rs of Jove with sleep, to free her mind.
Neptune assists the Greeks, and of the foe
Slaughter inflicts a mighty overthrow.
Ajax so sore strikes Hector with a stone,
It makes him spit blood, and his sense sets gone.

ANOTHER ARGUMENT

In with sleep, and bed, heav'n's Queen
Ev'n Jove himself makes overseen.
Not wine, nor feasts, could lay their soft chains on old Nestor's ear

To this high clamour, who requir'd Machaon's thoughts to bear
His care in part, about the cause; "For, methink, still," said he,
"The cry increases. I must needs the watchtow'r mount, to see
Which way the flood of war doth drive. Still drink thou wine, and eat,
Till fair-hair'd Hecamed hath giv'n a little water heat
To cleanse the quitture from thy wound." This said, the goodly shield
Of warlike Thrasymed, his son, who had his own in field,
He took, snatch'd up a mighty lance, and so stept forth to view
Cause of that clamour. Instantly th' unworthy cause he knew,
The Grecians wholly put in rout, the Trojans routing still,
Close at the Greeks' backs, their wall raz'd. The old man mourn'd this ill;
And, as when with unwieldy waves the great sea fore-feels winds
That both ways murmur, and no way her certain current finds,
But pants and swells confusedly, here goes, and there will stay,
Till on it air casts one firm wind, and then it rolls away;
So stood old Nestor in debate, two thoughts at once on wing
In his discourse, if first to take direct course to the king,
Or to the multitude in fight. At last he did conclude
To visit Agamemnon first. Mean time both hosts imbrued
Their steel in one another's blood, nought wrought their healths but harms,
Swords, huge stones, double-headed darts, still thumping on their arms.
And now the Jove-kept kings, whose wounds were yet in cure, did meet
Old Nestor, Diomed, Ithacus, and Atreus' sons, from fleet
Bent for the fight which was far off, the ships being drawn to shore
On heaps at first, till all their sterns a wall was rais'd before,
Which, though not great, it yet suffic'd to hide them, though their men
Were something straited; for whose scope, in form of battle then,
They drew them through the spacious shore, one by another still,
Till all the bosom of the strand their sable bulks did fill,
Ev'n till they took up all the space 'twixt both the promont'ries.
These kings, like Nestor, in desire to know for what those cries
Became so violent, came along, all leaning on their darts,
To see, though not of pow'r to fight, sad and suspicious hearts
Distemp'ring them; and, meeting now Nestor, the king in fear
Cried out: "O Nestor our renown! Why shows thy presence here,
The harmful fight abandoned? Now Hector will make good
The threat'ning vow he made, I fear, that, till he had our blood,
And fir'd our fleet, he never more would turn to Ilion.
Nor is it long, I see, before his whole will will be done.
O Gods! I now see all the Greeks put on Achilles' ire
Against my honour; no mean left to keep our fleet from fire."
He answer'd: "'Tis an evident truth, not Jove himself can now,
With all the thunder in his hands, prevent our overthrow.
The wall we thought invincible, and trusted more than Jove,
Is scal'd, raz'd, enter'd; and our pow'rs (driv'n up) past breathing, prove
A most inevitable fight; both slaughters so commix'd,
That for your life you cannot put your diligent'st thought betwixt
The Greeks and Trojans, and as close their throats cleave to the sky.

Consult we then, if that will serve. For fight advise not I;
It fits not wounded men to fight." Atrides answer'd him:
"If such a wall as cost the Greeks so many a tiréd limb,
And such a dike be pass'd, and raz'd, that, as yourself said well,
We all esteem'd invincible, and would past doubt repell
The world from both our fleet and us; it doth directly show
That here Jove vows our shames and deaths. I evermore did know
His hand from ours when he help'd us, and now I see as clear
That, like the blesséd Gods, he holds our hated enemies dear,
Supports their arms, and pinions ours. Conclude then, 'tis in vain
To strive with him. Our ships drawn up, now let us launch again,
And keep at anchor till calm night, that then, perhaps, our foes
May calm their storms, and in that time our scape we may dispose.
'It is not any shame to fly from ill, although by night.
Known ill he better does that flies, than he it takes in fight.'"
Ulysses frown'd on him, and said: "Accurs'd, why talk'st thou thus?
Would thou hadst led some barb'rous host, and not commanded us
Whom Jove made soldiers from our youth, that age might scorn to fly
From any charge it undertakes, and ev'ry dazzled eye
The honour'd hand of war might close. Thus wouldst thou leave this town,
For which our many mis'ries felt entitle it our own?
Peace, lest some other Greek give ear, and hear a sentence such;
As no man's palate should profane; at least that knew how much
His own right weigh'd, and being a prince, and such a prince as bears
Rule of so many Greeks as thou. This counsel loathes mine ears,
Let others toil in fight and cries, and we so light of heels
Upon their very noise, and groans, to hoise away our keels.
Thus we should fit the wish of Troy, that, being something near
The victory, we give it clear; and we were sure to bear
A slaughter to the utmost man, for no man will sustain
A stroke, the fleet gone, but at that, look still, and wish him slain.
And therefore, prince of men, be sure, thy censure is unfit."
"O Ithacus," replied the king, "thy bitter terms have smit
My heart in sunder. At no hand, 'gainst any prince's will
Do I command this. Would to God, that any man of skill
To give a better counsel would, or old, or younger man!
My voice should gladly go with his." Then Diomed began:
"The man not far is, nor shall ask much labour to bring in,
That willingly would speak his thoughts, if spoken they might win
Fit ear, and suffer no impair, that I discover them,
Being youngest of you; since my sire, that heir'd a diadem,
May make my speech to diadems decent enough, though he
Lies in his sepulchre at Thebes. I boast this pedigree:
Portheus three famous sons begot, that in high Calydon
And Pleuron kept, with state of kings, their habitatión;
Agrius, Melas, and the third the horseman Oeneus,
My father's father, that excell'd in actions generous
The other two. But these kept home, my father being driv'n

With wand'ring and advent'rous spirits, for so the King of heav'n
And th' other Gods set down their wills, and he to Argos came,
Where he begun the world, and dwelt. There marrying a dame,
One of Adrastus' female race, he kept a royal house,
For he had great demesnes, good land, and, being industrious,
He planted many orchard-grounds about his house, and bred
Great store of sheep. Besides all this, he was well qualitied,
And pass'd all Argives, for his spear. And these digressive things
Are such as you may well endure, since (being deriv'd from kings,
And kings not poor nor virtueless) you cannot hold me base,
Nor scorn my words, which oft, though true, in mean men meet disgrace.
However, they are these in short: Let us be seen at fight,
And yield to strong necessity, though wounded, that our sight
May set those men on that, of late, have to Achilles' spleen
Been too indulgent, and left blows; but be we only seen,
Not come within the reach of darts, lest wound on wound we lay;
Which rev'rend Nestor's speech implied, and so far him obey."
This counsel gladly all observ'd, went on, Atrides led.
Nor Neptune this advantage lost, but closely followéd,
And like an aged man appear'd t' Atrides; whose right hand
He seiz'd, and said: "Atrides, this doth passing fitly stand
With stern Achilles' wreakful spirit, that he can stand astern
His ship, and both in fight and death the Grecian bane discern,
Since not in his breast glows one spark of any human mind.
But be that his own bane. Let God by that loss make him find
How vile a thing he is. For know, the blest Gods have not giv'n
Thee ever over, but perhaps the Trojans may from heav'n
Receive that justice. Nay, 'tis sure, and thou shalt see their falls,
Your fleet soon freed, and for fights here they glad to take their walls."
This said, he made known who he was, and parted with a cry
As if ten thousand men had join'd in battle then, so high
His throat flew through the host; and so this great Earth-shaking God
Cheer'd up the Greek hearts, that they wish their pains no period.
Saturnia from Olympus' top saw her great brother there,
And her great husband's brother too, exciting ev'rywhere
The glorious spirits of the Greeks; which as she joy'd to see,
So, on the fountful Ida's top, Jove's sight did disagree
With her contentment, since she fear'd that his hand would descend,
And check the Sea-god's practices. And this she did contend
How to prevent, which thus seem'd best: To deck her curiously,
And visit the Idalian hill, that so the Lightner's eye
She might enamour with her looks, and his high temples steep,
Ev'n to his wisdom, in the kind and golden juice of sleep.
So took she chamber, which her son, the God of ferrary,
With firm doors made, being joinèd close, and with a privy key
That no God could command but Jove; where, enter'd, she made fast
The shining gates, and then upon her lovely body cast
Ambrosia, that first made it clear, and after laid on it

An od'rous, rich, and sacred oil, that was so wond'rous sweet
That ever, when it was but touch'd, it sweeten'd heav'n and earth.
Her body being cleans'd with this, her tresses she let forth,
And comb'd, her comb dipp'd in the oil, then wrapp'd them up in curls;
And, thus her deathless head adorn'd, a heav'nly veil she hurls
On her white shoulders, wrought by Her that rules in housewif'ries,
Who wove it full of antique works, of most divine device;
And this with goodly clasps of gold she fasten'd to her breast.
Then with a girdle, whose rich sphere a hundred studs impress'd,
She girt her small waist. In her ears, tenderly pierc'd, she wore
Pearls, great and orient. On her head, a wreath not worn before
Cast beams out like the sun. At last, she to her feet did tie
Fair shoes. And thus entire attir'd, she shin'd in open sky,
Call'd the fair Paphian Queen apart from th' other Gods, and said:
"Lov'd daughter! Should I ask a grace, should I, or be obey'd?
Or wouldst thou cross me, being incens'd, since I cross thee and take
The Greeks' part, thy hand helping Troy?" She answer'd, "That shall make
No diff'rence in a diff'rent cause. Ask, ancient Deity,
What most contents thee. My mind stands inclin'd as liberally
To grant it as thine own to ask; provided that it be
A favour fit and in my pow'r." She, giv'n deceitfully,
Thus said: "Then give me those two pow'rs, with which both men and Gods
Thou vanquishest, Love and Desire; for now the periods
Of all the many-feeding earth, and the original
Of all the Gods, Oceanus, and Thetis whom we call
Our Mother, I am going to greet. They nurst me in their court,
And brought me up, receiving me in most respectful sort
From Phæa, when Jove under earth and the unfruitful seas
Cast Saturn. These I go to see, intending to appease
Jars grown betwixt them, having long abstain'd from speech and bed;
Which jars, could I so reconcile, that in their anger's stead
I could place love, and so renew their first society,
I should their best lov'd be esteem'd, and honour'd endlessly."
She answer'd: "'Tis not fit, nor just, thy will should be denied,
Whom Jove in his embraces holds." This spoken, she untied,
And from her od'rous bosom took, her Ceston, in whose sphere
Were all enticements to delight, all loves, all longings were,
Kind conference, fair speech, whose pow'r the wisest doth inflame.
This she resigning to her hands, thus urg'd her by her name:
"Receive this bridle, thus fair-wrought, and put it 'twixt thy breasts,
Where all things to be done are done; and whatsoever rests
In thy desire return with it." The great-ey'd Juno smil'd,
And put it 'twixt her breasts. Love's Queen, thus cunningly beguil'd,
To Jove's court flew. Saturnia, straight stooping from heav'n's height,
Pieria and Emathia, those countries of delight,
Soon reach'd, and to the snowy mounts, where Thracian soldiers dwell,
Approaching, pass'd their tops untouch'd. From Athos then she fell,
Pass'd all the broad sea, and arriv'd in Lemnos, at the tow'rs

Of godlike Thoas, where she met the Prince of all men's pow'rs,
Death's brother, Sleep; whose hand she took, and said: "Thou king of men,
Prince of the Gods too, if before thou heard'st my suits, again
Give helpful ear, and through all times I'll offer thanks to thee.
Lay slumber on Jove's fi'ry eyes, that I may comfort me
With his embraces; for which grace I'll grace thee with a throne
Incorruptible, all of gold, and elegantly done
By Mulciber, to which he forg'd a footstool for the ease
Of thy soft feet, when wine and feasts thy golden humours please."
Sweet Sleep replied: "Satunia, there lives not any God,
Besides Jove, but I would becalm; aye if it were the Flood,
That fathers all the Deities, the great Oceanus;
But Jove we dare not come more near, than he commandeth us.
Now you command me as you did, when Jove's great-minded son,
Alcides, having sack'd the town of stubborn Ilion,
Took sail from thence; when by your charge I pour'd about Jove's mind
A pleasing slumber, calming him, till thou drav'st up the wind,
In all his cruelties, to sea, that set his son ashore
In Cous, far from all his friends. Which, waking, vex'd so sore
The supreme Godhead, that he cast the Gods about the sky,
And me, above them all, he sought, whom he had utterly
Hurl'd from the sparkling firmament, if all-gods-taming Night
(Whom, flying, I besought for aid) had suffer'd his despite,
And not preserv'd me; but his wrath with my offence dispens'd,
For fear t' offend her, and so ceas'd, though never so incens'd.
And now another such escape, you wish I should prepare."
She answer'd: "What hath thy deep rest to do with his deep care?
As though Jove's love to Ilion in all degrees were such
As 'twas to Hercules his son, and so would storm as much
For their displeasure as for his? Away, I will remove
Thy fear with giving thee the dame, that thou didst ever love,
One of the fair young Graces born, divine Pasithae."
This started Somnus into joy, who answer'd: "Swear to me,
By those inviolable springs, that feed the Stygian lake,
With one hand touch the nourishing earth, and in the other take
The marble sea, that all the Gods, of the infernal state,
Which circle Saturn, may to us be witnesses, and rate
What thou hast vow'd; That with all truth, thou wilt bestow on me,
The dame I grant I ever lov'd, divine Pasithae."
She swore, as he enjoin'd, in all, and strengthen'd all his joys
By naming all th' infernal Gods, surnam'd the Titanois.
The oath thus taken, both took way, and made their quick repair
To Ida from the town, and isle, all hid in liquid air.
At Lecton first they left the sea, and there the land they trod;
The fountful nurse of savages, with all her woods, did nod
Beneath their feet; there Somnus stay'd, lest Jove's bright eye should see,
And yet, that he might see to Jove, he climb'd the goodliest tree
That all th' Idalian mountain bred, and crown'd her progeny,

A fir it was, that shot past air, and kiss'd the burning sky;
There sate he hid in his dark arms, and in the shape with all
Of that continual prating bird, whom all the Deities call
Chalcis, but men Cymmindis name. Saturnia tripp'd apace,
Up to the top of Gargarus, and show'd her heav'nly face
To Jupiter, who saw, and lov'd, and with as hot a fire,
Being curious in her tempting view, as when with first desire
(The pleasure of it being stol'n) they mix'd in love and bed;
And, gazing on her still, he said: "Saturnia, what hath bred
This haste in thee from our high court, and whither tends thy gait,
That void of horse and chariot, fit for thy sov'reign state,
Thou lackiest here?" Her studied fraud replied: "My journey now
Leaves state and labours to do good; and where in right I owe
All kindness to the Sire of Gods, and our good Mother Queen
That nurst and kept me curiously in court (since both have been
Long time at discord) my desire is to atone their hearts;
And therefore go I now to see those earth's extremest parts.
For whose far-seat I spar'd my horse the scaling of this hill,
And left them at the foot of it; for they must taste their fill
Of travail with me, and must draw my coach through earth and seas,
Whose far-intended reach, respect, and care not to displease
Thy graces, made me not attempt, without thy gracious leave."
The cloud-compelling God her guile in this sort did receive:
"Juno, thou shalt have after leave, but, ere so far thou stray,
Convert we our kind thoughts to love, that now doth ev'ry way
Circle with victory my pow'rs, nor yet with any dame,
Woman, or Goddess, did his fires my bosom so inflame
As now with thee. Not when it lov'd the parts so generous
Ixion's wife had, that brought forth the wise Pirithous;
Nor when the lovely dame Acrisius' daughter stirr'd
My amorous pow'rs, that Perseus bore to all men else preferr'd;
Nor when the dame, that Phenix got, surpris'd me with her sight,
Who the divine-soul'd Rhadamanth and Minos brought to light;
Nor Semele, that bore to me the joy of mortal men,
The sprightly Bacchus; nor the dame that Thebes renownéd then,
Alcmena, that bore Hercules; Latona, so renown'd;
Queen Ceres, with the golden hair; nor thy fair eyes did wound
My entrails to such depth as now with thirst of amorous ease."
The cunning Dame seem'd much incens'd, and said: "What words are these,
Unsufferable Saturn's son? What! Here! In Ida's height!
Desir'st thou this? How fits it us? Or what if in the sight
Of any God thy will were pleas'd, that he the rest might bring
To witness thy incontinence? 'Twere a dishonour'd thing.
I would not show my face in heav'n, and rise from such a bed.
But, if love be so dear to thee, thou hast a chamberstead,
Which Vulcan purposely contriv'd with all fit secrecy;
There sleep at pleasure." He replied: "I fear not if the eye
Of either God or man observe, so thick a cloud of gold

I'll cast about us that the sun, who furthest can behold,
Shall never find us." This resolv'd, into his kind embrace
He took his wife. Beneath them both fair Tellus strew'd the place
With fresh-sprung herbs, so soft and thick that up aloft it bore
Their heav'nly bodies; with his leaves, did dewy lotus store
Th' Elysian mountain; saffron flow'rs and hyacinths help'd make
The sacred bed; and there they slept. When suddenly there brake
A golden vapour out of air, whence shining dews did fall,
In which they wrapt them close, and slept till Jove was tam'd withal.
Mean space flew Somnus to the ships, found Neptune out, and said:
"Now cheerfully assist the Greeks; and give them glorious head,
At least a little, while Jove sleeps; of whom through ev'ry limb
I pour'd dark sleep, Saturnia's love hath so illuded him."
This news made Neptune more secure in giving Grecians heart,
And through the first fights thus he stirr'd the men of most desert:
"Yet, Grecians, shall we put our ships, and conquest, in the hands
Of Priam's Hector by our sloth? He thinks so, and commands
With pride according; all because, Achilles keeps away.
Alas, as we were nought but him! We little need to stay
On his assistance, if we would our own strengths call to field,
And mutually maintain repulse. Come on then, all men yield
To what I order. We that bear best arms in all our hosts,
Whose heads sustain the brightest helms, whose hands are bristled most
With longest lances, let us on. But stay, I'll lead you all;
Nor think I but great Hector's spirits will suffer some appall,
Though they be never so inspir'd. The ablest of us then,
That on our shoulders worst shields bear, exchange with worser men
That fight with better." This propos'd, all heard it, and obey'd.
The kings, ev'n those that suffer'd wounds, Ulysses, Diomed,
And Agamemnon, helpt t' instruct the cómplete army thus:
To good gave good arms, worse to worse, yet none were mutinous.
Thus, arm'd with order, forth they flew; the great Earth-shaker led,
A long sword in his sinewy hand, which when he brandishéd
It lighten'd still, there was no law for him and it, poor men
Must quake before them. These thus mann'd, illustrious Hector then
His host brought up. The blue-hair'd God and he stretch'd through the prease
A grievous fight; when to the ships and tents of Greece the seas
Brake loose, and rag'd. But when they join'd, the dreadful clamour rose
To such a height, as not the sea, when up the North-spirit blows
Her raging billows, bellows so against the beaten shore;
Nor such a rustling keeps a fire, driven with violent blore
Through woods that grow against a hill; nor so the fervent strokes
Of almost-bursting winds resound against a grove of oaks;
As did the clamour of these hosts, when both the battles clos'd.
Of all which noble Hector first at Ajax' breast dispos'd
His jav'lin, since so right on him the great-soul'd soldier bore;
Nor miss'd it, but the bawdricks both that his broad bosom wore,
To hang his shield and sword, it strook; both which his flesh preserv'd.

Hector, disdaining that his lance had thus as good as swerv'd,
Trode to his strength; but, going off, great Ajax with a stone,
One of the many props for ships, that there lay trampled on,
Strook his broad breast above his shield, just underneath his throat,
And shook him piecemeal; when the stone sprung back again, and smote
Earth, like a whirlwind, gath'ring dust with whirring fiercely round,
For fervour of his unspent strength, in settling on the ground.
And as when Jove's bolt by the roots rends from the earth an oak,
His sulphur casting with the blow a strong unsavoury smoke,
And on the fall'n plant none dare look but with amazéd eyes,
(Jove's thunder being no laughing game) so bow'd strong Hector's thighs,
And so with tost-up heels he fell, away his lance he flung,
His round shield follow'd, then his helm, and out his armour rung.
The Greeks then shouted, and ran in, and hop'd to hale him off,
And therefore pour'd on darts in storms, to keep his aid aloof;
But none could hurt the people's Guide, nor stir him from his ground;
Sarpedon, prince of Lycia, and Glaucus so renown'd,
Divine Agenor, Venus' son, and wise Polydamas,
Rush'd to his rescue, and the rest. No one neglective was
Of Hector's safety. All their shields, they couch'd about him close,
Rais'd him from earth, and (giving him, in their kind arms, repose)
From off the labour carried him, to his rich chariot,
And bore him mourning towards Troy. But when the flood they got
Of gulfy Xanthus, that was got by deathless Jupiter,
There took they him from chariot, and all besprinkled there
His temples with the stream. He breath'd, look'd up, assay'd to rise,
And on his knees stay'd spitting blood. Again then clos'd his eyes,
And back again his body fell. The main blow had not done
Yet with his spirit. When the Greeks saw worthy Hector gone,
Then thought they of their work, then charg'd with much more cheer the foe,
And then, far first, Oïliades began the overthrow.
He darted Satnius Enops' son, whom famous Nais bore
As she was keeping Enops' flocks on Satnius' river's shore,
And strook him in his belly's rim, who upwards fell, and rais'd
A mighty skirmish with his fall. And then Panthœdés seiz'd
Prothenor Areilycides, with his revengeful spear,
On his right shoulder, strook it through, and laid him breath less there;
For which he insolently bragg'd, and cried out: "Not a dart
From great-soul'd Panthus' son, I think, shall ever vainlier part,
But some Greek's bosom it shall take, and make him give his ghost."
This brag the Grecians stomach'd much; but Telamonius most,
Who stood most near Prothenor's fall, and out he sent a lance,
Which Panthus' son, declining, 'scap'd, yet took it to sad chance
Archilochus, Antenor's son, whom heav'n did destinate
To that stern end; 'twixt neck and head the jav'lin wrought his fate,
And ran in at the upper joint of all the back long bone,
Cut both the nerves; and such a load of strength laid Ajax on,
As that small part he seiz'd outweigh'd all th' under limbs, and strook

His heels up, so that head and face the earth's possessions took,
When all the low parts sprung in air; and thus did Ajax quit
Panthœdes' brave: "Now, Panthus' son, let thy prophetic wit
Consider, and disclose a truth, if this man do not weigh
Ev'n with Prothenor. I conceive, no one of you will say
That either he was base himself, or sprung of any base;
Antenor's brother, or his son, he should be by his face;
One of his race, past question, his likeness shows he is,"
This spake he, knowing it well enough. The Trojans storm'd at this,
And then slew Acamas, to save his brother yet engag'd,
Bœotius, dragging him to spoil; and thus the Greeks enrag'd:
"O Greeks, ev'n born to bear our darts, yet ever breathing threats,
Not always under tears and toils ye see our fortune sweats,
But sometimes you drop under death. See now your quick among
Our dead, intranc'd with my weak lance, to prove I have ere long
Reveng'd my brother. 'Tis the wish of ev'ry honest man
His brother, slain in Mars's field, may rest wreak'd in his fane."
This stirr'd fresh envy in the Greeks, but urg'd Peneleus most,
Who hurl'd his lance at Acamas; he 'scap'd; nor yet it lost
The force he gave it, for it found the flock-rich Phorbas' son,
Ilionëus, whose dear sire, past all in Ilion,
Was lov'd of Hermes, and enrich'd, and to him only bore
His mother this now slaughter'd man. The dart did undergore
His eye-lid, by his eye's dear roots, and out the apple fell,
The eye pierc'd through. Nor could the nerve that stays the neck repell
His strong-wing'd lance, but neck and all gave way, and down he dropp'd.
Peneleus then unsheath'd his sword, and from the shoulders chopp'd
His luckless head; which down he threw, the helm still sticking on,
And still the lance fix'd in his eye; which not to see alone
Contented him, but up again he snatch'd, and show'd it all,
With this stern brave: "Ilians, relate brave Ilionëus' fall
To his kind parents, that their roofs their tears may overrun;
For so the house of Promachus, and Alegenor's son,
Must with his wife's eyes overflow, she never seeing more
Her dear lord, though we tell his death, when to our native shore
We bring from ruin'd Troy our fleet, and men so long forgone."
This said, and seen, pale fear possess'd all those of Ilion,
And ev'ry man cast round his eye to see where death was not,
That he might fly him. Let not then his grac'd hand be forgot,
O Muses, you that dwell in heav'n, that first imbru'd the field
With Trojan spoil, when Neptune thus had made their irons yield.
First Ajax Telamonius the Mysian captain slew,
Great Hyrtius Gyrtiades. Antilochus o'erthrew
Phalces and Mermer, to their spoil. Meriones gave end
To Morys and Hyppotion. Teucer to fate did send
Prothoon and Periphetes. Atrides' jav'lin chac'd
Duke Hyperenor, wounding him in that part that is plac'd
Betwixt the short ribs and the bones, that to the triple gut

Have pertinence; the jav'lin's head did out his entrails cut,
His forc'd soul breaking through the wound; night's black hand
clos'd his eyes.
Then Ajax, great Oïleus' son, had divers victories,
For when Saturnius suffer'd flight, of all the Grecian race
Not one with swiftness of his feet could so enrich a chace.

[1] This first verse (after the first four syllables) is to be read as one of our tens.

THE END OF THE FOURTEENTH BOOK.

THE ARGUMENT

Jove waking, and beholding Troy in flight,
Chides Juno, and sends Iris to the fight
To charge the Sea-god to forsake the field,
And Phœbus to invade it, with his shield
Recov'ring Hector's bruis'd and eraséd pow'rs,
To field he goes, and makes new conquerors,
The Trojans giving now the Grecians chace
Ev'n to their fleet. Then Ajax turns his face,
And feeds, with many Trojan lives, his ire;
Who then brought brands to set the fleet on fire.

ANOTHER ARGUMENT

Jove sees in O his oversight,
Chides Juno, Neptune calls from fight.
The Trojans, beat past pale and dike, and numbers prostrate laid,
All got to chariot, fear-driv'n all, and fear'd as men dismay'd.
Then Jove on Ida's top awak'd, rose from Saturnia's side,
Stood up, and look'd upon the war; and all inverted spied
Since he had seen it; th' Ilians now in rout, the Greeks in fight;
King Neptune, with his long sword, chief; great Hector put down quite,
Laid flat in field, and with a crown of princes compasséd
So stopp'd up that he scarce could breathe, his mind's sound habit fled,
And he still spitting blood. Indeed, his hurt was not set on
By one that was the weakest Greek. But him Jove look'd upon
With eyes of pity; on his wife with horrible aspéct,
To whom he said: "O thou in ill most cunning architect,
All arts and comments that exceed'st! not only to enforce
Hector from fight, but, with his men, to show the Greeks a course.
I fear, as formerly, so now, these ills have with thy hands

Their first fruits sown, and therefore could load all thy limbs with bands,
Forgett'st thou, when I hang'd thee up, how to thy feet I tied
Two anvils, golden manacles on thy false wrists implied,
And let thee mercilessly hang from our refinéd heav'n
Ev'n to earth's vapours; all the Gods in great Olympus giv'n
To mutinies about thee, yet, though all stood staring on,
None durst dissolve thee, for these hands, had they but seiz'd upon
Thy friend, had headlong thrown him off from our star-bearing round,
Till he had tumbled out his breath, and piece-meal dash'd the ground?
Nor was my angry spirit calm'd so soon, for those foul seas,
On which, inducing northern flaws, thou shipwrack'dst Hercules,
And toss'd him to the Coan shore, that thou shouldst tempt again
My wrath's importance, when thou seest, besides, how grossly vain
My pow'rs can make thy policies; for from their utmost force
I freed my son, and set him safe in Argos, nurse of horse.
These I remember to thy thoughts, that thou may'st shun these sleights,
And know how badly bed-sports thrive, procur'd by base deceits."
This frighted the offending queen, who with this state excus'd
Her kind unkindness: "Witness Earth, and Heav'n so far diffus'd,
Thou Flood whose silent gliding waves the under ground doth bear,
(Which is the great'st and gravest oath, that any God can swear)
Thy sacred head, those secret joys that our young bed gave forth,
By which I never rashly swore! that He who shakes the earth
Not by my counsel did this wrong to Hector and his host,
But, pitying th' oppresséd Greeks, their fleet being nearly lost,
Reliev'd their hard conditión, yet utterly impell'd
By his free mind. Which since I see is so offensive held
To thy high pleasure, I will now advise him not to tread
But where thy tempest-raising feet, O Jupiter, shall lead."
Jove laugh'd to hear her so submiss, and said: "My fair-ey'd love,
If still thus thou and I were one, in counsels held above,
Neptune would still in word and fact be ours, if not in heart.
If then thy tongue and heart agree, from hence to heav'n depart,
To call the excellent-in-bows, the Rain-bow, and the Sun,
That both may visit both the hosts; the Grecian army one,
And that is Iris, let her haste, and make the Sea-god cease
T' assist the Greeks, and to his court retire from war in peace;
Let Phœbus, on the Trojan part, inspire with wonted pow'r
Great Hector's spirits, make his thoughts forget the late stern hour,
And all his anguish, setting on his whole recover'd man
To make good his late grace in fight, and hold in constant wane
The Grecian glories, till they fall, in flight before the fleet
Of vex'd Achilles. Which extreme will prove the mean to greet
Thee with thy wish, for then the eyes of great Æacides
(Made witness of the gen'ral ill, that doth so near him prease)
Will make his own particular look out, and by degrees
Abate his wrath, that, though himself for no extremities
Will seem reflected, yet his friend may get of him the grace

To help his country in his arms; and he shall make fit place
For his full presence with his death, which shall be well fore-run;
For I will first renown his life with slaughter of my son,
Divine Sarpedon, and his death great Hector's pow'r shall wreak,
Ending his ends. Then, at once, out shall the fury break
Of fierce Achilles, and, with that, the flight now felt shall turn,
And then last, till in wrathful flames the long-sieg'd Ilion burn.
Minerva's counsel shall become grave mean to this my will,
Which no God shall neglect before Achilles take his fill
Of slaughter for his slaughter'd friend; ev'n Hector's slaughter thrown
Under his anger; that these facts may then make fully known
My vow's performance, made of late, and, with my bowéd head,
Confirm'd to Thetis, when her arms embrac'd my knees, and pray'd
That to her city-razing son I would all honour show."
This heard, his charge she seem'd t' intend, and to Olympus flew.
But, as the mind of such a man that hath a great way gone,
And either knowing not his way, or then would let alone
His purpos'd journey, is distract, and in his vexéd mind
Resolves now not to go, now goes, still many ways inclin'd;
So rev'rend Juno headlong flew, and 'gainst her stomach striv'd,
For, being amongst th' immortal Gods in high heav'n soon arriv'd,
All rising, welcoming with cups her little absence thence,
She all their courtships overpass'd with solemn negligence,
Save that which fair-cheek'd Themis show'd, and her kind cup she took,
For first she ran and met with her, and ask'd: "What troubled look
She brought to heav'n? She thought, for truth, that Jove had terrified
Her spirits strangely since she went." The fair-arm'd Queen replied:
"That truth may eas'ly be suppos'd; you, Goddess Themis, know
His old severity and pride, but you bear't out with show,
And like the banquet's arbiter amongst th' Immortals' fare,
Though well you hear amongst them all, how bad his actions are;
Nor are all here, or anywhere, mortals, nor Gods, I fear,
Entirely pleas'd with what he does, though thus ye banquet here."
Thus took she place, displeasedly; the feast in general
Bewraying privy spleens at Jove; and then, to colour all,
She laugh'd, but merely from her lips, for over her black brows
Her still-bent forehead was not clear'd; yet this her passion's throes
Brought forth in spite, being lately school'd: "Alas, what fools are we
That envy Jove! Or that by act, word, thought, can fantasy
Any resistance to his will! He sits far off, nor cares,
Nor moves, but says he knows his strength, to all degrees compares
His greatness past all other Gods, and that in fortitude,
And ev'ry other godlike pow'r, he reigns past all indu'd.
For which great eminence all you Gods, whatever ill he does,
Sustain with patience. Here is Mars, I think, not free from woes,
And yet he bears them like himself. The great God had a son,
Whom he himself yet justifies, one that from all men won
Just surname of their best belov'd, Ascalaphus; yet he,

By Jove's high grace to Troy, is slain." Mars started horribly,
As Juno knew he would, at this, beat with his hurl'd-out hands
His brawny thighs, cried out, and said: "O you that have commands
In these high temples, bear with me, if I revenge the death
Of such a son. I'll to the fleet, and though I sink beneath
The fate of being shot to hell, by Jove's fell thunder-stone,
And lie all grim'd amongst the dead with dust and blood, my son
Revenge shall honour." Then he charg'd Fear and Dismay to join
His horse and chariot. He got arms, that over heav'n did shine
And then a wrath more great and grave in Jove had been prepar'd
Against the Gods than Juno caus'd, if Pallas had not car'd
More for the peace of heav'n than Mars; who leap'd out of her throne,
Rapt up her helmet, lance, and shield, and made her fane's porch groan
With her egression to his stay, and thus his rage defers:
"Furious and foolish, th' art undone! Hast thou for nought thine ears?
Heard'st thou not Juno being arriv'd from heav'n's great King but now?
Or wouldst thou he himself should rise, forc'd with thy rage, to show
The dreadful pow'r she urg'd in him, so justly being stirr'd?
Know, thou most impudent and mad, thy wrath had not inferr'd
Mischief to thee, but to us all. His spirit had instantly
Left both the hosts, and turn'd his hands to uproars in the sky,
Guilty and guiltless both to wrack in his high rage had gone.
And therefore, as thou lov'st thyself, cease fury for thy son;
Another, far exceeding him in heart and strength of hand,
Or is, or will be shortly, slain. It were a work would stand
Jove in much trouble, to free all from death that would not die."
This threat ev'n nail'd him to his throne; when heav'n's chief Majesty
Call'd bright Apollo from his fane, and Iris that had place
Of internunciess from the Gods, to whom she did the grace
Of Jupiter, to this effect: "It is Saturnius' will,
That both, with utmost speed, should stoop to the Idalian hill,
To know his further pleasure there. And this let me advise,
When you arrive, and are in reach of his refulgent eyes,
His pleasure heard, perform it all, of whatsoever kind."
Thus mov'd she back, and us'd her throne. Those two outstripp'd the wind,
And Ida all-enchas'd with springs they soon attain'd, and found
Where far-discerning Jupiter, in his repose, had crown'd
The brows of Gargarus, and wrapt an odorif'rous cloud
About his bosom. Coming near, they stood. Nor now he show'd
His angry count'nance, since so soon he saw they made th' access
That his lov'd wife enjoin'd; but first the fair ambassadress
He thus commanded: "Iris, go to Neptune, and relate
Our pleasure truly, and at large. Command him from the fate
Of human war, and either greet the Gods' society,
Or the divine sea make his seat. If proudly he deny,
Let better counsels be his guides, than such as bid me war,
And tempt my charge, though he be strong, for I am stronger far,
And elder born. Nor let him dare, to boast even state with me

Whom all Gods else prefer in fear." This said, down hasted she
From Ida's top to Ilion; and like a mighty snow,
Or gelid hail, that from the clouds the northern spirit doth blow;
So fell the windy-footed dame, and found with quick repair
The wat'ry God, to whom she said: "God with the sable hair,
I came from Ægis-bearing Jove, to bid thee cease from fight,
And visit heav'n, or th' ample seas. Which if, in his despite,
Or disobedience, thou deniest, he threatens thee to come,
In opposite fight, to field himself; and therefore warns thee home,
His hands eschewing, since his pow'r is far-superior,
His birth before thee; and affirms, thy lov'd heart should abhor
To vaunt equality with him, whom ev'ry Deity fears."
He answer'd: "O unworthy thing! Though he be great, he bears
His tongue too proudly, that ourself, born to an equal share
Of state and freedom, he would force. Three brothers born we are
To Saturn, Rhea brought us forth, this Jupiter, and I.
And Pluto, God of under-grounds. The world indiff'rently
Dispos'd betwixt us; ev'ry one his kingdom; I the seas,
Pluto the black lot, Jupiter the principalities
Of broad heav'n, all the sky and clouds, was sorted out. The earth
And high Olympus common are, and due to either's birth.
Why then should I be aw'd by him? Content he his great heart
With his third portion, and not think, to amplify his part,
With terrors of his stronger hands, on me, as if I were
The most ignoble of us all. Let him contain in fear
His daughters and his sons, begot by his own person, This
Holds more convenience. They must hear these violent threats of his."
"Shall I," said Iris, "bear from thee, an answer so austere?
Or wilt thou change it? Changing minds, all noble natures bear.
And well thou know'st, these greatest born, the Furies follow still."
He answer'd: "Iris, thy reply keeps time, and shows thy skill.
O 'tis a most praiseworthy thing, when messengers can tell,
Besides their messages, such things, as fit th' occasion well.
But this much grieves my heart and soul, that being in pow'r and state
All-ways his equal, and so fix'd by one decree in fate,
He should to me, as under him, ill language give, and chide.
Yet now, though still incens'd, I yield, affirming this beside,
And I enforce it with a threat: That if without consent
Of me, Minerva, Mercury, the Queen of regiment,
And Vulcan, he will either spare high Ilion, or not race
Her turrets to the lowest stone, and, with both these, not grace
The Greeks as victors absolute, inform him this from me—
His pride and my contempt shall live at endless enmity."
This said, he left the Greeks, and rush'd into his wat'ry throne,
Much miss'd of all th' heroic host. When Jove discern'd him gone,
Apollo's service he employ'd, and said: "Lov'd Phœbus, go
To Hector; now th' earth-shaking God hath taken sea, and so
Shrunk from the horrors I denounc'd; which standing, he, and all

The under-seated Deities, that circle Saturn's fall,
Had heard of me in such a fight as had gone hard for them.
But both for them and me 'tis best, that thus they fly th' extreme,
That had not pass'd us without sweat. Now then, in thy hands take
My adder-fring'd affrighting shield, which with such terror shake,
That fear may shake the Greeks to flight. Besides this, add thy care,
O Phœbus, far-off shooting God, that this so sickly fare
Of famous Hector be recur'd, and quickly so excite
His amplest pow'rs, that all the Greeks may grace him with their flight,
Ev'n to their ships, and Hellespont; and then will I devise
All words and facts again for Greece, that largely may suffice
To breathe them from their instant toils." Thus from th' Idæan height,
Like air's swift pigeon-killer, stoop'd the far-shot God of light,
And found great Hector sitting up, not stretch'd upon his bed,
Not wheezing with a stopp'd-up spirit, not in cold sweats, but fed
With fresh and comfortable veins, but his mind all his own,
But round about him all his friends, as well as ever known.
And this was with the mind of Jove, that flew to him before
Apollo came; who, as he saw no sign of any sore,
Ask'd, like a cheerful visitant: "Why in this sickly kind,
Great Hector, sitt'st thou so apart? Can any grief of mind
Invade thy fortitude?" He spake, but with a feeble voice:
"O thou, the best of Deities! Why, since I thus rejoice
By thy so serious benefit, demand'st thou, as in mirth,
And to my face, if I were ill? For, more than what thy worth
Must needs take note of, doth not Fame from all mouths fill thine ears,
That, as my hand at th' Achive fleet was making massacres
Of men whom valiant Ajax led, his strength strook with a stone
All pow'r of more hurt from my breast? My very soul was gone,
And once to-day I thought to see the house of Dis and Death."
"Be strong," said he, "for such a spirit now sends the God of breath
From airy Ida, as shall run through all Greek spirits in thee.
Apollo with the golden sword, the clear Far-seer, see,
Him, who betwixt death and thy life, 'twixt ruin and those tow'rs,
Ere this day oft hath held his shield. Come then, be all thy pow'rs
In wonted vigour, let thy knights with all their horse assay
The Grecian fleet, myself will lead, and scour so clear the way,
That flight shall leave no Greek a rub." Thus instantly inspir'd
Were all his nerves with matchless strength; and then his friends he fir'd
Against their foes, when to his eyes his ears confirm'd the God.
Then, as a goodly-headed hart, or goat, bred in the wood,
A rout of country huntsmen chase, with all their hounds in cry,
The beast yet or the shady woods, or rocks excessive high,
Keep safe, or our unwieldy fates (that ev'n in hunters sway)
Bar them the poor beast's pulling down; when straight the clam'rous fray
Calls out a lion, hugely-man'd, and his abhorréd view
Turns headlong in unturning flight (though vent'rous) all the crew;
So hitherto the chasing Greeks their slaughter dealt by troops;

But, after Hector was beheld range here and there, then stoops
The boldest courage, then their heels took in their drooping hearts,
And then spake Andræmonides, a man of far-best parts
Of all the Ætolians, skill'd in darts, strenuous in fights of stand,
And one of whom few of the Greeks could get the better hand
For rhetoric, when they fought with words; with all which being wise,
Thus spake he to his Grecian friends: "O mischief! Now mine eyes
Discern no little miracle; Hector escap'd from death,
And all-recover'd, when all thought his soul had sunk beneath
The hands of Ajax. But some God hath sav'd and freed again
Him that but now dissolv'd the knees of many a Grecian,
And now I fear will weaken more; for, not without the hand
Of Him that thunders, can his pow'rs thus still the forefights stand,
Thus still triumphant. Hear me then: Our troops in quick retreat
Let's draw up to our fleet, and we, that boast ourselves the great,
Stand firm, and try if these that raise so high their charging darts
May be resisted. I believe, ev'n this great heart of hearts
Will fear himself to be too bold, in charging thorow us."
They eas'ly heard him, and obey'd; when all the generous
They call'd t' encounter Hector's charge, and turn'd the common men
Back to the fleet. And these were they, that bravely furnish'd then
The fierce forefight: Th' Ajaces both, the worthy Cretan king,
The Mars-like Meges, Merion, and Teucer. Up then bring
The Trojan chiefs their men in heaps; before whom, amply-pac'd,
March'd Hector, and in front of him Apollo, who had cast
About his bright aspect a cloud, and did before him bear
Jove's huge and each-where-shaggy shield, which, to contain in fear
Offending men, the God-smith gave to Jove; with this he led
The Trojan forces. The Greeks stood. A fervent clamour spread
The air on both sides as they join'd. Out flew the shafts and darts,
Some falling short, but other some found butts in breasts and hearts.
As long as Phœbus held but out his horrid shield, so long
The darts flew raging either way, and death grew both ways strong;
But when the Greeks had seen his face, and, who it was that shook
The bristled targe, knew by his voice, then all their strengths forsook
Their nerves and minds. And then look how a goodly herd of neat,
Or wealthy flock of sheep, being close, and dreadless at their meet,
In some black midnight, suddenly, and not a keeper near,
A brace of horrid bears rush in, and then fly here and there
The poor affrighted flocks or herds; so ev'ry way dispers'd
The heartless Grecians, so the Sun their headstrong chace revers'd
To headlong flight, and that day rais'd, with all grace, Hector's head.
Arcesilaus then he slew, and Stichius; Stichius led
Bœotia's brazen-coated men; the other was the friend
Of mighty-soul'd Menestheüs. Æneas brought to end
Medon and Jasus; Medon was the brother, though but base,
Of swift Oïliades, and dwelt, far from his breeding place,
In Phylace; the other led th' Athenian bands, his sire

Was Spelus, Bucolus's son. Mecistheus did expire
Beneath Polydamas's hand. Polites, Echius slew,
Just at the joining of the hosts. Agenor overthrew
Clonius. Bold Deïochus felt Alexander's lance;
It strook his shoulder's upper part, and did his head advance
Quite through his breast, as from the fight he turn'd him for retreat.
While these stood spoiling of the slain, the Greeks found time to get
Beyond the dike and th' undik'd pales; all scapes they gladly gain'd,
Till all had pass'd the utmost wall; Necessity so reign'd.
Then Hector cried out: "Take no spoil, but rush on to the fleet;
From whose assault, for spoil or flight, if any man I meet,
He meets his death; nor in the fire of holy funeral
His brother's or his sister's hands shall cast within our wall
His loathéd body; but, without, the throats of dogs shall grave
His manless limbs." This said, the scourge his forward horses drave
Through ev'ry order; and, with him, all whipp'd their chariots on,
All threat'ningly, out-thund'ring shouts as earth were overthrown.
Before them march'd Apollo still, and, as he march'd, digg'd down,
Without all labour, with his feet the dike, till, with his own,
He fill'd it to the top, and made way both for man and horse
As broad and long as with a lance, cast out to try one's force,
A man could measure. Into this they pour'd whole troops as fast
As num'rous; Phœbus still, before, for all their haste,
Still shaking Jove's unvalu'd shield, and held it up to all.
And then, as he had chok'd their dike, he tumbled down their wall.
And look how eas'ly any boy, upon the sea-ebb'd shore,
Makes with a little sand a toy, and cares for it no more,
But as he rais'd it childishly, so in his wanton vein,
Both with his hands and feet he pulls, and spurns it down again;
So slight, O Phœbus, thy hands made of that huge Grecian toil,
And their late stand, so well-resolv'd, as eas'ly mad'st recoil.
Thus stood they driv'n up at their fleet; where each heard other's thought,
Exhorted, passing humbly pray'd, all all the Gods besought,
With hands held up to heav'n, for help. 'Mongst all the good old man,
Grave Nestor, for his counsels call'd the Argives' guardian,
Fell on his aged knees, and pray'd, and to the starry host
Stretch'd out his hands for aid to theirs, of all thus moving most:
"O father Jove, if ever man, of all our host, did burn
Fat thighs of oxen or of sheep, for grace of safe return,
In fruitful Argos, and obtain'd the bowing of thy head
For promise of his humble pray'rs, O now remember him,
Thou merely heav'nly, and clear up the foul brows of this dim
And cruel day; do not destroy our zeal for Trojan pride."
He pray'd, and heav'n's great Counsellor with store of thunder tried
His former grace good, and so heard the old man's hearty pray'rs.
The Trojans took Jove's sign for them, and pour'd out their affairs
In much more violence on the Greeks, and thought on nought but fight.
And as a huge wave of a sea, swoln to his rudest height,

Breaks over both sides of a ship, being all-urg'd by the wind,
For that's it makes the wave so proud; in such a borne-up kind
The Trojans overgat the wall, and, getting in their horse,
Fought close at fleet, which now the Greeks ascended for their force.
Then from their chariots they with darts, the Greeks with bead-hooks fought,
Kept still aboard for naval fights, their heads with iron wrought
In hooks and pikes. Achilles' friend, still while he saw the wall,
That stood without their fleet, afford employment for them all,
Was never absent from the tent of that man-loving Greek,
Late-hurt Eurypylus, but sate, and ev'ry way did seek,
To spend the sharp time of his wound, with all the ease he could
In med'cines, and in kind discourse. But when he might behold
The Trojans past the wall, the Greeks flight-driv'n, and all in cries,
Then cried he out, cast down his hands, and beat with grief his thighs,
Then, "O Eurypylus," he cried, "now all thy need of me
Must bear my absence, now a work of more necessity
Calls hence, and I must haste to call Achilles to the field.
Who knows, but, God assisting me, my words may make him yield?
The motion of a friend is strong." His feet thus took him thence.
The rest yet stood their enemies firm; but all their violence
(Though Troy fought there with fewer men) lack'd vigour to repell
Those fewer from their navy's charge, and so that charge as well
Lack'd force to spoil their fleet or tents. And as a shipwright's line
(Dispos'd by such a hand as learn'd from th' Artizan divine
The perfect practice of his art) directs or guards so well
The naval timber then in frame, that all the laid-on steel
Can hew no further than may serve, to give the timber th' end
Fore-purpos'd by the skilful wright; so both hosts did contend
With such a line or law applied, to what their steel would gain.
At other ships fought other men; but Hector did maintain
His quarrel firm at Ajax' ship. And so did both employ
About one vessel all their toil; nor could the one destroy
The ship with fire, nor force the man, nor that man yet get gone
The other from so near his ship, for God had brought him on.
But now did Ajax, with a dart, wound deadly in the breast
Caletor, son of Clytius, as he with fire address'd
To burn the vessel; as he fell, the brand fell from his hand.
When Hector saw his sister's son lie slaughter'd in the sand,
He call'd to all his friends, and pray'd they would not in that strait
Forsake his nephew, but maintain about his corse the fight,
And save it from the spoil of Greece. Then sent he out a lance
At Ajax, in his nephew's wreak; which miss'd, but made the chance
On Lycophron Mastorides, that was the household friend
Of Ajax, born in Cythera; whom Ajax did defend,
Being fled to his protectión, for killing of a man
Amongst the god-like Cytherans. The vengeful jav'lin ran
Quite through his head, above his ear, as he was standing by
His fautour then astern his ship, from whence his soul did fly,

And to the earth his body fell. The hair stood up an end
On Ajax, who to Teucer call'd (his brother) saying: "Friend
Our lovéd consort, whom we brought from Cythera, and grac'd
So like our father, Hector's hand hath made him breathe his last.
Where then are all thy death-borne shafts, and that unvalu'd bow
Apollo gave thee?" Tencer straight his brother's thoughts did know,
Stood near him, and dispatch'd a shaft, amongst the Trojan fight.
It strook Pisenor's goodly son, young Clitus, the delight
Of the renown'd Polydamas, the bridle in his hand,
As he was labouring his horse, to please the high command
Of Hector and his Trojan friends, and bring him where the fight
Made greatest tumult; but his strife, for honour in their sight,
Wrought not what sight or wishes help'd; for, turning back his look,
The hollow of his neck the shaft came singing on, and strook,
And down he fell; his horses back, and hurried through the field
The empty chariot. Panthus' son made all haste, and withheld
Their loose career, disposing them to Protiaon's son,
Astynous, with special charge, to keep them ever on,
And in his sight. So he again, amongst the foremost went.
At Hector then another shaft, incenséd Teucer sent,
Which, had it hit him, sure had hurt, and, had it hurt him, slain,
And, had it slain him, it had driv'n all those to Troy again.
But Jove's mind was not sleeping now, it wak'd to Hector's fame,
And Teucer's infamy; himself (in Teucer's deadly aim)
His well-wrought string dissevering, that serv'd his bravest bow;
His shaft flew quite another way, his bow the earth did strow.
At all which Teucer stood amaz'd, and to his brother cried:
"O prodigy! Without all doubt, our angel doth deride
The counsels of our fight; he brake a string my hands put on
This morning, and was newly made, and well might have set gone
A hundred arrows; and, beside, he strook out of my hand
The bow Apollo gave." He said: "Then, good friend, do not stand
More on thy archery, since God, preventer of all grace
Desir'd by Grecians, slights it so. Take therefore in the place
A good large lance, and on thy neck a target cast as bright,
With which come fight thyself with some, and other some excite,
That without labour at the least, though we prove worser men,
Troy may not brag it took our ships. Come, mind our business, then."
This said, he hasted to his tent, left there his shafts and bow,
And then his double double shield did on his shoulders throw;
Upon his honour'd head he plac'd his helmet thickly-plum'd,
And then his strong and well-pil'd lance in his fair hand assum'd,
Return'd; and boldly took his place, by his great brother's side.
When Hector saw his arrows broke, out to his friends he cried:
"O friends, be yet more comforted; I saw the hands of Jove
Break the great Grecian archer's shafts. 'Tis easy to approve
That Jove's pow'r is direct with men; as well in those set high
Upon the sudden, as in those depress'd as suddenly,

And those not put in state at all. As now he takes away
Strength from the Greeks, and gives it us; then use it, and assay
With join'd hands this approachéd fleet. If any bravely buy
His fame or fate with wounds or death, in Jove's name let him die.
Who for his country suffers death, sustains no shameful thing,
His wife in honour shall survive, his progeny shall spring
In endless summers, and their roofs with patrimony swell.
And all this, though, with all their freight, the Greek ships we repell."
His friends thus cheer'd; on th' other part, strong Ajax stirr'd his friends:
"O Greeks," said he, "what shame is this, that no man more defends
His fame and safety, than to live, and thus be forc'd to shrink!
Now either save your fleet, or die; unless ye vainly think
That you can live and they destroy'd. Perceives not ev'ry ear
How Hector heartens up his men, and hath his fire-brands here
Now ready to inflame our fleet? He doth not bid them dance,
That you may take your ease and see, but to the fight advance.
No counsel can serve us but this: To mix both hands and hearts,
And bear up close. 'Tis better much, t' expose our utmost parts
To one day's certain life or death, than languish in a war
So base as this, beat to our ships by our inferiors far."
Thus rous'd he up their spirits and strengths. To work then both sides went,
When Hector the Phocensian duke to fields of darkness sent,
Fierce Schedius, Perimedes' son; which Ajax did requite
With slaughter of Laodamas, that led the foot to fight,
And was Antenor's famous son. Polydamas did end
Otus, surnam'd Cyllenius, whom Phydas made his friend,
Being chief of the Epeians' bands. Whose fall when Meges view'd,
He let fly at his feller's life; who, shrinking in, eschew'd
The well-aim'd lance; Apollo's will denied that Panthus' son
Should fall amongst the foremost fights; the dart the mid-breast won
Of Crasmus; Meges won his arms. At Meges, Dolops then
Bestow'd his lance; he was the son of Lampus, best of men,
And Lampus of Laomedon, well-skill'd in strength of mind,
He strook Phylides' shield quite through, whose curets, better lin'd,
And hollow'd fitly, sav'd his life. Phyleus left him them,
Who from Epirus brought them home, on that part where the stream
Of famous Seléés doth run; Euphetes did bestow,
Being guest with him, those well-prov'd arms, to wear against the foe,
And now they sav'd his son from death. At Dolops, Meges threw
A spear well-pil'd, that strook his casque full in the height; off flew
His purple feather, newly made, and in the dust it fell.
While these thus striv'd for victory, and either's hope serv'd well,
Atrides came to Meges' aid, and, hidden with his side,
Let loose a jav'lin at his foe, that through his back implied
His lusty head, ev'n past his breast; the ground receiv'd his weight.
While these made in to spoil his arms, great Hector did excite
All his allies to quick revenge; and first he wrought upon
Strong Manalippus, that was son to great Hycetaon,

With some reproof. Before these wars, he in Percote fed
Clov'n-foot'd oxen, but did since return where he was bred,
Excell'd amongst the Ilians, was much of Priam lov'd,
And in his court kept as his son. Him Hector thus reprov'd:
"Thus, Menalippus, shall our blood accuse us of neglect?
Nor moves it thy lov'd heart, thus urg'd, thy kinsman to protect?
Seest thou not how they seek his spoil? Come, follow, now no more
Our fight must stand at length, but close; nor leave the close before
We close the latest eye of them, or they the lowest stone
Tear up, and sack the citizens of lofty Ilion."
He led; he follow'd, like a God. And then must Ajax needs,
As well as Hector, cheer his men, and thus their spirits he feeds:
"Good friends, bring but yourselves to feel the noble stings of shame
For what ye suffer, and be men. Respect each other's fame;
For which who strives in shame's fit fear, and puts on ne'er so far,
Comes oft'ner off. Then stick engag'd; these fugitives of war
Save neither life, nor get renown, nor bear more mind than sheep."
This short speech fir'd them in his aid, his spirit touch'd them deep,
And turn'd them all before the fleet into a wall of brass;
To whose assault Jove stirr'd their foes, and young Atrides was
Jove's instrument, who thus set on the young Antilochus:
"Antilochus, in all our host, there is not one of us
More young than thou, more swift of foot, nor, with both those, so strong.
O would thou wouldst then, for thou canst, one of this lusty throng,
That thus comes skipping out before (whoever, any where)
Make stick, for my sake, 'twixt both hosts, and leave his bold blood there!"
He said no sooner, and retir'd, but forth he rush'd before
The foremost fighters, yet his eye did ev'ry way explore
For doubt of odds; out flew his lance; the Trojans did abstain
While he was darting; yet his dart he cast not off in vain,
For Menalippus, that rare son of great Hycetaon,
As bravely he put forth to fight, it fiercely flew upon;
And at the nipple of his breast, his breast and life did part.
And then, much like an eager hound, cast off at some young hart
Hurt by the hunter, that had left his covert then but new,
The great-in-war Antilochus, O Menalippus, flew
On thy torn bosom for thy spoil. But thy death could not lie
Hid to great Hector; who all haste made to thee, and made fly
Antilochus, although in war he were at all parts skill'd.
But as some wild beast, having done some shrewd turn (either kill'd
The herdsman, or the herdsman's dog) and skulks away before
The gather'd multitude makes in; so Nestor's son forbore,
But after him, with horrid cries, both Hector and the rest
Show'rs of tear-thirsty lances pour'd; who having arm'd his breast
With all his friends, he turn'd it then. Then on the ships all Troy,
Like raw-flesh-nourish'd lions, rush'd, and knew they did employ
Their pow'rs to perfect Jove's high will; who still their spirits enflam'd,
And quench'd the Grecians'; one renown'd, the other often sham'd.

For Hector's glory still he stood, and ever went about
To make him cast the fleet such fire, as never should go out;
Heard Thetis' foul petitión, and wish'd in any wise
The splendour of the burning ships might satiate his eyes.
From him yet the repulse was then to be on Troy conferr'd,
The honour of it giv'n the Greeks; which thinking on, he stirr'd,
With such addition of his spirit, the spirit Hector bore
To burn the fleet, that of itself was hot enough before.
But now he far'd like Mars himself, so brandishing his lance
As, through the deep shades of a wood, a raging fire should glance,
Held up to all eyes by a hill; about his lips a foam
Stood as when th' ocean is enrag'd, his eyes were overcome
With fervour, and resembled flames, set off by his dark brows,
And from his temples his bright helm abhorréd lightnings throws;
For Jove, from forth the sphere of stars, to his state put his own,
And all the blaze of both the hosts confin'd in him alone.
And all this was, since after this he had not long to live,
This lightning flew before his death, which Pallas was to give
(A small time thence, and now prepar'd) beneath the violence
Of great Pelides. In mean time, his present eminence
Thought all things under it; and he, still where he saw the stands
Of greatest strength and bravest arm'd, there he would prove his hands,
Or nowhere; off'ring to break through, but that pass'd all his pow'r,
Although his will were past all theirs, they stood him like a tow'r
Conjoin'd so firm, that as a rock, exceeding high and great,
And standing near the hoary sea, bears many a boist'rous threat
Of high-voic'd winds and billows huge, belch'd on it by the storms;
So stood the Greeks great Hector's charge, nor stirr'd their battellous forms.
He, girt in fire borne for the fleet, still rush'd at ev'ry troop,
And fell upon it like a wave, high rais'd, that then doth stoop
Out from the clouds, grows, as it stoops, with storms, then down doth come
And cuff a ship, when all her sides are hid in brackish foam,
Strong gales still raging in her sails, her sailors' minds dismay'd,
Death being but little from their lives; so Jove-like Hector fray'd
And plied the Greeks, who knew not what would chance, for all their guards.
And as the baneful king of beasts, leapt into oxen herds
Fed in the meadows of a fen, exceeding great; the beasts
In number infinite; 'mongst whom (their herdsmen wanting breasts
To fight with lions, for the price of a black ox's life)
He here and there jumps, first and last, in his blood-thirsty strife,
Chas'd and assaulted; and, at length, down in the midst goes one,
And all the rest spers'd through the fen; so now all Greece was gone;
So Hector, in a flight from heav'n upon the Grecians cast,
Turn'd all their backs; yet only one his deadly lance laid fast,
Brave Mycenæus Periphes, Cypræus' dearest son,
Who of the heav'n's-Queen-lovéd king, great Eurysthæus, won
The grace to greet in ambassy the strength of Hercules,
Was far superior to his sire in feet, fight, nobleness

Of all the virtues, and all those did such a wisdom guide
As all Mycena could not match; and this man dignified,
Still making greater his renown, the state of Priam's son,
For his unhappy hasty foot, as he address'd to run,
Stuck in th' extreme ring of his shield, that to his ankles reach'd,
And down he upwards fell, his fall up from the centre fetch'd
A huge sound with his head and helm; which Hector quickly spied,
Ran in, and in his worthy breast his lance's head did hide;
And slew about him all his friends, who could not give him aid,
They griev'd, and of his god-like foe fled so extreme afraid.
And now amongst the nearest ships, that first were drawn to shore,
The Greeks were driv'n; beneath whose sides, behind them, and before,
And into them they pour'd themselves, and thence were driv'n again
Up to their tents, and there they stood; not daring to maintain
Their guards more outward, but, betwixt the bounds of fear and shame,
Cheer'd still each other; when th' old man, that of the Grecian name
Was call'd the Pillar, ev'ry man thus by his parents pray'd:
"O friends, be men, and in your minds let others' shames be weigh'd.
Know you have friends besides yourselves, possessions, parents, wives,
As well those that are dead to you, as those ye love with lives;
All sharing still their good, or bad, with yours. By these I pray,
That are not present (and the more should therefore make ye weigh
Their miss of you, as yours of them) that you will bravely stand,
And this forc'd flight you have sustain'd, at length yet countermand."
Supplies of good words thus supplied the deeds and spirits of all.
And so at last Minerva clear'd, the cloud that Jove let fall
Before their eyes; a mighty light flew beaming ev'ry way,
As well about their ships, as where their darts did hottest play,
Then saw they Hector great in arms, and his associates,
As well all those that then abstain'd, as those that help'd the fates,
And all their own fight at the fleet. Nor did it now content
Ajax to keep down like the rest; he up the hatches went,
Stalk'd here and there, and in his hand a huge great bead-hook held,
Twelve cubits long, and full of iron. And as a man well-skill'd
In horse, made to the martial race, when, of a number more,
He chooseth four, and brings them forth, to run them all before
Swarms of admiring citizens, amids their town's high way,
And, in their full career, he leaps from one to one, no stay
Enforc'd on any, nor fails he, in either seat or leap;
So Ajax with his bead-hook leap'd nimbly from ship to ship,
As actively commanding all, them in their men as well
As men in them, most terribly exhorting to repell,
To save their navy and their tents. But Hector nothing needs
To stand on exhortations now at home, he strives for deeds.
And look how Jove's great queen of birds, sharp-set, looks out for prey,
Knows floods that nourish wild-wing'd fowls, and, from her airy way,
Beholds where cranes, swans, cormorants, have made their foody fall,
Darkens the river with her wings, and stoops amongst them all;

So Hector flew amongst the Greeks, directing his command,
In chief, against one opposite ship; Jove with a mighty hand
Still backing him and all his men. And then again there grew
A bitter conflict at the fleet. You would have said none drew
A weary breath, nor ever would, they laid so freshly on.
And this was it that fir'd them both: The Greeks did build upon
No hope but what the field would yield, flight an impossible course;
The Trojans all hope entertain'd, that sword and fire should force
Both ships and lives of all the Greeks. And thus, unlike affects
Bred like strenuity in both. Great Hector still directs
His pow'rs against the first near ship. 'Twas that fair bark that brought
Protesilaus to those wars, and now her self to nought,
With many Greek and Trojan lives, all spoil'd about her spoil.
One slew another desp'rately, and close the deadly toil
Was pitch'd on both parts. Not a shaft, nor far-off striking dart
Was us'd through all. One fight fell out, of one despiteful heart.
Sharp axes, twybills, two-hand swords, and spears with two heads borne,
Were then the weapons; fair short swords, with sanguine hilts still worn,
Had use in like sort; of which last, ye might have numbers view'd
Drop with dissolv'd arms from their hands, as many down-right hew'd
From off their shoulders as they fought, their bawdrics cut in twain.
And thus the black blood flow'd on earth, from soldiers hurt and slain.
When Hector once had seiz'd the ship, he clapt his fair broad hand
Fast on the stern, and held it there, and there gave this command:
"Bring fire, and all together shout. Now Jove hath drawn the veil
From such a day as makes amends, for all his storms of hail;
By whose blest light we take those ships, that, in despite of heav'n,
Took sea, and brought us worlds of woe, all since our peers were giv'n
To such a laziness and fear; they would not let me end
Our ling'ring banes, and charge thus home, but keep home and defend,
And so they rul'd the men I led. But though Jove then withheld
My natural spirit, now by Jove 'tis freed, and thus impell'd."
This more inflam'd them; in so much that Ajax now no more
Kept up, he was so drown'd in darts; a little he forbore
The hatches to a seat beneath, of sev'n foot long, but thought
It was impossible to scape; he sat yet where he fought,
And hurl'd out lances thick as hail, at all men that assay'd
To fire the ship; with whom he found his hands so overlaid,
That on his soldiers thus he cried: "O friends, fight I alone?
Expect ye more walls at your backs? Towns rampir'd here are none,
No citizens to take ye in, no help of any kind.
We are, I tell you, in Troy's fields; have nought but seas behind,
And foes before; far, far from Greece. For shame, obey commands,
There is no mercy in the wars; your healths lie in your hands."
Thus rag'd he, and pour'd out his darts. Whoever he espied
Come near the vessel arm'd with fire, on his fierce dart he died.
All that pleas'd Hector made him mad, all that his thanks would earn;
Of which twelve men, his most resolv'd, lay dead before his stern.

THE END OF THE FIFTEENTH BOOK.

THE ARGUMENT

Achilles, at Patroclus' suit, doth yield
His arms and Myrmidons; which brought to field,
The Trojans fly. Patroclus hath the grace
Of great Sarpedon's death, sprung of the race
Of Jupiter, he having slain the horse
Of Thetis' son, fierce Pedasus. The force
Of Hector doth revenge the much-rued end
Of most renown'd Sarpedon on the friend
Of Thetides, first by Euphorbus harm'd,
And by Apollo's personal pow'r disarm'd.

ANOTHER ARGUMENT

In Ṁ Patroclus bears the chance
Of death, impos'd by Hector's lance.
Thus fighting for this well-built ship; Patroclus all that space
Stood by his friend, preparing words to win the Greeks his grace,
With pow'r of uncontainéd tears; and, like a fountain pour'd
In black streams from a lofty rock, the Greeks so plagu'd deplor'd.
Achilles, ruthful for his tears, said: "Wherefore weeps my friend
So like a girl, who, though she sees her mother cannot tend
Her childish humours, hangs on her, and would be taken up,
Still viewing her with tear-drown'd eyes, when she hath made her stoop,
To nothing liker I can shape thy so unseemly tears.
What causeth them? Hath any ill solicited thine ears
Befall'n my Myrmidons? Or news from lovéd Phthia brought,
Told only thee, lest I should grieve, and therefore thus hath wrought
On thy kind spirit? Actor's son, the good Menœtius,
Thy father, lives, and Peleus, mine, great son of Æacus,
Amongst his Myrmidons; whose deaths, in duty we should mourn,
Or is it what the Greeks sustain, that doth thy stomach turn,
On whom, for their injustice' sake, plagues are so justly laid?
Speak, man, let both know either's heart." Patroclus, sighing, said:
"O Peleus' son, thou strongest Greek by all degrees that lives,
Still be not angry, our sad state such cause of pity gives,
Our greatest Greeks lie at their ships sore wounded; Ithacus,
King Agamemnon, Diomed, and good Eurypylus;
But these much-med'cine-knowing men, physicians, can recure,

Thou yet unmed'cinable still, though thy wound all endure,
Heav'n bless my bosom from such wrath as thou sooth'st as thy bliss,
Unprofitably virtuous. How shall our progenies,
Born in thine age, enjoy thine aid, when these friends, in thy flow'r,
Thou leav'st to such unworthy death? O idle, cruel pow'r!
Great Peleus never did beget, nor Thetis bring forth thee,
Thou from the blue sea, and her rocks, deriv'st thy pedigree,
What so declines thee? If thy mind shuns any augury,
Related by thy mother-queen from heav'n's foreseeing eye,
And therefore thou forsak'st thy friends, let me go ease their moans
With those brave relics of our host, thy mighty Myrmidons,
That I may bring to field more light to conquest than hath been.
To which end grace me with thine arms, since, any shadow seen
Of thy resemblance, all the pow'r of perjur'd Troy will fly,
And our so-tiréd friend's will breathe; our fresh-set-on supply
Will eas'ly drive their wearied off." Thus, foolish man, he sued
For his sure death; of all whose speech Achilles first renew'd
The last part thus: "O worthy friend, what have thy speeches been?
I shun the fight for oracles, or what my mother queen
Hath told from Jove? I take no care, nor note of one such thing!
But this fit anger stings me still, that the insulting king
Should from his equal take his right, since he exceeds in pow'r.
This, still his wrong, is still my grief: He took my paramour
That all men gave, and whom I won by virtue of my spear,
That, for her, overturn'd a town. This rape he made of her,
And used me like a fugitive, an inmate in a town,
That is no city libertine, nor capable of their gown.
But bear we this as out of date; 'tis past, nor must we still
Feed anger in our noblest parts; yet thus, I have my will
As well as our great king of men, for I did ever vow
Never to cast off my disdain till, as it falls out now,
Their miss of me knock'd at my fleet, and told me in their cries
I was reveng'd, and had my wish of all my enemies.
And so of this repeat enough. Take thou my fame-blaz'd arms,
And my fight-thirsty Myrmidons lead to these hot alarms.
Whole clouds of Trojans circle us with hateful eminence;
The Greeks shut in a little shore, a sort of citizens
Skipping upon them; all because their proud eyes do not see
The radiance of my helmet there, whose beams had instantly
Thrust back, and all these ditches fill'd with carrion of their flesh,
If Agamemnon had been kind; where now they fight as fresh,
As thus far they had put at ease, and at our tents contend.
And may; for the repulsive hand of Diomed doth not spend
His raging darts there, that their death could fright out of our fleet;
Nor from that head of enmity, can my poor hearers meet
The voice of great Atrides now. Now Hector's only voice
Breaks all the air about both hosts, and, with the very noise
Bred by his loud encouragements, his forces fill the field,

And fight the poor Achaians down. But on, put thou my shield
Betwixt the fire-plague and our fleet. Rush bravely on, and turn
War's tide as headlong on their throats. No more let them ajourn
Our sweet home-turning. But observe the charge I lay on thee
To each least point, that thy rul'd hand may highly honour me,
And get such glory from the Greeks, that they may send again
My most sweet wench, and gifts to boot, when thou hast cast a rein
On these so headstrong citizens, and forc'd them from our fleet.
With which grace if the God of sounds thy kind egression greet; [1]
Retire, and be not tempted on (with pride to see thy hand
Rain slaughter'd carcasses on earth) to run forth thy command
As far as Ilion, lest the Gods, that favour Troy, come forth
To thy encounter, for the Sun much loves it; and my worth,
In what thou suffer'st, will be wrong'd, that I would let my friend
Assume an action of such weight without me, and transcend
His friend's prescription. Do not then affect a further fight
Than I may strengthen. Let the rest, when thou hast done this right,
Perform the rest. O would to Jove, thou Pallas, and thou Sun,
That not a man hous'd underneath those tow'rs of Ilion,
Nor anyone of all the Greeks, how infinite a sum
Soever all together make, might live unovercome;
But only we two, 'scaping death, might have the thund'ring down
Of ev'ry stone stuck in the walls of this so sacred town!"
Thus spake they only 'twixt themselves. And now the foe no more
Could Ajax stand, being so oppress'd with all the iron store
The Trojans pour'd on; with whose darts, and with Jove's will beside,
His pow'rs were cloy'd, and his bright helm did deaf'ning blows abide,
His plume, and all bead-ornaments, could never hang in rest.
His arm yet labour'd up his shield, and having done their best,
They could not stir him from his stand, although he wrought it out
With short respirings, and with sweat, that ceaseless flow'd about
His reeking limbs; no least time giv'n to take in any breath;
Ill strengthen'd ill; when one was up, another was beneath.
Now, Muses, you that dwell in heav'n, the dreadful mean inspire,
That first enforc'd the Grecian fleet, to take in Trojan fire.
First Hector, with his huge broad sword, cut off, at setting on,
The head of Ajax' ashen lance; which Ajax seeing gone,
And that he shook a headless spear, a little while unware,
His wary spirits told him straight the hand of Heav'n was there;
And trembling under his conceit, which was that 'twas Jove's deed,
Who, as be poll'd off his dart's heads, so sure he had decreed
That all the counsels of their war, he would poll off like it,
And give the Trojans victory; so trusted he his wit,
And left his darts. And then the ship was heap'd with horrid brands
Of kindling fire; which instantly was seen through all the strands
In unextinguishable flames, that all the ship embrac'd.
And then Achilles beat his thighs, cried out, "Patroclus, haste,
Make way with horse. I see at fleet, a fire of fearful rage.

Arm, arm, lest all our fleet it fire, and all our pow'r engage.
Arm quickly, I'll bring up the troops." To these so dreadful wars
Patroclus, in Achilles' arms, enlighten'd all with stars,
And richly amell'd, all haste made. He wore his sword, his shield,
His huge-plum'd helm, and two such spears, as he could nimbly wield.
But the most fam'd Achilles' spear, big, solid, full of weight,
He only left of all his arms; for that far pass'd the might
Of any Greek to shake but his; Achilles' only ire
Shook that huge weapon, that was giv'n by Chiron to his sire,
Cut from the top of Pelion, to be heroës' deaths.
His steeds Automedon straight join'd; like whom no man that breathes,
Next Peleus' son, Patroclus lov'd; for, like him, none so great
He found in faith at ev'ry fight, nor to out-look a threat,
Automedon did therefore guide for him Achilles' steeds,
Xanthius and Balius swift as wind, begotten by the seeds
Of Zephyr, and the Harpy born, Podarge, in a mead
Close to the wavy oceán, where that fierce Harpy fed.
Automedon join'd these before, and with the hindmost gears
He fasten'd famous Pedasus, whom, from the massacres
Made by Achilles, when he took Eëtion's wealthy town,
He brought, and, though of mortal race, yet gave him the renown
To follow his immortal horse. And now, before his tents,
Himself had seen his Myrmidons, in all habiliments
Of dreadful war. And when ye see, upon a mountain bred, [2]
A den of wolves, about whose hearts unmeasur'd strengths are fed,
New come from currie of a stag, their jaws all blood-besmear'd,
And when from some black-water fount they all together herd,
There having plentifully lapp'd, with thin and thrust out tongues,
The top and clearest of the spring, go belching from their lungs
The clotter'd gore, look dreadfully, and entertain no dread,
Their bellies gaunt all taken up, with being so rawly fed;
Then say, that such, in strength and look, were great Achilles' men
Now order'd for the dreadful fight; and so with all them then
Their princes and their chiefs did show, about their Gen'ral's friend;
His friend, and all, about himself; who chiefly did intend
Th' embattelling of horse and foot. To that siege, held so long,
Twice-five-and-twenty sail he brought, twice-five-and-twenty strong
Of able men was ev'ry sail. Five colonels he made
Of all those forces; trusty men, and all of pow'r to lead,
But he of pow'r beyond them all. Menesthius was one,
That ever wore discolour'd arms; he was a river's son
That fell from heav'n, and good to drink was his delightful stream,
His name unwearied Sperchius, he lov'd the lovely dame
Fair Polydora, Peleus' seed, and dear in Borus' sight,
And she to that celestial Flood gave this Menesthius light,
A woman mixing with a God. Yet Borus bore the name
Of father to Menesthius, he marrying the dame,
And giving her a mighty dow'r; he was the kind descent

Of Perieres. The next man, renown'd with regiment,
Was strong Eudorus, brought to life by one suppos'd a maid,
Bright Polymela, Phylas' seed, but had the wanton play'd
With Argus-killing Mercury; who (fir'd with her fair eyes,
As she was singing in the quire of Her that makes the cries
In clam'rous hunting, and doth bear the crooked bow of gold)
Stole to her bed in that chaste room, that Phœbe chaste did hold,
And gave her that swift-warlike son, Eudorus, brought to light
As she was dancing; but as soon, as She that rules the plight
Of labouring women eas'd her throes, and show'd her son the sun,
Strong Echecæus, Actor's heir, woo'd earnestly, and won
Her second favour, feeing her with gifts of infinite prize;
And after brought her to his house, where, in his grandsire's eyes,
Old Phylas, Polymela's son obtain'd exceeding grace,
And found as careful bringing up, as of his natural race
He had descended. The third chief was fair Mæmalides
Pisandrus, who in skill of darts obtain'd supremest praise
Of all the Myrmidons, except their lord's companion.
The fourth charge, aged Phœnix had. The fifth, Alcimedon,
Son of Laerces, and much fam'd. All these digested thus
In fit place by the mighty son of royal Peleüs,
This stern remembrance he gave all: "You, Myrmidons," said he,
"Lest any of you should forget his threat'nings us'd to me
In this place, and, through all the time, that my just anger
reign'd,
Attempting me with bitter words, for being so restrain'd,
For my hot humour, from the fight, remember them as these:
'Thou cruel son of Peleüs, whom She that rules the seas
Did only nourish with her gall, thou dost ungently hold
Our hands against our wills from fight. We will not be controll'd,
But take our ships, and sail for home, before we loiter here
And feed thy fury.' These high words exceeding often were
The threats that, in your mutinous troops, ye us'd to me for wrath
To be detain'd so from the field. Now then, your spleens may bathe
In sweat of those great works ye wish'd; now, he that can employ
A gen'rous heart, go fight, and fright these bragging sons of Troy."
This set their minds and strengths on fire, the speech enforcing well,
Being us'd in time; but, being their king's, it much more did impell,
And closer rush'd in all the troops. And as, for buildings high,
The mason lays his stones more thick, against th' extremity
Of wind and weather, and ev'n then, if any storm arise,
He thickens them the more for that, the present act so plies
His honest mind to make sure work; so, for the high estate
This work was brought to, these men's minds, according to the rate,
Were rais'd, and all their bodies join'd; but their well-spoken king,
With his so timely-thought-on speech, more sharp made valour's sting,
And thicken'd so their targets boss'd, so all their helmets then,
That shields propp'd shields, helms helmets knock'd, and men encourag'd men.

Patroclus and Automedon did arm before them all,
Two bodies with one mind inform'd; and then the General
Betook him to his private tent, where from a coffer wrought
Most rich and curiously, and giv'n by Thetis to be brought
In his own ship, top-fill'd with vests, warm robes to check cold wind,
And tapestries all gold'n-fring'd, and curl'd with thrumbs behind,
He took a most unvalu'd bowl, in which none drank but he;
Nor he but to the Deities, nor any Deity
But Jove himself was serv'd with that; and that he first did cleanse
With sulphur, then with fluences of sweetest water rense;
Then wash'd his hands, and drew himself a mighty bowl of wine,
Which (standing midst the place enclos'd for services divine,
And looking up to heav'n and Jove, who saw him well) he pour'd
Upon the place of sacrifice, and humbly thus implor'd:
"Great Dodonæus, president of cold Dodone's tow'rs,
Divine Pelasgicus, that dwellest far hence; about whose bow'rs
Th' austere prophetic Selli dwell, that still sleep on the ground,
Go bare, and never cleanse their feet; as I before have found
Grace to my vows, and hurt to Greece, so now my pray'rs intend.
I still stay in the gather'd fleet, but have dismiss'd my friend,
Amongst my many Myrmidons, to danger of the dart;
O grant his valour my renown, arm with my mind his heart!
That Hector's self may know my friend can work in single war,
And not then only show his hands, so hot and singular,
When my kind presence seconds him. But, fight he ne'er so well,
No further let him trust his fight, but, when he shall repell
Clamour and danger from our fleet, vouchsafe a safe retreat
To him and all his companies, with fames and arms complete."
He pray'd, and heav'n's great Counsellor gave satisfying ear
To one part of his orisons, but left the other there;
He let him free the fleet of foes, but safe retreat denied.
Achilles left that utter part where he his zeal applied,
And turn'd into his inner tent, made fast his cup, and then
Stood forth, and with his mind beheld the foes fight; and his men,
That follow'd his great-minded friend, embattled till they brake
With gallant spirit upon the foe. And as fell wasps, that make
Their dwellings in the broad high-way, which foolish children use
(Their cottages being near their nests) to anger and abuse
With ever vexing them, and breed (to soothe their childish war)
A common ill to many men, since if a traveller
(That would his journey's end apply, and pass them unassay'd)
Come near and vex them, upon him the children's faults are laid,
For on they fly as he were such, and still defend their own;
So far'd it with the fervent mind of ev'ry Myrmidon,
Who pour'd themselves out of their fleet upon their wanton foes,
That needs would stir them, thrust so near, and cause the overthrows
Of many others, that had else been never touch'd by them,
Nor would have touch'd. Patroclus then put his wind to the stream,

And thus exhorted: "Now, my friends, remember you express
Your late-urg'd virtue, and renown our great Æacides.
That, he being strong'st of all the Greeks, his eminence may dim
All others likewise in our strengths, that far off imitate him:
And Agamemnon now may see his fault as general
As his place high, dishonouring him that so much honours all."
Thus made he sparkle their fresh fire, and on they rush'd; the fleet
Fill'd full her hollow sides with sounds, that terribly did greet
Th' amazed Trojans; and their eyes did second their amaze
When great Menœtius' son they saw, and his friend's armour blaze.
All troops stood troubled, with conceit that Peleus' son was there,
His anger cast off at the ships; and each look'd ev'rywhere
For some authority to lead the then preparéd flight.
Patroclus greeted with a lance the region where the fight
Made strongest tumult, near the ship Protesilaus brought,
And strook Pyræchmen; who before the fair-helmed Pæons fought,
Led from Amydon, near whose walls the broad-stream'd Axius flows.
Through his right shoulder flew the dart, whose blow strook all the blows
In his pow'r from his pow'rless arm, and down he groaning fell;
His men all flying, their leader fled. This one dart did repell
The whole guard plac'd about the ship, whose fire extinct, half burn'd
The Pæons left her, and full cry to clam'rous flight return'd.
Then spread the Greeks about their ships; triumphant tumult flow'd:
And, as from top of some steep hill the Lightner strips a cloud,
And lets a great sky out from heav'n, in whose delightsome light
All prominent foreheads, forests, tow'rs, and temples cheer the sight;
So clear'd these Greeks this Trojan cloud, and at their ships and tents
Obtain'd a little time to breathe, but found no present vents
To their inclusions; nor did Troy, though these Pæonians fled,
Lose any ground, but from this ship they needfully turn'd head.
Then ev'ry man a man subdu'd. Patroclus in the thigh
Strook Areilycus; his dart the bone did break, and fly
Quite through, and sunk him to the earth. Good Menelaus slew
Accomplish'd Thoas, in whose breast, being nak'd, his lance he threw
Above his shield, and freed his soul. Phylides, taking note
That bold Amphiclus bent at him, prevented him, and smote
His thigh's extreme part, where of man his fattest muscle lies,
The nerves torn with his lance's pile, and darkness clos'd his eyes.
Antilochus Atymnius seiz'd, his steel lance did impress
His first three guts, and loos'd his life. At young Nestorides,
Maris, Atymnius' brother, flew; and at him Thrasymed
The brother to Antilochus; his eager jav'lin's head
The muscles of his arm cut out, and shiver'd all the bone;
Night clos'd his eyes, his lifeless corse his brother fell upon.
And so by two kind brothers' hands, did two kind brothers bleed;
Both being divine Sarpedon's friends, and were the darting seed
Of Amisodarus, that kept the bane of many men
Abhorr'd Chimæra; and such bane now caught his childeren.

Ajax Oïliades did take Cleobulus alive,
Invading him stay'd by the press; and at him then let drive
With his short sword that cut his neck; whose blood warm'd all the steel,
And cold Death with a violent fate his sable eyes did seel.
Peneleüs, and Lycon cast together off their darts;
Both miss'd, and both together then went with their swords; in parts
The blade and hilt went, laying on upon the helmet's height.
Peneleus' sword caught Lycon's neck, and cut it thorough quite.
His head hung by the very skin. The swift Meriones,
Pursuing flying Acamas, just as he got access
To horse and chariot overtook, and took him such a blow
On his right shoulder, that he left his chariot, and did strow
The dusty earth; life left his limbs, and night his eyes possess'd.
Idomenæus his stern dart at Erymas address'd,
As, like to Acamas, he fled; it cut the sundry bones
Beneath his brain, betwixt his neck, and foreparts; and so runs,
Shaking his teeth out, through his mouth, his eyes all drown'd in blood,
So through his nostrils and his mouth, that now dart-open stood,
He breath'd his spirit. Thus had death from ev'ry Grecian chief
A chief of Troy. For, as to kids, or lambs, their cruell'st thief,
The wolf, steals in, and, when he sees that by the shepherd's sloth
The dams are spers'd about the hills, then serves his rav'nous tooth
With ease, because his prey is weak; so serv'd the Greeks their foes,
Discerning well how shrieking flight did all their spirits dispose,
Their biding virtues quite forgot. And now the natural spleen
That Ajax bore to Hector still, by all means, would have been
Within his bosom with a dart; but he that knew the war,
Well-cover'd in a well-lin'd shield, did well perceive how far
The arrows and the jav'lins reach'd, by being within their sounds
And ominous singings; and observ'd the there-in-clining bounds
Of Conquest in her aid of him, and so obey'd her change,
Took safest course for him and his, and stood to her as strange.
And as, when Jove intends a storm, he lets out of the stars,
From steep Olympus, a black cloud, that all heav'n's splendour bars
From men on earth; so from the hearts of all the Trojan host
All comfort lately found from Jove, in flight and cries was lost.
Nor made they any fair retreat. Hector's unruly horse
Would needs retire him, and he left engag'd his Trojan force,
Forc'd by the steepness of the dike, that in ill place they took,
And kept them that would fain have gone. Their horses quite forsook
A number of the Trojan kings, and left them in the dike;
Their chariots in their foreteams broke. Patroclus then did strike
While steel was hot, and cheer'd his friends; nor meant his enemies good,
Who, when they once began to fly, each way receiv'd a flood,
And chok'd themselves with drifts of dust. And now were clouds begot
Beneath the clouds; with flight and noise the horse neglected not
Their home intendments; and, where rout was busiest, there pour'd on
Patroclus most exhorts and threats; and then lay overthrown

Numbers beneath their axle-trees; who, lying in flight's stream,
Made th' after chariots jot and jump, in driving over them.
Th' immortal horse Patroclus rode, did pass the dike with ease,
And wish'd the depth and danger more; and Menœtiades
As great a spirit had to reach, retiring Hector's haste,
But his fleet horse had too much law, and fetch'd him off too fast.
And as in Autumn the black earth is loaden with the storms
That Jove in gluts of rain pours down, being angry with the forms
Of judgment in authoriz'd men, that in their courts maintain,
With violent office, wrested laws, and (fearing Gods, nor men)
Exile all justice; for whose fault, whole fields are overflown,
And many valleys cut away with torrents headlong thrown
From neighbour mountains, till the sea receive them roaring in,
And judg'd men's labours then are vain, plagu'd for their judge's sin;
So now the foul defaults of some all Troy were laid upon;
So like those torrents roar'd they back to windy Ilion;
And so like tempests blew the horse with ravishing back again
Those hot assailants, all their works at fleet now render'd vain.
Patroclus, when he had dispers'd the foremost phalanxes,
Call'd back his forces to the fleet, and would not let them prease,
As they desir'd, too near the town; but 'twixt the ships and flood,
And their steep rampire, his hand steep'd Revenge in seas of blood.
Then Pronous was first that fell beneath his fi'ry lance,
Which strook his bare breast, near his shield. The second Thestor's chance,
Old Enops' son, did make himself; who shrinking, and set close
In his fair seat, ev'n with th' approach Patroclus made, did lose
All manly courage, insomuch that from his hands his reins
Fell flowing down, and his right jaw Patroclus' lance attains,
Strock through his teeth, and there it stuck, and by it to him drew
Dead Thestor to his chariot. It show'd, as when you view
An angler from some prominent rock draw with his line and hook
A mighty fish out of the sea; for so the Greek did pluck
The Trojan gaping from his seat, his jaws op'd with the dart;
Which when Patroclus drew, he fell; his life and breast did part.
Then rush'd he on Erylaus; at whom he hurl'd a stone,
Which strake his head so in the midst, that two was made of one;
Two ways it fell, cleft through his casque. And then Tlepolemus,
Epaltes, Damastorides, Evippus, Echius,
Ipheas, bold Amphoterus, and valiant Erymas,
And Polymelus, by his sire surnam'd Argeadas,
He heap'd upon the much-fed earth. When Jove's most worthy son,
Divine Sarpedon, saw these friends thus stay'd, and others run,
"O shame! Why fly ye?" then he cried, "Now show ye feet enow.
On, keep your way, myself will meet the man that startles you,
To make me understand his name that flaunts in conquest thus,
And hath so many able knees so soon dissolv'd to us."
Down jump'd he from his chariot; down leap'd his foe as light.
And as, on some far-looking rock, a cast of vultures fight,

Fly on each other, strike and truss, part, meet, and then stick by,
Tug both with crooked beaks and seres, cry, fight, and fight and cry;
So fiercely fought these angry kings, and show'd as bitter galls.
Jove, turning eyes to this stern fight, his wife and sister calls,
And much mov'd for the Lycian Prince, said: "O that to my son
Fate, by this day and man, should cut a thread so nobly spun!
Two minds distract me; if I should now ravish him from fight,
And set him safe in Lycia; or give the Fates their right."
"Austere Saturnius," she replied, "what unjust words are these?
A mortal, long since mark'd by fate, wouldst thou immortalize?
Do, but by no God be approv'd. Free him, and numbers more,
Sons of Immortals, will live free, that death must taste before
These gates of Ilion; ev'ry God will have his son a God,
Or storm extremely. Give him then an honest period
In brave fight by Patroclus' sword, if he be dear to thee,
And grieves thee for his danger'd life; of which when he is free,
Let Death and Somnus bear him hence, till Lycia's natural womb
Receive him from his brother's hands, and citizens'; a tomb
And column rais'd to him. This is the honour of the dead."
She said, and her speech rul'd his pow'r; but in his safety's stead,
For sad ostent of his near death, he steep'd his living name
In drops of blood heav'n swet for him, which earth drunk to his fame.
And now, as this high combat grew to this too humble end,
Sarpedon's death had this state more; 'twas usher'd by his friend
And charioteer, brave Thrasymed; whom in his belly's rim
Patroclus wounded with his lance, and endless ended him.
And then another act of name foreran his princely fate.
His first lance missing, he let fly a second that gave date
Of violent death to Pedasus; who, as he joy'd to die
By his so honourable hand, did ev'n in dying neigh.
His ruin startled th' other steeds, the gears crack'd, and the reins
Strappled his fellows; whose misrule Automedon restrains
By cutting the intangling gears, and so dissund'ring quite
The brave slain beast; when both the rest obey'd, and went foreright.
And then the royal combatants fought for the final stroke;
When Lycia's Gen'ral miss'd again, his high-rais'd jav'lin took
Above his shoulder empty way. But no such speedless flight
Patroclus let his spear perform, that on the breast did light
Of his brave foe, where life's strings close about the solid heart,
Impressing a recureless wound; his knees then left their part,
And let him fall; when like an oak, a poplar, or a pine,
New fell'd by arts-men on the hills, he stretch'd his form divine
Before his horse and chariot. And as a lion leaps
Upon a goodly yellow bull, drives all the herd in heaps,
And, under his unconquer'd jaws, the brave beast sighing dies;
So sigh'd Sarpedon underneath this prince of enemies,
Call'd Glaucus to him, his dear friend, and said: "Now, friend, thy hands
Much duty owe to fight and arms; now for my love it stands

Thy heart in much hand to approve that war is harmful; now
How active all thy forces are, this one hour's act must show.
First call our Lycian captains up, look round, and bring up all,
And all exhort to stand, like friends, about Sarpedon's fall,
And spend thyself thy steel for me; for be assur'd no day
Of all thy life, to thy last hour, can clear thy black dismay
In woe and infamy for me, if I be taken hence
Spoil'd of mine arms, and thy renown despoil'd of my defence.
Stand firm then, and confirm thy men." This said, the bounds of death
Concluded all sight to his eyes, and to his nosthrils breath.
Patroclus, though his guard was strong, forc'd way through ev'ry doubt,
Climb'd his high bosom with his foot, and pluck'd his jav'lin out,
And with it drew the film and strings of his yet panting heart;
And last, together with the pile, his princely soul did part.
His horse, spoil'd both of guide and king, thick snoring and amaz'd,
And apt to flight, the Myrmidons made nimbly to, and seiz'd.
Glaucus, to hear his friend ask aid, of him past all the rest,
Though well he knew his wound uncur'd, confusion fill'd his breast
Not to have good in any pow'r, and yet so much good will.
And (laying his hand upon his wound, that pain'd him sharply still,
And was by Teucer's hand set on from their assail'd steep wall,
In keeping hurt from other men) he did on Phœbus call,
The God of med'cines, for his cure: "Thou King of cures," said he,
"That art perhaps in Lycia with her rich progeny,
Or here in Troy; but any where, since thou hast pow'r to hear,
O give a hurt and woeful man, as I am now, thine ear.
This arm sustains a cruel wound, whose pains shoot ev'ry way,
Afflict this shoulder, and this hand, and nothing long can stay
A flux of blood still issuing; nor therefore can I stand
With any enemy in fight, nor hardly make my hand
Support my lance; and here lies dead the worthiest of men,
Sarpedon, worthy son to Jove, whose pow'r could yet abstain
From all aid in this deadly need; give thou then aid to me,
O King of all aid to men hurt; assuage th' extremity
Of this arm's anguish, give it strength, that by my precedent
I may excite my men to blows, and this dead corse prevent
Of further violence." He pray'd, and kind Apollo heard,
Allay'd his anguish, and his wound of all the black blood clear'd
That vex'd it so, infus'd fresh pow'rs into his weaken'd mind;
And all his spirits flow'd with joy that Phœbus stood inclin'd,
In such quick bounty, to his pray'rs. Then, as Sarpedon will'd,
He cast about his greedy eye; and first of all instill'd
To all his captains all the stings, that could inflame their fight
For good Sarpedon. And from them, he stretch'd his speedy pace
T' Agenor, Hector, Venus' son, and wise Polydamas;
And (only naming Hector) said: "Hector, you now forget
Your poor auxiliary friends, that in your toils have swet
Their friendless souls out far from home. Sarpedon, that sustain'd

With justice, and his virtues all, broad Lycia, hath not gain'd
The like guard for his person here; for yonder dead he lies
Beneath the great Patroclus' lance. But come, let your supplies,
Good friends, stand near him. O disdain to see his corse defil'd
With Grecian fury; and his arms, by their oppressions spoil'd.
These Myrmidons are come enrag'd, that such a mighty boot
Of Greeks Troy's darts have made at fleet." This said, from head to foot
Grief strook their pow'rs past patience, and not to be restrain'd,
To hear news of Sarpedon's death; who, though he appertain'd
To other cities, yet to theirs he was the very fort,
And led a mighty people there, of all whose better sort
Himself was best. This made them run in flames upon the foe;
The first man Hector, to whose heart Sarpedon's death did go.
Patroclus stirr'd the Grecian spirits; and first th' Ajaces, thus:
"Now, brothers, be it dear to you, to fight and succour us,
As ever heretofore ye did, with men first excellent.
The man lies slain that first did scale, and raze the battlement
That crown'd our wall, the Lycian prince. But if we now shall add
Force to his corse, and spoil his arms, a prise may more be had
Of many great ones, that for him will put on to the death."
To this work these were prompt enough; and each side ordereth
Those phalanxes that most had rate of resolutions;
The Trojans and the Lycian pow'rs; the Greeks and Myrmidons.
These ran together for the corse, and clos'd with horrid cries,
Their armours thund'ring with the claps laid on about the prise.
And Jove, about th' impetuous broil, pernicious night pour'd out,
As long as for his lovéd son, pernicious Labour fought.
The first of Troy the first Greeks foil'd; when, not the last indeed
Amongst the Myrmidons, was slain, the great Agacleus' seed,
Divine Epigeus, that before had exercis'd command
In fair Budeiüs; but because he laid a bloody hand
On his own sister's valiant son, to Peleus and his queen
He came for pardon, and obtain'd; his slaughter being the mean
He came to Troy, and so to this. He ventur'd ev'n to touch
The princely carcass; when a stone did more to him by much,
Sent out of able Hector's hand; it cut his skull in twain,
And strook him dead. Patroclus, griev'd to see his friend so slain,
Before the foremost thrust himself. And as a falcon frays
A flock of stares or caddesses; such fear brought his assays
Amongst the Trojans and their friends; and, angry at the heart,
As well as griev'd, for him so slain, another stony dart
As good as Hector's he let fly, that dusted in the neck
Of Sthenelaus, thrust his head to earth first, and did break
The nerves in sunder with his fall; off fell the Trojans too,
Ev'n Hector's self, and all as far as any man can throw
(Provok'd for games, or in the wars to shed an enemy's soul)
A light long dart. The first that turn'd, was he that did control
The targeteers of Lycia, prince Glaucus; who to hell

Sent Bathyclæus, Chalcon's son; he did in Hellas dwell,
And shin'd for wealth and happiness amongst the Myrmidons;
His bosom's midst the jav'lin strook, his fall gat earth with groans.
The Greeks griev'd, and the Trojans joy'd, for so renown'd a man;
About whom stood the Grecians firm. And then the death began
On Troy's side by Meriones; he slew one great in war,
Laogonus, Onetor's son, the priest of Jupiter,
Created in th' Idæan hill. Betwixt his jaw and ear
The dart stuck fast, and loos'd his soul; sad mists of hate and fear
Invading him. Anchises' son despatch'd a brazen lance
At bold Meriones; and hop'd to make an equal chance
On him with bold Laogonus, though under his broad shield
He lay so close. But he discern'd, and made his body yield
So low, that over him it flew, and trembling took the ground,
With which Mars made it quench his thirst; and since the head could wound
No better body, and yet thrown from ne'er the worse a hand,
It turn'd from earth, and look'd awry. Æneas let it stand,
Much angry at the vain event, and told Meriones
He scap'd but hardly, nor had cause to hope for such success
Another time, though well he knew his dancing faculty,
By whose agility he scap'd; for, had his dart gone by
With any least touch, instantly he had been ever slain.
He answer'd: "Though thy strength be good, it cannot render vain
The strength of others with thy jests; nor art thou so divine,
But when my lance shall touch at thee, with equal speed to thine,
Death will share with it thy life's pow'rs; thy confidence can shun
No more than mine what his right claims." Menœtius' noble son
Rebuk'd Meriones, and said: "What need'st thou use this speech?
Nor thy strength is approv'd with words, good friend, nor can we reach
The body, nor make th' enemy yield, with these our counterbraves.
We must enforce the binding earth, to hold them in her graves.
If you will war, fight. Will you speak? Give counsel Counsel, blows,
Are th' ends of wars and words. Talk here, the time in vain bestows."
He said, and led; and, nothing less for any thing he said,
(His speech being season'd with such right) the worthy seconded.
And then, as in a sounding vale, near neighbour to a hill,
Wood-fellers make a far-heard noise, with chopping, chopping still,
And laying on, on blocks and trees; so they on men laid load,
And beat like noises into air, both as they strook and trode.
But, past their noise, so full of blood, of dust, of darts, lay smit
Divine Sarpedon, that a man must have an excellent wit
That could but know him, and might fail, so from his utmost head,
Ev'n to the low plants of his feet, his form was alteréd.
All thrusting near it ev'ry way, as thick as flies in spring,
That in a sheep-cote, when new milk assembles them, make wing,
And buzz about the top-full pails. Nor ever was the eye
Of Jove averted from the fight; he view'd, thought, ceaselessly
And diversly upon the death of great Achilles' friend,

If Hector there, to wreak his son, should with his jav'lin end
His life, and force away his arms, or still augment the field;
He then concluded that the flight of much more soul should yield
Achilles' good friend more renown, and that ev'n to their gates
He should drive Hector and his host; and so disanimates
The mind of Hector that he mounts his chariot, and takes Flight
Up with him, tempting all to her; affirming his insight
Knew evidently that the beam of Jove's all-ord'ring scoles
Was then in sinking on their side, surcharg'd with flocks of souls.
Then not the noble Lycians stay'd, but left their slaughter'd lord
Amongst the corses' common heap; for many more were pour'd
About and on him, while Jove's hand held out the bitter broil.
And now they spoil'd Sarpedon's arms, and to the ships the spoil
Was sent by Menœtiades. Then Jove thus charg'd the Sun:
"Haste, honour'd Phœbus, let no more Greek violence be done
To my Sarpedon; but his corse of all the sable blood
And jav'lins purg'd; then carry him, far hence to some clear flood,
With whose waves wash, and then embalm each thorough-cleanséd limb
With our ambrosia; which perform'd, divine weeds put on him,
And then to those swift mates and twins, sweet Sleep and Death, commit
His princely person, that with speed they both may carry it
To wealthy Lycia; where his friends and brothers will embrace,
And tomb it in some monument, as fits a prince's place."
Then flew Apollo to the fight, from the Idalian hill,
At all parts putting into act his great Commander's will;
Drew all the darts, wash'd, balm'd the corse; which, deck'd with ornament,
By Sleep and Death, those feather'd twins, he into Lycia sent.
Patroclus then Automedon commands to give his steeds
Large reins, and all way to the chace; so madly he exceeds
The strict commission of his friend; which had he kept had kept
A black death from him. But Jove's mind hath evermore outstept
The mind of man; who both affrights, and takes the victory
From any hardiest hand with ease; which he can justify,
Though he himself commands him fight, as now he put this chace
In Menœtiades's mind. How much then weighs the grace,
Patroclus, that Jove gives thee now, in scoles put with thy death,
Of all these great and famous men the honourable breath!
Of which Adrestus first he slew, and next Autonous,
Epistora, and Perimus, Pylartes, Elasus,
Swift Menalippus, Molius; all these were overthrown
By him, and all else put in rout; and then proud Ilion
Had stoop'd beneath his glorious hand, he rag'd so with his lance,
If Phœbus had not kept the tow'r, and help'd the Ilians,
Sustaining ill thoughts 'gainst the prince. Thrice to the prominence
Of Troy's steep wall he bravely leap'd; thrice Phœbus thrust him thence,
Objecting his all-dazzling shield, with his resistless hand;
But fourthly, when, like one of heav'n, he would have stirr'd his stand,
Apollo threaten'd him, and said: "Cease, it exceeds thy fate,

Forward, Patroclus, to expugn with thy bold lance this state;
Nor under great Achilles' pow'rs, to thine superior far,
Lies Troy's grave ruin." When he spake, Patroclus left that war,
Leap'd far back, and his anger shunn'd. Hector detain'd his horse
Within the Scæan port, in doubt to put his personal force
Amongst the rout, and turn their heads, or shun in Troy the storm.
Apollo, seeing his suspense, resum'd the goodly form
Of Hector's uncle, Asius; the Phrygian Dymas' son,
Who near the deep Sangarius had habitation,
Being brother to the Trojan queen. His shape Apollo took,
And ask'd of Hector, why his spirit so clear the fight forsook?
Affirming 'twas unfit for him, and wish'd his forces were
As much above his, as they mov'd in an inferior sphere.
He should, with shame to him, be gone; and so bade drive away
Against Patroclus, to approve, if He that gave them day
Would give the glory of his death to his preferréd lance.
So left he him, and to the fight did his bright head advance,
Mix'd with the multitude, and stirr'd foul tumult for the foe.
Then Hector bade Cebriones put on; himself let go
All other Greeks within his reach, and only gave command
To front Patroclus. He at him; jump'd down; his strong left hand
A jav'lin held, his right a stone, a marble sharp and such
As his large hand had pow'r to gripe, and gave it strength as much
As he could lie to; nor stood long, in fear of that huge man
That made against him, but full on with his huge stone he ran,
Discharg'd, and drave it 'twixt the brows of bold Cebriones.
Nor could the thick bone there prepar'd extenuate so th' access,
But out it drave his broken eyes, which in the dust fell down,
And he div'd after; which conceit of diving took the son
Of old Menœtius, who thus play'd upon the other's bane.
"O heav'ns! For truth, this Trojan was a passing active man!
With what exceeding ease he dives, as if at work he were
Within the fishy seas! This man alone would furnish cheer
For twenty men, though 'twere a storm, to leap out of a sail,
And gather oysters for them all, he does it here as well,
And there are many such in Troy." Thus jested he so near
His own grave death; and then made in, to spoil the charioteer,
"With such a lion's force and fate, as, often ruining
Stalls of fat oxen, gets at length a mortal wound to sting
His soul out of that rav'nous breast, that was so insolent,
And so his life's bliss proves his bane; so deadly confident
Wert thou, Patroclus, in pursuit of good Cebriones,
To whose defence now Hector leap'd. The opposite address,
These masters of the cry in war now made, was of the kind
Of two fierce kings of beasts, oppos'd in strife about a hind
Slain on the forehead of a hill, both sharp and hungry set
And to the currie never came but like two deaths they met;
Nor these two entertain'd less mind of mutual prejudice

About the body, close to which when each had press'd for prise,
Hector the head laid hand upon, which, once grip'd, never could
Be forc'd from him; Patroclus then upon the feet got hold,
And he pinch'd with as sure a nail. So both stood tugging there,
While all the rest made eager fight, and grappled ev'ry where.
And as the east and south winds strive, to make a lofty wood
Bow to their greatness, barky elms, wild ashes, beeches, bow'd
Ev'n with the earth, in whose thick arms the mighty vapours lie,
And toss by turns, all, either way, their leaves at random fly,
Boughs murmur, and their bodies crack, and with perpetual din
The sylvans falter, and the storms are never to begin;
So rag'd the fight, and all from Flight pluck'd her forgotten wings,
While some still stuck, still new-wing'd shafts flew dancing from their strings,
Huge stones sent after that did shake the shields about the corse,
Who now, in dust's soft forehead stretch'd, forgat his guiding horse.
As long as Phœbus turn'd his wheels about the midst of heaven,
So long the touch of either's darts the falls of both made even;
But, when his wain drew near the west, the Greeks past measure were
The abler soldiers, and so swept the Trojan tumult clear
From off the body, out of which they drew the hurl'd-in darts,
And from his shoulders stripp'd his arms; and then to more such parts
Patroclus turn'd his striving thoughts, to do the Trojans ill.
Thrice, like the God of war, he charg'd, his voice as horrible,
And thrice-nine those three charges slew; but in the fourth assay,
O then, Patroclus, show'd thy last; the dreadful Sun made way
Against that onset; yet the prince discern'd no Deity,
He kept the press so, and, besides, obscur'd his glorious eye
With such felt darkness. At his back, he made a sudden stand,
And 'twixt his neck and shoulders laid down-right with either hand
A blow so weighty, that his eyes a giddy darkness took,
And from his head his three-plum'd helm the bounding violence shook,
That rung beneath his horses' hooves, and, like a water-spout,
Was crush'd together with the fall; the plumes that set it out,
All spatter'd with black blood and dust; when ever heretofore
It was a capital offence to have or dust or gore
Defile a triple-feather'd helm, but on the head divine
And youthful temples of their prince it us'd, untouch'd, to shine.
Yet now Jove gave it Hector's hands, the other's death was near.
Besides whose lost and filéd helm his huge long weighty spear,
Well-bound with iron, in his hand was shiver'd, and his shield
Fell from his shoulders to his feet, the bawdrick strewing the field;
His curets left him, like the rest. And all this only done
By great Apollo. Then his mind took in confusion,
The vig'rous knittings of his joints dissolv'd; and, thus dismay'd,
A Dardan, one of Panthus' sons, and one that overlaid
All Trojans of his place with darts, swift footing, skill, and force
In noble horsemanship, and one that tumbled from their horse,
One after other, twenty men, and when he did but learn

The art of war; nay when he first did in the field discern
A horse and chariot of his guide; this man, with all these parts,
(His name Euphorbus) comes behind, and 'twixt the shoulders darts
Forlorn Patroclus, who yet liv'd, and th' other (getting forth
His jav'lin) took him to his strength; nor durst he stand the worth
Of thee, Patroclus, though disarm'd, who yet (discomfited
By Phœbus' and Euphorbus' wound) the red heap of the dead
He now too late shunn'd, and retir'd. When Hector saw him yield,
And knew he yielded with a wound, he scour'd the arméd field,
Came close up to him, and both sides strook quite through with his lance.
He fell, and his most weighty fall gave fit tune to his chance;
For which all Greece extremely mourn'd. And as a mighty strife
About a little fount begins, and riseth to the life
Of some fell boar resolv'd to drink; when likewise to the spring
A lion comes alike dispos'd, the boar thirsts, and his king,
Both proud, and both will first be serv'd; and then the lion takes
Advantage of his sov'reign strength, and th' other, fainting, makes
Resign his thirst up with his blood; Patroclus, so enforc'd
When he had forc'd so much brave life, was from his own divorc'd.
And thus his great divorcer brav'd: "Patroclus, thy conceit
Gave thee th' eversion of our Troy, and to thy fleet a freight
Of Trojan ladies, their free lives put all in bands by thee;
But (too much prizer of thy self) all these are propp'd by me,
For these have my horse stretch'd their hoofs to this so long a war,
And I (far best of Troy in arms) keep off from Troy as far,
Ev'n to the last beam of my life, their necessary day.
And here, in place of us and ours, on thee shall vultures prey,
Poor wretch; nor shall thy mighty friend afford thee any aid,
That gave thy parting much deep charge, and this perhaps be said:
'Martial Patroclus, turn not face, nor see my fleet before
The curets from great Hector's breast, all gilded with his gore,
Thou hew'st in pieces.' If thus vain were his far-stretched commands,
As vain was thy heart to believe his words lay in thy hands."
He, languishing, replied: "This proves, thy glory worse than vain,
That when two Gods have giv'n thy hands what their pow'rs did obtain,
(They conqu'ring, and they spoiling me both of my arms and mind,
It being a work of ease for them) thy soul should be so blind
To oversee their evident deeds, and take their pow'rs to thee;
When, if the pow'rs of twenty such had dar'd t' encounter me,
My lance had strew'd earth with them all. Thou only dost obtain
A third place in my death; whom, first, a harmful hate hath slain
Effected by Latona's son; second, and first of men,
Euphorbus. And this one thing more concerns thee; note it then;
Thou shalt not long survive thyself; nay, now death calls for thee,
And violent fate; Achilles' lance shall make this good for me."
Thus death join'd to his words his end; his soul took instant wing,
And to the house that hath no lights descended) sorrowing
For his sad fate, to leave him young, and in his ablest age.

He dead, yet Hector ask'd him why, in that prophetic rage,
He so forespake him, when none knew but great Achilles might
Prevent his death, and on his lance receive his latest light?
Thus setting on his side his foot, he drew out of his wound
His brazen lance, and upwards cast the body on the ground;
When quickly, while the dart was hot, he charg'd Automedon,
Divine guide of Achilles' steeds, in great contention
To seize him too; but his so swift and deathless horse, that fetch'd
Their gift to Peleus from the Gods, soon rapt him from his reach.

[1] *Jupiter called the God of sounds, for the chief sound his thunder.*

[2] *A simile most lively expressive.*

THE END OF THE SIXTEENTH BOOK.

THE SEVENTEENTH BOOK OF HOMER'S ILIADS

THE ARGUMENT

A dreadful fight about Patroclus' corse;
Euphorbus slain by Menelaus' force;
Hector in th' armour of Æacides;
Antilochus relating the decease
Of slain Patroclus to fair Thetis' son;
The body from the striving Trojans won;
Th' Ajaces making good the after field;
Make all the subject that this book doth yield,

ANOTHER ARGUMENT

In Rho the vent'rous hosts maintain
A slaught'rous conflict for the slain.
Nor could his slaughter rest conceal'd from Menelaus' ear;
Who flew amongst the foremost fights, and with his targe and spear
Circled the body, as much griev'd, and with as tender heed
To keep it theirs, as any dam about her first-born seed,
Not proving what the pain of birth would make the love before,
Nor to pursue his first attaint Euphorbus' spirit forbore; [1]
But, seeing Menelaus chief in rescue of the dead,
Assay'd him thus: "Atrides, cease, and leave the slaughteréd
With his embru'd spoil to the man, that first, of all our state,
And famous succours, in fair fight, made passage to his fate;
And therefore suffer me to wear the good name I have won
Amongst the Trojans, lest thy life repay what his hath done."

"O Jupiter," said he, incens'd, "thou art no honest man
To boast so past thy pow'r to do. Not any lion can,
Nor spotted leopard, nor boar, whose mind is mightiest
In pouring fury from his strength, advance so proud a crest
As Panthus' fighting progeny. But Hyperenor's pride,
That joy'd so little time his youth, when he so vilified
My force in arms, and call'd me worst of all our chivalry,
And stood my worst, might teach ye all to shun this surcuidrie;
I think he came not safely home, to tell his wife his acts.
Nor less right of thy insolence my equal fate exacts,
And will obtain me, if thou stay'st. Retire then, take advice:
A fool sees nought before 'tis done, and still too late is wise."
This mov'd not him but to the worse, since it renew'd the sting
That his slain brother shot in him, remember'd by the king,
To whom he answer'd: "Thou shalt pay, for all the pains endur'd
By that slain brother, all the wounds sustain'd for him, recur'd
With one made in thy heart by me. 'Tis true thou mad'st his wife
A heavy widow, when her joys of wedlock scarce had life,
And hurt'st our parents with his grief; all which thou gloriest in,
Forespeaking so thy death, that now their grief's end shall begin.
To Panthus, and the snowy hand of Phrontes, I will bring
Those arms, and that proud head of thine. And this laborious thing
Shall ask no long time to perform. Nor be my words alone,
But their performance; Strength, and Fight, and Terror thus sets on."
This said, he strook his all-round shield; nor shrunk that, but his lance
That turn'd head in it. Then the king assay'd the second chance;
First praying to the King of Gods; and his dart entry got
(The force much driving back his foe) in low part of his throat,
And ran his neck through. Then fell pride, and he; and all with gore
His locks, that like the Graces were, and which he ever wore
In gold and silver ribands wrapp'd, were piteously wet.
And when alone in some choice place, a husbandman hath set
The young plant of an olive tree, whose root being ever fed
With plenty of delicious springs, his branches bravely spread,
And all his fresh and lovely head, grown curl'd with snowy flow'rs,
That dance and flourish with the winds, that are of gentlest pow'rs;
But when a whirlwind, got aloft, stoops with a sudden gale,
Tears from his head his tender curls, and tosseth therewithal
His fix'd root from his hollow mines; it well presents the force
Of Sparta's king; and so the plant, Euphorbus and his corse.
He slain, the king stripp'd off his arms; and with their worthy prise,
All fearing him, had clearly pass'd, if heaven's fair Eye of eyes
Had not, in envy of his acts, to his encounter stirr'd
The Mars-like Hector; to whose pow'rs the rescue he preferr'd
Of those fair arms, and took the shape of Mentas, colonel
Of all the Cicones that near the Thracian Hebrus dwell.
Like him, he thus puts forth his voice: "Hector, thou scour'st the field
In headstrong púrsuit of those horse, that hardly are compell'd

To take the draught of chariots, by any mortal's hand;
The great grandchild of Æacus hath only their command,
Whom an immortal mother bore. While thou attend'st on these,
The young Atrides, in defence of Menœtiades,
Hath slain Euphorbus." Thus the God took troop with men again;
And Hector, heartily perplex'd, look'd round, and saw the slain
Still shedding rivers from his wound; and then took envious view
Of brave Atrides with his spoil; in way to whom he flew
Like one of Vulcan's quenchless flames. Atrides heard the cry
That ever usher'd him, and sigh'd, and said: "O me, if I [2]
Should leave these goodly arms, and him, that here lies dead for me,
I fear I should offend the Greeks; if I should stay and be
Alone with Hector and his men, I may be compass'd in,
Some sleight or other they may use, many may quickly win
Their wills of one, and all Troy comes ever where Hector leads.
But why, dear mind, dost thou thus talk? When men dare set their heads
Against the Gods, as sure they do that fight with men they love,
Straight one or other plague ensues. It cannot therefore move
The grudge of any Greek that sees I yield to Hector, he
Still fighting with a spirit from heav'n. And yet if I could see
Brave Ajax, he and I would stand, though 'gainst a God; and sure
'Tis best I seek him, and then see if we two can procure
This corse's freedom through all these. A little then let rest
The body, and my mind be still. Of two bads choose the best."
In this discourse, the troops of Troy were in with him, and he
Made such a lion-like retreat, as when the herdsmen see
The royal savage, and come on, with men, dogs, cries, and spears,
To clear their hornéd stall, and then the kingly heart he bears
(With all his high disdain) falls off; so from this odds of aid
The golden-hair'd Atrides fled, and in his strength display'd
Upon his left hand him he wish'd, extremely busiéd
About encouraging his men, to whom an extreme dread
Apollo had infus'd. The king reach'd Ajax instantly,
And said: "Come, friend, let us two haste, and from the tyranny
Of Hector free Patroclus' corse." He straight and gladly went;
And then was Hector haling off the body, with intent
To spoil the shoulders of the dead, and give the dogs the rest,
His arms he having pris'd before; when Ajax brought his breast
To bar all further spoil. With that he had, sure Hector thought
'Twas best to satisfy his spleen; which temper Ajax wrought
With his mere sight, and Hector fled. The arms he sent to Troy,
To make his citizens admire, and pray Jove send him joy.
Then Ajax gather'd to the corse, and hid it with his targe,
There setting down as sure a foot, as, in the tender charge
Of his lov'd whelps, a lion doth; two hundred hunters near
To give him onset, their more force makes him the more austere,
Drowns all their clamours in his roars, darts, dogs, doth all despise,
And lets his rough brows down so low, they cover all his eyes;

So Ajax look'd, and stood, and stay'd for great Priamides.
When Glaucus Hippolochides saw Ajax thus depress
The spirit of Hector, thus he chid: "O goodly man at arms,
In fight a Paris, why should fame make thee fort 'gainst our harms,
Being such a fugitive? Now mark, how well thy boasts defend
Thy city only with her own. Be sure it shall descend
To that proof wholly. Not a man of any Lycian rank
Shall strike one stroke more for thy town; for no man gets a thank
Should he eternally fight here, nor any guard of thee.
How wilt thou, worthless that thou art, keep off an enemy
From our poor soldiers, when their prince, Sarpedon, guest and friend
To thee, and most deservedly, thou flew'st from in his end,
And left'st to all the lust of Greece? O Gods, a man that was
(In life) so huge a good to Troy, and to thee such a grace,
(In death) not kept by thee from dogs! If my friends will do well,
We'll take our shoulders from your walls, and let all sink to hell;
As all will, were our faces turn'd. Did such a spirit breathe
In all you Trojans, as becomes all men that fight beneath
Their country's standard, you would see, that such a prop your cause
With like exposure of their lives, have all the honour'd laws
Of such a dear confederacy kept to them to a thread,
As now ye might reprise the arms Sarpedon forfeited
By forfeit of your rights to him, would you but lend your hands,
And force Patroclus to your Troy. Ye know how dear he stands
In his love, that of all the Greeks is, for himself, far best,
And leads the best near-fighting men; and therefore would at least
Redeem Sarpedon's arms; nay him, whom you have likewise lost.
This body drawn to Ilion would after draw and cost
A greater ransom if you pleas'd; but Ajax startles you;
'Tis his breast bars this right to us; his looks are darts enow
To mix great Hector with his men. And not to blame ye are,
You choose foes underneath your strengths, Ajax exceeds ye far."
Hector look'd passing sour at this, and answer'd: "Why dar'st thou,
So under, talk above me so? O friend, I thought till now
Thy wisdom was superior to all th' inhabitants
Of gleby Lycia; but now impute apparent wants
To that discretion thy words show, to say I lost my ground
For Ajax' greatness. Nor fear I the field in combats drown'd,
Nor force of chariots, but I fear a Pow'r much better seen
In right of all war than all we. That God, that holds between
Our victory and us his shield, lets conquest come and go
At his free pleasure, and with fear converts her changes so
Upon the strongest. Men must fight when his just spirit impels,
Not their vain glories. But come on, make thy steps parallels
To these of mine, and then be judge, how deep the work will draw.
If then I spend the day in shifts, or thou canst give such law
To thy detractive speeches then, or if the Grecian host
Holds any that in pride of strength holds up his spirit most,

Whom, for the carriage of this prince, that thou enforcest so,
I make not stoop in his defence. You, friends, ye hear and know
How much it fits ye to make good this Grecian I have slain,
For ransom of Jove's son, our friend. Play then the worthy men,
Till I indue Achilles' arms." This said, he left the fight,
And call'd back those that bore the arms, not yet without his sight,
In convoy of them towards Troy. For them he chang'd his own,
Remov'd from where it rained tears, and sent them back to town.
Then put he on th' eternal arms, that the Celestial States
Gave Peleus; Peleus, being old, their use appropriates
To his Achilles, that, like him, forsook them not for age.
When He, whose empire is in clouds, saw Hector bent to wage
War in divine Achilles' arms, he shook his head, and said:
"Poor wretch, thy thoughts are far from death, though he so near hath laid
His ambush for thee. Thou putt'st on those arms, as braving him
Whom others fear; hast slain his friend, and from his youthful limb
Torn rudely off his heav'nly arms, himself being gentle, kind,
And valiant. Equal measure then, thy life in youth must find.
Yet since the justice is so strict, that not Andromache,
In thy denied return from fight, must ever take of thee
Those arms, in glory of thy acts; thou shalt have that frail blaze
Of excellence that neighbours death, a strength ev'n to amaze."
To this His sable brows did bow; and he made fit his limb
To those great arms, to fill which up the War-god enter'd him
Austere and terrible, his joints and ev'ry part extends
With strength and fortitude; and thus to his admiring friends
High Clamour brought him. He so shin'd, that all could think no less
But he resembled ev'ry way great-soul'd Æacides.
Then ev'ry way he scour'd the field, his captains calling on;
Asteropæus, Eunomus, that foresaw all things done,
Glaucus, and Medon, Desinor, and strong Thersilochus,
Phorcis, and Mesthles, Chromius, and great Hippothous;
To all these, and their populous troops, these his excitements were:
"Hear us, innumerable friends, near-bord'ring nations, hear.
We have not call'd you from our towns, to fill our idle eye
With number of so many men (no such vain empery
Did ever joy us) but to fight; and of our Trojan wives,
With all their children, manfully to save the innocent lives.
In whose cares we draw all our towns of aiding soldiers dry,
With gifts, guards, victual, all things fit; and hearten their supply
With all like rights; and therefore now let all sides set down this,
Or live, or perish; this of war the special secret is.
In which most resolute design, whoever bears to town
Patroclus, laid dead to his hand, by winning the renown
Of Ajax' slaughter, the half-spoil we wholly will impart
To his free use, and to ourself the other half convert;
And so the glory shall be shar'd, ourself will have no more
Then he shall shine in." This drew all to bring abroad their store

Before the body. Ev'ry man had hope it would be his,
And forc'd from Ajax. Silly fools, Ajax prevented this
By raising rampires to his friend with half their carcasses.
And yet his humour was to roar, and fear, and now no less
To startle Sparta's king, to whom he cried out: "O my friend!
O Menelaus! Now no hope to get off; here's the end
Of all our labours. Not so much I fear to lose the corse
(For that's sure gone, the fowls of Troy and dogs will quickly force
That piece-meal) as I fear my head, and thine, O Atreus' son.
Hector a cloud brings will hide all. Instant destructión,
Grievous and heavy, comes. O call our peers to aid us; fly."
He hasted, and us'd all his voice, sent far and near his cry:
"O princes, chief lights of the Greeks, and you that publicly
Eat with our General and me, all men of charge, O know
Jove gives both grace and dignity to any that will show
Good minds for only good itself, though presently the eye
Of him that rules discern him not. 'Tis hard for me t'espy,
Through all this smoke of burning fight, each captain in his place,
And call assistance to our need. Be then each other's grace,
And freely follow each his next. Disdain to let the joy
Of great Æacides be forc'd to feed the beasts of Troy."
His voice was first heard and obey'd by swift Oïliades;
Idomenëus and his mate, renown'd Meriones,
Were seconds to Oïleus' son; but, of the rest, whose mind
Can lay upon his voice the names, that after these combin'd
In setting up this fight on end? The Trojans first gave on.
And as into the sea's vast mouth, when mighty rivers run,
Their billows and the sea resound, and all the utter shore
Rebellows in her angry shocks the sea's repulsive roar;
With such sounds gave the Trojans charge, so was their charge repress'd.
One mind fill'd all Greeks, good brass shields close couch'd toev'ry breast,
And on their bright helms Jove pour'd down a mighty deal of night,
To hide Patroclus; whom alive, and when he was the knight
Of that grandchild of Æacus, Saturnius did not hate,
Nor dead would see him dealt to dogs, and so did instigate
His fellows to his worthy guard. At first the Trojans drave
The black-ey'd Grecians from the corse; but not a blow they gave
That came at death. Awhile they hung about the body's heels,
The Greeks quite gone. But all that while, did Ajax whet the steels
Of all his forces, that cut back way to the corse again.
Brave Ajax (that for form and fact, pass'd all that did maintain
The Grecian fame, next Thetis' son) now flew before the first.
And as a sort of dogs and youths are by a boar disperst
About a mountain; so fled these from mighty Ajax, all
That stood in conflict for the corse, who thought no chance could fall
Betwixt them and the prise at Troy; for both Hippothous,
Lethus' Pelasgus' famous son, was so adventurous
That he would stand to bore the corse about the ancle-bone,

Where all the nervy fibres meet and ligaments in one,
That make the motion of those parts; through which he did convey
The thong or bawdric of his shield, and so was drawing away
All thanks from Hector and his friends; but in their stead he drew
An ill that no man could avert; for Telamonius threw
A lance that strook quite through his helm, his brain came leaping out;
Down fell Letheides, and with him the body's hoisted foot.
Far from Larissa's soil he fell; a little time allow'd
To his industrious spirits to quit the benefits bestow'd
By his kind parents. But his wreak Priamides assay'd,
And threw at Ajax; but his dart, discover'd, pass'd, and stay'd
At Schedius, son of Iphitus, a man of ablest hand
Of all the strong Phocensians, and liv'd with great command
In Panopëus. The fell dart fell through his channel-bone,
Pierc'd through his shoulder's upper part, and set his spirit gone.
When after his another flew, the same hand giving wing
To martial Phorcis' startled soul, that was the after spring
Of Phænops' seed. The jav'lin strook his curets through, and tore
The bowels from the belly's midst. His fall made those before
Give back a little, Hector's self enforc'd to turn his face.
And then the Greeks bestow'd their shouts, took vantage of the chace,
Drew off, and spoil'd Hippothous and Phorcis of their arms.
And then ascended Ilion had shaken with alarms,
Discov'ring th' impotence of Troy, ev'n past the will of Jove,
And by the proper force of Greece, had Phœbus fail'd to move
Æneas in similitude of Periphas (the son
Of grave Epytes) king at arms, and had good service done
To old Anchises, being wise, and ev'n with him in years.
But, like this man, the far-seen God to Venus' son appears,
And ask'd him how he would maintain steep Ilion in her height,
In spite of Gods, as he presum'd; when men approv'd so slight
All his presumptions, and all theirs that puff'd him with that pride,
Believing in their proper strengths, and gen'rally supplied
With such unfrighted multitudes? But he well knew that Jove,
Besides their self-conceits, sustain'd their forces with more love
Than theirs of Greece; and yet all that lack'd pow'r to hearten them.
Æneas knew the God, and said: "It was a shame extreme,
That those of Greece should beat them so, and by their cowardice,
Not want of man's aid nor the Gods'; and this before his eyes
A Deity stood ev'n now and vouch'd, affirming Jove their aid;
And so bade Hector and the rest, to whom all this he said,
Turn head, and not in that quick ease part with the corse to Greece."
This said, before them all he flew, and all as of a piece
Against the Greeks flew. Venus' son Leocritus did end,
Son of Arisbas, and had place of Lycomedes' friend;
Whose fall he friendly pitied, and, in revenge, bestow'd
A lance that Apisaon strook, so sore that straight he strow'd
The dusty centre, it did stick in that congealéd blood

That forms the liver. Second man he was of all that stood
In name for arms amongst the troop that from Pæonia came,
Asteropæus being the first; who was in ruth the same
That Lycomedes was; like whom, he put forth for the wreak
Of his slain friend; but wrought it not, because he could not break
That bulwark made of Grecian shields, and bristled wood of spears,
Combin'd about the body slain. Amongst whom Ajax bears
The greatest labour, ev'ry way exhorting to abide,
And no man fly the corse a foot, nor break their ranks in pride
Of any foremost daring spirit, but each foot hold his stand,
And use the closest fight they could. And this was the command
Of mighty Ajax; which observ'd, they steep'd the earth in blood.
The Trojans and their friends fell thick. Nor all the Grecians stood
(Though far the fewer suffer'd fate) for ever they had care
To shun confusion, and the toil that still oppresseth there.
So set they all the field on fire; with which you would have thought
The sun and moon had been put out, in such a smoke they fought
About the person of the prince. But all the field beside
Fought underneath a lightsome heav'n; the sun was in his pride,
And such expansure of his beams he thrust out of his throne,
That not a vapour durst appear in all that region,
No, not upon the highest hill. There fought they still, and breath'd,
Shunn'd danger, cast their darts aloof, and not a sword unsheath'd.
The other plied it, and the war and night plied them as well,
The cruel steel afflicting all; the strongest did not dwell
Unhurt within their iron roofs. Two men of special name.
Antilochus and Thrasymed, were yet unserv'd by Fame
With notice of Patroclus' death. They thought him still alive
In foremost tumult, and might well, for (seeing their fellows thrive
In no more comfortable sort than fight and death would yield)
They fought apart; for so their sire, old Nestor, strictly will'd,
Enjoining fight more from the fleet. War here increas'd his heat
The whole day long, continually the labour and the sweat
The knees, calves, feet, hands, faces, smear'd, of men that Mars applied
About the good Achilles' friend. And as a huge ox-hide [3]
A currier gives amongst his men, to supple and extend
With oil till it be drunk withall; they tug, stretch out, and spend
Their oil and liquor lib'rally, and chafe the leather so
That out they make a vapour breathe, and in their oil doth go,
A number of them set on work, and in an orb they pull,
That all ways all parts of the hide they may extend at full;
So here and there did both parts hale the corse in little place,
And wrought it all ways with their sweat; the Trojans hop'd for grace
To make it reach to Ilion, the Grecians to their fleet,
A cruel tumult they stirr'd up, and such as should Mars see't
(That horrid hurrier of men) or She that betters him,
Minerva, never so incens'd, they could not disesteem.
So baneful a contention did Jove that day extend

Of men and horse about the slain. Of whom his god-like friend
Had no instruction, so far off, and underneath the wall
Of Troy, that conflict was maintain'd; which was not thought at all
By great Achilles, since he charg'd, that having set his foot
Upon the ports, he would retire, well knowing Troy no boot
For his assaults without himself, since not by him as well
He knew it was to be subdu'd. His mother oft would tell
The mind of mighty Jove therein, oft hearing it in heav'n;
But of that great ill to his friend was no instruction giv'n
By careful Thetis. By degrees must ill events be known.
The foes cleft one to other still, about the overthrown.
His death with death infected both. Ev'n private Greeks would say
Either to other: "'Twere a shame, for us to go our way,
And let the Trojans bear to Troy the praise of such a prise!
Which, let the black earth gasp, and drink our blood for sacrifice,
Before we suffer. 'Tis an act much less infortunate,
And then would those of Troy resolve, though certainly our fate
Will fell us altogether here. Of all not turn a face."
Thus either side his fellows' strength excited past his place,
And thus through all th' unfruitful air, an iron sound ascended
Up to the golden firmament; when strange affects contended
In these immortal heav'n-bred horse of great Æacides,
Whom (once remov'd from forth the fight) a sudden sense did seize
Of good Patroclus' death, whose hands they oft had undergone,
And bitterly they wept for him. Nor could Automedon
With any manage make them stir, oft use the scourge to them,
Oft use his fairest speech, as oft threats never so extreme,
They neither to the Hellespont would bear him, nor the fight;
But still as any tombstone lays his never stirréd weight
On some good man or woman's grave for rites of funeral;
So unremovéd stood these steeds, their heads to earth let fall,
And warm tears gushing from their eyes, with passionate desire
Of their kind manager; their manes, that flourish'd with the fire
Of endless youth allotted them, fell through the yoky sphere,
Ruthfully ruffled and defil'd, Jove saw their heavy cheer,
And, pitying them, spake to his mind: "Poor wretched beasts," saidhe,
"Why gave we you t' a mortal king, when immortality
And incapacity of age so dignifies your states?
Was it to haste the miseries pour'd out on human fates?
Of all the miserablest things that breathe and creep on earth,
No one more wretched is than man. And for your deathless birth,
Hector must fail to make you prise. Is't not enough he wears,
And glories vainly in those arms? Your chariots and rich gears,
Besides you, are too much for him. Your knees and spirits again
My care of you shall fill with strength, that so ye may sustain
Automedon, and bear him off. To Troy I still will give
The grace of slaughter, till at fleet their bloody feet arrive,
Till Phœbus drink the western sea, and sacred Darkness throws

Her sable mantle 'twixt their points." Thus in the steeds he blows
Excessive spirit; and through the Greeks and Ilians they rapt
The whirring chariot, shaking off the crumbled centre wrapt
Amongst their tresses. And with them, Automedon let fly
Amongst the Trojans, making way through all as frightfully
As through a jangling flock of geese a lordly vulture beats,
Giv'n way with shrikes by ev'ry goose, that comes but near his threats;
With such state fled he through the press, pursuing as he fled;
But made no slaughter; nor he could, alone being carried
Upon the sacred chariot. How could he both works do,
Direct his jav'lin, and command his fi'ry horses too?
At length he came where he beheld his friend Alcimedon,
That was the good Laercius', the son of Æmon's, son;
Who close came to his chariot side, and ask'd: "What God is he
That hath so robb'd thee of thy soul, to run thus franticly
Amongst these fore fights, being alone; thy fighter being slain,
And Hector glorying in his arms?" He gave these words again:
"Alcimedon, what man is he, of all the Argive race,
So able as thyself to keep, in use of press and pace,
These deathless horse; himself being gone, that like the Gods had th' art
Of their high manage? Therefore take to thy command his part,
And ease me of the double charge, which thou hast blam'd with right."
He took the scourge and reins in hand, Automedon the fight.
Which Hector seeing, instantly, Æneas standing near,
He told him, he discern'd the horse, that mere immortal were,
Address'd to fight with coward guides, and therefore hop'd to make
A rich prise of them, if his mind would help to undertake,
For those two could not stand their charge. He granted, and both cast
Dry solid hides upon their necks, exceeding soundly brast;
And forth they went, associate with two more god-like men,
Aretus and bold Chromius; nor made they question then
To prise the goodly-crested horse, and safely send to hell
The souls of both their guardians. O fools, that could not tell
They could not work out their return from fierce Automedon
Without the lib'ral cost of blood; who first made orison
To father Jove, and then was fill'd with fortitude and strength;
When (counselling Alcimedon to keep at no great length
The horse from him, but let them breathe upon his back, because
He saw th' advance that Hector made, whose fury had no laws
Propos'd to it, but both their lives and those horse made his prise,
Or his life theirs) he call'd to friend these well-approv'd supplies,
Th' Ajaces, and the Spartan king, and said, "Come, princes, leave
A sure guard with the corse, and then to your kind care receive
Our threaten'd safeties. I discern the two chief props of Troy
Prepar'd against us. But herein, what best men can enjoy
Lies in the free knees of the Gods. My dart shall lead ye all [4]
The sequel to the care of Jove I leave, whatever fall."
All this spake good Automedon; then, brandishing his lance,

He threw, and strook Aretus' shield, that gave it enterance
Through all the steel, and, by his belt, his belly's inmost part
It pierc'd, and all his trembling limbs gave life up to his dart.
Then Hector at Automedon a blazing lance let fly,
Whose flight he saw, and falling flat, the compass was too high,
And made it stick beyond in earth, th' extreme part burst, and there
Mars buried all his violence. The sword then for the spear
Had chang'd the conflict, had not haste sent both th' Ajaces in,
Both serving close their fellows' call, who, where they did begin,
There drew the end. Priamides, Æneas, Chromius
(In doubt of what such aid might work) left broken hearted thus
Aretus to Automedon, who spoil'd his arms, and said:
"A little this revives my life for him so lately dead,
Though by this nothing countervail'd." And with this little vent
Of inward grief, he took the spoil; with which he made ascent
Up to his chariot, hands and feet of bloody stains so full
That lion-like he look'd, new turn'd from tearing up a bull.
And now another bitter fight about Patroclus grew,
Tear-thirsty, and of toil enough; which Pallas did renew,
Descending from the cope of stars, dismiss'd by sharp-ey'd Jove
To animate the Greeks; for now, inconstant change did move
His mind from what he held of late. And as the purple bow
Jove bends at mortals, when of war he will the signal show,
Or make it a presage of cold, in such tempestuous sort
That men are of their labours eas'd, but labouring cattle hurt;
So Pallas in a purple cloud involv'd herself, and went
Amongst the Grecians, stirr'd up all; but first encouragement
She breath'd in Atreus' younger son, and, for disguise, made choice
Of aged Phœnix' shape, and spake with his unwearied voice:
"O Menelaus, much defame, and equal heaviness,
Will touch at thee, if this true friend of great Æacides
Dogs tear beneath the Trojan walls; and therefore bear thee well.
Toil through the host, and ev'ry man with all thy spirit impell."
He answer'd: "O thou long-since born, O Phœnix, that hast won
The honour'd foster-father's name of Thetis' god-like son,
I would Minerva would but give strength to me, and but keep
These busy darts off; I would then make in indeed, and steep
My income in their bloods, in aid of good Patroclus; much
His death afflicts me, much. But yet, this Hector's grace is such
With Jove, and such a fi'ry strength and spirit he has, that still
His steel is killing, killing still." The king's so royal will
Minerva joy'd to hear, since she did all the Gods outgo
In his remembrance. For which grace she kindly did bestow
Strength on his shoulders, and did fill his knees as lib'rally
With swiftness, breathing in his breast the courage of a fly,
Which loves to bite so, and doth bear man's blood so much good will,
That still though beaten from a man she flies upon him still;
With such a courage Pallas fill'd the black parts near his heart,

And then he hasted to the slain, cast off a shining dart,
And took one Podes, that was heir to old Eetion,
A rich man and a strenuous, and by the people done
Much honour, and by Hector too, being consort and his guest;
And him the yellow-headed king laid hold on at his waist
In off'ring flight, his iron pile strook through him, down he fell,
And up Atrides drew his corse. Then Phœbus did impell
The spirit of Hector, Phænops like, surnam'd Asiades,
Whom Hector us'd, of all his guests, with greatest friendliness,
And in Abydus stood his house; in whose form thus he spake:
"Hector! What man of all the Greeks will any terror make
Of meeting thy strength any more, when thou art terrified
By Menelaus, who, before he slew thy friend, was tried
A passing easy soldier, where now (besides his end
Impos'd by him) he draws him off, and not a man to friend.
From all the Trojans? This friend is Podes, Eetion's son."
This hid him in a cloud of grief, and set him foremost on.
And then Jove took his snake-fring'd shield, and Ida cover'd all
With sulphury clouds, from whence he let abhorréd lightnings fall,
And thunder'd till the mountains shook; and with this dreadful state
He usher'd victory to Troy, to Argos flight and fate.
Peneleüs Bœotius was he that foremost fled,
Being wounded in his shoulder's height; but there the lance's head
Strook lightly, glancing to his mouth, because it strook him near,
Thrown from Polydamas. Leitus next left the fight in fear
(Being hurt by Hector in his hand) because he doubted sore
His hand in wishéd fight with Troy would hold his lance no more.
Idomenëus sent a dart at Hector (rushing in,
And following Leitus) that strook his bosom near his chin,
And brake at top. The Ilians for his escape did shout.
When Hector at Deucalides another lance sent out,
As in his chariot he stood; it miss'd him narrowly,
For, as it fell, Cœranus drave his speedy chariot by,
And took the Trojan lance himself; he was the charioteer
Of stern Meriones, and first on foot did service there,
Which well he left to govern horse, for saving now his king,
With driving 'twixt him and his death, though thence his own didspring,
Which kept a mighty victory from Troy, in keeping death
From his great sov'reign. The fierce dart did enter him beneath
His ear, betwixt his jaw and it, drave down, cut through his tongue,
And strook his teeth out; from his hands the horses' reins he flung,
Which now Meriones receiv'd as they bestrew'd the field,
And bade his sov'reign scourge away, he saw that day would yield
No hope of victory for them. He fear'd the same, and fled.
Nor from the mighty-minded son of Telamon lay hid,
For all his clouds, high Jove himself, nor from the Spartan king.
They saw Him in the victory, He still was varying
For Troy. For which sight Ajax said: "O heav'ns, what fool is he

That sees not Jove's hand in the grace now done our enemy?
Not any dart they touch but takes, from whomsoever thrown,
Valiant or coward; what he wants Jove adds, not any one
Wants his direction to strike sure; nor ours to miss as sure.
But come, let us be sure of this, to put the best in ure
That lies in us; which two-fold is, both to fetch off our friend,
And so to fetch him off as we may likeliest contend
To fetch ourselves off; that our friends surviving may have right
In joy of our secure retreat, as he that fell in fight,
Being kept as sure from further wrong. Of which perhaps they doubt,
And looking this way, grieve for us, not able to work out
Our pass from this man-slaughterer, great Hector, and his hands
That are too hot for men to touch, but that these thirsty sands
Before our fleet will be enforc'd to drink our headlong death.
Which to prevent by all fit means, I would the parted breath
Of good Patroclus, to his friend, with speed imparted were,
By some he loves; for, I believe, no heavy messenger
Hath yet inform'd him. But alas! I see no man to send,
Both men and horse are hid in mists that ev'ry way descend.
O father Jupiter, do thou the sons of Greece release
Of this felt darkness; grace this day with fit transparences;
And give the eyes thou giv'st, their use; destroy us in the light,
And work thy will with us, since needs thou wilt against us fight."
This spake he weeping, and his tears Saturnius pity show'd,
Dispers'd the darkness instantly, and drew away the cloud
From whence it fell; the sun shin'd out, and all the host appear'd;
And then spake Ajax, whose heard pray'r his spirits highly cheer'd:
"Brave Menelaus, look about; and if thou canst descry
Nestor's Antilochus alive, incite him instantly
To tell Achilles that his friend, most dear to him, is dead."
He said, nor Menelaus stuck at any thing he said,
As loth to do it, but he went. As from a grazier's stall
A lion goes, when overlaid with men, dogs, darts, and all,
Not eas'ly losing a fat ox, but strong watch all night held,
His teeth yet wat'ring, oft he comes, and is as oft repell'd,
The adverse darts so thick are pour'd before his brow-hid eyes,
And burning firebrands which, for all his great heart's heat, he flies,
And, grumbling, goes his way betimes; so from Patroclus went
Atrides, much against his mind, his doubts being vehement
Lest, he gone from his guard, the rest would leave for very fear
The person to the spoil of Greece. And yet his guardians were
Th' Ajaces and Meriones; whom much his care did press,
And thus exhort: "Ajaces both, and you Meriones,
Now let some true friend call to mind the gentle and sweet nature
Of poor Patroclus; let him think, how kind to ev'ry creature
His heart was living, though now dead." Thus urg'd the fair-hair'd king,
And parted, casting round his eye. As when upon her wing
An eagle is, whom men affirm to have the sharpest sight

Of all air's region of fowls, and, though of mighty height,
Sees yet within her leavy form of humble shrubs, close laid,
A light-foot hare, which straight she stoops, trusses, and strikes her dead;
So dead thou strook'st thy charge, O king, through all war's thickets so
Thou look'dst, and swiftly found'st thy man exhorting 'gainst the foe,
And heart'ning his plied men to blows us'd in the war's left wing;
To whom thou saidst: "Thou god-lov'd man, come here, and hear a thing
Which I wish never were to hear. I think ev'n thy eye sees
What a destruction God hath laid upon the sons of Greece,
And what a conquest he gives Troy; in which the best of men,
Patroclus, lies exanimate, whose person passing fain
The Greeks would rescue and bear home; and therefore give thy speed
To his great friend, to prove if he will do so good a deed
To fetch the naked person off, for Hector's shoulders wear
His priséd arms." Antilochus was highly griev'd to hear
This heavy news, and stood surpris'd with stupid silence long;
His fair eyes standing full of tears; his voice, so sweet and strong
Stuck in his bosom; yet all this wrought in him no neglect
Of what Atrides gave in charge, but for that quick effect
He gave Laodocus his arms (his friend that had the guide
Of his swift horse) and then his knees were speedily applied
In his sad message, which his eyes told all the way in tears.
Nor would thy gen'rous heart assist his sore charg'd soldiers,
O Menelaus, in mean time, though left in much distress;
Thou sent'st them god-like Thrasymede, and mad'st thy kind regress
Back to Patroclus; where arriv'd, half breathless thou didst say
To both th' Ajaces: "I have sent this messenger away
To swift Achilles, who, I fear, will hardly help us now,
Though mad with Hector; without arms he cannot fight, ye know.
Let us then think of some best mean, both how we may remove
The body, and get off ourselves from this vocif'rous drove,
And fate of Trojans." "Bravely spoke at all parts," Ajax said,
"O glorious son of Atreus. Take thou then straight the dead,
And thou, Meriones; we two, of one mind as one name,
Will back ye soundly, and on us receive the wild-fire flame
That Hector's rage breathes after you, before it come at you."
This said, they took into their arms the body; all the show,
That might be, made to those of Troy; at arm's end bearing it.
Out shriek'd the Trojans when they saw the body borne to fleet,
And rush'd on. As at any boar, gash'd with the hunter's wounds,
A kennel of the sharpest set and sorest bitten hounds
Before their youthful huntsmen haste, and eagerly awhile
Pursue, as if they were assur'd of their affected spoil;
But when the savage, in his strength as confident as they,
Turns head amongst them, back they fly, and ev'ry one his way;
So troop-meal Troy pursu'd awhile, laying on with swords and darts;
But when th' Ajaces turn'd on them, and made their stand, theirhearts
Drunk from their faces all their bloods, and not a man sustain'd

The forechace, nor the after-fight. And thus Greece nobly gain'd
The person towards home. But thus, the changing war was rack'd
Out to a passing bloody length; for as, once put in act,
A fire, invading city roofs, is suddenly engrost,
And made a wondrous mighty flame, in which is quickly lost
A house long building, all the while a boist'rous gust of wind
Lumb'ring amongst it; so the Greeks, in bearing off their friend,
More and more foes drew, at their heels a tumult thund'ring still
Of horse and foot. Yet as when mules, in haling from a hill
A beam or mast, through foul deep way, well-clapp'd, and hearten'd, close
Lie to their labour, tug and sweat, and passing hard it goes,
Urg'd by their drivers to all haste; so dragg'd they on the corse,
Still both th' Ajaces at their backs, who back still turn'd the force,
Though after it grew still the more. Yet as a sylvan hill
Thrusts back a torrent, that hath kept a narrow channel still,
Till at his oaken breast it beats, but there a check it takes,
That sends it over all the vale, with all the stir it makes,
Nor can with all the confluence break through his rooty sides;
In no less firm and brave repulse, th' Ajaces curb'd the prides
Of all the Trojans; yet all held the pursuit in his strength,
Their chiefs being Hector, and the son of Venus, who at length
Put all the youth of Greece besides in most amazeful rout,
Forgetting all their fortitudes, distraught, and shrieking out
A number of their rich arms lost, fall'n from them here and there,
About, and in the dike; and yet, the war concludes not here.

[1] This Euphorbus was he that, in Ovid, Pythagoras saith he was in the wars of Troy.

[2] Note the manly and wise discourse of Menelaus with himself seeing Hector advancing towards him.

[3] An inimitable simile.

[4] In the Greek always this phrase is used, not in the hands, but ἐν γούνασι κεῖται, in the knees of the Gods lies our help, etc.

THE END OF THE SEVENTEENTH BOOK.

THE EIGHTEENTH BOOK OF HOMER'S ILIADS

THE ARGUMENT

Achilles mourns, told of Patroclus' end;
When Thetis doth from forth the sea ascend
And comfort him, advising to abstain
From any fight till her request could gain
Fit arms of Vulcan. Juno yet commands

To show himself. And at the dike he stands
In sight of th' enemy, who with his sight
Flies; and a number perish in the flight.
Patroclus' person (safe brought from the wars)
His soldiers wash. Vulcan the arms prepares.

Sigma continues the alarms,
And fashions the renownéd arms.
They fought still like the rage of fire. And now Antilochus
Came to Æacides, whose mind was much solicitous
For that which, as he fear'd, was fall'n. He found him near the fleet
With upright sail-yards, utt'ring this to his heroic conceit:
"Ah me! Why see the Greeks themselves thus beaten from the field,
And routed headlong to their fleet? O let not heaven yield
Effect to what my sad soul fears, that, as I was foretold,
The strongest Myrmidon next me, when I should still behold
The sun's fair light, must part with it. Past doubt Menœtius' son
Is he on whom that fate is wrought. O wretch, to leave undone
What I commanded; that, the fleet once freed of hostile fire,
Not meeting Hector, instantly he should his pow'rs retire."
As thus his troubled mind discours'd, Antilochus appear'd,
And told with tears the sad news thus: "My lord, that must be heard
Which would to heav'n I might not tell! Menœtius' son lies dead,
And for his naked corse (his arms already forfeited,
And worn by Hector) the debate is now most vehement."
This said, grief darken'd all his pow'rs. With both his hands he rent
The black mould from the forcéd earth, and pour'd it on his head,
Smear'd all his lovely face; his weeds, divinely fashionéd,
All fil'd and mangled; and himself he threw upon the shore,
Lay, as laid out for funeral, then tumbled round, and tore
His gracious curls. His ecstasy he did so far extend,
That all the ladies won by him and his now slaughter'd friend,
Afflicted strangely for his plight, came shrieking from the tents,
And fell about him, beat their breasts, their tender lineaments
Dissolv'd with sorrow. And with them wept Nestor's warlike son,
Fell by him, holding his fair hands, in fear he would have done
His person violence; his heart, extremely straiten'd, burn'd,
Beat, swell'd, and sigh'd as it would burst. So terribly he mourn'd,
That Thetis, sitting in the deeps of her old father's seas,
Heard, and lamented. To her plaints the bright Nereides
Flock'd all, how many those dark gulfs soever comprehend.
There Glauce, and Cymodoce, and Spio, did attend,
Nessea, and Cymothoe, and calm Amphithoe,
Thalia, Thoa, Panope, and swift Dynamene,
Actæa, and Limnoria, and Halia the fair

Fam'd for the beauty of her eyes, Amathia for her hair,
Iæra, Proto, Clymene, and curl'd Dexamene,
Pherusa, Doris, and with these the smooth Amphinome,
Chaste Galatea so renown'd, and Callianira, came,
With Doto and Orythia, to cheer the mournful dame.
Apseudes likewise visited, and Callianassa gave
Her kind attendance, and with her Agave grac'd the cave,
Nemertes, Mæra, followéd, Melita, Ianesse,
With Ianira, and the rest of those Nereides
That in the deep seas make abode; all which together beat
Their dewy bosoms; and to all, thus Thetis did repeat
Her cause of mourning: "Sisters, hear, how much the sorrows weigh,
Whose cries now call'd ye. Hapless I brought forth unhappily
The best of all the sons of men; who, like a well-set plant
In best soils, grew and flourishéd; and when his spirit did want
Employment for his youth and strength, I sent him with a fleet
To fight at Ilion; from whence his fate-confinéd feet
Pass all my deity to retire. The court of his high birth,
The glorious court of Peleüs, must entertain his worth
Never hereafter. All the life he hath to live with me
Must waste in sorrows. And this son I now am bent to see,
Being now afflicted with some grief not usually grave,
Whose knowledge and recure I seek." This said, she left her cave,
Which all left with her; swimming forth, the green waves, as they sworn,
Cleft with their bosoms, curl'd, and gave quick way to Troy. Being come,
They all ascended, two and two, and trod the honour'd shore,
Till where the fleet of Myrmidons, drawn up in heaps, it bore.
There stay'd they at Achilles' ship; and there did Thetis lay
Her fair hand on her son's curl'd head, sigh'd, wept, and bade him say
What grief drew from his eyes those tears? "Conceal it not," said she,
"Till this hour thy uplifted hands have all things granted thee.
The Greeks, all thrust up at their sterns, have pour'd out tears enow,
And in them seen how much they miss remission of thy vow."
He said, "'Tis true, Olympius hath done me all that grace,
But what joy have I of it all, when thus thrusts in the place
Loss of my whole self in my friend? Whom, when his foe had slain,
He spoil'd of those profanéd arms, that Peleus did obtain
From heav'n's high Pow'rs, solemnizing thy sacred nuptial bands,
As th' only present of them all, and fitted well their hands,
Being lovely, radiant, marvellous. O would to heav'n thy throne,
With these fair Deities of the sea, thou still hadst sat upon,
And Peleus had a mortal wife; since by his means is done
So much wrong to thy grievéd mind, my death being set so soon,
And never suff'ring my return to grace of Peleus' court!
Nor do I wish it; nor to live in any man's resort,
But only that the crying blood, for vengeance of my friend
Mangled by Hector, may be still'd; his foe's death paying his end."
She, weeping, said: "That hour is near, and thy death's hour then nigh;

Which, in thy wish serv'd of thy foe, succeedeth instantly."
"And instantly it shall succeed," he answer'd "since my fate
Allow'd not to my will a pow'r to rescue, ere the date
Of his late slaughter, my true friend. Far from his friends he died,
Whose wrong therein my eyes had light and right to see denied.
Yet now I neither light myself, nor have so spent my light,
That either this friend or the rest (in numbers infinite
Slaughter'd by Hector) I can help, nor grace with wish'd repair
To our dear country, but breathe here unprofitable air,
And only live a load to earth with all my strength, though none
Of all the Grecians equal it. In counsel many a one
Is my superior; what I have, no grace gets; what I want
Disgraceth all. How then too soon can hastiest death supplant
My fate-curst life? Her instrument to my indignity
Being that black fiend Contention; whom would to God might die
To Gods and men; and Anger too, that kindles tyranny
In men most wise, being much more sweet than liquid honey is
To men of pow'r to satiate their watchful enmities;
And like a pliant fume it spreads through all their breasts; as late
It stole stern passage thorough mine, which he did instigate
That is our Gen'ral. But the fact so long past, the effect
Must vanish with it, though both griev'd; nor must we still respect
Our soothéd humours. Need now takes the rule of either's mind.
And when the loser of my friend his death in me shall find,
Let death take all. Send him, ye Gods, I'll give him my embrace.
Not Hercules himself shunn'd death, though dearest in the grace
Of Jupiter; ev'n him Fate stoop'd, and Juno's cruelty.
And if such fate expect my life, where death strikes I will lie.
Meantime I wish a good renown that these deep breasted dames
Of Ilion and Dardania may, for the extinguish'd flames
Of their friends' lives, with both their hands wipe miserable tears
From their so-curiously-kept cheeks, and be the officers
To execute my sighs on Troy, when (seeing my long retreat
But gather'd strength, and gives my charge an answerable heat)
They well may know 'twas I lay still, and that my being away
Presented all their happiness. But any further stay
(Which your much love perhaps may wish) assay not to persuade;
All vows are kept, all pray'rs heard; now, free way for fight is made."
The silver-footed Dame replied: "It fits thee well, my son,
To keep destruction from thy friends; but those fair arms are won
And worn by Hector, that should keep thyself in keeping them,
Though their fruition be but short, a long death being near him,
Whose cruel glory they are yet. By all means then forbear
To tread the massacres of war, till I again appear
From Mulciber with fit new arms; which, when thy eye shall see
The sun next rise, shall enter here with his first beams and me."
Thus to her Sisters of the Sea she turn'd, and bade them ope
The doors and deeps of Nereüs; she in Olympus' top

Must visit Vulcan for new arms to serve her wreakful son,
And bade inform her father so, with all things further done.
This said, they underwent the sea, herself flew up to heav'n.
In mean space, to the Hellespont and ships the Greeks were driv'n
In shameful rout; nor could they yet, from rage of Priam's son,
Secure the dead of new assaults, both horse and men made on
With such impression. Thrice the feet the hands of Hector seiz'd,
And thrice th' Ajaces thump'd him off. With whose repulse displeas'd,
He wreak'd his wrath upon the troops, then to the corse again
Made horrid turnings, crying out of his repulséd men,
And would not quit him quite for death. A lion almost sterv'd
Is not by upland herdsman driv'n, from urging to be serv'd,
With more contention, than his strength by those two of a name;
And had perhaps his much-prais'd will, if th' airy-footed Dame,
Swift Iris, had not stoop'd in haste, ambassadress from heav'n
To Peleus' son, to bid him arm; her message being giv'n
By Juno, kept from all the Gods; she thus excited him:
"Rise, thou most terrible of men, and save the precious limb
Of thy belov'd; in whose behalf, the conflict now runs high
Before the fleet, the either host fells other mutually,
These to retain, those to obtain. Amongst whom most of all
Is Hector prompt, he's apt to drag thy friend home, he your pall
Will make his shoulders; his head forc'd, he'll be most famous; rise,
No more lie idle, set the foe a much more costly prize
Of thy friend's value than let dogs make him a monument,
Where thy name will be grav'n." He ask'd, "What Deity hath sent
Thy presence hither?" She replied: "Saturnia, she alone,
Not high Jove knowing, nor one God that doth inhabit on
Snowy Olympus." He again: "How shall I set upon
The work of slaughter, when mine arms are worn by Priam's son?
How will my Goddess-mother grieve, that bade I should not arm
Till she brought arms from Mulciber! But should I do such harm
To her and duty, who is he, but Ajax, that can vaunt
The fitting my breast with his arms; and he is conversant
Amongst the first in use of his, and rampires of the foe
Slain near Patroclus builds to him?" "All this," said she, "we know,
And wish thou only wouldst but show thy person to the eyes
Of these hot Ilians, that, afraid of further enterprise,
The Greeks may gain some little breath." She woo'd, and he was won;
And straight Minerva honour'd him, who Jove's shield clapp'd upon
His mighty shoulders, and his head girt with a cloud of gold
That cast beams round about his brows. And as when arms enfold
A city in an isle, from thence a fume at first appears,
Being in the day, but, when the even her cloudy forehead rears,
Thick show the fires, and up they cast their splendour, that men nigh,
Seeing their distress, perhaps may set ships out to their supply;
So (to show such aid) from his head a light rose, scaling heav'n,
And forth the wall he stept and stood, nor brake the precept giv'n

By his great mother, mix'd in fight, but sent abroad his voice;
Which Pallas far-off echoéd, who did betwixt them hoise
Shrill tumult to a topless height. And as a voice is heard
With emulous affectión, when any town is spher'd
With siege of such a foe as kills men's minds, and for the town
Makes sound his trumpet; so the voice from Thetis' issue thrown
Won emulously th' ears of all. His brazen voice once heard,
The minds of all were startled so they yielded; and so fear'd
The fair-man'd horses, that they flew back, and their chariots turn'd,
Presaging in their augurous hearts the labours that they mourn'd
A little after; and their guides a repercussive dread
Took from the horrid radiance of his refulgent head,
Which Pallas set on fire with grace. Thrice great Achilles spake,
And thrice (in heat of all the charge) the Trojans started back.
Twelve men, of greatest strength in Troy, left with their lives exhal'd
Their chariots and their darts, to death with his three summons call'd.
And then the Grecians spritefully drew from the darts the corse,
And hears'd it, bearing it to fleet; his friends with all remorse
Marching about it. His great friend dissolving then in tears
To see his truly-lov'd return'd, so hors'd upon an hearse,
Whom with such horse and chariot he set out safe and whole,
Now wounded with unpitying steel, now sent without a soul,
Never again to be restor'd, never receiv'd but so,
He follow'd mourning bitterly. The sun (yet far to go)
Juno commanded to go down; who, in his pow'r's despite,
Sunk to the ocean, over earth dispersing sudden night.
And then the Greeks and Trojans both gave up their horse and darts.
The Trojans all to council call'd, ere they refresh'd their hearts
With any supper, nor would sit; they grew so stiff with fear
To see, so long from heavy fight, Æacides appear.
Polydamas began to speak, who only could discern
Things future by things past, and was vow'd friend to Hector, born
In one night both. He thus advis'd: "Consider well, my friends,
In this so great and sudden change, that now itself extends,
What change is best for us t' oppose. To this stands my command:
Make now the town our strength, not here abide light's rosy hand,
Our wall being far off, and our foe, much greater, still as near.
Till this foe came, I well was pleas'd to keep our watches here,
My fit hope of the fleet's surprise inclin'd me so; but now
'Tis stronglier guarded, and, their strength increas'd, we must allow
Our own proportionate amends. I doubt exceedingly
That this indiff'rency of fight 'twixt us and th' enemy,
And these bounds we prefix to them, will nothing so confine
Th' uncurb'd mind of Æacides. The height of his design
Aims at our city and our wives; and all bars in his way
(Being back'd with less than walls) his pow'r will scorn to make his stay,
And over-run, as over-seen and not his object. Then
Let Troy be freely our retreat; lest, being enforc'd, our men

'Twixt this and that be taken up by vultures, who by night
May safe come off, it being a time untimely for his might
To spend at random; that being sure. If next light show us here
To his assaults, each man will wish, that Troy his refuge were,
And then feel what he hears not now. I would to heav'n mine ear
Were free ev'n now of those complaints, that you must after hear
If ye remove not! If ye yield, though wearied with a fight
So late and long, we shall have strength in council and the night.
And (where we here have no more force, than need will force us to,
And which must rise out of our nerves) high ports, tow'rs, walls will do
What wants in us; and in the morn, all arm'd upon our tow'rs,
We all will stand out to our foe. 'Twill trouble all his pow'rs,
To come from fleet and give us charge, when his high-crested horse
His rage shall satiate with the toil of this and that way's course,
Vain entry seeking underneath our well-defended walls,
And he be glad to turn to fleet, about his funerals.
For of his entry here at home, what mind will serve his thirst,
Or ever feed him with sack'd Troy? The dogs shall eat him first."
At this speech Hector bent his brows, and said: "This makes not great
Your grace with me, Polydamas, that argue for retreat
To Troy's old prison. Have we not enough of those tow'rs yet?
And is not Troy yet charg'd enough, with impositions set
Upon her citizens, to keep our men from spoil without,
But still we must impose within? That houses with our rout
As well as purses may be plagu'd? Before time, Priam's town
Traffick'd with divers-languag'd men, and all gave the renown
Of rich Troy to it, brass and gold abounding; but her store
Is now from ev'ry house exhaust; possessions evermore
Are sold out into Phrygia and lovely Mæony;
And have been ever since Jove's wrath. And now his clemency
Gives me the mean to quit our want with glory, and conclude
The Greeks in sea-bords and our seas, to slack it, and extrude
His offer'd bounty by our flight. Fool that thou art, bewray
This counsel to no common ear, for no man shall obey;
If any will, I'll check his will. But what our self command,
Let all observe. Take suppers all, keep watch of ev'ry hand.
If any Trojan have some spoil, that takes his too much care,
Make him dispose it publicly; 'tis better any fare
The better for him, than the Greeks. When light then decks the skies,
Let all arm for a fierce assault. If great Achilles rise,
And will enforce our greater toil, it may rise so to him.
On my back he shall find no wings, my spirit shall force my limb
To stand his worst, and give or take. Mars is our common lord,
And the desirous swordsman's life he ever puts to sword."
This counsel gat applause of all, so much were all unwise;
Minerva robb'd them of their brains, to like the ill advice
The great man gave, and leave the good since by the meaner given.
All took their suppers; but the Greeks spent all the heavy even

About Patroclus' mournful rites, Pelides leading all
In all the forms of heaviness. He by his side did fall,
And his man-slaught'ring hands impos'd into his oft-kiss'd breast,
Sighs blew up sighs; and lion-like, grac'd with a goodly crest,
That in his absence being robb'd by hunters of his whelps,
Returns to his so desolate den, and, for his wanted helps,
Beholding his unlook'd-for wants, flies roaring back again,
Hunts the sly hunter, many a vale resounding his disdain;
So mourn'd Pelides his late loss, so weighty were his moans,
Which, for their dumb sounds, now gave words to all his Myrmidons:
"O Gods," said he, "how vain a vow I made, to cheer the mind
Of sad Menœtius, when his son his hand to mine resign'd,
That high-tow'r'd Opus he should see, and leave ras'd Ilion
With spoil and honour, ev'n with me! But Jove vouchsafes to none
Wish'd passages to all his vows; we both were destinate
To bloody one earth here in Troy; nor any more estate
In my return hath Peleüs or Thetis; but because
I last must undergo the ground, I'll keep no fun'ral laws,
O my Patroclus, for thy corse, before I hither bring
The arms of Hector and his head to thee for offering.
Twelve youths, the most renown'd of Troy, I'll sacrifice beside,
Before thy heap of funeral, to thee unpacified.
In mean time, by our crooked sterns lie, drawing tears from me,
And round about thy honour'd corse, these dames of Dardanie,
And Ilion, with the ample breasts (whom our long spears and pow'rs
And labours purchas'd from the rich and by-us-ruin'd tow'rs,
And cities strong and populous with divers-languag'd men)
Shall kneel, and neither day nor night be licens'd to abstain
From solemn watches, their toil'd eyes held ope with endless tears."
This passion past, he gave command to his near soldiers
To put a tripod to the fire, to cleanse the fester'd gore
From off the person. They obey'd, and presently did pour
Fresh water in it, kindled wood, and with an instant flame
The belly of the tripod girt, till fire's hot quality came
Up to the water. Then they wash'd, and fill'd the mortal wound
With wealthy oil of nine years old; then wrapp'd the body round
In largeness of a fine white sheet, and put it then in bed;
When all watch'd all night with their lord, and spent sighs on the dead.
Then Jove ask'd Juno: "If at length she had sufficed her spleen,
Achilles being won to arms? Or if she had not been
The natural mother of the Greeks, she did so still prefer
Their quarrel?" She, incens'd, ask'd: "Why he still was taunting her,
For doing good to those she lov'd? since man to man might show
Kind offices, though thrall to death, and though they did not know
Half such deep counsels as disclos'd beneath her far-seeing state,
She, reigning queen of Goddesses, and being in generate
Of one stock with himself, besides the state of being his wife
And must her wrath, and ill to Troy, continue such a strife

From time to time 'twixt him and her?" This private speech they had.
And now the Silver-footed Queen had her ascension made
To that incorruptible house, that starry golden court
Of fi'ry Vulcan, beautiful amongst th' immortal sort,
Which yet the lame God built himself. She found him in a sweat
About his bellows, and in haste had twenty tripods beat.
To set for stools about the sides of his well-builded hall,
To whose feet little wheels of gold he put, to go withal,
And enter his rich dining room, alone, their motion free,
And back again go out alone, miraculous to see.
And thus much he had done of them, yet handles were to add,
For which he now was making studs. And while their fashion had
Employment of his skilful hand, bright Thetis was come near;
Whom first fair well-hair'd Charis saw, that was the nuptial fere
Of famous Vulcan, who the hand of Thetis took, and said:
"Why, fair-train'd, lov'd, and honour'd dame, are we thus visited
By your kind presence? You, I think, were never here before.
Come near, that I may banquet you, and make you visit more."
She led her in, and in a chair of silver (being the fruit
Of Vulcan's hand) she made her sit, a footstool of a suit
Apposing to her crystal feet; and call'd the God of fire,
For Thetis was arriv'd, she said, and entertain'd desire
Of some grace that his art might grant. "Thetis to me," said he,
"Is mighty, and most reverend, as one that nourish'd me,
When grief consum'd me, being cast from heaven by want of shame
In my proud mother, who, because she brought me forth so lame,
Would have me made away; and then, had I been much distress'd
Had Thetis and Eurynome in either's silver breast
Not rescu'd me; Eurynome that to her father had
Reciprocal Oceanus. Nine years with them I made
A number of well-arted things, round bracelets, buttons brave,
Whistles, and carquenets. My forge stood in a hollow cave,
About which, murmuring with foam, th' unmeasur'd ocean
Was ever beating; my abode known nor to God nor man,
But Thetis and Eurynome, and they would see me still,
They were my loving guardians. Now then the starry hill,
And our particular roof, thus grac'd with bright-hair'd Thetis here,
It fits me always to repay, a recompense as dear
To her thoughts, as my life to me. Haste, Charis, and appose
Some dainty guest-rites to our friend, while I my bellows loose
From fire, and lay up all my tools." Then from an anvil rose
Th' unwieldy monster, halt'd down, and all awry he went.
He took his bellows from the fire, and ev'ry instrument
Lock'd safe up in a silver chest. Then with a sponge he drest
His face all over, neck and hands, and all his hairy breast;
Put on his coat, his sceptre took, and then went halting forth,
Handmaids of gold attending him, resembling in all worth
Living young damsels, fill'd with minds and wisdom, and were train'd

In all immortal ministry, virtue and voice contain'd,
And mov'd with voluntary pow'rs; and these still wait'd on
Their fi'ry sov'reign, who (not apt to walk) sate near the throne
Of fair-hair'd Thetis, took her hand, and thus he court'd her:
"For what affair, O fair-train'd queen, rev'rend to me, and dear,
Is our court honour'd with thy state, that hast not heretofore
Perform'd this kindness? Speak thy thoughts, thy suit can be no more
Than my mind gives me charge to grant. Can my pow'r get it wrought?
Or that it have not only pow'r of only act in thought?"
She thus: "O Vulcan, is there one, of all that are of heav'n,
That in her never-quiet mind Saturnius hath giv'n
So much affliction as to me: whom only he subjects,
Of all the sea-nymphs, to a man; and makes me bear th' affects
Of his frail bed; and all against the freedom of my will;
And he worn to his root with age? From him another ill
Ariseth to me; Jupiter, you know, hath giv'n a son,
The excellent'st of men, to me; whose education
On my part well hath answered his own worth, having grown
As in a fruitful soil a tree, that puts not up alone
His body to a naked height, but jointly gives his growth
A thousand branches; yet to him so short a life I brought,
That never I shall see him more return'd to Peleus' court.
And all that short life he hath spent in most unhappy sort;
For first he won a lovely dame, and had her by the hands
Of all the Grecians, yet this dame Atrides countermands;
For which in much disdain he mourn'd, and almost pin'd away.
And yet for this wrong he receiv'd some honour, I must say;
The Greeks, being shut up at their ships, not suffer'd to advance
A head out of their batter'd sterns; and mighty suppliance
By all their grave men hath been made, gifts, honours, all propos'd
For his reflection; yet he still kept close, and saw enclos'd
Their whole host in this gen'ral plague. But now his friend put on
His arms, being sent by him to field, and many a Myrmidon
In conduct of him. All the day, they fought before the gates
Of Scæa, and, most certainly, that day had seen the dates
Of all Troy's honours in her dust, if Phœbus (having done
Much mischief more) the envied life of good Menœtius' son
Had not with partial hands enforc'd, and all the honour giv'n
To Hector, who hath pris'd his arms. And therefore I am driv'n
T' embrace thy knees for new defence to my lov'd son. Alas!
His life, prefix'd so short a date, had need spent that with grace.
A shield then for him, and a helm, fair greaves, and curets, such
As may renown thy workmanship, and honour him as much,
I sue for at thy famous hands." "Be confident," said he,
"Let these wants breed thy thoughts no care. I would it lay in me
To hide him from his heavy death, when fate shall seek for him,
As well as with renownéd arms to fit his goodly limb;
Which thy hands shall convey to him; and all eyes shall admire,

See, and desire again to see, thy satisfied desire."
This said, he left her there, and forth did to his bellows go,
Appos'd them to the fire again, commanding them to blow.
Through twenty holes made to his hearth at once blew twenty pair,
That fir'd his coals, sometimes with soft, sometimes with vehement, air,
As he will'd, and his work requir'd. Amids the flame he cast
Tin, silver, precious gold, and brass; and in a stock he plac'd
A mighty anvil; his right hand a weighty hammer held,
His left his tongs. And first he forg'd a strong and spacious shield
Adorn'd with twenty sev'ral hues; about whose verge he beat
A ring, three-fold and radiant, and on the back he set
A silver handle; five-fold were the equal lines he drew
About the whole circumference, in which his hand did shew
(Directed with a knowing mind) a rare variety;
For in it he presented Earth; in it the Sea and Sky;
In it the never-wearied Sun, the Moon exactly round,
And all those Stars with which the brows of ample heav'n are crown'd,
Orion, all the Pleiades, and those sev'n Atlas got,
The close-beam'd Hyades, the Bear, surnam'd the Chariot,
That turns about heav'n's axle-tree, holds ope a constant eye
Upon Orion, and, of all the cressets in the sky,
His golden forehead never bows to th' Ocean empery.
Two cities in the spacious shield he built, with goodly state
Of divers-languag'd men. The one did nuptials celebrate,
Observing at them solemn feasts, the brides from forth their bow'rs
With torches usher'd through the streets, a world of paramours
Excited by them; youths and maids in lovely circles danc'd,
To whom the merry pipe and harp their spritely sounds advanc'd,
The matrons standing in their doors admiring. Other where
A solemn court of law was kept, where throngs or people were.
The case in question was a fine, impos'd on one that slew
The friend of him that follow'd it, and for the fine did sue;
Which th' other pleaded he had paid. The adverse part denied,
And openly affirm'd he had no penny satisfied.
Both put it to arbitrement. The people cried 'twas best
For both parts, and th' assistants too gave their dooms like the rest.
The heralds made the people peace. The seniors then did bear
The voiceful heralds' sceptres, sat within a sacred sphere,
On polish'd stones, and gave by turns their sentence. In the court
Two talents' gold were cast, for him that judg'd in justest sort.
The other city other wars employ'd as busily;
Two armies glittering in arms, of one confed'racy,
Besieg'd it; and a parlè had with those within the town.
Two ways they stood resolv'd; to see the city overthrown,
Or that the citizens should heap in two parts all their wealth,
And give them half. They neither lik'd, but arm'd themselves by stealth,
Left all their old men, wives, and boys, behind to man their walls,
And stole out to their enemy's town. The Queen of martials,

And Mars himself, conducted them; both which, being forg'd of gold,
Must needs have golden furniture, and men might so behold
They were presented Deities. The people, Vulcan forg'd
Of meaner metal. When they came, where that was to be urg'd
For which they went, within a vale close to a flood, whose stream
Us'd to give all their cattle drink, they there enambush'd them,
And sent two scouts out to descry, when th' enemy's herds and sheep
Were setting out. They straight came forth, with two that us'd to keep
Their passage always; both which pip'd, and went on merrily,
Nor dream'd of ambuscadoes there. The ambush then let fly,
Slew all their white-fleec'd sheep, and neat, and by them laid their guard.
When those in siege before the town so strange an uproar heard,
Behind, amongst their flocks and herds (being then in council set)
They then start up, took horse, and soon their subtle enemy met,
Fought with them on the river's shore, where both gave mutual blows
With well-pil'd darts. Amongst them all perverse Contention rose,
Amongst them Tumult was enrag'd, amongst them ruinous Fate
Had her red-finger; some they took in an unhurt estate,
Some hurt yet living, some quite slain, and those they tugg'd to them
By both the feet, stripp'd off and took their weeds, with all the stream
Of blood upon them that their steels had manfully let out.
They far'd as men alive indeed drew dead indeed about.
To these the fi'ry Artizan did add a new-ear'd field,
Large and thrice plough'd, the soil being soft, and of a wealthy yield;
And many men at plough he made, that drave earth here and there,
And turn'd up stitches orderly; at whose end when they were,
A fellow ever gave their hands full cups of luscious wine;
Which emptied, for another stitch, the earth they undermine,
And long till th' utmost bound be reach'd of all the ample close.
The soil turn'd up behind the plough, all black like earth arose,
Though forg'd of nothing else but gold, and lay in show as light
As if it had been plough'd indeed, miraculous to sight.
There grew by this a field of corn, high, ripe, where reapers wrought,
And let thick handfuls fall to earth, for which some bought
Bands, and made sheaves. Three binders stood, and took the handfuls reap'd
From boys that gather'd quickly up, and by them armfuls heap'd.
Amongst these at furrow's end, the king stood pleas'd at heart,
Said no word, but his sceptre show'd. And from him, much apart,
His harvest-bailiffs underneath an oak a feast prepar'd
And having kill'd a mighty ox, stood there to see him shar'd
Which women for their harvest folks (then come to sup) had dress'd,
And many white wheat-cakes bestow'd, to make it up a feast.
He set near this a vine of gold, that crack'd beneath the weight
Of bunches black with being ripe; to keep which at the height,
A silver rail ran all along, and round about it flow'd
An azure moat, and to this guard, a quickset was bestow'd
Of tin, one only path to all, by which the pressmen came
In time of vintage. Youths and maids, that bore not yet the flame

Of manly Hymen, baskets bore, of grapes and mellow fruit.
A lad that sweetly touch'd a harp, to which his voice did suit,
Center'd the circles of that youth, all whose skill could not do
The wanton's pleasure to their minds, that danc'd, sung, whistled too.
A herd of oxen then he carv'd, with high rais'd heads, forg'd all
Of gold and tin, for colour mix'd, and bellowing from their stall
Rush'd to their pastures at a flood, that echo'd all their throats,
Exceeding swift, and full of reeds; and all in yellow coats
Four herdsmen follow'd; after whom, nine mastiffs went. In head
Of all the herd, upon a bull, that deadly bellowéd,
Two horrid lions rampt, and seiz'd, and tugg'd off bellowing still;
Both men and dogs came; yet they tore the hide, and lapp'd their fill
Of black blood, and the entrails ate. In vain the men assay'd
To set their dogs on; none durst pinch, but cur-like stood and bay'd
In both the faces of their kings, and all their onsets fled.
Then in a passing pleasant vale, the famous Artsman fed,
Upon a goodly pasture ground, rich flocks of white-fleec'd sheep,
Built stables, cottages, and cotes, that did the shepherds keep
From wind and weather. Next to these, he cut a dancing place,
All full of turnings, that was like the admirable maze
For fair-hair'd Ariadne made, by cunning Dædalus;
And in it youths and virgins danc'd, all young and beauteous,
And glewéd in another's palms. Weeds that the wind did toss
The virgins wore; the youths wov'n coats, that cast a faint dim gloss
Like that of oil. Fresh garlands too, the virgins' temples crown'd;
The youths gilt swords wore at their thighs, with silver bawdrics bound.
Sometimes all wound close in a ring, to which as fast they spun
As any wheel a turner makes, being tried how it will run,
While he is set; and out again, as full of speed they wound,
Not one left fast, or breaking hands. A multitude stood round,
Delighted with their nimble sport; to end which two begun,
Mids all, a song, and turning sung the sports conclusión,
All this he circled in the shield, with pouring round about,
In all his rage, the Ocean, that it might never out.
This shield thus done, he forg'd for him, such curets as outshin'd
The blaze of fire. A helmet then (through which no steel could find
Forc'd passage) he compos'd, whose hue a hundred colours took,
And in the crest a plume of gold, that each breath stirr'd, he stuck.
All done, he all to Thetis brought, and held all up to her.
She took them all, and like t' the hawk, surnam'd the osspringer,
From Vulcan to her mighty son, with that so glorious show,
Stoop'd from the steep Olympian hill, hid in eternal snow.

THE END OF THE EIGHTEENTH BOOK.

THE NINETEENTH BOOK OF HOMER'S ILIADS

Thetis presenting armour to her son,
He calls a court, with full reflection
Of all his wrath; takes of the king of men
Free-offer'd gifts. All take their breakfast then;
He only fasting, arms, and brings abroad
The Grecian host, and (hearing the abode
Of his near death by Xanthus prophesied)
The horse, for his so bold presage, doth chide.

ANOTHER ARGUMENT

Ταῦ gives the anger period,
And great Achilles comes abroad.
The morn arose, and from the ocean, in her saffron robe,
Gave light to all, as well to Gods, as men of th' under globe.
Thetis stoop'd home, and found the prostrate person of her son
About his friend, still pouring out himself in passión;
A number more being heavy consorts to him in his cares.
Amongst them all Thetis appear'd and, sacred comforters,
Made these short words: "Though we must grieve, yet bear it thus, my son,
It was no man that prostrated, in this sad fashión,
Thy dearest friend; it was a God that first laid on his hand,
Whose will is law. The Gods' decrees, no human must withstand.
Do thou embrace this fabric of a God, whose hand before
Ne'er forg'd the like; and such as yet, no human shoulder wore."
Thus, setting down, the precious metal of the arms was such
That all the room rung with the weight of every slend'rest touch.
Cold tremblings took the Myrmidons; none durst sustain, all fear'd
T' oppose their eyes; Achilles yet, as soon as they appear'd,
Stern Anger enter'd. From his eyes, as if the day-star rose,
A radiance terrifying men did all the state enclose.
At length he took into his hands the rich gift of the God,
And, much pleas'd to behold the art that in the shield he show'd,
He brake forth into this applause: "O mother, these right well
Show an immortal finger's touch; man's hand must never deal
With arms again. Now I will arm; yet, that no honour make
My friend forgotten, I much fear, lest with the blows of flies
His brass-inflicted wounds are fil'd; life gone, his person lies
All apt to putrefactión." She bade him doubt no harm
Of those offences, she would care, to keep the petulant swarm
Of flies, that usually taint the bodies of the slain,
From his friend's person. Though a year, the earth's top should sustain
His slaughter'd body, it should still rest sound, and rather hold
A better state than worse, since time that death first made him cold.

And so bade call a council, to dispose of new alarms,
Where, to the king, that was the pastor of that flock in arms,
He should depose all anger, and put on a fortitude
Fit for his arms. All this his pow'rs with dreadful strength indued.
She, with her fair hand, still'd into the nostrils of his friend
Red nectar and ambrosia; with which she did defend
The corse from putrefactión. He trod along the shore,
And summon'd all th' heroic Greeks, with all that spent before
The time in exercise with him, the masters, pilots too,
Vict'lers, and all. All, when they saw Achilles summon so,
Swarm'd to the council, having long left the laborious wars.
To all these came two halting kings, true servitors of Mars,
Tydides and wise Ithacus, both leaning on their spears,
Their wounds still painful; and both these sat first of all the peers.
The last come was the king of men, sore wounded with the lance
Of Coon Antenorides. All set, the first in utterance
Was Thetis' son, who rose and said: "Atrides, had not this
Conferr'd most profit to us both, when both our enmities
Consum'd us so, and for a wench, whom, when I choos'd for prise,
In laying Lyrnessus' ruin'd walls amongst our victories,
I would to heav'n, as first she set her dainty foot aboard,
Diana's hand had tumbled off, and with a jav'lin gor'd!
For then th' unmeasurable earth had not so thick been gnawn,
In death's convulsions, by our friends, since my affects were drawn
To such distemper. To our foe, and to our foe's chief friend,
Our jar brought profit; but the Greeks will never give an end
To thought of what it prejudic'd them. Past things yet past our aid;
Fit grief for what wrath rul'd in them, must make th' amends repaid
With that necessity of love, that now forbids our ire;
Which I with free affects obey. 'Tis for the senseless fire
Still to be burning, having stuff; but men must curb rage still,
Being fram'd with voluntary pow'rs, as well to check the will
As give it reins. Give you then charge, that for our instant fight
The Greeks may follow me to field, to try if still the night
Will bear out Trojans at our ships. I hope there is some one,
Amongst their chief encouragers, will thank me to be gone,
And bring his heart down to his knees in that submissión."
The Greeks rejoic'd to hear the heart of Peleus' mighty son
So qualified. And then the king (not rising from his throne
For his late hurt) to get good ear, thus order'd his reply:
"Princes of Greece, your states shall suffer no indignity,
If, being far off, ye stand and hear; nor fits it such as stand
At greater distance, to disturb the council now in hand
By uproar, in their too much care of hearing. Some, of force,
Must lose some words; for hard it is, in such a great concourse
(Though hearers' ears be ne'er so sharp) to touch at all things spoke;
And in assemblies of such thrust, how can a man provoke
Fit pow'r to hear, or leave to speak? Best auditors may there

Lose fittest words, and the most vocal orator fit ear.
My main end then, to satisfy Pelides with reply,
My words shall prosecute; to him my speech especially
Shall bear direction. Yet I wish, the court in general
Would give fit ear; my speech shall need attention of all.
Oft have our peers of Greece much blam'd my forcing of the prise
Due to Achilles; of which act, not I, but destinies,
And Jove himself, and black Erinnys (that casts false mists still
Betwixt us and our actions done, both by her pow'r and will)
Are authors. What could I do then? The very day and hour
Of our debate, that Fury stole in that act on my pow'r.
And more; all things are done by strife; that ancient seed of Jove,
Ate, that hurts all, perfects all, her feet are soft, and move
Not on the earth, they bear her still aloft men's heads, and there
The harmful hurts them. Nor was I alone her prisoner,
Jove, best of men and Gods, hath been; not he himself hath gone
Beyond her fetters, no, she made a woman put them on;
For when Alcmena was to vent the force of Hercules
In well-wall'd Thebes, thus Jove triumph'd: 'Hear, Gods and Goddesses,
The words my joys urg'd: In this day, Lucina, bringing pain
To labouring women, shall produce into the light of men
A man that all his neighbour kings shall in his empire hold,
And vaunt that more than manly race whose honour'd veins enfold
My eminent blood.' Saturnia conceiv'd a present sleight,
And urg'd confirmance of his vaunt t' infringe it; her conceit
In this sort urg'd: 'Thou wilt not hold thy word with this rare man;
Or, if thou wilt, confirm it with the oath Olympian,
That whosoever falls this day betwixt a woman's knees,
Of those men's stocks that from thy blood derive their pedigrees,
Shall all his neighbour towns command.' Jove, ignorant of fraud,
Took that great oath, which his great ill gave little cause t' applaud.
Down from Olympus' top she stoop'd, and quickly reach'd the place
In Argos where the famous wife of Sthenelus, whose race
He fetch'd from Jove by Perseus, dwelt. She was but sev'n months gone
With issue, yet she brought it forth; Alcmena's matchless son
Delay'd from light, Saturnia repress'd the teeming throes
Of his great mother. Up to heav'n she mounts again, and shows,
In glory, her deceit to Jove. 'Bright-light'ning Jove,' said she,
'Now th' Argives have an emperor; a son deriv'd from thee
Is born to Persean Sthenelus, Eurystheus his name,
Noble and worthy of the rule thou swor'st to him.' This came
Close to the heart of Jupiter; and Ate, that had wrought
This anger by Saturnia, by her bright hair he caught,
Held down her head, and over her made this infallible vow:
'That never to the cope of stars should reascend that brow,
Being so infortunate to all.' Thus, swinging her about,
He cast her from the fi'ry heav'n; who ever since thrust out
Her fork'd sting in th' affairs of men. Jove ever since did grieve,

Since his dear issue Hercules did by his vow achieve
The unjust toils of Eurystheus. Thus fares it now with me,
Since under Hector's violence the Grecian progeny
Fell so unfitly by my spleen; whose falls will ever stick
In my griev'd thoughts: my weakness yet (Saturnius making sick
The state my mind held) now recur'd, th' amends shall make ev'n weight
With my offence. And therefore rouse thy spirits to the fight
With all thy forces; all the gifts, propos'd thee at thy tent
Last day by royal Ithacus, my officers shall present.
And, if it like thee, strike no stroke, though never so on thorns
Thy mind stands to thy friend's revenge, till my command adorns
Thy tents and coffers with such gifts, as well may let thee know
How much I wish thee satisfied." He answer'd: "Let thy vow,
Renown'd Atrides, at thy will be kept, as justice would,
Or keep thy gifts; 'tis all in thee. The council now we hold
Is for repairing our main field with all our fortitude.
My fair show made brooks no retreat, nor must delays delude
Our deed's expectance. Yet undone the great work is. All eyes
Must see Achilles in first fight depeopling enemies,
As well as counsel it in court; that ev'ry man set on
May choose his man to imitate my exercise upon."
Ulysses answer'd: "Do not yet, thou man made like the Gods,
Take fasting men to field. Suppose, that whatsoever odds
It brings against them with full men, thy boundless eminence
Can amply answer, yet refrain to tempt a violence.
The conflict wearing out our men was late, and held as long,
Wherein, though most Jove stood for Troy, he yet made our part strong
To bear that most. But 'twas to bear, and that breeds little heart.
Let wine and bread then add to it; they help the twofold part,
The soul and body, in a man, both force and fortitude.
All day men cannot fight and fast, though never so indued
With minds to fight, for, that suppos'd, there lurks yet secretly
Thirst, hunger, in th' oppresséd joints, which no mind can supply.
They take away a marcher's knees. Men's bodies throughly fed,
Their minds share with them in their strength; and, all day combated,
One stirs not, till you call off all. Dismiss them then to meat,
And let Atrides tender here, in sight of all this seat,
The gifts he promis'd. Let him swear before us all, and rise
To that oath, that he never touch'd in any wanton wise
The lady he enforc'd. Besides, that he remains in mind
As chastely satisfied; not touch'd, or privily inclin'd
With future vantages. And last, 'tis fit he should approve
All these rites at a solemn feast in honour of your love,
That so you take no mangled law for merits absolute.
And thus the honours you receive, resolving the pursuit
Of your friend's quarrel, well will quit your sorrow for your friend.
And thou, Atrides, in the taste of so severe an end,
Hereafter may on others hold a juster government;

Nor will it aught impair a king, to give a sound content
To any subject soundly wrong'd." "I joy," replied the king,
"O Laertiades, to hear thy lib'ral counselling;
In which is all decorum kept, nor any point lacks touch
That might be thought on to conclude a reconcilement such
As fits example, and us two. My mind yet makes me swear,
Not your impulsion; and that mind shall rest so kind and clear,
That I will not forswear to God. Let then Achilles stay,
Though never so inflam'd for fight, and all men here I pray
To stay, till from my tents these gifts be brought here, and the truce
At all parts finish'd before all. And thou of all I choose,
Divine Ulysses, and command to choose of all your host
Youths of most honour, to present, to him we honour most,
The gifts we late vow'd, and the dames. Mean space about our tents
Talthybius shall provide a boar, to crown these kind events
With thankful sacrifice to Jove, and to the God of Light."
Achilles answer'd: "These affairs will show more requisite,
Great king of men, some other time, when our more free estates
Yield fit cessation from the war, and when my spleen abates;
But now, to all our shames besides, our friends by Hector slain
(And Jove to friend) lie unfetch'd off. Haste, then, and meat your men;
Though, I must still say, my command would lead them fasting forth,
And all together feast at night. Meat will be something worth,
When stomachs first have made it way with venting infamy,
And other sorrows late sustain'd, with long'd-for wreaks, that lie
Heavy upon them, for right's sake. Before which load be got
From off my stomach, meat nor drink, I vow, shall down my throat,
My friend being dead, who digg'd with wounds, and bor'd through both his feet,
Lies in the entry of my tent, and in the tears doth fleet
Of his associates. Meat and drink have little merit then
To comfort me; but blood, and death, and deadly groans of men."
The great in counsels yet made good his former counsels thus:
"O Peleus' son, of all the Greeks by much most valorous,
Better and mightier than myself no little with thy lance
I yield thy worth; in wisdom, yet, no less I dare advance
My right above thee, since above in years, and knowing more.
Let then thy mind rest in thy words. We quickly shall have store
And all satiety of fight, whose steel heaps store of straw
And little corn upon a floor, when Jove, that doth withdraw
And join all battles, once begins t' incline his balances,
In which he weighs the lives of men. The Greeks you must not press
To mourning with the belly; death hath nought to do with that
In healthful men that mourn for friends. His steel we stumble at,
And fall at, ev'ry day, you see, sufficient store, and fast.
What hour is it that any breathes? We must not use; more haste,
Than speed holds fit for our revenge. Nor should we mourn too much.
Who dead is, must be buriéd. Men's patience should be such,
That one day's moan should serve one man. The dead must end with death,

And life last with what strengthens life. All those that held their breath
From death in fight the more should eat, that so they may supply
Their fellows that have stuck in field, and fight incessantly.
Let none expect reply to this, nor stay; for this shall stand
Or fall with some offence to him that looks for new command,
Whoever in dislike holds back. All join then, all things fit
Allow'd for all; set on a charge, at all parts answering it."
This said, he chose, for noblest youths to bear the presents, these:
The sons of Nestor, and with them renown'd Meriones,
Phylides, Thoas, Lycomed, and Meges, all which went,
And Menalippus, following Ulysses to the tent
Of Agamemnon. He but spake, and with the word the deed
Had join'd effect. The fitness well was answer'd in the speed.
The presents, added to the dame the Gen'ral did enforce,
Were twenty caldrons, tripods sev'n, twelve young and goodly horse;
Sev'n ladies excellently seen in all Minerva's skill,
The eighth Briseis who had pow'r to ravish ev'ry will;
Twelve talents of the finest gold, all which Ulysses weigh'd
And carried first; and after him, the other youths convey'd
The other presents, tender'd all in face of all the court.
Up rose the king. Talthybius, whose voice had a report
Like to a God, call'd to the rites. There having brought the boar,
Atrides with his knife took say upon the part before,
And lifting up his sacred hands, to Jove to make his vows,
Grave silence strook the cómplete court; when, casting his high brows
Up to the broad heav'n, thus he spake: "Now witness, Jupiter,
First, highest, and thou best of Gods; thou Earth that all dost bear;
Thou Sun; ye Furies under earth that ev'ry soul torment
Whom impious perjury distains; that nought incontinent
In bed, or any other act to any slend'rest touch
Of my light vows, hath wrong'd the dame; and, let my plagues be such
As are inflicted by the Gods, in all extremity
Of whomsoever perjur'd men, if godless perjury
In least degree dishonour me." This said, the bristled throat
Of the submitted sacrifice, with ruthless steel he cut;
Which straight into the hoary sea Talthybius cast, to feed
The sea-born nation. Then stood up the half-celestial seed
Of fair-hair'd Thetis, strength'ning thus Atrides' innocence:
"O father Jupiter, from thee descends the confluence
Of all man's ill; for now I see the mighty king of men
At no hand forc'd away my prise, nor first inflam'd my spleen
With any set ill in himself, but thou, the King of Gods,
Incens'd with Greece, made that the mean to all their periods.
Which now amend we as we may, and give all suffrages
To what wise Ithacus advis'd; take breakfasts, and address
For instant conflict." Thus he rais'd the court, and all took way
To sev'ral ships. The Myrmidons the presents did convey
T' Achilles' fleet, and in his tents dispos'd them; doing grace

Of seat and all rights to the dames; the horses put in place
With others of Æacides. When, like love's golden Queen,
Briseis all in ghastly wounds had dead Patroclus seen,
She fell about him, shrieking out, and with her white hands tore
Her hair, breasts, radiant cheeks, and, drown'd in warm tears, did deplore
His cruel destiny. At length she gat pow'r to express
Her violent passion, and thus spake this like-the-goddesses:
"O good Patroclus, to my life the dearest grace it had,
I, wretched dame, departing hence, enforc'd, and dying sad,
Left thee alive, when thou hadst cheer'd my poor captivity,
And now return'd I find thee dead; misery on misery
Ever increasing with my steps. The lord to whom my sire
And dearest mother gave my life in nuptials, his life's fire
I saw before our city gates extinguish'd: and his fate
Three of my worthy brothers' lives, in one womb generate,
Felt all in that black day of death. And when Achilles' hand
Had slain all these, and ras'd the town Mynetes did command,
(All cause of never-ending griefs presented) thou took'st all
On thy endeavour to convert to joy as general,
Affirming, he that hurt should heal, and thou wouldst make thy friend,
Brave captain that thou wert, supply my vowéd husband's end,
And in rich Phthia celebrate, amongst his Myrmidons,
Our nuptial banquets; for which grace, with these most worthy moans
I never shall be satiate, thou ever being kind,
Ever delightsome, one sweet grace fed still with one sweet mind."
Thus spake she weeping; and with her, did th' other ladies moan
Patroclus' fortunes in pretext, but in sad truth their own.
About Æacides himself the kings of Greece were plac'd,
Entreating him to food; and he entreated them as fast,
Still intermixing words and sighs, if any friend were there
Of all his dearest, they would cease, and offer him no cheer
But his due sorrows; for before the sun had left that sky
He would not eat, but of that day sustain th' extremity.
Thus all the kings, in res'lute grief and fasting, he dismiss'd;
But both th' Atrides, Ithacus, and war's old Martialist,
Idomenëus and his friend, and Phœnix, these remain'd
Endeavouring comfort, but no thought of his vow'd woe restrain'd.
Nor could, till that day's bloody fight had calm'd his blood; he still
Remember'd something of his friend, whose good was all his ill.
Their urging meat the diligent fashion of his friend renew'd
In that excitement: "Thou," said he, "when this speed was pursued
Against the Trojans, evermore apposedst in my tent
A pleasing breakfast; being so free, and sweetly diligent,
Thou mad'st all meat sweet. Then the war was tearful to our foe
But now to me; thy wounds so wound me, and thy overthrow;
For which my ready food I fly, and on thy longings feed.
Nothing could more afflict me; Fame relating the foul deed
Of my dear father's slaughter, blood drawn from my sole son's heart,

No more could wound me. Curséd man, that in this foreign part
(For hateful Helen) my true love, my country, sire, and son,
I thus should part with. Scyros now gives educatión, [1]
O Neoptolemus, to thee, if living yet; from whence
I hop'd, dear friend, thy longer life safely return'd from hence,
And my life quitting thine, had pow'r to ship him home, and show
His young eyes Phthia, subjects, court; my father being now
Dead, or most short-liv'd, troublous age oppressing him, and fear
Still of my death's news." These sad words, he blew into the ear
Of ev'ry visitant with sighs, all echo'd by the peers,
Rememb'ring who they left at home. All whose so humane tears
Jove pitied; and, since they all would in the good of one
Be much reviv'd, he thus bespake Minerva: "Thetis' son,
Now, daughter, thou hast quite forgot. O, is Achilles care
Extinguish'd in thee? Prostrated in most extreme ill fare,
He lies before his high-sail'd fleet, for his dead friend; the rest
Are strength'ning them with meat, but he lies desp'rately oppress'd
With heartless fasting. Go thy ways, and to his breast instill
Red nectar and ambrosia, that fast procure no ill
To his near enterprise." This spur he added to the free,
And, like a harpy, with a voice that shrieks so dreadfully,
And feathers that like needles prick'd, she stoop'd through all the stars,
Amongst the Grecians, all whose tents were now fill'd for the wars;
Her seres strook through Achilles' tent, and closely she instill'd
Heav'n's most-to-be-desired feast to his great breast, and fill'd
His sinews with that sweet supply, for fear unsavoury fast
Should creep into his knees. Herself the skies again enchas'd.
The host set forth, and pour'd his steel waves far out of the fleet.
And as from air the frosty north wind blows a cold thick sleet,
That dazzles eyes, flakes after flakes incessantly descending;
So thick, helms, curets, ashen darts, and round shields, never ending,
Flow'd from the navy's hollow womb. Their splendours gave heav'n's eye
His beams again. Earth laugh'd to see her face so like the sky;
Arms shin'd so hot, and she such clouds made with the dust she cast,
She thunder'd, feet of men and horse importun'd her so fast.
In midst of all, divine Achilles his fair person arm'd,
His teeth gnash'd as he stood, his eyes so full of fire they warm'd,
Unsuffer'd grief and anger at the Trojans so combin'd.
His greaves first us'd, his goodly curets on his bosom shin'd,
His sword, his shield that cast a brightness from it like the moon.
And as from sea sailors discern a harmful fire let run
By herdsmen's faults, till all their stall flies up in wrestling flame;
Which being on hills is seen far off; but being alone, none came
To give it quench, at shore no neighbours, and at sea their friends
Driv'n off with tempests; such a fire, from his bright shield extends
His ominous radiance, and in heav'n impress'd his fervent blaze.
His crested helmet, grave and high, had next triumphant place
On his curl'd head, and like a star it cast a spurry ray,

About which a bright thicken'd bush of golden hair did play,
Which Vulcan forg'd him for his plume. Thus cómplete arm'd, he tried
How fit they were, and if his motion could with ease abide
Their brave instruction; and so far they were from hind'ring it,
That to it they were nimble wings, and made so light his spirit,
That from the earth the princely captain they took up to air.
Then from his armoury he drew his lance, his father's spear,
Huge, weighty, firm, that not a Greek but he himself alone
Knew how to shake; it grew upon the mountain Pelion,
From whóse height Chiron hew'd it for his sire, and fatal 'twas
To great-soul'd men, of Peleus and Pelion surnam'd Pelias.
Then from the stable their bright horse, Automedon withdraws
And Alcymus; put poitrils on, and cast upon their jaws
Their bridles, hurling back the reins, and hung them on the seat.
The fair scourge then Automedon takes up, and up doth get
To guide the horse. The fight's seat last, Achilles took behind;
Who look'd so arm'd as if the sun, there fall'n from heav'n, had shin'd,
And terribly thus charg'd his steeds: "Xanthus and Balius,
Seed of the Harpy, in the charge ye undertake of us,
Discharge it not as when Patroclus ye left dead in field,
But, when with blood, for this day's fast observ'd, revenge shall yield
Our heart satiety, bring us off." Thus, since Achilles spake
As if his aw'd steeds understood, 'twas Juno's will to make
Vocal the palate of the one; who, shaking his fair head,
(Which in his mane, let fall to earth, he almost buried)
Thus Xanthus spake: "Ablest Achilles, now, at least, our care
Shall bring thee off; but not far hence the fatal minutes are
Of thy grave ruin. Nor shall we be then to be reprov'd,
But mightiest Fate, and the great God. Nor was thy best belov'd
Spoil'd so of arms by our slow pace, or courage's impair;
The best of Gods, Latona's son, that wears the golden hair,
Gave him his death's wound; though the grace he gave to Hector's hand.
We, like the spirit of the west, that all spirits can command
For pow'r of wing, could run him off; but thou thyself must go,
So fate ordains; God and a man must give thee overthrow."
This said, the Furies stopp'd his voice. Achilles, far in rage,
Thus answer'd him: "It fits not thee, thus proudly to presage
My overthrow. I know myself, it is my fate to fall
Thus far from Phthia; yet that fate shall fail to vent her gall,
Till mine vent thousands." These words us'd, he fell to horrid deeds,
Gave dreadful signal, and forthright made fly his one-hoof'd steeds.

[1] Scyros was an isle in the sea Ægeum, where Achilles himself was brought up, as well as his son.

THE END OF THE NINETEENTH BOOK.

THE ARGUMENT

By Jove's permission, all the Gods descend
To aid on both parts. For the Greeks contend
Juno, Minerva, Neptune, Mulciber,
And Mercury. The Deities that prefer
The Trojan part are Phœbus, Cyprides,
Phœbe, Latona, and the Foe to peace,
With bright Scamander. Neptune in a mist
Preserves Æneas daring to resist
Achilles; by whose hand much scathe is done;
Besides the slaughter of old Priam's son
Young Polydor, whose rescue Hector makes;
Him flying, Phœbus to his rescue takes.
The rest, all shunning their importun'd fates,
Achilles beats even to the Ilian gates.

ANOTHER ARGUMENT

In Upsilon, Strife stirs in heav'n;
The day's grace to the Greeks is giv'n.
The Greeks thus arm'd, and made insatiate with desire of fight,
About thee, Peleus' son, the foe, in ground of greatest height,
Stood opposite, rang'd. Then Jove charg'd Themis from Olympus' top
To call a court. She ev'ry way dispers'd, and summon'd up
All Deities; not any flood, besides Oceanus,
But made appearance; not a nymph (that arbours odorous,
The heads of floods, and flow'ry meadows, make their sweet abodes)
Was absent there; but all at his court, that is King of Gods,
Assembled, and, in lightsome seats of admirable frame,
Perform'd for Jove by Vulcan, sat. Ev'n angry Neptune came,
Nor heard the Goddess with unwilling ear, but with the rest
Made free ascension from the sea, and did his state invest
In midst of all, began the council, and inquir'd of Jove
His reason for that sessión, and on what point did move
His high intention for the foes; he thought the heat of war
Was then near breaking out in flames? To him the Thunderer:
"Thou knowest this council by the rest of those fore-purposes
That still inclin'd me; my cares still must succour the distress
Of Troy; though in the mouth of Fate, yet vow I not to stir
One step from off this top of heav'n, but all th' affair refer
To anyone. Here I'll hold state, and freely take the joy
Of either's fate. Help whom ye please; for 'tis assur'd that Troy
Not one day's conflict can sustain against Æacides,
If Heav'n oppose not. His mere looks threw darts enow t' impress

Their pow'rs with trembling; but when blows, sent from his fi'ry hand,
(Thrice heat by slaughter of his friend) shall come and countermand
Their former glories, we have fear, that though Fate keep their wall,
He'll overturn it. Then descend; and cease not till ye all
Add all your aids; mix earth and heav'n together with the fight
Achilles urgeth." These his words did such a war excite
As no man's pow'r could wrastle down; the Gods with parted hearts
Departed heav'n, and made earth war. To guide the Grecian darts,
Juno and Pallas, with the God that doth the earth embrace,
And most-for-man's-use Mercury (whom good wise inwards grace)
Were partially and all employ'd; and with them halted down
(Proud of his strength) lame Mulciber, his walkers quite misgrown,
But made him tread exceeding sure. To aid the Ilian side,
The changeable in arms went, Mars; and him accompanied
Diana that delights in shafts, and Phœbus never shorn,
And Aphrodite laughter-pleas'd, and She of whom was born
Still young Apollo, and the Flood that runs on golden sands
Bright Xanthus. All these aided Troy; and, till these lent their hands,
The Grecians triumph'd in the aid Æacides did add;
The Trojans trembling with his sight; so gloriously clad
He overshin'd the field, and Mars no harmfuller than he,
He bore the iron stream on clear. But when Jove's high decree
Let fall the Gods amongst their troops, the field swell'd, and the fight
Grew fierce and horrible. The Dame, that armies doth excite,
Thunder'd with clamour, sometimes set at dike without the wall,
And sometimes on the bellowing shore. On th' other side, the call
Of Mars to fight was terrible, he cried out like a storm,
Set on the city's pinnacles; and there he would inform
Sometimes his heart'nings, other times where Simois pours on
His silver current at the foot of high Callicolon.
And thus the bless'd Gods both sides urg'd; they all stood in the mids,
And brake contention to the hosts. And over all their heads
The Gods' King in abhorréd claps his thunder rattled out.
Beneath them Neptune toss'd the earth; the mountains round about
Bow'd with affright and shook their heads; Jove's hill the earthquake felt,
(Steep Ida) trembling at her roots, and all her fountains spilt,
Their brows all crannied; Troy did nod; the Grecian navy play'd
As on the sea; th' Infernal King, that all things frays, was fray'd,
And leap'd affrighted from his throne, cried out, lest over him
Neptune should rend in two the earth, and so his house, so dim,
So loathsome, filthy, and abhorr'd of all the Gods beside,
Should open both to Gods and men. Thus all things shook and cried,
When this black battle of the Gods was joining. Thus array'd
'Gainst Neptune, Phœbus with wing'd shafts; 'gainst Mars, the blue-ey'd Maid;
'Gainst Juno, Phœbe, whose white hands bore singing darts of gold,
Her side arm'd with a sheaf of shafts, and (by the birth twofold
Of bright Latona) sister twin to Him that shoots so far.
Against Latona, Hermes stood, grave guard, in peace and war,

Of human beings. 'Gainst the God, whose empire is in fire,
The wat'ry Godhead, that great Flood, to show whose pow'r entire
In spoil as th' other, all his stream on lurking whirlpits trod,
Xanthus by Gods, by men Scamander, call'd. Thus God 'gainst God
Enter'd the field. Æacides sustain'd a fervent mind
To cope with Hector; past all these, his spirit stood inclin'd
To glut Mars with the blood of him. And at Æacides
Apollo sent Anchises' son; but first he did impress
A more than natural strength in him, and made him feel th' excess
Infus'd from heav'n; Lycaon's shape gave show to his address,
(Old Priam's son) and thus he spake: "Thou counsellor of Troy,
Where now fly out those threats that late put all our peers in joy
Of thy fight with Æacides? Thy tongue once, steep'd in wine,
Durst vaunt as much." He answer'd him: "But why wouldst thou incline
My pow'rs 'gainst that proud enemy, and 'gainst my present heat?
I mean not now to bid him blows. That fear sounds my retreat,
That heretofore discourag'd me, when after he had ras'd
Lyrnessus, and strong Pedasus, his still breath'd fury chas'd
Our oxen from th' Idæan hill, and set on me; but Jove
Gave strength and knees, and bore me off, that had not walk'd above
This centre now but propp'd by him; Minerva's hand (that held
A light to this her favourite, whose beams show'd and impell'd
His pow'rs to spoil) had ruin'd me, for these ears heard her cry:
'Kill, kill the seed of Ilion, kill th' Asian Lelegi.'
Mere man then must not fight with him that still hath Gods to friend,
Averting death on others' darts, and giving his no end
But with the ends of men. If God like fortune in the fight
Would give my forces, not with ease wing'd victory should light
On his proud shoulders, nor he 'scape, though all of brass he boasts
His plight consisteth." He replied: "Pray thou those Gods of hosts,
Whom he implores, as well as he; and his chance may be thine;
Thou cam'st of Gods like him; the Queen that reigns in Salamine
Fame sounds thy mother; he deriv'd of lower Deity,
Old Nereus' daughter bearing him. Bear then thy heart as high,
And thy unwearied steel as right; nor utterly be beat
With only cruelty of words, not proof against a threat."
This strengthen'd him, and forth like rush'd; nor could his strength'ning fly
White-wristed Juno, nor his drifts. She ev'ry Deity
Of th' Achive faction called to her, and said: "Ye must have care,
Neptune and Pallas, for the frame of this important war
Ye undertake here. Venus' son, by Phœbus being impell'd,
Runs on Achilles; turn him back, or see our friend upheld
By one of us. Let not the spirit of Æacides
Be over-dar'd, but make him know the mightiest Deities
Stand kind to him; and that the Gods, protectors of these tow'rs
That fight against Greece, and were here before our eminent pow'rs,
Bear no importance. And besides, that all we stoop from heav'n,
To curb this fight, that no impair be to his person giv'n

By any Trojans, nor their aids, while this day bears the sun.
Hereafter, all things that are wrapp'd in his birth-thread, and spun
By Parcas in that point of time his mother gave him air,
He must sustain. But if report perform not the repair
Of all this to him, by the voice of some Immortal State,
He may be fearful (if some God should set on him) that Fate
Makes him her minister. The Gods, when they appear to men,
And manifest their proper forms, are passing dreadful then."
Neptune replied: "Saturnia, at no time let your care
Exceed your reason; 'tis not fit. Where only humans are,
We must not mix the hands of Gods, our odds is too extreme.
Sit we by, in some place of height, where we may see to them,
And leave the wars of men to men. But if we see from thence
Or Mars or Phœbus enter fight, or offer least offence
To Thetis' son, not giving free way to his conqu'ring rage,
Then comes the conflict to our cares; we soon shall disengage
Achilles, and send them to heav'n, to settle their abode
With equals, flying under-strifes." This said, the black-hair'd God
Led to the tow'r of Hercules, built circular and high
By Pallas and the Ilians, for fit security
To Jove's divine son 'gainst the whale, that drave him from the shore
To th' ample field. There Neptune sat, and all the Gods that bore
The Greeks good meaning, casting all thick mantles made of clouds
On their bright shoulders. Th' oppos'd Gods sat hid in other shrouds
On top of steep Callicolon, about thy golden sides,
O Phœbus, brandisher of darts, and thine, whose rage abides
No peace in cities. In this state, these Gods in council sate,
All ling'ring purpos'd fight, to try who first would elevate
His heav'nly weapon. High-thron'd Jove cried out to set them on,
Said, all the field was full of men, and that the earth did groan
With feet of proud encounterers, burn'd with the arms of men
And barbed horse. Two champions for both the armies then
Met in their midst prepar'd for blows; divine Æacides,
And Venus' son. Æneas first stepp'd threat'ning forth the prease,
His high helm nodding, and his breast barr'd with a shady shield,
And shook his jav'lin. Thetis' son did his part to the field.
As when the harmful king of beasts (sore threaten'd to be slain
By all the country up in arms) at first makes coy disdain
Prepare resistance, but at last, when anyone hath led
Bold charge upon him with his dart, he then turns yawning head,
Fell anger lathers in his jaws, his great heart swells, his stern
Lasheth his strength up, sides and thighs waddled with stripes to learn
Their own pow'r, his eyes glow, he roars, and in he leaps to kill,
Secure of killing; so his pow'r then rous'd up to his will
Matchless Achilles, coming on to meet Anchises' son.
Both near, Achilles thus inquir'd: "Why stand'st thou thus alone,
Thou son of Venus? Calls thy heart to change of blows with me?
Sure Troy's whole kingdom is propos'd: some one hath promis'd thee

The throne of Priam for my life; but Priam's self is wise,
And, for my slaughter, not so mad to make his throne thy prise.
Priam hath sons to second him. Is't then some piece of land,
Past others fit to set and sow, that thy victorious hand
The Ilians offer for my head? I hope that prise will prove
No easy conquest. Once, I think, my busy jav'lin drove,
With terror, those thoughts from your spleen. Retain'st thou not the time,
When single on th' Idæan hill I took thee with the crime
Of runaway, thy oxen left, and when thou hadst no face
That I could see; thy knees bereft it, and Lyrnessus was
The mask for that? Then that mask, too, I open'd to the air
(By Jove and Pallas' help) and took the free light from the fair,
Your ladies bearing prisoners; but Jove and th' other Gods
Then saft thee. Yet again I hope, they will not add their odds
To save thy wants, as thou presum'st. Retire then, aim not at
Troy's throne by me; fly ere thy soul flies; fools are wise too late."
He answer'd him: "Hope not that words can child-like terrify
My stroke-proof breast. I well could speak in this indecency,
And use tart terms; but we know well what stock us both put out,
Too gentle to bear fruits so rude. Our parents ring about
The world's round bosom, and by fame their dignities are blown
To both our knowledges, by sight neither to either known,
Thine to mine eyes, nor mine to thine. Fame sounds thy worthiness
From famous Peleus; the sea-nymph, that hath the lovely tress,
Thetis, thy mother; I myself affirm my sire to be
Great-soul'd Anchises; she that holds the Paphian Deity,
My mother. And of these this light is now t' exhale the tears
For their lov'd issue; thee or me; childish, unworthy, dares
Are not enough to part our pow'rs; for if thy spirits want
Due excitation, by distrust of that desert I vaunt,
To set up all rests for my life, I'll lineally prove
(Which many will confirm) my race. First, cloud-commanding Jove
Was sire to Dardanus, that built Dardania; for the walls
Of sacred Ilion spread not yet these fields; those fair-built halls
Of divers-languag'd men, not rais'd; all then made populous
The foot of Ida's fountful hill. This Jove-got Dardanus
Begot king Erichthonius, for wealth past all compares
Of living mortals; in his fens he fed three thousand mares,
All neighing by their tender foals, of which twice-six were bred
By lofty Boreas, their dams lov'd by him as they fed,
He took the brave form of a horse that shook an azure mane,
And slept with them. These twice-six colts had pace so swift, they ran
Upon the top-ayles of corn-ears, nor bent them any whit;
And when the broad back of the sea their pleasure was to sit,
The superficies of his waves they slid upon, their hoves
Not dipp'd in dank sweat of his brows. Of Erichthonius' loves
Sprang Tros, the king of Trojans. Tros three young princes bred,
Ilus, renown'd Assaracus, and heav'nly Ganymed

The fairest youth of all that breath'd, whom, for his beauty's love,
The Gods did ravish to their state, to bear the cup to Jove.
Ilus begot Laomedon, God-like Laomedon
Got Tithon, Priam, Clytius, Mars-like Hycetaon,
And Lampus. Great Assaracus, Capys begot; and he
Anchises. Prince Anchises, me. King Priam, Hector. We
Sprang both of one high family. Thus fortunate men give birth,
But Jove gives virtue; he augments, and he impairs the worth
Of all men; and his will their rule; he, strong'st, all strength affords.
Why then paint we, like dames, the face of conflict with our words?
Both may give language that a ship, driv'n with a hundred oars,
Would overburthen. A man's tongue is voluble, and pours
Words out of all sorts ev'ry way. Such as you speak you hear.
What then need we vie calumnies, like women that will wear
Their tongues out, being once incens'd, and strive for strife to part
(Being on their way) they travel so? From words, words may avert;
From virtue, not. It is your steel, divine Æacides,
Must prove my proof, as mine shall yours." Thus amply did he ease
His great heart of his pedigree; and sharply sent away
A dart that caught Achilles' shield, and rung so it did fray
The son of Thetis, his fair hand far-thrusting out his shield,
For fear the long lance had driv'n through. O fool, to think 'twould yield,
And not to know the God's firm gifts want want to yield so soon
To men's poor pow'rs. The eager lance had only conquest won
Of two plates, and the shield had five, two forg'd of tin, two brass,
One, that was centre-plate, of gold; and that forbad the pass
Of Anchisiades's lance. Then sent Achilles forth
His lance, that through the first fold strook, where brass of little worth
And no great proof of hides was laid; through all which Pelias ran
His iron head, and after it his ashen body wan
Pass to the earth, and there it stuck, his top on th' other side,
And hung the shield up; which hard down Æneas pluck'd, to hide
His breast from sword blows, shrunk up round, and in his heavy eye
Was much grief shadow'd, much afraid that Pelias stuck so nigh.
Then prompt Achilles rushing in, his sword drew; and the field
Rung with his voice. Æneas now, left and let hang his shield,
And all-distracted, up he snatch'd a two-men's strength of stone,
And either at his shield or casque he set it rudely gone,
Nor car'd where, so it strook a place that put on arms for death.
But he (Achilles came so close) had doubtless sunk beneath
His own death had not Neptune seen and interpos'd the odds
Of his divine pow'r, utt'ring this to the Achaian Gods:
"I grieve for this great-hearted man; he will be sent to hell,
Ev'n instantly, by Peleus' son, being only mov'd to deal
By Phœbus' words. What fool is he! Phœbus did never mean
To add to his great words his guard against the ruin then
Summon'd against him. And what cause, hath he to head him on
To others' mis'ries, he being clear of any trespass done

Against the Grecians? Thankful gifts he oft hath giv'n to us.
Let us then quit him, and withdraw this combat; for if thus
Achilles end him, Jove will rage; since his escape in fate
Is purpos'd, lest the progeny of Dardanus take date,
Whom Jove, past all his issue, lov'd, begot of mortal dames.
All Priam's race he hates; and this must propagate the names
Of Trojans, and their sons' sons' rule, to all posterity."
Saturnia said: "Make free your pleasure. Save, or let him die.
Pallas and I have taken many, and most public, oaths,
That th' ill day never shall avert her eye, red with our wroths,
From hated Troy; no, not when all in studied fire she flames
The Greek rage, blowing her last coal." This nothing turn'd his aims
From present rescue, but through all the whizzing spears he pass'd,
And came where both were combating; when instantly he cast
A mist before Achilles' eyes, drew from the earth and shield
His lance, and laid it at his feet; and then took up and held
Aloft the light Anchises' son, who pass'd, with Neptune's force,
Whole orders of heroës' heads, and many a troop of horse
Leap'd over, till the bounds he reach'd of all the fervent broil,
Where all the Caucons' quarters lay. Thus, far freed from the toil,
Neptune had time to use these words: "Æneas, who was he
Of all the Gods, that did so much neglect thy good and thee
To urge thy fight with Thetis' son, who in immortal rates
Is better and more dear than thee? Hereafter, lest, past fates,
Hell be thy headlong home, retire, make bold stand never near
Where he advanceth. But his fate once satisfied, then bear
A free and full sail; no Greek else shall end thee." This reveal'd,
He left him, and dispers'd the cloud, that all this act conceal'd
From vex'd Achilles; who again had clear light from the skies,
And, much disdaining the escape, said: "O ye Gods, mine eyes
Discover miracles! My lance submitted, and he gone
At whom I sent it with desire of his confusion!
Æneas sure was lov'd of heav'n. I thought his vaunt from thence
Had flow'd from glory. Let him go, no more experience
Will his mind long for of my hands, he flies them now so clear.
Cheer then the Greeks, and others try." Thus rang'd he ev'rywhere
The Grecian orders; ev'ry man (of which the most look'd on
To see their fresh lord shake his lance) he thus put charge upon:
"Divine Greeks, stand not thus at gaze, but man to man apply
Your sev'ral valours. 'Tis a task laid too unequally
On me left to so many men, one man oppos'd to all.
Not Mars, immortal and a God, not war's She-General,
A field of so much fight could chase, and work it out with blows.
But what a man may execute, that all limbs will expose,
And all their strength to th' utmost nerve (though now I lost some play
By some strange miracle) no more shall burn in vain the day
To any least beam. All this host, I'll ransack, and have hope,
Of all not one again will scape, whoever gives such scope

To his adventure, and so near dares tempt my angry lance."
Thus he excited. Hector then as much strives to advance
The hearts of his men, adding threats, affirming he would stand
In combat with Æacides: "Give fear," said he, "no hand
Of your great hearts, brave Ilians, for Peleus' talking son,
I'll fight with any God with words; but when their spears put on,
The work runs high, their strength exceeds mortality so far,
And they may make works crown their words; which holds not in the war
Achilles makes; his hands have bounds; this word he shall make good,
And leave another to the field. His worst shall be withstood
With sole objection of myself; though in his hands he bear
A rage like fire, though fire itself his raging fingers were,
And burning steel flew in his strength." Thus he incited his;
And they rais'd lances, and to work with mixéd courages;
And up flew Clamour. But the heat in Hector, Phœbus gave
This temper: "Do not meet," said he, "in any single brave
The man thou threaten'st, but in press; and in thy strength impeach
His violence; for, far off, or near, his sword or dart will reach."
The God's voice made a difference in Hector's own conceit
Betwixt his and Achilles' words, and gave such over-weight
As weigh'd him back into his strength, and curb'd his flying out.
At all threw fierce Æacides, and gave a horrid shout.
The first, of all he put to dart, was fierce Iphition,
Surnam'd Otryntides, whom Nais the water-nymph made son
To town-destroy'r Otrynteüs. Beneath the snowy hill
Of Tmolus, in the wealthy town of Hyda, at his will
Were many able men at arms. He, rushing in, took full
Pelides' lance in his head's midst, that cleft in two his skull.
Achilles knew him one much fam'd, and thus insulted then:
"Th' art dead, Otryntides, though call'd the terriblest of men.
Thy race runs at Gygæus' lake, there thy inheritance lay,
Near fishy Hyllus and the gulfs of Hermus; but this day
Removes it to the fields of Troy." Thus left he night to seize
His closéd eyes, his body laid in course of all the prease,
Which Grecian horse broke with the strakes nail'd to their chariot wheels.
Next, through the temples, the burst eyes his deadly jav'lin seels
Of great-in-Troy Antenor's son, renown'd Demoleon,
A mighty turner of a field. His overthrow set gone
Hippodamas; who leap'd from horse, and, as he fled before
Æacides's turnéd back, he made fell Pelias gore,
And forth he puff'd his flying soul. And as a tortur'd bull,
To Neptune brought for sacrifice, a troop of youngsters pull
Down to the earth, and drag him round about the hallow'd shore,
To please the wat'ry Deity with forcing him to roar,
And forth he pours his utmost throat; so bellow'd this slain friend
Of flying Ilion, with the breath that gave his being end.
Then rush'd he on, and in his eye had heav'nly Polydore,
Old Priam's son, whom last of all his fruitful princess bore,

And for his youth, being dear to him, the king forbad to fight.
Yet (hot of unexperienc'd blood, to show how exquisite
He was of foot, for which of all the fifty sons he held
The special name) he flew before the first heat of the field,
Ev'n till he flew out breath and soul; which, through the back, the lance
Of swift Achilles put in air, and did his head advance
Out at his navel. On his knees the poor prince crying fell,
And gather'd with his tender hands his entrails, that did swell
Quite through the wide wound, till a cloud as black as death conceal'd
Their sight, and all the world from him. When Hector had beheld
His brother tumbled so to earth, his entrails still in hand,
Dark sorrow overcast his eyes; nor far off could he stand
A minute longer, but like fire he brake out of the throng,
Shook his long lance at Thetis' son; and then came he along
To feed th' encounter: "O," said he, "here comes the man that most
Of all the world destroys my mind, the man by whom I lost
My dear Patroclus. Now not long the crooked paths of war
Can yield us any privy scapes. 'Come, keep not off so far,'
He cried to Hector, 'make the pain of thy sure death as short,
As one so desp'rate of his life hath reason.'" In no sort
This frighted Hector, who bore close, and said: "Æacides,
Leave threats for children. I have pow'r to thunder calumnies
As well as others, and well know thy strength superior far
To that my nerves hold; but the Gods, not nerves, determine war.
And yet, for nerves, there will be found a strength of pow'r in mine
To drive a lance home to thy life. My lance as well as thine
Hath point and sharpness, and 'tis this." Thus brandishing his spear,
He set it flying; which a breath of Pallas back did bear
From Thetis' son to Hector's self, and at his feet it fell.
Achilles us'd no dart, but close flew in; and thought to deal
With no strokes but of sure dispatch, but, what with all his blood
He labour'd, Phœbus clear'd with ease, as being a God, and stood
For Hector's guard, as Pallas did, Æacides, for thine.
He rapt him from him, and a cloud of much night cast between
His person and the point oppos'd. Achilles then exclaim'd:
"O see, yet more Gods are at work. Apollo's hand hath fram'd,
Dog that thou art, thy rescue now; to whom go pay thy vows
Thy safety owes him, I shall vent in time those fatal blows
That yet beat in my heart on thine, if any God remain
My equal fautor. In mean time, my anger must maintain
His fire on other Ilians." Then laid he at his feet
Great Demuchus, Philetor's son; and Dryope did greet
With like encounter. Dardanus and strong Laogonus,
Wise Bias' sons, he hurl'd from horse; of one victorious
With his close sword, the other's life he conquer'd with his lance.
Then Tros, Alastor's son, made in, and sought to scape their chance
With free submission. Down he fell, and pray'd about his knees
He would not kill him, but take ruth, as one that destinies

Made to that purpose, being a man born in the self same year
That he himself was. O poor fool, to sue to him to bear
A ruthful mind! He well might know, he could not fashion him
In ruth's soft mould, he had no spirit to brook that interim
In his hot fury, he was none of these remorseful men,
Gentle and affable, but fierce at all times, and mad then.
He gladly would have made a pray'r, and still so hugg'd his knee
He could not quit him; till at last his sword was fain to free
His fetter'd knees, that made a vent for his white liver's blood
That caus'd such pitiful affects; of which it pour'd a flood
About his bosom, which it fill'd, ev'n till it drown'd his eyes,
And all sense fail'd him. Forth then flew this prince of tragedies;
Who next stoop'd Mulius ev'n to death with his insatiate spear;
One ear it enter'd, and made good his pass to th' other ear.
Echeclus then, Agenor's son, he strook betwixt the brows;
Whose blood set fire upon his sword, that cool'd it till the throes
Of his then labouring brain let out his soul to fixéd fate,
And gave cold entry to black death. Deucalion then had state
In these men's beings, where the nerves about the elbow knit,
Down to his hand his spear's steel pierc'd, and brought such pain to it
As led death jointly; whom he saw before his fainting eyes,
And in his neck felt, with a stroke, laid on so, that off flies
His head. One of the twice-twelve bones, that all the backbone make,
Let out his marrow; when the head he, helm and all, did take,
And hurl'd amongst the Ilians; the body stretch'd on earth.
Rhigmus of fruitful Thrace next fell. He was the famous birth
Of Pireüs; his belly's midst the lance took, whose stern force
Quite tumbled him from chariot. In turning back the horse,
Their guider Areithous receiv'd another lance
That threw him to his lord. No end was put to the mischance
Achilles enter'd. But as fire, fall'n in a flash from heav'n,
Inflames the high woods of dry hills, and with a storm is driv'n
Through all the sylvan deeps; and raves, till down goes ev'rywhere
The smother'd hill; so ev'ry way Achilles and his spear
Consum'd the champain, the black earth flow'd with the veins he tore.
And look how oxen, yok'd and driv'n about the circular floor
Of some fair barn, tread suddenly the thick sheaves thin of corn,
And all the corn consum'd with chaff; so mix'd and overborne,
Beneath Achilles' one-hoof'd horse, shields, spears, and men, lay trod,
His axle-trees and chariot wheels, all spatter'd with the blood
Hurl'd from the steeds' hooves and the strakes. Thus, to be magnified,
His most inaccessible hands in human blood he dyed.

THE END OF THE TWENTIETH BOOK.

THE TWENTY-FIRST BOOK OF HOMER'S ILIADS

In two parts Troy's host parted; Thetis' son
One to Scamander, one to Ilion,
Pursues. Twelve lords he takes alive, to end
In sacrifice for vengeance to his friend.
Asteropæus dies by his fierce hand,
And, Priam's son, Lycaon. Over land
The Flood breaks where Achilles being engag'd,
Vulcan preserves him, and with spirit enrag'd
Sets all the champain and the floods on fire.
Contention then doth all the Gods inspire.
Apollo in Agenor's shape doth stay
Achilles' fury, and, by giving way,
Makes him pursue, till the deceit gives leave
That Troy in safety might her friends receive.

ANOTHER ARGUMENT

Phy at the flood's shore doth express
The labours of Æacides.
And now they reach'd the goodly swelling channel of the flood,
Gulf-eating Xanthus, whom Jove mix'd with his immortal brood;
And there Achilles cleft the host of Ilion; one side fell
On Xanthus, th' other on the town; and that did he impell
The same way that the last day's rage put all the Greeks in rout,
When Hector's fury reign'd; these now Achilles pour'd about
The scatter'd field. To stay the flight, Saturnia cast before
Their hasty feet a standing fog; and then flight's violence bore
The other half full on the flood. The silver-gulféd deep
Receiv'd them with a mighty cry, the billows vast and steep
Roar'd at their armours, which the shores did round about resound;
This way and that they swum, and shriek'd as in the gulfs they drown'd
And as in fir'd fields locusts rise, as the unwearied blaze
Plies still their rising, till in swarms all rush as in amaze,
For scape into some neighbour flood; so th' Achilleian stroke
Here drave the foe, the gulfy flood with men and horse did choke.
Then on the shore the Worthy hid and left his horrid lance
Amids the tamarisks, and sprite-like did with his sword advance
Up to the river; ill affairs took up his furious brain
For Troy's engagements; ev'ry way he doubled slain on slain.
A most unmanly noise was made, with those he put to sword,
Of groans and outcries. The flood blush'd, to be so much engor'd
With such base souls. And as small fish the swift-finn'd dolphin fly,
Filling the deep pits in the ports, on whose close strength they lie,
And there he swallows them in shoals; so here, to rocks and holes

About the flood, the Trojans fled, and there most lost their souls,
Ev'n till he tir'd his slaught'rous arm. Twelve fair young princes then
He chose of all to take alive, to have them freshly slain
On that most solemn day of wreak, resolv'd on for his friend.
These led he trembling forth the flood, as fearful of their end
As any hind calves. All their hands he pinioned behind
With their own girdles worn upon their rich weeds, and resign'd
Their persons to his Myrmidons to bear to fleet; and he
Plung'd in the stream again to take more work of tragedy.
He met, then issuing the flood with all intent of flight,
Lycaon, Dardan Priam's son; whom lately in the night
He had surpris'd, as in a wood of Priam's he had cut
The green arms of a wild fig-tree, to make him spokes to put
In naves of his new chariot. An ill then, all unthought,
Stole on him in Achilles' shape, who took him thence, and brought
To well-built Lemnos, selling him to famous Jason's son.
From whom a guest then in his house (Imbrius Eetion)
Redeem'd at high rate, and sent home t' Arisba, whence he fled,
And saw again his father's court; elev'n days banqueted
Amongst his friends; the twelfth God thrust his hapless head again
In t' hands of stern Æacides, who now must send him slain
To Pluto's court, and 'gainst his will. Him, when Achilles knew,
Naked of helmet, shield, sword, lance (all which for ease he threw
To earth, being overcome with sweat, and labour wearying
His flying knees) he storm'd, and said: "O heav'n, a wondrous thing
Invades mine eyes! Those Ilians, that heretofore I slew,
Rise from the dark dead quick again. This man Fate makes eschew
Her own steel fingers. He was sold in Lemnos, and the deep
Of all seas 'twixt this Troy, and that (that many a man doth keep
From his lov'd country) bars not him. Come then, he now shall taste
The head of Pelias, and try if steel will down as fast
As other fortunes, or kind earth can any surer seize
On his sly person, whose strong arms have held down Hercules."
His thoughts thus mov'd, while he stood firm, to see if he, he spied,
Would offer flight (which first he thought) but when he had descried
He was descried and flight was vain, fearful, he made more nigh,
With purpose to embrace his knees, and now long'd much to fly
His black fate and abhorréd death by coming in. His foe
Observ'd all this, and up he rais'd his lance as he would throw;
And then Lycaon close ran in, fell on his breast, and took
Achilles' knees; whose lance, on earth now staid, did overlook
His still turn'd back, with thirst to glut his sharp point with the blood
That lay so ready. But that thirst Lycaon's thirst withstood
To save his blood; Achilles' knee in his one hand he knit,
His other held the long lance hard, and would not part with it,
But thus besought: "I kiss thy knees, divine Æacides!
Respect me, and my fortunes rue. I now present th' access
Of a poor suppliant for thy ruth; and I am one that is

Worthy thy ruth, O Jove's belov'd. First hour my miseries
Fell into any hand, 'twas thine. I tasted all my bread
By thy gift since, O since that hour that thy surprisal led
From forth the fair wood my sad feet, far from my lov'd allies,
To famous Lemnos, where I found a hundred oxen's prize
To make my ransom; for which now I thrice the worth will raise.
This day makes twelve, since I arriv'd in Ilion, many days
Being spent before in sufferance; and now a cruel fate
Thrusts me again into thy hands. I should haunt Jove with hate,
That with such set malignity gives thee my life again.
There were but two of us for whom Laothoe suffer'd pain,
Laothoe, old Alte's seed; Alte, whose palace stood
In height of upper Pedasus, near Satnius' silver flood,
And rul'd the war-like Lelegi. Whose seed (as many more)
King Priam married, and begot the god-like Polydore,
And me accurs'd. Thou slaughter'dst him; and now thy hand on me
Will prove as mortal. I did think, when here I met with thee,
I could not 'scape thee; yet give ear, and add thy mind to it:
I told my birth to intimate, though one sire did beget
Yet one womb brought not into light Hector that slew thy friend,
And me. O do not kill me then, but let the wretched end
Of Polydore excuse my life. For half our being bred
Brothers to Hector, he (half) paid, no more is forfeited."
Thus sued he humbly; but he heard, with this austere reply:
"Fool, urge not ruth nor price to me, till that solemnity,
Resolv'd on for Patroclus' death, pay all his rites to fate.
Till his death I did grace to Troy, and many lives did rate
At price of ransom; but none now, of all the brood of Troy,
(Whoever Jove throws to my hands) shall any breath enjoy
That death can beat out, specially that touch at Priam's race.
Die, die, my friend. What tears are these? What sad looks spoil thy face?
Patroclus died, that far pass'd thee. Nay, seest thou not beside,
Myself, ev'n I, a fair young man, and rarely magnified,
And, to my father being a king, a mother have that sits
In rank with Goddesses; and yet, when thou hast spent thy spirits,
Death and as violent a fate must overtake ev'n me,
By twilight, morn-light, day, high noon, whenever destiny
Sets on her man to hurl a lance, or knit out of his string
An arrow that must reach my life." This said, a languishing
Lycaon's heart bent like his knees, yet left him strength t' advance
Both hands for mercy as he kneel'd. His foe yet leaves his lance,
And forth his sword flies, which he hid in furrow of a wound
Driv'n through the jointure of his neck; flat fell he on the ground,
Stretch'd with death's pangs, and all the earth imbru'd with timeless blood.
Then gript Æacides his heel, and to the lofty flood
Flung, swinging, his unpitied corse, to see it swim, and toss
Upon the rough waves, and said; "Go, feed fat the fish with loss
Of thy left blood, they clean will suck thy green wounds; and this saves

Thy mother tears upon thy bed. Deep Xanthus on his waves
Shall hoise thee bravely to a tomb, that in her burly breast
The sea shall open, where great fish may keep thy fun'ral feast
With thy white fat, and on the waves dance at thy wedding fate,
Clad in black horror, keeping close inaccessible state,
So perish Ilians, till we pluck the brows of Ilion
Down to her feet, you flying still, I flying still upon
Thus in the rear, and (as my brows were fork'd with rabid horns) [1]
Toss ye together. This brave flood, that strengthens and adorns
Your city with his silver gulfs, to whom so many bulls
Your zeal hath offer'd, which blind zeal his sacred current gulls,
With casting chariots and horse quick to his pray'd-for aid,
Shall nothing profit. Perish then, till cruell'st death hath laid
All at the red feet of Revenge for my slain friend, and all
With whom the absence of my hands made yours a festival."
This speech great Xanthus more enrag'd, and made his spirit contend
For means to shut up the op'd vein against him, and defend
The Trojans in it from his plague. In mean time Peleus' son,
And now with that long lance he hid, for more blood set upon
Asteropæus, the descent of Pelegon, and he
Of broad-stream'd Axius, and the dame, of first nativity
To all the daughters that renown'd Acesamenus' seed,
Bright Peribœa, whom the Flood, arm'd thick with lofty reed,
Compress'd. At her grandchild now went Thetis' great son, whose foe
Stood arm'd with two darts, being set on by Xanthus anger'd so
For those youths' blood shed in his stream by vengeful Thetis' son
Without all mercy. Both being near, great Thetides begun
With this high question; "Of what race art thou that dar'st oppose
Thy pow'r to mine thus? Curséd wombs they ever did disclose,
That stood my anger." He replied: "What makes thy fury's heat
Talk, and seek pedigrees? Far hence lies my innative seat,
In rich Pæonia. My race from broad-stream'd Axius runs;
Axius, that gives earth purest drink, of all the wat'ry sons
Of great Oceanus, and got the famous for his spear,
Pelegonus, that father'd me; and these Pæonians here,
Arm'd with long lances, here I lead; and here th' elev'nth fair light
Shines on us since we enter'd Troy. Come now, brave man, let's fight."
Thus spake he, threat'ning; and to him Pelides made reply
With shaken Pelias; but his foe with two at once let fly,
For both his hands were dexterous. One jav'lin strook the shield
Of Thetis' son, but strook not through; the gold, God's gift, repell'd
The eager point; the other lance fell lightly on the part
Of his fair right hand's cubit; forth the black blood spun; the dart
Glanc'd over, fast'ning on the earth, and there his spleen was spent
That wish'd the body. With which wish Achilles his lance sent,
That quite miss'd, and infix'd itself fast in steep-up shore;
Ev'n to the midst it enter'd it. Himself then fiercely bore
Upon his enemy with his sword. His foe was tugging hard

To get his lance out; thrice he pluck'd, and thrice sure Pelias barr'd
His wish'd evulsion; the fourth pluck, he bow'd and meant to break
The ashen plant, but, ere that act, Achilles' sword did check
His bent pow'r, and brake out his soul. Full in the navel-stead
He ripp'd his belly up, and out his entrails fell, and dead
His breathless body; whence his arms Achilles drew, and said:
"Lie there, and prove it dangerous to lift up adverse head
Against Jove's sons, although a Flood were ancestor to thee.
Thy vaunts urg'd him, but I may vaunt a higher pedigree
From Jove himself. King Peleüs was son to Æacus,
Infernal Æacus to Jove, and I to Peleüs.
Thunder-voic'd Jove far passeth floods, that only murmurs raise
With earth and water as they run with tribute to the seas;
And his seed theirs exceeds as far. A Flood, a mighty Flood,
Rag'd near thee now, but with no aid; Jove must not be withstood.
King Achelous yields to him, and great Oceanus,
Whence all floods, all the sea, all founts, wells, all deeps humorous,
Fetch their beginnings; yet ev'n he fears Jove's flash, and the crack
His thunder gives, when out of heav'n it tears atwo his rack." [2]
Thus pluck'd he from the shore his lance, and left the waves to wash
The wave-sprung entrails, about which fausens and other fish
Did shoal, to nibble at the fat which his sweet kidneys hid.
This for himself. Now to his men, the well-rode Pæons, did
His rage contend, all which cold fear shook into flight, to see
Their captain slain. At whose maz'd flight, as much enrag'd, flew he.
And then fell all these, Thrasius, Mydon, Astypylus,
Great Ophelestes, Ænius, Mnesus, Thersilochus.
And on these many more had fall'n, unless the angry Flood
Had took the figure of a man, and in a whirlpit stood,
Thus speaking to Æacides: "Past all, pow'r feeds thy will,
Thou great grandchild of Æacus, and, past all, th' art in ill,
And Gods themselves confederates, and Jove, the best of Gods,
All deaths gives thee, all places not. Make my shores periods
To all shore service. In the field let thy field-acts run high,
Not in my waters. My sweet streams choke with mortality
Of men slain by thee. Carcasses so glut me, that I fail
To pour into the sacred sea my waves; yet still assail
Thy cruel forces. Cease, amaze affects me with thy rage,
Prince of the people." He replied: "Shall thy command assuage,
Gulf-fed Scamander, my free wrath? I'll never leave pursu'd
Proud Ilion's slaughters, till this hand in her fill'd walls conclude
Her flying forces, and hath tried in single fight the chance
Of war with Hector; whose event with stark death shall advance
One of our conquests." Thus again he like a fury flew
Upon the Trojans; when the flood his sad plaint did pursue
To bright Apollo, telling him he was too negligent
Of Jove's high charge, importuning by all means vehement
His help of Troy till latest even should her black shadows pour

On Earth's broad breast. In all his worst, Achilles yet from shore
Leapt to his midst. Then swell'd his waves, then rag'd, then boil'd again
Against Achilles. Up flew all, and all the bodies slain
In all his deeps (of which the heaps made bridges to his waves)
He belch'd out, roaring like a bull. The unslain yet he saves
In his black whirlpits vast and deep. A horrid billow stood
About Achilles. On his shield the violence of the Flood
Beat so, it drave him back, and took his feet up, his fair palm
Enforc'd to catch into his stay a broad and lofty elm,
Whose roots he toss'd up with his hold, and tore up all the shore.
With this then he repell'd the waves, and those thick arms it bore
He made a bridge to bear him off; (for all fell in) when he
Forth from the channel threw himself. The rage did terrify [3]
Ev'n his great spirit, and made him add wings to his swiftest feet,
And tread the land. And yet not there the Flood left his retreat,
But thrust his billows after him, and black'd them all at top,
To make him fear, and fly his charge, and set the broad field ope
For Troy to 'scape in. He sprung out a dart's cast, but came on
Again with a redoubled force. As when the swiftest flown,
And strong'st of all fowls, Jove's black hawk, the huntress, stoops upon
A much lov'd quarry; so charg'd he; his arms with horror rung
Against the black waves. Yet again he was so urg'd, he flung
His body from the Flood, and fled; and after him again
The waves flew roaring. As a man that finds a water-vein,
And from some black fount is to bring his streams through plants and groves,
Goes with his mattock, and all checks, set to his course, removes;
When that runs freely, under it the pebbles all give way,
And, where it finds a fall, runs swift; nor can the leader stay
His current then, before himself full-pac'd it murmurs on;
So of Achilles evermore the strong Flood vantage won;
Though most deliver, Gods are still above the pow'rs of men.
As oft as th' able god-like man endeavour'd to maintain
His charge on them that kept the flood, and charg'd as he would try
If all the Gods inhabiting the broad unreachéd sky
Could daunt his spirit; so oft still, the rude waves charg'd him round,
Rampt on his shoulders; from whose depth his strength and spirit would bound
Up to the free air, vex'd in soul. And now the vehement Flood
Made faint his knees; so overthwart his waves were, they withstood
All the denied dust, which he wish'd, and now was fain to cry,
Casting his eyes to that broad heav'n, that late he long'd to try,
And said: "O Jove, how am I left! No God vouchsafes to free
Me, miserable man. Help now, and after torture me
With any outrage. "Would to heaven, Hector, the mightiest
Bred in this region, had imbru'd his jav'lin in my breast,
That strong may fall by strong! Where now weak water's luxury
Must make my death blush, one, heav'n-born, shall like a hog-herd die,
Drown'd in a dirty torrent's rage. Yet none of you in heav'n
I blame for this, but She alone by whom this life was giv'n

That now must die thus. She would still delude me with her tales,
Affirming Phœbus' shafts should end within the Trojan walls
My curs'd beginning." In this strait, Neptune and Pallas flew,
To fetch him off. In men's shapes both close to his danger drew,
And, taking both both hands, thus spake the Shaker of the world:
"Pelides, do not stir a foot, nor these waves, proudly curl'd
Against thy bold breast, fear a jot; thou hast us two thy friends,
Neptune and Pallas, Jove himself approving th' aid we lend.
'Tis nothing as thou fear'st with Fate; she will not see thee drown'd.
This height shall soon down, thine own eyes shall see it set aground.
Be rul'd then, we'll advise thee well; take not thy hand away
From putting all, indiff'rently, to all that it can lay
Upon the Trojans, till the walls of haughty Ilion
Conclude all in a desp'rate flight. And when thou hast set gone
The soul of Hector, turn to fleet; our hands shall plant a wreath
Of endless glory on thy brows." Thus to the free from death
Both made retreat. He, much impell'd by charge the Godheads gave,
The field, that now was overcome with many a boundless wave,
He overcame. On their wild breasts they toss'd the carcasses,
And arms, of many a slaughter'd man. And now the wingéd knees
Of this great captain bore aloft; against the Flood he flies
With full assault; nor could that God make shrink his rescu'd thighs.
Nor shrunk the Flood, but, as his foe grew pow'rful, he grew mad,
Thrust up a billow to the sky, and crystal Simoïs bad
To his assistance: "Simoïs, ho, brother," out he cried,
"Come, add thy current, and resist this man half-deified,
Or Ilion he will pull down straight; the Trojans cannot stand
A minute longer. Come, assist, and instantly command
All fountains in thy rule to rise, all torrents to make in,
And stuff thy billows; with whose height, engender such a din,
With trees torn up and justling stones, as so immane a man
May shrink beneath us; whose pow'r thrives do my pow'r all it can;
He dares things fitter for a God. But, nor his form, nor force,
Nor glorious arms shall profit it; all which, and his dead corse,
I vow to roll up in my sands, nay, bury in my mud,
Nay, in the very sinks of Troy, that, pour'd into my flood,
Shall make him drowning work enough; and, being drown'd, I'll set
A fort of such strong filth on him, that Greece shall never get
His bones from it. There, there shall stand Achilles' sepulchre,
And save a burial for his friends." This fury did transfer
His high-ridg'd billows on the prince, roaring with blood and foam
And carcasses. The crimson stream did snatch into her womb
Surpris'd Achilles; and her height stood, held up by the hand
Of Jove himself. Then Juno cried, and call'd (to countermand
This wat'ry Deity) the God that holds command in fire,
Afraid lest that gulf-stomach'd Flood would satiate his desire
On great Achilles: "Mulciber, my best lov'd son!" she cried,
"Rouse thee, for all the Gods conceive this Flood thus amplified

Is rais'd at thee, and shows as if his waves would drown the sky,
And put out all the sphere of fire. Haste, help thy empery.
Light flames deep as his pits. Ourself the west wind and the south
Will call out of the sea, and breathe in either's full-charg'd mouth
A storm t' enrage thy fires 'gainst Troy; which shall (in one exhal'd)
Blow flames of sweat about their brows, and make their armours scald.
Go thou then, and, 'gainst these winds rise, make work on Xanthus' shore,
With setting all his trees on fire, and in his own breast pour
A fervor that shall make it burn; nor let fair words or threats
Avert thy fury till I speak, and then subdue the heats
Of all thy blazes." Mulciber prepar'd a mighty fire,
First in the field us'd; burning up the bodies that the ire
Of great Achilles reft of souls; the quite-drown'd field it dried,
And shrunk the flood up. And as fields, that have been long time cloy'd
With catching weather, when their corn lies on the gavel heap,
Are with a constant north wind dried, with which for comfort leap
Their hearts that sow'd them; so this field was dried, the bodies burn'd,
And ev'n the flood into a fire as bright as day was turn'd.
Elms, willows, tam'risks, were inflam'd; the lote trees, sea-grass reeds,
And rushes, with the galingale roots, of which abundance breeds
About the sweet flood, all were fir'd; the gliding fishes flew
Upwards in flames; the grov'lling eels crept upright; all which slew
Wise Vulcan's unresisted spirit. The Flood out of a flame
Cried to him: "Cease, O Mulciber, no Deity can tame
Thy matchless virtue; nor would I, since thou art thus hot, strive.
Cease then thy strife; let Thetis' son, with all thy wish'd haste, drive
Ev'n to their gates these Ilians. What toucheth me their aid,
Or this contention?" Thus in flames the burning River pray'd.
And as a caldron, underput with store of fire, and wrought
With boiling of a well-fed brawn, up leaps his wave aloft,
Bavins of sere wood urging it, and spending flames apace,
Till all the caldron be engirt with a consuming blaze;
So round this Flood burn'd, and so sod his sweet and tortur'd streams,
Nor could flow forth, bound in the fumes of Vulcan's fi'ry beams;
Who, then not mov'd, his mother's ruth by all his means he craves,
And ask'd, why Vulcan should invade and so torment his waves
Past other floods, when his offence rose not to such degree
As that of other Gods for Troy; and that himself would free
Her wrath to it, if she were pleas'd; and pray'd her, that her son
Might be reflected; adding this, that he would ne'er be won
To help keep off the ruinous day, in which all Troy should burn,
Fir'd by the Grecians. This vow heard, she charg'd her son to turn
His fi'ry spirits to their homes, and said it was not fit
A God should suffer so for men. Then Vulcan did remit
His so unmeasur'd violence, and back the pleasant Flood
Ran to his channel. Thus these Gods she made friends; th' other stood
At weighty diff'rence; both sides ran together with a sound,
That earth resounded, and great heav'n about did surrebound,

Jove heard it, sitting on his hill, and laugh'd to see the Gods
Buckle to arms like angry men; and, he pleas'd with their odds,
They laid it freely. Of them all, thump-buckler Mars began,
And at Minerva with a lance of brass he headlong ran,
These vile words ushering his blows: "Thou dog-fly, what's the cause
Thou mak'st Gods fight thus? Thy huge heart breaks all our peaceful laws
With thy insatiate shamelessness, Rememb'rest thou the hour
When Diomed charg'd me, and by thee, and thou with all thy pow'r
Took'st lance thyself, and, in all sights, rush'd on me with a wound?
Now vengeance falls on thee for all." This said, the shield fring'd round
With fighting adders, borne by Jove, that not to thunder yields,
He clapt his lance on; and this God, that with the blood of fields
Pollutes his godhead, that shield pierc'd, and hurt the arméd Maid,
But back she leapt, and with her strong hand rapt a huge stone, laid
Above the champain, black and sharp, that did in old time break
Partitions to men's lands; and that she dusted in the neck
Of that impetuous challenger. Down to the earth he sway'd,
And overlaid sev'n acres' land. His hair was all beray'd
With dust and blood mix'd; and his arms rung out. Minerva laugh'd,
And thus insulted: "O thou fool, yet hast thou not been taught
To know mine eminence? Thy strength opposest thou to mine?
So pay thy mother's furies then, who for these aids of thine,
(Ever afforded perjur'd Troy, Greece ever left) takes spleen,
And vows thee mischief." Thus she turn'd her blue eyes, when love's Queen
The hand of Mars took, and from earth rais'd him with thick-drawn breath,
His spirits not yet got up again. But from the press of death
Kind Aphrodite was his guide. Which Juno seeing, exclaim'd:
"Pallas, see, Mars is help'd from field! Dog-fly, his rude tongue nam'd
Thyself ev'n now; but that his love, that dog-fly, will not leave
Her old consort. Upon her fly." Minerva did receive
This excitation joyfully, and at the Cyprian flew,
Strook with her hard hand her soft breast, a blow that overthrew
Both her and Mars; and there both lay together in broad field.
When thus she triumph'd: "So lie all, that any succours yield
To these false Trojans 'gainst the Greeks; so bold and patient
As Venus, shunning charge of me; and no less impotent
Be all their aids, than hers to Mars. So short work would be made
In our depopulating Troy, this hardiest to invade
Of all earth's cities." At this wish, white-wristed Juno smil'd.
Next Neptune and Apollo stood upon the point of field,
And thus spake Neptune: "Phœbus! Come, why at the lance's end
Stand we two thus? 'Twill be a shame, for us to re-ascend
Jove's golden house, being thus in field and not to fight. Begin;
For 'tis no graceful work for me; thou hast the younger chin,
I older and know more. O fool, what a forgetful heart
Thou bear'st about thee, to stand here, prest to take th' Ilian part,
And fight with me! Forgett'st thou then, what we two, we alone
Of all the Gods, have suffer'd here, when proud Laomedon

Enjoy'd our service a whole year, for our agreed reward?
Jove in his sway would have it so; and in that year I rear'd
This broad brave wall about this town, that (being a work of mine)
It might be inexpugnable. This service then was thine,
In Ida, that so many hills and curl'd-head forests crown,
To feed his oxen, crooked-shank'd, and headed like the moon.
But when the much-joy-bringing Hours brought term for our reward,
The terrible Laomedon dismiss'd us both, and scar'd
Our high deservings, not alone to hold our promis'd fee,
But give us threats too. Hands and feet he swore to fetter thee,
And sell thee as a slave, dismiss'd far hence to foreign isles.
Nay more, he would have both our ears. His vow's breach, and reviles,
Made us part angry with him then; and dost thou gratulate now
Such a king's subjects? Or with us not their destruction vow,
Ev'n to their chaste wives and their babes?" He answer'd: "He might hold,
His wisdom little, if with him, a God, for men he would
Maintain contention; wretched men that flourish for a time
Like leaves, eat some of that earth yields, and give earth in their prime
Their whole selves for it. Quickly then, let us fly fight for them,
Nor show it offer'd. Let themselves bear out their own extreme."
Thus he retir'd, and fear'd to change blows with his uncle's hands;
His sister therefore chid him much, the Goddess that commands
In games of hunting, and thus spake: "Fly'st thou, and leav'st the field
To Neptune's glory, and no blows? O fool, why dost thou wield
Thy idle bow? No more my ears shall hear thee vaunt in skies
Dares to meet Neptune, but I'll tell thy coward's tongue it lies."
He answer'd nothing; yet Jove's wife could put on no such reins,
But spake thus loosely: "How dar'st thou, dog, whom no fear contains,
Encounter me? 'Twill prove a match of hard conditión.
Though the great Lady of the bow and Jove hath set thee down
For lion of thy sex, with gift to slaughter any dame
Thy proud will envies; yet some dames will prove th' had'st better tame
Wild lions upon hills than them. But if this question rests
Yet under judgment in thy thoughts, and that thy mind contests,
I'll make thee know it." Suddenly with her left hand she catch'd
Both Cynthia's palms, lock'd fingers fast, and with her right she snatch'd
From her fair shoulders her gilt bow, and, laughing, laid it on
About her ears, and ev'ry way her turnings seiz'd upon,
Till all her arrows scatter'd out, her quiver emptied quite.
And as a dove, that, flying a hawk, takes to some rock her flight,
And in his hollow breasts sits safe, her fate not yet to die;
So fled she mourning, and her bow left there. Then Mercury
His opposite thus undertook: "Latona, at no hand
Will I bide combat. 'Tis a work right dangerous to stand
At diff'rence with the wives of Jove. Go, therefore, freely vaunt
Amongst the Deities, th' hast subdu'd, and made thy combatant
Yield with plain pow'r." She answer'd not, but gather'd up the bow
And shafts fall'n from her daughter's side, retiring. Up did go

Diana to Jove's starry hall, her incorrupted veil
Trembling about her so she shook. Phœbus, lest Troy should fail
Before her fate, flew to her walls; the other Deities flew
Up to Olympus, some enrag'd, some glad. Achilles slew
Both men and horse of Ilion. And as a city fir'd
Casts up a heat that purples heav'n, clamours and shrieks expir'd
In ev'ry corner, toil to all, to many misery,
Which fire th' incenséd Gods let fall; Achilles so let fly
Rage on the Trojans, toils and shrieks as much by him impos'd.
Old Priam in his sacred tow'r stood, and the flight disclos'd
Of his forc'd people, all in rout, and not a stroke return'd
By fled resistance. His eyes saw in what a fury burn'd
The son of Peleüs, and down went weeping from the tow'r
To all the port-guards, and their chiefs told of his flying pow'r.
Commanding th' op'ning of the ports, but not to let their hands
Stir from them, for Æacides would pour in with his bands.
"Destruction comes, O shut them strait, when we are in," he pray'd,
"For not our walls I fear will check this violent man." This said,
Off lifted they the bars, the ports hal'd open, and they gave
Safety her entry with the host; which yet they could not save,
Had not Apollo sallied out, and strook destructión,
Brought by Achilles in their necks, back; when they right upon
The ports bore all, dry, dusty, spent; and on their shoulders rode
Rabid Achilles with his lance, still glory being the goad
That prick'd his fury. Then the Greeks high-ported Ilion
Had seiz'd, had not Apollo stirr'd Antenor's famous son,
Divine Agenor, and cast in an undertaking spirit
To his bold bosom, and himself stood by to strengthen it,
And keep the heavy hand of death from breaking in. The God
Stood by him, leaning on a beech, and cover'd his abode.
With night-like darkness; yet for all the spirit he inspir'd,
When that great city-razer's force his thoughts strook, he retir'd,
Stood, and went on; a world of doubts still falling in his way;
When, angry with himself, he said: "Why suffer I this stay
In this so strong need to go on? If, like the rest, I fly,
'Tis his best weapon to give chace, being swift, and I should die
Like to a coward. If I stand, I fall too. These two ways
Please not my purpose; I would live. What if I suffer these
Still to be routed, and, my feet affording further length,
Pass all these fields of Ilion, till Ida's sylvan strength
And steep heights shroud me, and at even refresh me in the flood,
And turn to Ilion? O my soul? why drown'st thou in the blood
Of these discourses? If this course, that talks of further flight,
I give my feet, his feet more swift have more odds. Get he sight
Of that pass, I pass least; for pace, and length of pace, his thighs
Will stand out all men. Meet him then; my steel hath faculties
Of pow'r to pierce him; his great breast but one soul holds, and that
Death claims his right in, all men say; but he holds special state

In Jove's high bounty; that's past man, that ev'ry way will hold,
And that serves all men ev'ry way." This last heart made him bold
To stand Achilles, and stirr'd up a mighty mind to blows.
And as a panther, having heard the hounds' trail, doth disclose
Her freckled forehead, and stares forth from out some deep-grown wood
To try what strength dares her abroad; and when her fi'ry blood
The hounds have kindled, no quench serves of love to live or fear,
Though strook, though wounded, though quite through she feels the mortal spear,
But till the man's close strength she tries, or strows earth with his dart,
She puts her strength out; so it far'd with brave Agenor's heart,
And till Achilles he had prov'd, no thoughts, no deeds, once stirr'd
His fixéd foot. To his broad breast his round shield he preferr'd,
And up his arm went with his aim, his voice out with this cry:
"Thy hope is too great, Peleus' son, this day to show thine eye
Troy's Ilion at thy foot. O fool! the Greeks with much more woes,
More than are suffer'd yet, must buy great Ilion's overthrows.
We are within her many strong, that for our parents' sakes,
Our wives and children, will save Troy; and thou, though he that makes
Thy name so terrible, shalt make a sacrifice to her
With thine own ruins." Thus he threw, nor did his jav'lin err,
But strook his foe's leg near his knee; the fervent steel did ring
Against his tin greaves, and leapt back; the fire's strong-handed king
Gave virtue of repulse. And then Æacides assail'd
Divine Agenor; but in vain, Apollo's pow'r prevail'd,
And rapt Agenor from his reach; whom quietly he plac'd
Without the skirmish, casting mists to save from being chac'd
His tender'd person; and (he gone) to give his soldiers 'scape,
The Deity turn'd Achilles still, by putting on the shape
Of him he thirsted; evermore he fed his eye, and fled,
And he with all his knees pursu'd. So cunningly he led,
That still he would be near his reach, to draw his rage, with hope,
Far from the conflict; to the flood maintaining still the scope
Of his attraction. In mean time, the other frighted pow'rs
Came to the city, comforted; when Troy and all her tow'rs
Strooted with fillers; none would stand to see who stay'd without,
Who scap'd, and who came short. The ports cleft to receive the rout
That pour'd itself in. Ev'ry man was for himself. Most fleet
Most fortunate. Whoever scap'd, his head might thank his feet.

[1] The word is κεραΐζων, which they translate cædens, but properly signifies dissipans, ut boves infestis cornibus.

[2] The rack or motion of the clouds, for the clouds.

[3] Note the continued height and admired expression of Achilles' glory.

THE END OF THE TWENTY-FIRST BOOK.

THE ARGUMENT

All Trojans hous'd but Hector, only he
Keeps field, and undergoes th' extremity.
Æacides assaulting, Hector flies,
Minerva stays him, he resists, and dies.
Achilles to his chariot doth enforce,
And to the naval station drags his corse.

ANOTHER ARGUMENT

Hector, in Chi, to death is done,
By pow'r of Peleus' angry son.
Thus, chas'd like hinds, the Ilians took time to drink and eat,
And to refresh them, getting off the mingled dust and sweat,
And good strong rampires on instead. The Greeks then cast their shields
Aloft their shoulders; and now Fate their near invasion yields
Of those tough walls, her deadly hand compelling Hector's stay
Before Troy at the Scæan ports. Achilles still made way
At Phœbus, who his bright head turn'd, and ask'd: "Why, Peleus' son,
Pursu'st thou, being a man, a God? Thy rage hath never done.
Acknowledge not thine eyes my state? Esteems thy mind no more
Thy honour in the chase of Troy, but puts my chase before
Their utter conquest? They are all now hous'd in Ilion,
While thou hunt'st me. What wishest thou? My blood will never run
On thy proud jav'lin." "It is thou," replied Æacides,
"That putt'st dishonour thus on me, thou worst of Deities.
Thou turn'dst me from the walls, whose ports had never entertain'd
Numbers now enter'd, over whom thy saving hand hath reign'd,
And robb'd my honour; and all is, since all thy actions stand
Past fear of reck'ning. But held I the measure in my hand,
It should afford thee dear-bought scapes." Thus with elated spirits,
Steed-like, that at Olympus' games wears garlands for his merits,
And rattles home his chariot, extending all his pride,
Achilles so parts with the God. When aged Priam spied
The great Greek come, spher'd round with beams and showing as if the star,
Surnam'd Orion's hound, that springs in autumn, and sends far
His radiance through a world of stars, of all whose beams his own
Cast greatest splendour, the midnight that renders them most shown
Then being their foil; and on their points, cure-passing fevers then
Come shaking down into the joints of miserable men;
As this were fall'n to earth, and shot along the field his rays
Now towards Priam, when he saw in great Æacides,

Out flew his tender voice in shrieks, and with rais'd hands he smit
His rev'rend head, then up to heav'n he cast them, showing it
What plagues it sent him, down again then threw them to his son,
To make him shun them. He now stood without steep Ilion,
Thirsting the combat; and to him thus miserably cried
The kind old king: "O Hector, fly this man, this homicide,
That straight will stroy thee. He's too strong, and would to heav'n he were
As strong in heav'n's love as in mine! Vultures and dogs should tear
His prostrate carcass, all my woes quench'd with his bloody spirits.
He has robb'd me of many sons and worthy, and their merits
Sold to far islands. Two of them, ah me! I miss but now,
They are not enter'd, nor stay here. Laothoe, O 'twas thou,
O queen of women, from whose womb they breath'd. O did the tents
Detain them only, brass and gold would purchase safe events
To their sad durance; 'tis within; old Altes, young in fame,
Gave plenty for his daughter's dow'r; but if they fed the flame
Of this man's fury, woe is me, woe to my wretched queen!
But in our state's woe their two deaths will nought at all be seen,
So thy life quit them. Take the town, retire, dear son, and save
Troy's husbands and her wives, nor give thine own life to the grave
For this man's glory. Pity me, me, wretch, so long alive,
Whom in the door of age Jove keeps: that so he may deprive
My being, in fortune's utmost curse, to see the blackest thread
Of this life's mis'ries, my sons slain, my daughters ravishéd,
Their resting chambers sack'd, their babes, torn from them, on their knees
Pleading for mercy, themselves dragg'd to Grecian slaveries,
And all this drawn through my red eyes. Then last of all kneel I,
Alone, all helpless at my gates, before my enemy,
That ruthless gives me to my dogs, all the deformity
Of age discover'd; and all this thy death, sought wilfully,
Will pour on me. A fair young man at all parts it beseems,
Being bravely slain, to lie all gash'd, and wear the worst extremes
Of war's most cruelty; no wound, of whatsoever ruth,
But is his ornament; but I, a man so far from youth,
White head, white-bearded, wrinkled, pin'd, all shames must show the eye.
Live, prevent this then, this most shame of all man's misery."
Thus wept the old king, and tore off his white hair; yet all these
Retir'd not Hector. Hecuba then fell upon her knees,
Stripp'd nak'd her bosom, show'd her breasts, and bad him rev'rence them,
And pity her. If ever she had quieted his exclaim,
He would cease hers, and take the town, not tempting the rude field
When all had left it: "Think," said she, 'I gave thee life to yield
My life recomfort; thy rich wife shall have no rites of thee,
Nor do thee rites; our tears shall pay thy corse no obsequy,
Being ravish'd from us, Grecian dogs nourish'd with what I nurs'd."
Thus wept both these, and to his ruth propos'd the utmost worst
Of what could chance them; yet he stay'd. And now drew deadly near
Mighty Achilles; yet he still kept deadly station there.

Look how a dragon, when she sees a traveller bent upon
Her breeding den, her bosom fed with full contagión,
Gathers her forces, sits him firm, and at his nearest pace
Wraps all her cavern in her folds, and thrusts a horrid face
Out at his entry; Hector so, with unextinguish'd spirit,
Stood great Achilles, stirr'd no foot, but at the prominent turret
Bent to his bright shield, and resolv'd to bear fall'n heav'n on it.
Yet all this resolute abode did not so truly fit
His free election; but he felt a much more galling spur
To the performance, with conceit of what he should incur
Ent'ring, like others, for this cause; to which he thus gave way:
"O me, if I shall take the town, Polydamas will lay
This flight and all this death on me; who counsell'd me to lead
My pow'rs to Troy this last black night, when so I saw make head
Incens'd Achilles. I yet stay'd, though, past all doubt, that course
Had much more profited than mine; which; being by so much worse
As comes to all our flight and death, my folly now I fear
Hath bred this scandal, all our town now burns my ominous ear
With whisp'ring: 'Hector's self-conceit hath cast away his host.'
And, this true, this extremity that I rely on most
Is best for me: stay, and retire with this man's life; or die
Here for our city with renown, since all else fled but I.
And yet one way cuts both these ways: What if I hang my shield
My helm and lance here on these walls, and meet in humble field
Renown'd Achilles, off'ring him Helen and all the wealth,
Whatever in his hollow keels bore Alexander's stealth
For both th' Atrides? For the rest, whatever is possess'd
In all this city, known or hid, by oath shall be confess'd
Of all our citizens; of which one half the Greeks shall have,
One half themselves. But why, lov'd soul, would these suggestions save
Thy state still in me? I'll not sue; nor would he grant, but I,
Mine arms cast off, should be assur'd a woman's death to die.
To men of oak and rock, no words; virgins and youths talk thus,
Virgins and youths that love and woo; there's other war with us;
What blows and conflicts urge, we cry, hates and defiances,
And, with the garlands these trees bear, try which hand Jove will bless."
These thoughts employ'd his stay; and now Achilles comes, now near
His Mars-like presence terribly came brandishing his spear,
His right arm shook it, his bright arms like day came glitt'ring on,
Like fire-light, or the light of heav'n shot from the rising sun,
This sight outwrought discourse, cold fear shook Hector from his stand;
No more stay now; all ports were left; he fled in fear the hand
Of that Fear-Master; who, hawk-like, air's swiftest passenger,
That holds a tim'rous dove in chase, and with command doth bear
His fi'ry onset, the dove hastes, the hawk comes whizzing on,
This way and that he turns and winds, and cuffs the pigeón,
And, till he truss it, his great spirit lays hot charge on his wing;
So urg'd Achilles Hector's flight; so still fear's point did sting

His troubled spirit, his knees wrought hard, along the wall he flew,
In that fair chariot-way that runs, beneath the tow'r of view,
And Troy's wild fig-tree, till they reach'd where those two mother-springs
Of deep Scamander pour'd abroad their silver murmurings;
One warm and casts out fumes as fire; the other cold as snow,
Or hail dissolv'd. And when the sun made ardent summer glow,
There water's concrete crystal shin'd; near which were cisterns made,
All pav'd and clear, where Trojan wives and their fair daughters had
Laundry for their fine linen weeds, in times of cleanly peace,
Before the Grecians brought their siege. These captains noted these,
One flying, th' other in pursuit; a strong man flew before,
A stronger follow'd him by far, and close up to him bore;
Both did their best, for neither now ran for a sacrifice,
Or for the sacrificer's hide, our runners' usual prize;
These ran for tame-horse Hector's soul. And as two running steeds,
Back'd in some set race for a game, that tries their swiftest speeds,
(A tripod, or a woman, giv'n for some man's funerals)
Such speed made these men, and on foot ran thrice about the walls. [1]
The Gods beheld them, all much mov'd; and Jove said: "O ill sight!
A man I love much, I see forc'd in most unworthy flight
About great Ilion. My heart grieves; he paid so many vows,
With thighs of sacrificéd beeves, both on the lofty brows
Of Ida, and in Ilion's height. Consult we, shall we free
His life from death, or give it now t' Achilles' victory?"
Minerva answer'd: "Alter Fate? One long since mark'd for death?
Now take from death? Do thou; but know, he still shall run beneath
Our other censures." "Be it then," replied the Thunderer,
"My lov'd Tritonia, at thy will; in this I will prefer
Thy free intention, work it all." Then stoop'd She from the sky
To this great combat. Peleus' son pursu'd incessantly
Still-flying Hector. As a hound that having rous'd a hart,
Although he tappish ne'er so oft, and ev'ry shrubby part
Attempts for strength, and trembles in, the hound doth still pursue
So close that not a foot he fails, but hunts it still at view;
So plied Achilles Hector's steps; as oft as he assay'd
The Dardan ports and tow'rs for strength (to fetch from thence some aid
With wingéd shafts) so oft forc'd he amends of pace, and stept
'Twixt him and all his hopes, and still upon the field he kept
His utmost turnings to the town. And yet, as in a dream,
One thinks he gives another chase, when such a fain'd extreme
Possesseth both, that he in chase the chaser cannot fly,
Nor can the chaser get to hand his flying enemy; [2]
So nor Achilles' chase could reach the flight of Hector's pace,
Nor Hector's flight enlarge itself of swift Achilles' chace.
But how chanc'd this? How, all this time, could Hector bear the knees
Of fierce Achilles with his own, and keep off destinies,
If Phœbus, for his last and best, through all that course had fail'd
To add his succours to his nerves, and, as his foe assail'd

Near and within him, fed his 'scape? Achilles yet well knew
His knees would fetch him, and gave signs to some friends (making shew
Of shooting at him) to forbear, lest they detracted so
From his full glory in first wounds, and in the overthrow
Make his hand last. But when they reach'd the fourth time the two founts,
Then Jove his golden scales weigh'd up, and took the last accounts
Of fate for Hector, putting in for him and Peleus' son
Two fates of bitter death; of which high heav'n receiv'd the one,
The other hell; so low declin'd the light of Hector's life.
Then Phœbus left him, when war's Queen came to resolve the strife
In th' other's knowledge: "Now," said she, "Jove-lov'd Æacides,
I hope at last to make renown perform a brave access
To all the Grecians; we shall now lay low this champion's height,
Though never so insatiate was his great heart of fight.
Nor must he 'scape our púrsuit still, though at the feet of Jove
Apollo bows into a sphere, soliciting more love
To his most favour'd. Breathe thee then, stand firm, myself will haste
And hearten Hector to change blows." She went, and he stood fast,
Lean'd on his lance, and much was joy'd that single strokes should try
This fadging conflict. Then came close the changéd Deity
To Hector, like Deiphobus in shape and voice, and said:
"O brother, thou art too much urg'd to be thus combated
About our own walls; let us stand, and force to a retreat
Th' insulting chaser." Hector joy'd at this so kind deceit,
And said: "O good Deiphobus, thy love was most before
(Of all my brothers) dear to me, but now exceeding more
It costs me honour, that, thus urg'd, thou com'st to part the charge
Of my last fortunes; other friends keep town, and leave at large
My rack'd endeavours." She replied: "Good brother, 'tis most true,
One after other, king and queen, and all our friends, did sue,
Ev'n on their knees, to stay me there, such tremblings shake them all
With this man's terror; but my mind so griev'd to see our wall
Girt with thy chases, that to death I long'd to urge thy stay.
Come, fight we, thirsty of his blood; no more let's fear to lay
Cost on our lances, but approve, if, bloodied with our spoils,
He can bear glory to their fleet, or shut up all their toils
In his one suff'rance on thy lance." With this deceit she led,
And, both come near, thus Hector spake: "Thrice have I compasséd
This great town, Peleus' son, in flight, with aversation
That out of fate put off my steps; but now all flight is flown,
The short course set up, death or life. Our resolutions yet
Must shun all rudeness, and the Gods before our valour set
For use of victory; and they being worthiest witnesses
Of all vows, since they keep vows best, before their Deities
Let vows of fit respect pass both, when conquest hath bestow'd
Her wreath on either. Here I vow no fury shall be show'd,
That is not manly, on thy corse, but, having spoil'd thy arms,
Resign thy person; which swear thou." These fair and temp'rate terms

Far fled Achilles; his brows bent, and out flew this reply:
"Hector, thou only pestilence in all mortality
To my sere spirits, never set the point 'twixt thee and me
Any conditions; but as far as men and lions fly
All terms of cov'nant, lambs and wolves; in so far opposite state,
Impossible for love t' atone, stand we, till our souls satiate
The God of soldiers. Do not dream that our disjunction can
Endure condition. Therefore now, all worth that fits a man
Call to thee, all particular parts that fit a soldier,
And they all this include (besides the skill and spirit of war)
Hunger for slaughter, and a hate that eats thy heart to eat
Thy foe's heart. This stirs, this supplies in death the killing heat;
And all this need'st thou. No more flight. Pallas Athenia
Will quickly cast thee to my lance. Now, now together draw
All griefs for vengeance, both in me, and all my friends late dead
That bled thee, raging with thy lance." This said, he brandishéd
His long lance, and away it sung; which Hector giving view,
Stoop'd low, stood firm, foreseeing it best, and quite it overflew,
Fast'ning on earth. Athenia drew it, and gave her friend,
Unseen of Hector. Hector then thus spake: "Thou want'st thy end,
God-like Achilles. Now I see, thou hast not learn'd my fate
Of Jove at all, as thy high words would bravely intimate.
Much tongue affects thee. Cunning words well serve thee to prepare
Thy blows with threats, that mine might faint with want of spirit to dare.
But my back never turns with breath; it was not born to bear
Burthens of wounds; strike home before; drive at my breast thy spear,
As mine at thine shall, and try then if heav'n's will favour thee
With scape of my lance. O would Jove would take it after me,
And make thy bosom take it all! An easy end would crown
Our difficult wars, were thy soul fled, thou most bane of our town."
Thus flew his dart, touch'd at the midst of his black shield, and flew
A huge way from it; but his heart wrath enter'd with the view
Of that hard scape, and heavy thoughts strook through him, when he spied
His brother vanish'd, and no lance beside left; out he cried:
"Deiphobus, another lance." Lance nor Deiphobus
Stood near his call. And then his mind saw all things ominous,
And thus suggested: "Woe is me, the Gods have call'd, and I
Must meet death here! Deiphobus I well hop'd had been by
With his white shield; but our strong walls shield him, and this deceit
Flows from Minerva. Now, O now, ill death comes, no more flight,
No more recovery. O Jove, this hath been otherwise;
Thy bright son and thyself have set the Greeks a greater prize
Of Hector's blood than now; of which, ev'n jealous, you had care,
But Fate now conquers; I am hers; and yet not she shall share
In my renown; that life is left to every noble spirit,
And that some great deed shall beget that all lives shall inherit."
Thus, forth his sword flew, sharp and broad, and bore a deadly weight,
With which he rush'd in. And look how an eagle from her height

Stoops to the rapture of a lamb, or cuffs a tim'rous hare;
So fell in Hector; and at him Achilles; his mind's fare
Was fierce and mighty, his shield cast a sun-like radiance,
Helm nodded, and his four plumes shook, and, when he rais'd his lance,
Up Hesp'rus rose 'mongst th' evening stars. His bright and sparkling eyes
Look'd through the body of his foe, and sought through all that prise
The next way to his thirsted life. Of all ways, only one
Appear'd to him, and that was where th' unequal winding bone,
That joins the shoulders and the neck, had place, and where there lay
The speeding way to death; and there his quick eye could display
The place it sought, e'en through those arms his friend Patroclus wore
When Hector slew him. There he aim'd, and there his jav'lin tore
Stern passage quite through Hector's neck; yet miss'd it so his throat
It gave him pow'r to change some words; but down to earth it got
His fainting body. Then triumph'd divine Æacides:
"Hector," said he, "thy heart suppos'd that in my friend's decease
Thy life was safe; my absent arm not car'd for. Fool! he left
One at the fleet that better'd him, and he it is that reft
Thy strong knees thus; and now the dogs and fowls in foulest use
Shall tear thee up, thy corse expos'd to all the Greeks' abuse."
He, fainting, said: "Let me implore, ev'n by thy knees and soul,
And thy great parents, do not see a cruelty so foul
Inflicted on me. Brass and gold receive at any rate,
And quit my person, that the peers and ladies of our state
May tomb it, and to sacred fire turn thy profane decrees."
"Dog," he replied, "urge not my ruth, by parents, soul, nor knees.
I would to God that any rage would let me eat thee raw,
Slic'd into pieces, so beyond the right of any law
I taste thy merits! And, believe, it flies the force of man
To rescue thy head from the dogs. Give all the gold they can,
If ten or twenty times so much as friends would rate thy price
Were tender'd here, with vows of more, to buy the cruelties
I here have vow'd, and after that thy father with his gold
Would free thyself; all that should fail to let thy mother hold
Solemnities of death with thee, and do thee such a grace
To mourn thy whole corse on a bed; which piecemeal I'll deface
With fowls and dogs." He, dying, said: "I, knowing thee well, foresaw
Thy now tried tyranny, nor hop'd for any other law,
Of nature, or of nations; and that fear forc'd much more
Than death my flight, which never touch'd at Hector's foot before.
A soul of iron informs thee. Mark, what vengeance th' equal fates
Will give me of thee for this rage, when in the Scæan gates
Phœbus and Paris meet with thee." Thus death's hand clos'd his eyes,
His soul flying his fair limbs to hell, mourning his destinies,
To part so with his youth and strength. Thus dead, thus Thetis' son
His prophecy answer'd: "Die thou now. When my short thread is spun,
I'll bear it as the will of Jove." This said, his brazen spear
He drew, and stuck by; then his arms, that all embruéd were,

He spoil'd his shoulders of. Then all the Greeks ran in to him,
To see his person, and admir'd his terror-stirring limb;
Yet none stood by that gave no wound to his so goodly form;
When each to other said: "O Jove, he is not in the storm
He came to fleet in with his fire, he handles now more soft."
"O friends," said stern Æacides, "now that the Gods have brought
This man thus down, I'll freely say, he brought more bane to Greece
Than all his aiders. Try we then, thus arm'd at ev'ry piece,
And girding all Troy with our host, if now their hearts will leave
Their city clear, her clear stay slain, and all their lives receive,
Or hold yet, Hector being no more. But why use I a word
Of any act but what concerns my friend? Dead, undeplor'd,
Unsepulchred, he lies at fleet, unthought on! Never hour
Shall make his dead state, while the quick enjoys me, and this pow'r
To move these movers. Though in hell, men say, that such as die
Oblivion seizeth, yet in hell in me shall Memory
Hold all her forms still of my friend. Now, youths of Greece, to fleet
Bear we this body, pæans sing, and all our navy greet
With endless honour; we have slain Hector, the period
Of all Troy's glory, to whose worth all vow'd as to a God."
This said, a work not worthy him he set to; of both feet
He bor'd the nerves through from the heel to th' ankle, and then knit
Both to his chariot with a thong of whitleather, his head [3]
Trailing the centre. Up he got to chariot, where he laid
The arms repurchas'd, and scourg'd on his horse that freely flew.
A whirlwind made of startled dust drave with them as they drew,
With which were all his black-brown curls knotted in heaps and fil'd.
And there lay Troy's late Gracious, by Jupiter exil'd
To all disgrace in his own land, and by his parents seen;
When, like her son's head, all with dust Troy's miserable queen
Distain'd her temples, plucking off her honour'd hair, and tore
Her royal garments, shrieking out. In like kind Priam bore
His sacred person, like a wretch that never saw good day,
Broken with outcries. About both the people prostrate lay,
Held down with clamour; all the town veil'd with a cloud of tears.
Ilion, with all his tops on fire, and all the massacres,
Left for the Greeks, could put on looks of no more overthrow
Than now fraid life. And yet the king did all their looks outshow.
The wretched people could not bear his sov'reign wretchedness,
Plaguing himself so, thrusting out, and praying all the press
To open him the Dardan ports, that he alone might fetch
His dearest son in, and (all fil'd with tumbling) did beseech
Each man by name, thus: "Lov'd friends, be you content, let me,
Though much ye grieve, be that poor mean to our sad remedy
Now in our wishes; I will go and pray this impious man,
Author of horrors, making proof if age's rev'rence can
Excite his pity. His own sire is old like me; and he
That got him to our griefs, perhaps, may, for my likeness, be

Mean for our ruth to him. Alas, you have no cause of cares,
Compar'd with me! I many sons, grac'd with their freshest years,
Have lost by him, and all their deaths in slaughter of this one
(Afflicted man) are doubled. This will bitterly set gone
My soul to hell. O would to heav'n, could but hold him dead
In these pin'd arms, then tears on tears might fall, till all were shed
In common fortune! Now amaze their natural course doth stop,
And pricks a mad vein." Thus he mourn'd, and with him all break ope
Their store of sorrows. The poor Queen amongst the women wept
Turn'd into anguish: "O my son," she cried out, "why still kept
Patient of horrors is my life, when thine is vanishéd?
My days thou glorifi'dst, my nights rung of some honour'd deed
Done by thy virtues, joy to me, profit to all our care.
All made a God of thee, and thou mad'st them all that they are,
Now under fate, now dead." These two thus vented as they could
There sorrow's furnace; Hector's wife not having yet been told
So much as of his stay without. She in her chamber close
Sat at her loom; a piece of work, grac'd with a both sides' gloss,
Strew'd curiously with varied flowers, her pleasure was; her care,
To heat a caldron for her lord, to bathe him turn'd from war,
Of which she chief charge gave her maids. Poor dame, she little knew
How much her cares lack'd of his case! But now the clamour flew
Up to her turret; then she shook, her work fell from her hand,
And up she started, call'd her maids, she needs must understand
That ominous outcry: "Come," said she, I hear through all this cry
My mother's voice shriek; to my throat my heart bounds; ecstasy
Utterly alters me; some fate is near the hapless sons
Of fading Priam. Would to God my words' suspicións
No ear had heard yet! O I fear, and that most heartily,
That, with some stratagem, the son of Peleus hath put by
The wall of Ilion my lord, and, trusty of his feet,
Obtain'd the chase of him alone, and now the curious heat
Of his still desp'rate spirit is cool'd. It let him never keep
In guard of others; before all his violent foot must step,
Or his place forfeited he held." Thus fury-like she went,
Two women, as she will'd, at hand; and made her quick ascent
Up to the tow'r and press of men, her spirit in uproar. Round
She cast her greedy eye, and saw her Hector slain, and bound
T' Achilles' chariot, manlessly dragg'd to the Grecian fleet.
Black night strook through her, under her trance took away her feet,
And back she shrunk with such a sway that off her head-tire flew,
Her coronet, caul, ribands, veil that golden Venus threw
On her white shoulders that high day when warlike Hector won
Her hand in nuptials in the court of king Eetion,
And that great dow'r then giv'n with her. About her, on their knees,
Her husband's sisters, brothers' wives, fell round, and by degrees
Recover'd her. Then, when again her respirations found
Free pass (her mind and spirit met) these thoughts her words did sound:

"O Hector, O me, curséd dame, both born beneath one fate,
Thou here, I in Cilician Thebes, where Placus doth elate
His shady forehead, in the court where king Eetion,
Hapless, begot unhappy me; which would he had not done,
To live past thee! Thou now art div'd to Pluto's gloomy throne,
Sunk through the coverts of the earth; I, in a hell of moan,
Left here thy widow; one poor babe born to unhappy both,
Whom thou leav'st helpless as he thee, he born to all the wroth
Of woe and labour. Lands left him will others seize upon;
The orphan day of all friends' helps robs ev'ry mother's son.
An orphan all men suffer sad; his eyes stand still with tears;
Need tries his father's friends, and fails; of all his favourers,
If one the cup gives, 'tis not long, the wine he finds in it
Scarce moists his palate; if he chance to gain the grace to sit,
Surviving fathers' sons repine, use contumelies, strike,
Bid, 'leave us, where's thy father's place?' He, weeping with dislike,
Retires to me, to me, alas! Astyanax is he
Born to these mis'ries; he that late fed on his father's knee,
To whom all knees bow'd, daintiest fare appos'd him; and when sleep
Lay on his temples, his cries still'd, his heart ev'n laid in steep
Of all things precious, a soft bed, a careful nurse's arms,
Took him to guardiance. But now as huge a world of harms
Lies on his suff'rance; now thou want'st thy father's hand to friend,
O my Astyanax; O my lord, thy hand that did defend
These gates of Ilion, these long walls by thy arm measur'd still
Amply and only. Yet at fleet thy naked corse must fill
Vile worms, when dogs are satiate, far from thy parents' care,
Far from those fun'ral ornaments that thy mind would prepare
(So sudden being the chance of arms) ever expecting death.
Which task, though my heart would not serve t' employ my hands beneath,
I made my women yet perform. Many, and much in price,
Were those integuments they wrought t' adorn thy exequies;
Which, since they fly thy use, thy corse not laid in their attire,
Thy sacrifice they shall be made; these hands in mischievous fire
Shall vent their vanities. And yet, being consecrate to thee,
They shall be kept for citizens, and their fair wives, to see."
Thus spake she weeping; all the dames endeavouring to cheer
Her desert state, fearing their own, wept with her tear for tear.

[1] Up and down the walls, it is to be understood.

[2] A most ingenious simile, used (as all our Homer besides) by Virgil, but this as a translator merely.

[3] Achilles' tyranny to Hector's person, which we lay on his fury and love to his slain friend, for whom himself living suffered so much.

THE END OF THE TWENTY-SECOND BOOK.

THE TWENTY-THIRD BOOK OF HOMER'S ILIADS

THE ARGUMENT

Achilles orders justs of exsequies
For his Patroclus; and doth sacrifice
Twelve Trojan princes, most lov'd hounds and horse,
And other off'rings, to the honour'd corse.
He institutes, besides, a Funeral Game;
Where Diomed, for horse-race, wins the fame;
For foot, Ulysses; others otherwise
Strive, and obtain; and end the Exsequies.

ANOTHER ARGUMENT

Psi sings the rites of the decease,
Ordain'd by great Æacides.
Thus mourn'd all Troy. But when at fleet and Hellespontus' shore
The Greeks arriv'd, each to his ship; only the Conqueror
Kept undispers'd his Myrmidons, and said, "Lov'd countrymen
Disjoin not we chariots and horse, but, bearing hard our rein,
With state of both, march soft and close, and mourn about the corse;
'Tis proper honour to the dead. Then take we out our horse,
When with our friends' kind woe our hearts have felt delight to do
A virtuous soul right, and then sup." This said, all full of woe
Circled the corse; Achilles led, and thrice, about him close,
All bore their goodly-coated horse. Amongst all Thetis rose,
And stirr'd up a delight in grief, till all their arms with tears,
And all the sands, were wet; so much they lov'd that Lord of Fears.
Then to the centre fell the prince; and, putting in the breast
Of his slain friend his slaught'ring hands, began to all the rest
Words to their tears: "Rejoice, said he, "O my Patroclus, thou
Courted by Dis now. Now I pay to thy late overthrow
All my revenges vow'd before. Hector lies slaughter'd here
Dragg'd at my chariot, and our dogs shall all in pieces tear
His hated limbs. Twelve Trojan youths, born of their noblest strains,
I took alive; and, yet enrag'd, will empty all their veins
Of vital spirits, sacrific'd before thy heap of fire."
This said, a work unworthy him he put upon his ire,
And trampled Hector under foot at his friend's feet. The rest
Disarm'd, took horse from chariot, and all to sleep address'd
At his black vessel. Infinite were those that rested there.
Himself yet sleeps not, now his spirits were wrought about the cheer
Fit for so high a funeral. About the steel us'd then
Oxen in heaps lay bellowing, preparing food for men;
Bleating of sheep and goats fill'd air; numbers of white-tooth'd swine,

Swimming in fat, lay singeing there. The person of the slain
Was girt with slaughter. All this done, all the Greek kings convey'd
Achilles to the King of men; his rage not yet allay'd
For his Patroclus. Being arriv'd at Agamemnon's tent,
Himself bade heralds put to fire a caldron, and present
The service of it to the prince, to try if they could win
His pleasure to admit their pains to cleanse the blood soak'd in
About his conqu'ring hands and brows. "Not by the King of Heav'n,"
He swore. "The laws of friendship damn this false-heart licence giv'n
To men that lose friends. Not a drop shall touch me till I put
Patroclus in the fun'ral pile, before these curls be cut,
His tomb erected. 'Tis the last of all care I shall take,
While I consort the careful. Yet, for your entreaties' sake,
And though I loathe food, I will eat. But early in the morn,
Atrides, use your strict command that loads of wood be borne
To our design'd place, all that fits to light home such a one
As is to pass the shades of death, that fire enough set gone
His person quickly from our eyes, and our diverted men
May ply their business." This all ears did freely entertain,
And found observance. Then they supp'd with all things fit, and all
Repair'd to tents and rest. The friend the shores maritimal
Sought for his bed, and found a place, fair, and upon which play'd
The murmuring billows. There his limbs to rest, not sleep, he laid,
Heavily sighing. Round about, silent and not too near,
Stood all his Myrmidons; when straight, so over-labour'd were
His goodly lineaments with chase of Hector, that, beyond
His resolution not to sleep, Sleep cast his sudden bond
Over his sense, and loos'd his care. Then of his wretched friend
The Soul appear'd; at ev'ry part the form did comprehend
His likeness; his fair eyes, his voice, his stature, ev'ry weed
His person wore, it fantasied; and stood above his head,
This sad speech utt'ring: "Dost thou sleep? Æacides, am I
Forgotten of thee? Being alive, I found thy memory
Ever respectful; but now, dead, thy dying love abates.
Inter me quickly, enter me in Pluto's iron gates,
For now the souls (the shades) of men, fled from this being, beat
My spirit from rest, and stay my much-desir'd receipt
Amongst souls plac'd beyond the flood. Now ev'ry way I err
About this broad-door'd house of Dis. O help then to prefer
My soul yet further! Here I mourn, but, had the fun'ral fire
Consum'd my body, never more my spirit should retire
From hell's low región; from thence souls never are retriev'd
To talk with friends here; nor shall I; a hateful fate depriv'd
My being here, that at my birth was fix'd; and to such fate
Ev'n thou, O god-like man, art mark'd; the deadly Ilion gate
Must entertain thy death. O then, I charge thee now, take care
That our bones part not; but as life combin'd in equal fare
Our loving beings, so let death. When from Opunta's tow'rs

My father brought me to your roofs (since, 'gainst my will, my pow'rs
Incens'd, and indiscreet at dice, slew fair Amphidamas)
Then Peleus entertain'd me well; then in thy charge I was
By his injunction and thy love; and therein let me still
Receive protection. Both our bones, provide in thy last will,
That one urn may contain; and make that vessel all of gold,
That Thetis gave thee, that rich urn." This said, Sleep ceas'd to hold
Achilles' temples, and the Shade thus he receiv'd: "O friend,
What needed these commands? My care, before, meant to commend
My bones to thine, and in that urn. Be sure thy will is done.
A little stay yet, let's delight, with some full passión
Of woe enough, either's affects; embrace we." Op'ning thus
His greedy arms, he felt no friend; like matter vaporous
The Spirit vanish'd under earth, and murmur'd in his stoop.
Achilles started, both his hands he clapp'd, and lifted up,
In this sort wond'ring: "O ye Gods, I see we have a soul
In th' under-dwellings, and a kind of man-resembling idol;
The soul's seat yet, all matter felt, stays with the carcass here.
O friends, hapless Patroclus' soul did all this night appear
Weeping and making moan to me, commanding ev'rything
That I intended towards him; so truly figuring
Himself at all parts, as was strange." This accident did turn
To much more sorrow, and begat a greediness to mourn
In all that heard. When mourning thus, the rosy Morn arose,
And Agamemnon through the tents wak'd all, and did dispose
Both men and mules for carriage of matter for the fire;
Of all which work Meriones, the Cretan sov'reign's squire,
Was captain; and abroad they went. Wood-cutting tools they bore
Of all hands, and well-twisted cords. The mules march'd all before.
Uphill, and down hill, overthwarts, and break-neck cliffs they pass'd;
But, when the fountful Ida's tops they scal'd with utmost haste,
All fell upon the high-hair'd oaks, and down their curléd brows,
Fell bustling to the earth, and up went all the boles and boughs
Bound to the mules; and back again they parted the harsh way
Amongst them through the tangling shrubs, and long they thought the day
Till in the plain field all arriv'd, for all the woodmen bore
Logs on their necks; Meriones would have it so. The shore
At last they reach'd yet, and then down their carriages they cast,
And sat upon them, where the son of Peleüs had plac'd
The ground for his great sepulchre, and for his friend's, in one.
They rais'd a huge pile, and to arms went ev'ry Myrmidon,
Charg'd by Achilles; chariots and horse were harnesséd.
Fighters and charioteers got up, and they the sad march led,
A cloud of infinite foot behind. In midst of all was borne
Patroclus' person by his peers. On him were all heads shorn,
Ev'n till they cover'd him with curls. Next to him march'd his friend
Embracing his cold neck all sad, since now he was to send
His dearest to his endless home. Arriv'd all where the wood

Was heap'd for fun'ral, they set down. Apart Achilles stood,
And when enough wood was heap'd on, he cut his golden hair,
Long kept for Sperchius the flood, in hope of safe repair
To Phthia by that river's pow'r; but now left hopeless thus,
Enrag'd, and looking on the sea, he cried out: "Sperchius,
In vain my father's piety vow'd, at my implor'd return
To my lov'd country, that these curls should on thy shores be shorn,
Besides a sacred hecatomb, and sacrifice beside
Of fifty wethers, at those founts, where men have edified
A lofty temple, and perfum'd an altar to thy name.
There vow'd he all these offerings; but fate prevents thy fame,
His hopes not suff'ring satisfied. And since I never more
Shall see my lov'd soil, my friend's hands shall to the Stygian shore
Convey these tresses." Thus he put in his friend's hands the hair;
And this bred fresh desire of moan; and in that sad affair
The sun had set amongst them all, had Thetis' son not spoke
Thus to Atrides: "King of men, thy aid I still invoke,
Since thy command all men still hear. Dismiss thy soldiers now,
And let them victual; they have mourn'd sufficient; 'tis we owe
The dead this honour; and with us let all the captains stay."
This heard, Atrides instantly the soldiers sent away;
The fun'ral officers remain'd, and heap'd on matter still,
Till of an hundred foot about they made the fun'ral pile,
In whose hot height they cast the corse, and then they pour'd on tears.
Numbers of fat sheep, and like store of crooked-going steers,
They slew before the solemn fire; stripp'd off their hides and dress'd.
Of which Achilles took the fat, and cover'd the deceas'd
From head to foot; and round about he made the officers pile
The beasts' nak'd bodies, vessels full of honey and of oil
Pour'd in them, laid upon a bier, and cast into the fire.
Four goodly horse; and of nine hounds, two most in the desire
Of that great prince, and trencher-fed; all fed that hungry flame.
Twelve Trojan princes last stood forth, young, and of toward fame,
All which (set on with wicked spirits) there strook he, there he slew,
And to the iron strength of fire their noble limbs he threw.
Then breath'd his last sighs, and these words: "Again rejoice, my friend,
Ev'n in the joyless depth of hell. Now give I cómplete end
To all my vows. Alone thy life sustain'd not violence,
Twelve Trojan princes wait on thee, and labour to incense
Thy glorious heap of funeral. Great Hector I'll excuse,
The dogs shall eat him." These high threats perform'd not their abuse;
Jove's daughter, Venus, took the guard of noble Hector's corse,
And kept the dogs off, night and day applying sov'reign force
Of rosy balms, that to the dogs were horrible in taste,
And with which she the body fill'd. Renown'd Apollo cast
A cloud from heav'n, lest with the sun the nerves and lineaments
Might dry and putrefy. And now some Pow'rs denied consents
To this solemnity; the Fire (for all the oily fuel

It had injected) would not burn; and then the loving Cruel
Studied for help, and, standing off, invok'd the two fair Winds,
Zephyr and Boreas, to afford the rage of both their kinds
To aid his outrage. Precious gifts his earnest zeal did vow
Pour'd from' a golden bowl much wine, and pray'd them both to blow,
That quickly his friend's corse might burn, and that heap's sturdy breast
Embrace consumption. Iris heard. The Winds were at a feast,
All in the court of Zephyrus, that boist'rous blowing Air,
Gather'd together. She that wears the thousand-colour'd hair
Flew thither, standing in the porch. They, seeing her, all arose,
Call'd to her, ev'ry one desir'd she would awhile repose,
And eat with them. She answer'd: "No, no place of seat is here;
Retreat calls to the Ocean and Æthiopia, where
A hecatomb is off'ring now to heav'n, and there must I
Partake the feast of sacrifice. I come to signify
That Thetis' son implores your aids, princes of North and West,
With vows of much fair sacrifice, if each will set his breast
Against his heap of funeral, and make it quickly burn;
Patroclus lies there, whose decease all the Achaians mourn."
She said, and parted; and out rush'd, with an unmeasur'd roar,
Those two Winds, tumbling clouds in heaps, ushers to either's blore,
And instantly they reach'd the sea; up flew the waves; the gale
Was strong; reach'd fruitful Troy; and full upon the fire they fall.
The huge heap thunder'd. All night long from his chok'd breast they blew
A lib'ral flame up; and all night swift-foot Achilles threw
Wine from a golden bowl on earth, and steep'd the soil in wine,
Still calling on Patroclus' soul. No father could incline
More to a son most dear, nor more mourn at his burnéd bones,
Than did the great prince to his friend at his combustións,
Still creeping near and near the heap, still sighing, weeping still.
But when the Day-star look'd abroad, and promis'd from hi hill
Light, which the saffron Morn made good, and sprinkled on the seas,
Then languish'd the great pile, then sunk the flames, and then calm Peace
Turn'd back the rough Winds to their homes; the Thracian billow rings.
Their high retreat, ruffled with cuffs of their triumphant wings.
Pelides then forsook the pile, and to his tired limb
Choos'd place of rest; where laid, sweet sleep fell to his wish on him.
When all the king's guard (waiting then, perceiving will to rise
In that great session) hurried in, and op'd again his eyes
With tumult of their troop, and haste. A little then he rear'd
His troubled person, sitting up, and this affair referr'd
To wish'd commandment of the kings: "Atrides, and the rest
Of our commanders general, vouchsafe me this request
Before your parting: Give in charge the quenching with black wine
Of this heap's relics, ev'ry brand the yellow fire made shine;
And then let search Patroclus' bones, distinguishing them well;
As well ye may, they kept the midst, the rest at random fell
About th' extreme part of the pile; men's bones and horses' mixed.

Being found, I'll find an urn of gold t' enclose them, and betwixt
The air and them two kels of fat lay on them, and to rest
Commit them, till mine own bones seal our love, my soul deceas'd.
The sepulchre I have not charg'd to make of too much state,
But of a model something mean, that you of younger fate,
When I am gone, may amplify with such a breadth and height
As fits your judgments and our worths." This charge receiv'd his weight
In all observance. First they quench'd with sable wine the heap,
As far as it had fed the flame. The ash fell wondrous deep,
In which his consorts, that his life religiously lov'd,
Search'd, weeping, for his bones; which found, they conscionably prov'd
His will made to Æacides, and what his love did add.
A golden vessel, double fat, contain'd them. All which, clad
In veils of linen, pure and rich, were solemnly convey'd
T' Achilles' tent. The platform then about the pile they laid
Of his fit sepulchre, and rais'd a heap of earth, and then
Offer'd departure. But the prince retain'd there still his men,
Employing them to fetch from fleet rich tripods for his games,
Caldrons, horse, mules, broad-headed beeves, bright steel, and brighter dames,
The best at horse-race he ordain'd a lady for his prize,
Gen'rally praiseful, fair and young, and skill'd in housewif'ries
Of all kinds fitting; and withal a trivet, that inclos'd
Twenty-two measures' room, with ears. The next prize he propos'd
Was (that which then had high respect) a mare of six years old,
Unhandled, horséd with a mule, and ready to have foal'd.
The third game was a caldron, new, fair, bright, and could for size
Contain two measures. For the fourth, two talents' quantities
Of finest gold. The fifth game was a great new standing bowl,
To set down both ways. These brought in, Achilles then stood up,
And said: "Atrides and my lords, chief horsemen of our host,
These games expect ye. If myself should interpose my most
For our horse-race, I make no doubt that I should take again
These gifts propos'd. Ye all know well, of how divine a strain
My horse are, and how eminent. Of Neptune's gift they are
To Peleus, and of his to me. Myself then will not share
In gifts giv'n others, nor my steeds breathe any spirit to shake
Their airy pasterns; so they mourn for their kind guider's sake,
Late lost; that us'd with humorous oil to slick their lofty manes,
Clear water having cleans'd them first; and, his bane being their banes,
Those lofty manes now strew the earth, their heads held shaken down.
You then that trust in chariots, and hope with horse to crown
Your conqu'ring temples, gird yourselves; now, fame and prize stretch for,
All that have spirits." This fir'd all. The first competitor
Was king Eumelus, whom the art of horsemanship did grace,
Son to Admetus. Next to him rose Diomed to the race,
That under reins rul'd Trojan horse, of late forc'd from the son
Of lord Anchises, himself freed of near confusion
By Phœbus. Next to him set forth the yellow-headed king

Of Lacedæmon, Jove's high seed; and, in his managing,
Podargus and swift Æthe trod, steeds to the King of men;
Æthe giv'n by Echepolus, the Anchisiaden,
As bribe to free him from the war resolv'd for Ilion;
So Delicacy feasted him, whom Jove bestow'd upon
A mighty wealth; his dwelling was in broad Sicyone.
Old Nestor's son, Antilochus, was fourth for chivalry
In this contention; his fair horse were of the Pylian breed,
And his old father, coming near, inform'd him, for good speed,
With good race notes, in which himself could good instruction give:
"Antilochus, though young thou art, yet thy grave virtues live
Belov'd of Neptune and of Jove. Their spirits have taught thee all
The art of horsemanship, for which the less thy merits fall
In need of doctrine. Well thy skill can wield a chariot
In all fit turnings, yet thy horse their slow feet handle not
As fits thy manage, which makes me cast doubts of thy success.
I well know all these are not seen in art of this address
More than thyself; their horses yet superior are to thine
For their parts, thine want speed to make discharge of a design
To please an artist. But go on, show but thy art and heart
At all points, and set them against their horses' heart and art;
Good judges will not see thee lose. A carpenter's desert
Stands more in cunning than in pow'r. A pilot doth avert
His vessel from the rock, and wrack, tost with the churlish winds,
By skill, not strength. So sorts it here; one charioteer that finds
Want of another's pow'r in horse must in his own skill set
An overplus of that to that; and so the proof will get
Skill, that still rests within a man, more grace; than pow'r without.
He that in horse and chariots trusts, is often hurl'd about
This way and that, unhandsomely, all-heaven wide of his end.
He, better skill'd, that rules worse horse, will all observance bend
Right on the scope still of a race, bear near, know ever when to rein,
When give rein, as his foe before, well noted in his vein
Of manage and his steeds' estate, presents occasion.
I'll give thee instance now, as plain as if thou saw'st it done:
Here stands a dry stub of some tree, a cubit from the ground; [1]
(Suppose the stub of oak or larch, for either are so sound
That neither rots with wet) two stones, white (mark you), white for view,
Parted on either side the stub; and these lay where they drew
The way into a strait; the race betwixt both lying clear.
Imagine them some monument of one long since tomb'd there,
Or that they had been lists of race for men of former years,
As now the lists Achilles sets may serve for charioteers
Many years hence. When near to these the race grows, then as right
Drive on them as thy eye can judge; then lay thy bridle's weight
Most of thy left side; thy right horse then switching, all thy throat,
Spent in encouragements, give him, and all the rein let float
About his shoulders; thy near horse will yet be he that gave

Thy skill the prize, and him rein so his head may touch the nave
Of thy left wheel; but then take care thou runn'st not on the stone
(With wrack of horse and chariot) which so thou bear'st upon.
Shipwrack within the hav'n avoid, by all means; that will breed
Others delight, and thee a shame. Be wise then, and take heed,
My lov'd son, get but to be first at turning in the course,
He lives not that can cote thee then, not if he back'd the horse
The Gods bred, and Adrastus ow'd; divine Arion's speed
Could not outpace thee, or the horse Laomedon did breed,
Whose race is famous, and fed here." Thus sat Neleides,
When all that could be said was said. And then Meriones; [2]
Set fifthly forth his fair-man'd horse. All leap'd to chariot;
And ev'ry man then for the start cast in his proper lot.
Achilles drew; Antilochus the lot set foremost forth;
Eumelus next; Atrides third; Meriones the fourth;
The fifth and last was Diomed, far first in excellence.
All stood in order, and the lists Achilles fix'd far thence
In plain field; and a seat ordain'd fast by, in which he set
Renownéd Phœnix, that in grace of Peleus was so great,
To see the race, and give a truth of all their passages.
All start together, scourg'd, and cried, and gave their business
Study and order. Through the field they held a wingéd pace.
Beneath the bosom of their steeds a dust so dimm'd the race,
It stood above their heads in clouds, or like to storms amaz'd.
Manes flew like ensigns with the wind. The chariots sometime graz'd,
And sometimes jump'd up to the air; yet still sat fast the men,
Their spirits ev'n panting in their breasts with fervour to obtain.
But when they turn'd to fleet again, then all men's skills were tried,
Then stretch'd the pasterns of their steeds. Eumelus' horse in pride
Still bore their sov'reign. After them came Diomed's coursers close,
Still apt to leap their chariot, and ready to repose
Upon the shoulders of their king their heads; his back ev'n burned
With fire that from their nostrils flew; and then their lord had turn'd
The race for him, or giv'n it doubt, if Phœbus had not smit
The scourge out of his hands, and tears of helpless wrath with it
From forth his eyes, to see his horse for want of scourge made slow,
And th' others, by Apollo's help, with much more swiftness go.
Apollo's spite Pallas discern'd, and flew to Tydeus' son,
His scourge reach'd, and his horse made fresh. Then took her angry run
At king Eumelus, brake his gears; his mares on both sides flew,
His draught-tree fell to earth, and him the toss'd-up chariot threw
Down to the earth, his elbows torn, his forehead, all his face
Strook at the centre, his speech lost. And then the turnéd race
Fell to Tydides; before all his conqu'ring horse he drave,
And first he glitter'd in the race; divine Athenia gave
Strength to his horse, and fame to him. Next him drave Sparta's king.
Antilochus his father's horse then urg'd with all his sting
Of scourge and voice: "Run low," said he, "stretch out your limbs, and fly;

With Diomed's horse I bid not strive, nor with himself strive I;
Athenia wings his horse, and him renowns; Atrides' steeds
Are they ye must not fail but reach; and soon, lest soon succeeds
The blot of all your fames, to yield in swiftness to a mare,
To female Æthe. What's the cause, ye best that ever were,
That thus ye fail us? Be assur'd, that Nestor's love ye lose
For ever, if ye fail his son. Through both your both sides goes
His hot steel, if ye suffer me to bring the last prize home.
Haste, overtake them instantly; we needs must overcome.
This harsh way next us, this my mind will take, this I despise
For peril, this I'll creep through. Hard the way to honour lies,
And that take I, and that shall yield." His horse by all this knew
He was not pleas'd, and fear'd his voice, and for a while they flew.
But straight more clear appear'd the strait Antilochus foresaw,
It was a gasp the earth gave, forc'd by humours cold and raw,
Pour'd out of Winter's wat'ry breast, met there, and cleaving deep
All that near passage to the lists. This Nestor's son would keep,
And left the roadway, being about. Atrides fear'd, and cried: [3]
"Antilochus, thy course is mad; contain thy horse, we ride
A way most dangerous; turn head, betime take larger field,
We shall be splitted." Nestor's son with much more scourge impell'd
His horse for this, as if not heard; and got as far before
As any youth can cast a quoit. Atrides would no more;
He back again, for fear himself, his goodly chariot,
And horse together, strew'd the dust, in being so dusty hot
Of thirsted conquest. But he chid, at parting, passing sore:
"Antilochus," said he, "a worse than thee earth never bore.
Farewell, we never thought thee wise that were wise; but not so
Without oaths shall the wreath, be sure, crown thy mad temples. Go."
Yet he bethought him, and went too, thus stirring up his steeds:
"Leave me not last thus, nor stand vex'd. Let these fail in the speeds
Of feet and knees, not you. Shall these, these old jades, past the flow'r
Of youth that you have, pass you?" This the horse fear'd, and more pow'r
Put to their knees, straight getting ground. Both flew, and so the rest.
All came in smokes, like spirits. The Greeks, set, to see who did best,
Without the race, aloft, now made a new discovery,
Other than that they made at first. Idomenëus' eye
Distinguish'd all, he knew the voice of Diomed, seeing a horse
Of special mark, of colour bay, and was the first in course,
His forehead putting forth a star, round like the moon, and white.
Up stood the Cretan, utt'ring this: "Is it alone my sight,
Princes and captains, that discerns another lead the race
With other horse than led of late? Eumelus made most pace
With his fleet mares, and he began the flexure as we thought;
Now all the field I search, and find nowhere his view; hath nought
Befall'n amiss to him? Perhaps he hath not with success
Perform'd his flexure; his reins lost, or seat, or with the tress
His chariot fail'd him, and his mares have outray'd with affright.

Stand up, try you your eyes, for mine hold with the second sight;
This seems to me th' Ætolian king, the Tydean Diomed."
"To you it seems so," rustically Ajax Oïleus said,
"Your words are suited to your eyes. Those mares lead still that led,
Eumelus owes them, and he still holds reins and place that did,
Not fall'n as you hop'd. You must prate before us all, though last
In judgment of all. Y' are too old, your tongue goes still too fast,
You must not talk so. Here are those that better thee, and look
For first place in the censure." This Idomenëus took
In much disdain, and thus replied: "Thou best in speeches worst,
Barbarous-languag'd, others here might have reprov'd me first,
Not thou, unfitt'st of all. I bold a tripod with thee here,
Or caldron, and our Gen'ral make our equal arbiter,
Those horse are first, that when thou pay'st thou then may'st know." This fir'd
Oïliades more, and more than words this quarrel had inspir'd,
Had not Achilles rose, and us'd this pacifying speech:
"No more. Away with words in war. It toucheth both with breach
Of that which fits ye. Your deserts should others reprehend
That give such foul terms. Sit ye still, the men themselves will end
The strife betwixt you instantly, and either's own load bear
On his own shoulders. Then to both the first horse will appear,
And which is second." These words us'd, Tydides was at hand,
His horse ran high, glanc'd on the way, and up they toss'd the sand
Thick on their coachman; on their pace their chariot deck'd with gold
Swiftly attended, no wheel seen, nor wheel's print in the mould.
Impress'd behind them. These horse flew a flight, not ran a race.
Arriv'd, amids the lists they stood, sweat trickling down apace
Their high manes and their prominent breasts; and down jumped Diomed,
Laid up his scourge aloft the seat, and straight his prize was led
Home to his tent. Rough Sthenelus laid quick hand on the dame,
And handled trivet, and sent both home by his men. Next came
Antilochus, that won with wiles, not swiftness of his horse,
Precedence of the gold-lock'd king, who yet maintained the course
So close, that not the king's own horse gat more before the wheel
Of his rich chariot, that might still the insecution feel
With the extreme hairs of his tail (and that sufficient close
Held to his leader, no great space it let him interpose
Consider'd in so great a field) that Nestor's wily son
Gat of the king, now at his heels, though at the breach he won
A quoit's cast of him, which the king again at th' instant gain'd.
Æthe Agamemnonides, that was so richly man'd,
Gat strength still as she spent; which words her worth had prov'd with deeds,
Had more ground been allow'd the race; and coted far his steeds,
No question leaving for the prize. And now Meriones
A dart's cast came behind the king, his horse of speed much less,
Himself less skill'd t' importune them, and give a chariot wing.
Admetus' son was last, whose plight Achilles pitying
Thus spake: "Best man comes last; yet right must see his prize not least,

The second his deserts must bear, and Diomed the best."
He said, and all allow'd; and sure the mare had been his own,
Had not Antilochus stood forth, and in his answer shown
Good reason for his interest: "Achilles," he replied,
"I should be angry with you much to see this ratified.
Ought you to take from me my right, because his horse had wrong,
Himself being good? He should have us'd, as good men do, his tongue
In pray'r to Their pow'rs that bless good, not trusting to his own,
Not to have been in this good last. His chariot overthrown
O'erthrew not me. Who's last? Who's first? Men's goodness without these
Is not our question. If his good you pity yet, and please
Princely to grace it, your tents hold a goodly deal of gold,
Brass, horse, sheep, women; out of these your bounty may be bold,
To take a much more worthy prize than my poor merit seeks,
And give it here before my face, and all these, that the Greeks
May glorify your lib'ral hands. This prize I will not yield.
Who bears this, whatsoever man, he bears a triéd field.
His hand and mine must change some blows." Achilles laugh'd, and said:
"If thy will be, Antilochus, I'll see Eumelus paid
Out of my tents. I'll give him th' arms, which late I conquer'd in
Asteropæus, forg'd of brass, and wav'd about with tin;
'Twill be a present worthy him." This said, Automedon
He sent for them. He went and brought; and to Admetus' son
Achilles gave them. He, well pleas'd, receiv'd them. Then arose
Wrong'd Menelaus, much incens'd with young Antilochus.
He bent to speak, a herald took his sceptre and gave charge
Of silence to the other Greeks; then did the king enlarge
The spleen he prison'd, utt'ring this: "Antilochus, till now [4]
We grant thee wise, but in this act what wisdom utter'st thou?
Thou hast disgrac'd my virtue, wrong'd my horse, preferring thine
Much their inferiors. But go to, Princes, nor his nor mine
Judge of with favour, him nor me; lest any Grecian use
This scandal: 'Menelaus won, with Nestor's son's abuse,
The prize in question, his horse worst; himself yet wan the best
By pow'r and greatness.' Yet, because I would not thus contest
To make parts taking, I'll be judge; and I suppose none here
Will blame my judgment, I'll do right: Antilochus, come near,
Come, noble gentleman, 'tis your place, swear by th' earth-circling God,
(Standing before your chariot and horse, and that self rod
With which you scourg'd them in your hand) if both with will and wile
You did not cross my chariot." He thus did reconcile
Grace with his disgrace, and with wit restor'd him to his wit:
"Now crave I patience. O king, whatever was unfit; [5]
Ascribe to much more youth in me than you. You, more in age
And more in excellence, know well, the outrays that engage
All young men's actions; sharper wits, but duller wisdoms, still
From us flow than from you; for which, curb, with your wisdom, will.
The prize I thought mine, I yield yours, and, if you please, a prize

Of greater value to my tent I'll send for, and suffice
Your will at full, and instantly; for, in this point of time,
I rather wish to be enjoin'd your favour's top to climb,
Than to be falling all my time from height of such a grace. [6]
O Jove-lov'd king, and of the Gods receive a curse in place."
This said, he fetch'd his prize to him; and it rejoic'd him so,
That as corn-ears shine with the dew, yet having time to grow,
When fields set all their bristles up; in such a ruff wert thou. [7]
O Menelaus, answ'ring thus: "Antilochus, I now,
Though I were angry, yield to thee, because I see th' hadst wit,
When I thought not; thy youth hath got the mast'ry of thy spirit.
And yet, for all this, 'tis more safe not to abuse at all
Great men, than, vent'ring, trust to wit to take up what may fall;
For no man in our host beside had eas'ly calm'd my spleen,
Stirr'd with like tempest. But thyself hast a sustainer been
Of much affliction in my cause; so thy good father too,
And so thy brother; at thy suit, I therefore let all go,
Give thee the game here, though mine own, that all these may discern
King Menelaus bears a mind at no part proud or stern."
The king thus calm'd, Antilochus receiv'd, and gave the steed
To lov'd Noemon to lead thence; and then receiv'd beside
The caldron. Next, Meriones, for fourth game, was to have
Two talents' gold. The fifth, unwon, renown'd Achilles gave
To rev'rend Nestor, being a bowl to set on either end;
Which through the press he carried him: "Receive," said he, "old friend,
This gift as fun'ral monument of my dear friend deceas'd,
Whom never you must see again. I make it his bequest
To you as, without any strife, obtaining it from all.
Your shoulders must not undergo the churlish whoorlbat's fall,
Wrestling is past you, strife in darts, the foot's celerity;
Harsh age in his years fetters you, and honour sets you free."
Thus gave he it. He took, and joy'd; but, ere he thank'd, he said:
"Now sure, my honourable son, in all points thou hast play'd
The comely orator; no more must I contend with nerves;
Feet fail, and hands; arms want that strength, that this and that swing serves
Under your shoulders. Would to heav'n, I were so young chinn'd now,
And strength threw such a many of bones, to celebrate this show,
As when the Epians brought to fire, actively honouring thus,
King Amaryncea's funerals in fair Buprasius!
His sons put prizes down for him; where not a man match'd me
Of all the Epians, or the sons of great-soul'd Ætolie,
No, nor the Pylians themselves, my countrymen. I beat
Great Clytomedeus, Enops' son, at buffets. At the feat
Of wrestling, I laid under me one that against me rose,
Ancæus, call'd Pleuronius. I made Iphiclus lose
The foot-game to me. At the spear, I conquer'd Polydore,
And strong Phylëus. Actor's sons, of all men, only bore
The palm at horse-race, conquering with lashing on more horse,

And envying my victory, because, before their course,
All the best games were gone with me. These men were twins; one was
A most sure guide, a most sure guide; the other gave the pass
With rod and mettle. This was then. But now young men must wage
These works, and my joints undergo the sad defects of age;
Though then I was another man. At that time I excell'd [8]
Amongst th' heroes. But forth now; let th' other rites be held
For thy deceas'd friend; this thy gift in all kind part I take,
And much it joys my heart, that still, for my true kindness' sake,
You give me mem'ry. You perceive, in what fit grace I stand
Amongst the Grecians; and to theirs you set your graceful hand.
The Gods give ample recompense of grace again to thee,
For this and all thy favours!" Thus, back through the thrust drave he,
When he had stay'd out all the praise of old Neleides. [9]
And now for buffets, that rough game, he order'd passages;
Proposing a laborious mule, of six years old, untam'd,
And fierce in handling, brought, and bound, in that place where they gam'd;
And, to the conquer'd, a round cup. Both which he thus proclaims:
"Atrides and all friends of Greece, two men, for these two games,
I bid stand forth. Who best can strike, with high contracted fists,
(Apollo giving him the wreath) know all about these lists,
Shall win a mule, patient of toil; the vanquish'd, this round cup."
This utter'd; Panopëus' son, Epëus, straight stood up,
A tall huge man, that to the nail knew that red sport of hand,
And, seizing the tough mule, thus spake: "Now let some other stand
Forth for the cup; this mule is mine, at cuffs I boast me best.
Is't not enough I am no soldier? Who is worthiest
At all works? None; not possible. At this yet this I say,
And will perform this: Who stands forth, I'll burst him, I will bray
His bones as in a mortar. Fetch surgeons enow to take [10]
His corse from under me." This speech did all men silent make.
At last stood forth Euryalus, a man god-like, and son
To king Mecisteus, the grandchild of honour'd Talaon.
He was so strong that, coming once to Thebes, when Œdipus
Had like rites solemniz'd for him, he went victorious
From all the Thebans. This rare man Tydides would prepare,
Put on his girdle, oxhide cords, fair wrought; and spent much care
That he might conquer, hearten'd him, and taught him tricks. Both dress'd
Fit for th' affair, both forth were brought; then breast oppos'd to breast,
Fists against fists rose, and, they join'd, rattling of jaws was there,
Gnashing of teeth, and heavy blows dash'd blood out ev'rywhere.
At length Epëus spy'd clear way, rush'd in, and such a blow
Drave underneath the other's ear, that his neat limbs did strow
The knock'd earth, no more legs had he; but as a huge fish laid
Near to the cold-weed-gath'ring shore, is with a north flaw fraid.
Shoots back, and in the black deep hides; so, sent against the ground,
Was foil'd Euryalus, his strength so bid in more profound
Deeps of Epëus, who took up th' intranc'd competitor;

About whom rush'd a crowd of friends, that through the clusters bore
His falt'ring knees, he spitting up thick clods of blood, his head
Totter'd of one side, his sense gone; when, to a by-place led,
Thither they brought him the round cup. Pelides then set forth
Prize for a wrastling; to the best a trivet, that was worth
Twelve oxen, great and fit for fire; the conquer'd was t' obtain
A woman excellent in works; her beauty, and her gain,
Priz'd at four oxen. Up he stood, and thus proclaim'd: "Arise,
You wrastlers, that will prove for these." Out stepp'd the ample size
Of mighty Ajax, huge in strength; to him Laertes' son,
The crafty one, as huge in sleight. Their ceremony done
Of making ready, forth they stepp'd, catch elbows with strong hands,
And as the beams of some high house crack with a storm, yet stands
The house, being built by well-skill'd men; so crack'd their
backbones, wrinch'd
With horrid twitches; in their sides, arms, shoulders, all bepinch'd,
Ran thick the wales, red with the blood, ready to start out. Both
Long'd for the conquest and the prize; yet show'd no play, being loth
To lose both. Nor could Ithacus stir Ajax; nor could he
Hale down Ulysses, being more strong than with mere strength to be
Hurl'd from all vantage of his sleight. Tir'd then with tugging play,
Great Ajax Telamonius said: "Thou wisest man, or lay
My face up, or let me lay thine; let Jove take care for these."
This said, he hois'd him up to air; when Laertiades
His wiles forgat not, Ajax' thigh he strook behind, and flat
He on his back fell; on his breast Ulysses. Wonder'd at
Was this of all; all stood amaz'd. Then the much-suff'ring man,
Divine Ulysses, at next close the Telamonian
A little rais'd from earth, not quite, but with his knee implied
Lock'd legs; and down fell both on earth, close by each other's side,
Both fil'd with dust; but starting up, the third close they had made,
Had not Achilles' self stood up, restraining them, and bade:
"No more tug one another thus, nor moil yourselves; receive
Prize equal; conquest crowns ye both; the lists to others leave."
They heard, and yielded willingly, brush'd off the dust, and on
Put other vests. Pelides then, to those that swiftest run,
Propos'd another prize; a bowl, beyond comparison,
Both for the size and workmanship, past all the bowls of earth.
It held six measures; silver all; but had his special worth
For workmanship, receiving form from those ingenious men
Of Sidon. The Phœnicians made choice, and brought it then
Along the green sea, giving it to Thoas; by degrees
It came t' Eunæus, Jason's son, who young Priamides,
Lycaon, of Achilles' friend bought with it; and this here
Achilles made best game for him, that best his feet could bear.
For second he propos'd an ox, a huge one, and a fat;
And half a talent gold for last. These thus he set them at:
"Rise, you that will assay for these." Forth stepp'd Oïliades;

Ulysses answer'd; and the third was, one esteem'd past these
For footmanship, Antilochus. All rank'd, Achilles show'd
The race-scope. From the start they glid. Oïliades bestow'd
His feet the swiftest; close to him flew god-like Ithacus.
And as a lady at her loom, being young and beauteous,
Her silk-shuttle close to her breast, with grace that doth inflame,
And her white hand, lifts quick and oft, in drawing from her frame
Her gentle thread, which she unwinds with ever at her breast
Gracing her fair hand; so close still, and with such interest
In all men's likings, Ithacus unwound, and spent the race
By him before, took out his steps with putting in their place
Promptly and gracefully his own, sprinkled the dust before,
And clouded with his breath his head. So facilie he bore
His royal person, that he strook shouts from the Greeks, with thirst
That he should conquer, though he flew: "Yet come, come, O come first,"
Ever they cried to him. And this ev'n his wise breast did move
To more desire of victory; it made him pray, and prove,
Minerva's aid, his fautress still: "O Goddess, hear," said he,
"And to my feet stoop with thy help, now happy fautress be."
She was, and light made all his limbs. And now, both near their crown,
Minerva tripp'd up Ajax' heels, and headlong he fell down
Amids the ordure of the beasts, there negligently left
Since they were slain there; and by this, Minerva's friend bereft
Oïliades of that rich bowl, and left his lips, nose, eyes,
Ruthfully smear'd. The fat ox yet he seiz'd for second prize,
Held by the horn, spit out the tail, and thus spake all-besmear'd:
"O villainous chance! This Ithacus so highly is endear'd
To his Minerva, that her hand is ever in his deeds.
She, like his mother, nestles him; for from her it proceeds,
I know, that I am us'd thus." This all in light laughter cast;
Amongst whom quick Antilochus laugh'd out his coming last
Thus wittily: "Know, all my friends, that all times past, and now,
The Gods most honour most-liv'd men. Oïliades ye know
More old than I, but Ithacus is of the foremost race,
First generation of men. Give the old man his grace,
They count him of the green-hair'd eld; they may; or in his flow'r;
For not our greatest flourisher can equal him in pow'r
Of foot-strife, but Æacides." Thus sooth'd he Thetis' son
Who thus accepted it: "Well, youth, your praises shall not run
With unrewarded feet on mine, your half a talent's prize
I'll make a whole one. Take you, sir." He took, and joy'd. Then flies
Another game forth. Thetis' son set in the lists a lance,
A shield, and helmet, being th' arms Sarpedon did advance
Against Patroclus, and he pris'd. And thus he nam'd th' address:
"Stand forth two the most excellent, arm'd, and before all these
Give mutual onset to the touch and wound of either's flesh.
Who first shall wound, through other's arms his blood appearing fresh,
Shall win this sword, silver'd, and hatch'd; the blade is right of Thrace;

Asteropæus yielded it. These arms shall part their grace
With either's valour; and the men I'll liberally feast
At my pavilion." To this game the first man that address'd
Was Ajax Telamonius; to him king Diomed.
Both, in oppos'd parts of the press, full arm'd, both enteréd
The lists amids the multitude, put looks on so austere,
And join'd so roughly, that amaze surpris'd the Greeks in fear
Of either's mischief. Thrice they threw their fierce darts, and clos'd thrice.
Then Ajax strook through Diomed's shield, but did no prejudice,
His curets saft him. Diomed's dart still over shoulders flew,
Still mounting with the spirit it bore. And now rough Ajax grew
So violent, that the Greeks cried: "Hold, no more. Let them no more.
Give equal prize to either." Yet the sword, propos'd before
For him did best, Achilles gave to Diomed. Then a stone,
In fashion of a sphere, he show'd; of no invention,
But natural, only melted through with iron. 'Twas the bowl
That king Eetion us'd to hurl; but he bereft of soul
By great Achilles, to the fleet, with store of other prise,
He brought it, and propos'd it now both for the exercise
And prize itself. He stood, and said: "Rise you that will approve
Your arms' strengths now in this brave strife. His vigour that can move
This furthest, needs no game but this; for reach he ne'er so far
With large fields of his own in Greece (and so needs for his car,
His plough, or other tools of thrift, much iron) I'll able this
For five revolvéd years; no need shall use his messages
To any town to furnish him, this only bowl shall yield
Iron enough for all affairs." This said; to try this field,
First Polypœtes issuéd; next Leontëus; third
Great Ajax; huge Epëus fourth, yet he was first that stirr'd
That mine of iron. Up it went, and up he toss'd it so,
That laughter took up all the field. The next man that did throw
Was Leontëus; Ajax third, who gave it such a hand,
That far past both their marks it flew. But now 'twas to be mann'd
By Polypœtes, and, as far as at an ox that strays
A herdsman can swing out his goad, so far did he outraise
The stone past all men; all the field rose in a shout to see't;
About him flock'd his friends, and bore the royal game to fleet.
For archery he then set forth ten axes edg'd two ways,
And ten of one edge. On the shore, far-off, he caus'd to raise
A ship-mast; to whose top they tied a fearful dove by th' foot,
At which all shot, the game put thus; He that the dove could shoot,
Nor touch the string that fasten'd her, the two-edg'd tools should bear
All to the fleet. Who touch'd the string, and miss'd the dove, should share
The one-edg'd axes. This propos'd; king Teucer's force arose,
And with him rose Meriones. And now lots must dispose
Their shooting first; both which let fall into a helm of brass,
First Teucer's came, and first he shot, and his cross fortune was
To shoot the string, the dove untouch'd; Apollo did envy

His skill, since not to him he vow'd, being God of archery,
A first-fall'n lamb. The bitter shaft yet cut in two the cord,
That down fell, and the dove aloft up to the welkin soar'd.
The Greeks gave shouts. Meriones first made a hearty vow
To sacrifice a first-fall'n lamb to Him that rules the bow,
And then fell to his aim, his shaft being ready nock'd before.
He spy'd her in the clouds that here, there, ev'rywhere, did soar,
Yet at her height he reach'd her side, strook her quite through, and down
The shaft fell at his feet; the dove the mast again did crown,
There hung the head, and all her plumes were ruffled, she stark dead,
And there, far off from him, she fell. The people wonderéd,
And stood astonish'd; th' archer pleas'd. Æacides then shows
A long lance, and a caldron new, engrail'd with twenty hues,
Priz'd at an ox. These games were show'd for men at darts; and then
Up rose the General of all, up rose the King of men,
Up rose late-crown'd Meriones. Achilles, seeing the King
Do him this grace, prevents more deed, his royal offering
Thus interrupting: "King of men, we well conceive how far
Thy worth superior is to all, how much most singular
Thy pow'r is, and thy skill in darts! Accept then this poor prize
Without contention, and (your will pleas'd with what I advise)
Afford Meriones the lance." The King was nothing slow
To that fit grace. Achilles then the brass lance did bestow
On good Meriones. The King his present would not save,
But to renown'd Talthybius the goodly caldron gave.

[1] A comment might well be bestowed upon this speech of Nestor.

[2] When all, etc.—Nestor's aged love of speech was here briefly noted.

[3] Menelaus in fear to follow Antilochus, who ye may see played upon him.

[4] Note Menelaus' ridiculous speech for conclusion of his character.

[5] Antilochus's ironical reply.

[6] Ironicè.

[7] This simile likewise is merely ironical.

[8] His desire of praise pants still.

[9] Another note of Nestor's humour, not so much being to be plainly observed in all these Iliads as in this book.

[10] Note the sharpness of wit in our Homer; if where you look not for it you can find it.

THE END OF THE TWENTY-THIRD BOOK.

THE TWENTY-FOURTH BOOK OF HOMER'S ILIADS

THE ARGUMENT

Jove, entertaining care of Hector's corse,
Sends Thetis to her son for his remorse,
And fit dismission of it. Iris then
He sends to Priam; willing him to gain
His son for ransom. He, by Hermes led,
Gets through Achilles' guards; sleeps deep and dead
Cast on them by his guide; when, with access
And humble suit made to Æacides,
He gains the body; which to Troy he bears,
And buries it with feasts, buried in tears.

ANOTHER ARGUMENT

Omega sings the Exsequies,
And Hector's redemptory prise.
The games perform'd; the soldiers wholly dispers'd to fleet,
Supper and sleep their only care. Constant Achilles yet
Wept for his friend, nor sleep itself, that all things doth subdue,
Could touch at him; this way and that he turn'd, and did renew
His friend's dear memory, his grace in managing his strength,
And his strength's greatness, how life rack'd into their utmost length
Griefs, battles, and the wraths of seas, in their joint sufferance.
Each thought of which turn'd to a tear. Sometimes he would advance,
In tumbling on the shore, his side; sometimes his face: then turn
Flat on his bosom; start upright. Although he saw the morn
Show sea and shore his ecstasy, he left not, till at last
Rage varied his distraction; horse, chariot, in haste
He call'd for; and, those join'd, the corse was to his chariot tied,
And thrice about the sepulchre he made his fury ride,
Dragging the person. All this past; in his pavilion
Rest seiz'd him, but with Hector's corse his rage had never done,
Still suff'ring it t' oppress the dust. Apollo yet, ev'n dead,
Pitied the prince, and would not see inhuman tyranny fed
With more pollution of his limbs; and therefore cover'd round
His person with his golden shield, that rude dogs might not wound
His manly lineaments, which threat Achilles cruelly
Had us'd in fury. But now Heav'n let fall a gen'ral eye
Of pity on him; the blest Gods persuaded Mercury,
Their good observer, to his stealth; and ev'ry Deity
Stood pleas'd with it; Juno except, green Neptune, and the Maid

Grac'd with the blue eyes, all their hearts stood hatefully appaid
Long since, and held it, as at first, to Priam, Ilion,
And all his subjects, for the rape of his licentious son,
Proud Paris, that despis'd these Dames in their divine access
Made to his cottage, and prais'd Her that his sad wantonness
So costly nourish'd. The twelfth morn now shin'd on the delay
Of Hector's rescue, and then spake the Deity of the Day
Thus to th' Immortals: "Shameless Gods, authors of ill ye are
To suffer ill. Hath Hector's life at all times show'd his care
Of all your rights, in burning thighs of beeves and goats to you,
And are your cares no more of him? Vouchsafe ye not ev'n now,
Ev'n dead, to keep him, that his wife, his mother, and his son,
Father, and subjects, may be mov'd to those deeds he hath done,
Seeing you preserve him that serv'd you, and sending to their hands
His person for the rites of fire? Achilles, that withstands
All help to others, you can help; one that hath neither heart
Nor soul within him, that will move or yield to any part
That fits a man, but lion-like, uplandish, and mere wild,
Slave to his pride, and all his nerves being naturally compil'd
Of eminent strength, stalks out and preys upon a silly sheep.
And so fares this man, that fit ruth that now should draw so deep
In all the world being lost in him; and shame, a quality [1]
Of so much weight, that both it helps and hurts excessively
Men in their manners, is not known, nor hath the pow'r to be,
In this man's being. Other men a greater loss than he
Have undergone, a son, suppose, or brother of one womb;
Yet, after dues of woes and tears, they bury in his tomb
All their deplorings. Fates have giv'n to all that are true men
True manly patience; but this man so soothes his bloody vein
That no blood serves it, he must have divine-soul'd Hector bound
To his proud chariot, and danc'd in a most barbarous round
About his lov'd friend's sepulchre, when he is slain. 'Tis vile,
And draws no profit after it. But let him now awhile
Mark but our angers; he is spent; let all his strength take heed
It tempts not our wraths; he begets, in this outrageous deed,
The dull earth with his fury's hate." White-wristed Juno said,
Being much incens'd, "This doom is one that thou wouldst have obey'd,
Thou bearer of the silver bow, that we in equal care
And honour should hold Hector's worth, with him that claims a share
In our deservings. Hector suck'd a mortal woman's breast,
Æacides a Goddess's; ourself had interest
Both in his infant nourishment, and bringing up with state,
And to the human Peleüs we gave his bridal mate,
Because he had th' Immortals' love. To celebrate the feast
Of their high nuptials, ev'ry God was glad to be a guest;
And thou fedd'st of his father's cates, touching thy harp in grace
Of that beginning of our friend, whom thy perfidious face,
In his perfection, blusheth not to match with Priam's son,

O thou that to betray and shame art still companion!"
Jove thus receiv'd her: "Never give these broad terms to a God.
Those two men shall not be compar'd; and yet, of all that trod
The well-pav'd Ilion, none so dear to all the Deities
As Hector was; at least to me, for off'rings most of prize
His hands would never pretermit. Our altars ever stood
Furnish'd with banquets fitting us, odours and ev'ry good
Smok'd in our temples; and for this, foreseeing it, his fate
We mark'd with honour, which must stand. But, to give stealth estate
In his deliv'rance, shun we that; nor must we favour one
To shame another. Privily, with wrong to Thetis' son,
We must not work out Hector's right. There is a ransom due,
And open course, by laws of arms; in which must humbly sue
The friends of Hector. Which just mean if any God would stay,
And use the other, 'twould not serve; for Thetis night and day
Is guardian to him. But would one call Iris hither, I
Would give directions that for gifts the Trojan king should buy
His Hector's body, which the son of Thetis shall resign."
This said, his will was done; the Dame that doth in vapours shine,
Dewy and thin, footed with storms, jump'd to the sable seas
'Twixt Samos and sharp Imber's cliffs; the lake groan'd with the press
Of her rough feet, and, plummet-like, put in an ox's horn
That bears death to the raw-fed fish, she div'd, and found forlorn
Thetis lamenting her son's fate, who was in Troy to have,
Far from his country, his death serv'd. Close to her Iris stood,
And said: "Rise, Thetis, prudent Jove, whose counsels thirst not blood,
Calls for thee." Thetis answer'd her with asking: "What's the cause
The great God calls? My sad pow'rs fear'd to break th' immortal laws,
In going fil'd with griefs to heav'n. But He sets snares for none
With colour'd counsels; not a word of him but shall be done."
She said, and took a sable veil (a blacker never wore
A heav'nly shoulder) and gave way. Swift Iris swum before.
About both roll'd the brackish waves. They took their banks, and flew
Up to Olympus; where they found Saturnius far-of-view
Spher'd with heav'n's ever-being States. Minerva rose, and gave
Her place to Thetis near to Jove; and Juno did receive
Her entry with a cup of gold, in which she drank to her,
Grac'd her with comfort, and the cup to her hand did refer.
She drank, resigning it; and then the Sire of men and Gods
Thus entertain'd her: "Com'st thou up to these our blest abodes,
Fair Goddess Thetis, yet art sad; and that in so high kind
As passeth suff'rance? This I know, and tried thee, and now find
Thy will by mine rul'd, which is rule to all worlds' government.
Besides this trial yet, this cause sent down for thy ascent,
Nine days' contention hath been held amongst th' Immortals here
For Hector's person and thy son; and some advices were
To have our good spy Mercury steal from thy son the corse;
But that reproach I kept far off, to keep in future force

Thy former love and reverence. Haste then, and tell thy son
The Gods are angry, and myself take that wrong he hath done
To Hector in worst part of all, the rather since he still
Detains his person. Charge him then, if he respect my will
For any reason, to resign slain Hector. I will send
Iris to Priam to redeem his son, and recommend
Fit ransom to Achilles' grace, in which right he may joy
And end his vain grief." To this charge bright Thetis did employ
Instant endeavour. From heav'n's tops she reach'd Achilles' tent,
Found him still sighing, and some friends with all their complement
Soothing his humour; other some with all contentión
Dressing his dinner, all their pains and skills consum'd upon
A huge wool-bearer, slaughter'd there. His rev'rend mother then
Came near, took kindly his fair hand, and ask'd him: "Dear son, when
Will sorrow leave thee? How long time wilt thou thus eat thy heart,
Fed with no other food, nor rest? 'Twere good thou wouldst divert
Thy friend's love to some lady, cheer thy spirits with such kind parts
As she can quit thy grace withal. The joy of thy deserts
I shall not long have, death is near, and thy all-conqu'ring fate,
Whose haste thou must not haste with grief, but understand the state
Of things belonging to thy life, which quickly order. I
Am sent from Jove t' advértise thee, that ev'ry Deity
Is angry with thee, himself most, that rage thus reigns in thee
Still to keep Hector. Quit him then, and, for fit ransom, free
His injur'd person." He replied: "Let him come that shall give
The ransom, and the person take. Jove's pleasure must deprive
Men of all pleasures." This good speech, and many more, the son
And mother us'd, in ear of all the naval statión.
And now to holy Ilion Saturnius Iris sent:
"Go, swift-foot Iris, bid Troy's king bear fit gifts, and content
Achilles for his son's release; but let him greet alone
The Grecian navy; not a man, excepting such a one
As may his horse and chariot guide, a herald, or one old,
Attending him; and let him take his Hector. Be he bold,
Discourag'd nor with death nor fear, wise Mercury shall guide
His passage till the prince be near; and, he gone, let him ride
Resolv'd ev'n in Achilles' tent. He shall not touch the state
Of his high person, nor admit the deadliest desperate
Of all about him; for, though fierce, he is not yet unwise,
Nor inconsid'rate, nor a man past awe of Deities,
But passing free and curious to do a suppliant grace,
This said, the Rainbow to her feet tied whirlwinds, and the place
Reach'd instantly. The heavy court Clamour and Mourning fill'd;
The sons all set about the sire; and there stood Grief, and still'd
Tears on their garments. In the midst the old king sate, his weed
All wrinkled, head and neck dust-fil'd; the princesses his seed,
The princesses his sons' fair wives, all mourning by; the thought
Of friends so many, and so good, being turn'd so soon to nought

By Grecian hands, consum'd their youth, rain'd beauty from their eyes.
Iris came near the king; her sight shook all his faculties,
And therefore spake she soft, and said: "Be glad, Dardanides;
Of good occurrents, and none ill, am I ambassadress.
Jove greets thee, who, in care, as much as he is distant, deigns
Eye to thy sorrows, pitying thee. My ambassy contains
This charge to thee from him: He wills thou shouldst redeem thy son,
Bear gifts t' Achilles, cheer him so; but visit him alone,
None but some herald let attend, thy mules and chariot
To manage for thee. Fear nor death let daunt thee, Jove hath got
Hermes to guide thee, who as near to Thetis' son as needs
Shall guard thee; and being once with him, nor his, nor others', deeds
Stand touch'd with, he will all contain; nor is he mad, nor vain,
Nor impious, but with all his nerves studious to entertain
One that submits with all fit grace." Thus vanish'd she like wind.
He mules and chariot calls, his sons bids see them join'd, and bind
A trunk behind it; he himself down to his wardrobe goes,
Built all of cedar, highly roof'd, and odoriferous,
That much stuff, worth the sight, contain'd. To him he call'd his queen,
Thus greeting her: "Come, hapless dame, an angel I have seen,
Sent down from Jove, that bade me free our dear son from the fleet
With ransom pleasing to our foe. What holds thy judgment meet?
My strength and spirit lays high charge on all my being to bear
The Greeks' worst, vent'ring through their host." The queen cried out to hear
His vent'rous purpose, and replied: "O whither now is fled
The late discretion that renown'd thy grave and knowing head
In foreign and thine own rul'd realms, that thus thou dar'st assay
Sight of that man, in whose brow sticks the horrible decay
Of sons so many, and so strong? Thy heart is iron I think.
If this stern man, whose thirst of blood makes cruelty his drink,
Take, or but see, thee, thou art dead. He nothing pities woe,
Nor honours age. Without his sight, we have enough to do
To mourn with thought of him. Keep we our palace, weep we here,
Our son is past our helps. Those throes, that my deliv'rers were
Of his unhappy lineaments, told me they should be torn
With black-foot dogs. Almighty Fate, that black hour he was born,
Spun in his springing thread that end; far from his parents' reach,
This bloody fellow then ordain'd to be their mean, this wretch,
Whose stony liver would to heav'n I might devour, my teeth
My son's revengers made! Curs'd Greek, he gave him not his death
Doing an ill work; he alone fought for his country, he
Fled not, nor fear'd, but stood his worst; and curséd policy
Was his undoing." He replied: "Whatever was his end
Is not our question, we must now use all means to defend
His end from scandal; from which act dissuade not my just will,
Nor let me nourish in my house a bird presaging ill
To my good actions; 'tis in vain. Had any earthly spirit
Giv'n this suggestion, if our priests, or soothsay'rs, challenging merit

Of prophets, I might hold it false, and be the rather mov'd
To keep my palace, but these ears and these self eyes approv'd
It was a Goddess. I will go; for not a word She spake
I know was idle. If it were, and that my fate will make
Quick riddance of me at the fleet, kill me, Achilles; come,
When getting to thee, I shall find a happy dying room
On Hector's bosom, when enough thirst of my tears finds there
Quench to his fervour." This resolv'd, the works most fair and dear
Of his rich screens he brought abroad; twelve veils wrought curiously;
Twelve plain gowns; and as many suits of wealthy tapestry;
As many mantles; horsemen's coats; ten talents of fine gold;
Two tripods; caldrons four; a bowl, whose value he did hold
Beyond all price, presented by th' ambassadors of Thrace.
The old king nothing held too dear, to rescue from disgrace
His gracious Hector. Forth he came. At entry of his court
The Trojan citizens so press'd, that this opprobrious sort
Of check he us'd: "Hence, cast-aways! Away, ye impious crew!
Are not your griefs enough at home? What come ye here to view?
Care ye for my griefs? Would ye see how miserable I am?
Is't not enough, imagine ye? Ye might know, ere ye came,
What such a son's loss weigh'd with me. But know this for your pains,
Your houses have the weaker doors; the Greeks will find their gains
The easier for his loss, be sure. But O Troy! ere I see
Thy ruin, let the doors of hell receive and ruin me!"
Thus with his sceptre set he on the crowding citizens,
Who gave back, seeing him so urge. And now he entertains
His sons as roughly, Helenus, Paris, Hippothous,
Pammon, divine Agathones, renown'd Deiphobus,
Agavus, and Antiphonus, and last, not least in arms,
The strong Polites: these nine sons the violence of his harms
Help'd him to vent in these sharp terms: "Haste, you infamous brood,
And get my chariot. Would to heav'n that all the abject blood
In all your veins had Hector 'scus'd! O me, accursèd man,
All my good sons are gone, my light the shades Cimmerian
Have swallow'd from me. I have lost Mestor, surnam'd the fair;
Troilus, that ready knight at arms, that made his field repair
Ever so prompt and joyfully; and Hector, amongst men
Esteem'd a God, not from a mortal's seed, but of th' Eternal strain,
He seem'd to all eyes. These are gone, you that survive are base,
Liars and common freebooters; all faulty, not a grace,
But in your heels, in all your parts; dancing companions
Ye all are excellent. Hence, ye brats! Love ye to hear my moans?
Will ye not get my chariot? Command it quickly, fly,
That I may perfect this dear work." This all did terrify;
And straight his mule-drawn chariot came, to which they fast did bind
The trunk with gifts. And then came forth, with an afflicted mind,
Old Hecuba. In her right hand a bowl of gold she bore
With sweet wine crown'd, stood near, and said: "Receive this, and implore,

With sacrificing it to Jove, thy safe return. I see
Thy mind likes still to go, though mine dislikes it utterly.
Pray to the black-cloud-gath'ring God, Idæan Jove, that views
All Troy, and all her miseries, that he will deign to use
His most-lov'd bird to ratify thy hopes, that, her broad wing
Spread on thy right hand, thou mayst know thy zealous offering
Accepted, and thy safe return confirm'd; but if he fail,
Fail thy intent, though never so it labours to prevail."
"This I refuse not," he replied, "for no faith is so great
In Jove's high favour, but it must with held-up hands intreat."
This said, the chambermaid, that held the ewer and basin by,
He bade pour water on his hands; when, looking to the sky,
He took the bowl, did sacrifice, and thus implor'd: "O Jove,
From Ida using thy commands, in all deserts above
All other Gods, vouchsafe me safe, and pity in the sight
Of great Achilles; and, for trust to that wish'd grace, excite
Thy swift-wing'd Messenger, most strong, most of air's region lov'd,
To soar on my right hand; which sight may firmly see approv'd
Thy former summons, and my speed." He pray'd, and heav'n's King heard,
And instantly cast from his fist air's all-commanding bird,
The black-wing'd huntress, perfectest of all fowls, which Gods call
Percnos, the eagle. And how broad the chamber nuptial
Of any mighty man hath doors, such breadth cast either wing;
Which now she us'd, and spread them wide on right hand of the king.
All saw it, and rejoic'd, and up to chariot he arose,
Drave forth, the portal and the porch resounding as he goes.
His friends all follow'd him, and mourn'd as if he went to die;
And bringing him past town to field, all left him; and the eye
Of Jupiter was then his guard, who pitied him, and us'd
These words to Hermes: "Mercury, thy help hath been profus'd
Ever with most grace in consorts of travellers distress'd,
Now cónsort Priam to the fleet; but so, that not the least
Suspicion of him be attain'd, till at Achilles' tent
The convoy hath arriv'd him safe." This charge incontinent
He put in practice. To his feet his feather'd shoes he tied,
Immortal, and made all of gold, with which he us'd to ride
The rough sea and th' unmeasur'd earth, and equall'd in his pace
The puffs of wind. Then took he up his rod, that hath the grace
To shut what eyes he lists with sleep, and open them again
In strongest trances. This he held, flew forth, and did attain
To Troy and Hellespontus straight. Then like a fair young prince,
First-down-chinn'd, and of such a grace as makes his looks convince
Contending eyes to view him, forth he went to meet the king.
He, having pass'd the mighty tomb of Ilus, watering
His mules in Xanthus, the dark even fell on the earth; and then
Idæus (guider of the mules) discern'd this grace of men,
And spake afraid to Priamus: "Beware, Dardanides,
Our states ask counsel; I discern the dangerous access

Of some man near us; now I fear we perish. Is it best
To fly, or kiss his knees and ask his ruth of men distress'd?"
Confusion strook the king, cold fear extremely quench'd his veins,
Upright upon his languishing head his hair stood, and the chains
Of strong amaze bound all his pow'rs. To both which then came near
The prince turn'd Deity, took his hand, and thus bespake the peer:
"To what place, father, driv'st thou out through solitary night,
When others sleep? Give not the Greeks sufficient cause of fright
To these late travels, being so near, and such vow'd enemies?
Of all which, if with all this load any should cast his eyes
On thy adventures, what would then thy mind esteem thy state,
Thyself old, and thy follow'r old? Resistance could not rate
At any value; as for me, be sure I mind no harm
To thy grave person, but against the hurt of others arm.
Mine own lov'd father did not get a greater love in me
To his good, than thou dost to thine." He answer'd: "The degree
Of danger in my course, fair son, is nothing less than that
Thou urgest; but some God's fair hand puts in for my safe state,
That sends so sweet a guardian in this so stern a time
Of night, and danger, as thyself, that all grace in his prime
Of body and of beauty show'st, all answer'd with a mind
So knowing, that it cannot be but of some blessed kind
Thou art descended." "Not untrue," said Hermes, "thy conceit
In all this holds; but further truth relate, if of such weight
As I conceive thy carriage be, and that thy care conveys
Thy goods of most price to more guard; or go ye all your ways
Frighted from holy Ilion, so excellent a son
As thou hadst (being your special strength) fallen to destructión,
Whom no Greek better'd for his fight?" "O, what art thou," said he,
"Most worthy youth, of what race born, that thus recount'st to me
My wretched son's death with such truth?" "Now, father," he replied,
"You tempt me far, in wond'ring how the death was signified
Of your divine son to a man so mere a stranger here
As you hold me; but I am one that oft have seen him bear
His person like a God in field; and when in heaps he slew
The Greeks, all routed to their fleet, his so victorious view
Made me admire, not feel his hand; because Æacides,
Incens'd, admitted not our fight, myself being of access
To his high person, serving him, and both to Ilion
In one ship sail'd. Besides, by birth I breathe a Myrmidon,
Polyctor, call'd the rich, my sire, declin'd with age like you.
Six sons he hath, and me a seventh; and all those six live now
In Phthia, since, all casting lots, my chance did only fall
To follow hither. Now for walk I left my General.
To-morrow all the sun-burn'd Greeks will circle Troy with arms,
The princes rage to be withheld so idly, your alarms
Not giv'n half hot enough they think, and can contain no more."
He answer'd: "If you serve the prince, let me be bold t' implore

This grace of thee, and tell me true: Lies Hector here at fleet,
Or have the dogs his flesh?" He said: "Nor dogs nor fowl have yet
Touch'd at his person; still he lies at fleet, and in the tent
Of our great Captain, who indeed is much too negligent
Of his fit usage. But, though now twelve days have spent their heat
On his cold body, neither worms with any taint have eat,
Nor putrefaction perish'd it; yet ever, when the Morn
Lifts her divine light from the sea, unmercifully borne
About Patroclus' sepulchre, it bears his friend's disdain,
Bound to his chariot; but no fits of further outrage reign
In his distemper. You would muse to see how deep a dew
Ev'n steeps the body, all the blood wash'd off, no slend'rest shew
Of gore or quitture, but his wounds all clos'd, though many were
Open'd about him. Such a love the blest Immortals bear,
Ev'n dead, to thy dear son, because his life show'd love to them."
He joyful answer'd: "O my son, it is a grace supreme
In any man to serve the Gods. And I must needs say this;
For no cause, having season fit, my Hector's hands would miss
Advancement to the Gods with gifts, and therefore do not they
Miss his remembrance after death. Now let an old man pray
Thy graces to receive this cup, and keep it for my love,
Nor leave me till the Gods and thee have made my pray'rs approve
Achilles' pity, by thy guide brought to his princely tent."
Hermes replied: "You tempt me now, old king, to a consent
Far from me, though youth aptly errs. I secretly receive
Gifts that I cannot broadly vouch, take graces that will give
My lord dishonour, or what he knows not, or will esteem
Perhaps unfit? Such briberies perhaps at first may seem
Sweet and secure; but futurely they still prove sour, and breed
Both fear and danger. I could wish thy grave affairs did need
My guide to Argos, either shipp'd, or lackeying by thy side,
And would be studious in thy guard, so nothing could be tried
But care in me to keep thee safe, for that I could excuse,
And vouch to all men." These words past, he put the deeds in use
For which Jove sent him; up he leapt to Priam's chariot,
Took scourge and reins, and blew in strength to his free steeds, and got
The naval tow'rs and deep dike straight. The guards were all at meat;
Those he enslumber'd, op'd the ports, and in he safely let
Old Priam with his wealthy prize. Forthwith they reach'd the tent
Of great Achilles, large and high, and in his most ascent
A shaggy roof of seedy reeds mown from the meads; a hall
Of state they made their king in it, and strengthen'd it withall
Thick with fir rafters; whose approach was let in by a door
That had but one bar, but so big that three men evermore
Rais'd it to shut, three fresh take down; which yet Æacides
Would shut and ope himself. And this with far more ease
Hermes set ope, ent'ring the king; then leapt from horse, and said:
"Now know, old king, that Mercury, a God, hath giv'n this aid

To thy endeavour, sent by Jove; and now away must I,
For men would envy thy estate to see a Deity
Affect a man thus. Enter thou, embrace Achilles' knee,
And by his sire, son, mother, pray his ruth and grace to thee."
This said, he high Olympus reach'd. The king then left his coach
To grave Idæus, and went on, made his resolv'd approach,
And enter'd in a goodly room, where with his princes sate
Jove-lov'd Achilles, at their feast; two only kept the state
Of his attendance, Alcimus, and lord Automedon,
At Priam's entry. A great time Achilles gaz'd upon
His wonder'd-at approach, nor ate; the rest did nothing see,
While close he came up, with his hands fast holding the bent knee
Of Hector's conqueror, and kiss'd that large man-slaught'ring hand
That much blood from his sons had drawn. And as in some strange land,
And great man's house, a man is driv'n (with that abhorr'd dismay
That follows wilful bloodshed still, his fortune being to slay
One whose blood cries aloud for his) to plead protectión,
In such a miserable plight as frights the lookers on;
In such a stupefied estate Achilles sat to see
So unexpected, so in night, and so incredibly,
Old Priam's entry. All his friends one on another star'd
To see his strange looks, seeing no cause. Thus Priam then prepar'd
His son's redemption: "See in me, O God-like Thetis' son,
Thy aged father; and perhaps ev'n now being out-run
With some of my woes, neighbour foes (thou absent) taking time
To do him mischief; no mean left to terrify the crime
Of his oppression; yet he hears thy graces still survive,
And joys to hear it, hoping still to see thee safe arrive
From ruin'd Troy; but I, curs'd man, of all my race shall live
To see none living. Fifty sons the Deities did give
My hopes to live in; all alive when near our trembling shore
The Greek ships harbour'd, and one womb nineteen of those sons bore.
Now Mars a number of their knees hath strength less left; and he
That was, of all, my only joy, and Troy's sole guard, by thee,
Late fighting for his country, slain; whose tender'd person now
I come to ransom. Infinite is that I offer you,
Myself conferring it, expos'd alone to all your odds,
Only imploring right of arms. Achilles! Fear the Gods,
Pity an old man like thy sire; diff'rent in only this,
That I am wretcheder, and bear that weight of miseries
That never man did, my curs'd lips enforc'd to kiss that hand
That slew my children." This mov'd tears; his father's name did stand,
Mention'd by Priam, in much help to his compassion,
And mov'd Æacides so much, he could not look upon
The weeping father. With his hand he gently put away
His grave face. Calm remission now did mutually display
Her pow'r in either's heaviness. Old Priam, to record
His son's death and his deathsman see, his tears and bosom pour'd

Before Achilles; at his feet he laid his rev'rend head.
Achilles' thoughts, now with his sire, now with his friend, were fed.
Betwixt both sorrow fill'd the tent. But now Æacides
(Satiate at all parts with the ruth of their calamities)
Start up, and up he rais'd the king. His milk-white head and beard
With pity he beheld, and said: "Poor man, thy mind is scar'd
With much afflictión. How durst thy person thus alone
Venture on his sight, that hath slain so many a worthy son,
And so dear to thee? Thy old heart is made of iron. Sit,
And settle we our woes, though huge, for nothing profits it.
Cold mourning wastes but our lives' heats. The Gods have destinate
That wretched mortals must live sad; 'tis the Immortal State
Of Deity that lives secure. Two tuns of gifts there lie
In Jove's gate, one of good, one ill, that our mortality
Maintain, spoil, order; which when Jove doth mix to any man,
One while he frolics, one while mourns. If of his mournful can
A man drinks only, only wrongs he doth expose him to,
Sad hunger in th' abundant earth doth toss him to and fro,
Respected nor of Gods nor men. The mix'd cup Peleus drank
Ev'n from his birth; Heav'n blest his life; he liv'd not that could thank
The Gods for such rare benefits as set forth his estate.
He reign'd among his Myrmidons most rich, most fortunate,
And, though a mortal, had his bed deck'd with a deathless dame.
And yet, with all this good, one ill God mix'd, that takes all name
From all that goodness; his name now, whose preservation here
Men count the crown of their most good, not bless'd with pow'r to bear
One blossom but myself, and I shaken as soon as blown;
Nor shall I live to cheer his age, and give nutritión
To him that nourish'd me. Far off my rest is set in Troy,
To leave thee restless and thy seed; thyself that did enjoy,
As we have heard, a happy life; what Lesbos doth contain,
In times past being a bless'd man's seat, what the unmeasur'd main
Of Hellespontus, Phrygia, holds, are all said to adorn
Thy empire, wealth and sons enow; but, when the Gods did turn
Thy blest state to partake with bane, war and the bloods of men
Circled thy city, never clear. Sit down and suffer then;
Mourn not inevitable things; thy tears can spring no deeds
To help thee, nor recall thy son; impatience ever breeds
Ill upon ill, makes worst things worse, and therefore sit." He said:
"Give me no seat, great seed of Jove, when yet unransomed
Hector lies riteless in thy tents, but deign with utmost speed
His resignation, that these eyes may see his person freed,
And thy grace satisfied with gifts. Accept what I have brought,
And turn to Phthia; 'tis enough thy conqu'ring hand hath fought
Till Hector falter'd under it, and Hector's father stood
With free humanity safe." He frown'd and said: "Give not my blood
Fresh cause of fury. I know well I must resign thy son,
Jove by my mother utter'd it; and what besides is done

I know as amply; and thyself, old Priam, I know too.
Some God hath brought thee; for no man durst use a thought to go
On such a service. I have guards, and I have gates to stay
Easy accesses; do not then presume thy will can sway,
Like Jove's will, and incense again my quench'd blood, lest nor thou
Nor Jove get the command of me." This made the old king bow,
And down he sat in fear. The prince leapt like a lion forth,
Automedon and Alcimus attending: all the worth
Brought for the body they took down and brought in, and with it
Idæus, herald to the king; a coat embroider'd yet,
And two rich cloaks, they left to hide the person. Thetis' son
Call'd out his women, to anoint and quickly overrun
The corse with water, lifting it in private to the coach,
Lest Priam saw, and his cold blood embrac'd a fi'ry touch
Of anger at the turpitude profaning it, and blew
Again his wrath's fire to his death. This done, his women threw
The coat and cloak on; but the corse Achilles' own hand laid
Upon a bed, and with his friends to chariot it convey'd.
For which forc'd grace, abhorring so from his free mind, he wept,
Cried out for anger, and thus pray'd: "O friend, do not except
Against this favour to our foe, if in the deep thou hear,
And that I give him to his sire; he gave fair ransom; dear
In my observance is Jove's will; and whatsoever part
Of all these gifts by any mean I fitly may convert
To thy renown here, and will there, it shall be pour'd upon
Thy honour'd sepulchre. This said, he went, and what was done
Told Priam, saying: "Father, now thy will's fit rites are paid,
Thy son is giv'n up; in the morn thine eyes shall see him laid
Deck'd in thy chariot on his bed; in mean space let us eat.
The rich-hair'd Niobe found thoughts that made her take her meat,
Though twelve dear children she saw slain, six daughters, six young sons.
The sons incens'd Apollo slew; the maids' confusions
Diana wrought; since Niobe her merits durst compare
With great Latona's, arguing that she did only bear
Two children, and herself had twelve; for which those only two
Slew all her twelve. Nine days they lay steep'd in their blood, her woe
Found no friend to afford them fire, Saturnius had turn'd
Humans to stones. The tenth day yet, the good Celestials burn'd
The trunks themselves, and Niobe, when she was tir'd with tears,
Fell to her food, and now with rocks and wild hills mix'd she bears
In Sipylus the Gods' wrath still, in that place where 'tis said
The Goddess Fairies use to dance about the fun'ral bed
Of Achelous, where, though turn'd with cold grief to a stone,
Heav'n gives her heat enough to feel what plague comparison
With his pow'rs made by earth deserves. Affect not then too far
Without grief, like a God, being a man, but for a man's life care,
And take fit food; thou shalt have time beside to mourn thy son;
He shall be tearful, thou being full; not here, but Ilion

Shall find thee weeping-rooms enow." He said, and so arose,
And caus'd a silver-fleec'd sheep kill'd; his friends' skills did dispose
The flaying, cutting of it up, and cookly spitted it,
Roasted, and drew it artfully. Automedon, as fit
Was for the rev'rend sewer's place; and all the brown joints serv'd
On wicker vessel to the board; Achilles' own hands kerv'd;
And close they fell to. Hunger stanch'd; talk, and observing time,
Was us'd of all hands. Priam sat amaz'd to see the prime
Of Thetis' son, accomplish'd so with stature, looks, and grace,
In which the fashion of a God he thought had chang'd his place.
Achilles fell to him as fast, admir'd as much his years
Told in his grave and good aspect; his speech ev'n charm'd his ears,
So order'd, so material. With this food feasted too,
Old Priam spake thus: "Now, Jove's seed, command that I may go,
And add to this feast grace of rest. These lids ne'er clos'd mine eyes,
Since under thy hands fled the soul of my dear son; sighs, cries,
And woes, all use from food and sleep have taken; the base courts
Of my sad palace made my beds, where all the abject sorts
Of sorrow I have variéd, tumbled in dust, and hid;
No bit, no drop, of sust'nance touch'd." Then did Achilles bid
His men and women see his bed laid down, and coveréd
With purple blankets, and on them an arras coverlid,
Waistcoats of silk plush laying by. The women straight took lights,
And two beds made with utmost speed, and all the other rites
Their lord nam'd us'd, who pleasantly the king in hand thus bore:
"Good father, you must sleep without; lest any counsellor
Make his access in depth of night, as oft their industry
Brings them t' impart our war-affairs; of whom should any eye
Discern your presence, his next steps to Agamemnon fly,
And then shall I lose all these gifts. But go to, signify,
And that with truth, how many days you mean to keep the state
Of Hector's funerals; because so long would I rebate
Mine own edge set to sack your town, and all our host contain
From interruption of your rites." He answer'd: "If you mean
To suffer such rites to my son, you shall perform a part
Of most grace to me. But you know with how dismay'd a heart
Our host took Troy; and how much fear will therefore apprehend
Their spirits to make out again, so far as we must send
For wood to raise our heap of death; unless I may assure
That this your high grace will stand good, and make their pass secure;
Which if you seriously confirm, nine days I mean to mourn;
The tenth keep funeral and feast; th' eleventh raise and adorn
My son's fit sepulchre; the twelfth, if we must needs, we'll fight."
"Be it," replied Æacides, "do Hector all this right;
I'll hold war back those whole twelve days; of which, to free all fear,
Take this my right hand." This confirm'd, the old king rested there;
His herald lodg'd by him; and both in forepart of the tent;
Achilles in an inmost room of wondrous ornament,

Whose side bright-cheek'd Briseis warm'd. Soft sleep tam'd Gods and men,
All but most-useful Mercury; sleep could not lay one chain
On his quick temples, taking care for getting off again
Engagéd Priam undiscern'd of those that did maintain
The sacred watch. Above his head he stood with this demand:
"O father, sleep'st thou so secure, still lying in the hand
Of so much ill, and being dismiss'd by great Æacides?
'Tis true thou hast redeem'd the dead; but for thy life's release,
Should Agamemnon hear thee here, three times the price now paid
Thy sons' hands must repay for thee." This said, the king, afraid,
Start from his sleep, Idæus call'd, and, for both, Mercury
The horse and mules, before loos'd, join'd so soft and curiously
That no ear heard, and through the host drave; but when they drew
To gulfy Xanthus' bright-wav'd stream, up to Olympus flew
Industrious Mercury. And now the saffron Morning rose,
Spreading her white robe over all the world; when, full of woes,
They scourg'd on with the corse to Troy, from whence no eye had seen,
Before Cassandra, their return. She, like love's golden Queen,
Ascending Pergamus, discern'd her father's person nigh,
His herald, and her brother's corse; and then she cast this cry
Round about Troy: "O Trojans, if ever ye did greet
Hector return'd from fight alive, now look ye out and meet
His ransom'd person. Then his worth was all your city's joy,
Now do it honour." Out all rush'd; woman nor man in Troy
Was left, a most unmeasur'd cry took up their voices. Close
To Scæa's ports they met the corse; and to it headlong goes
The rev'rend mother, the dear wife; upon it strow their hair,
And lie entrancéd. Round about the people broke the air
In lamentations; and all day had stay'd the people there,
If Priam had not cried "Give way, give me but leave to bear
The body home, and mourn your fills." Then cleft the press, and gave
Way to the chariot. To the court herald Idæus drave
Where on a rich bed they bestow'd the honour'd person, round
Girt it with singers that the woe with skilful voices crown'd.
A woeful elegy they sung, wept singing, and the dames
Sigh'd as they sung. Andromache the downright prose exclaims
Began to all; she on the neck of slaughter'd Hector fell,
And cried out: "O my husband, thou in youth bad'st youth farewell,
Left'st me a widow, thy sole son an infant; ourselves curs'd
In our birth made him right our child: for all my care that nurs'd
His infancy will never give life to his youth, ere that
Troy from her top will be destroy'd; thou guardian of our state,
Thou ev'n of all her strength the strength, thou, that in care wert past
Her careful mothers of their babes, being gone, how can she last?
Soon will the swoln fleet fill her womb with all their servitude,
Myself with them, and thou with me, dear son, in labours rude
Shalt be employ'd, sternly survey'd by cruel conquerors;
Or, rage not suff'ring life so long, some one, whose hate abhors

Thy presence (putting him in mind of his sire slain by thine,
His brother, son, or friend) shall work thy ruin before mine,
Toss'd from some tow'r, for many Greeks have ate earth from the hand
Of thy strong father; in sad fight his spirit was too much mann'd,
And therefore mourn his people; we, thy parents, my dear lord,
For that thou mak'st endure a woe, black, and to be abhorr'd.
Of all yet thou hast left me worst, not dying in thy bed,
And reaching me thy last-rais'd hand, in nothing counselléd
Nothing commanded by that pow'r thou hadst of me to do
Some deed for thy sake. O for these never will end my woe,
Never my tears cease." Thus wept she, and all the ladies clos'd
Her passion with a gen'ral shriek. Then Hecuba dispos'd
Her thoughts in like words; "O my son, of all mine much most dear,
Dear while thou liv'dst too ev'n to Gods, and after death they were
Careful to save thee. Being best, thou most wert envied;
My other sons Achilles sold; but thee he left not dead.
Imber and Samos, the false ports of Lemnos entertain'd
Their persons; thine, no port but death. Nor there in rest remain'd
Thy violated corse, the tomb of his great friend was spher'd
With thy dragg'd person; yet from death he was not therefore rear'd
But, all his rage us'd, so the Gods have tender'd thy dead state,
Thou liest as living, sweet and fresh, as he that felt the fate
Of Phœbus' holy shafts." These words the queen us'd for her moan,
And, next her, Helen held that state of speech and passión:
"O Hector, all my brothers more were not so lov'd of me
As thy most virtues. Not my lord I held so dear, as thee,
That brought me hither; before which I would I had been brought
To ruin; for what breeds that wish (which is the mischief wrought
By my access) yet never found one harsh taunt, one word's ill,
From thy sweet carriage. Twenty years do now their circles fill
Since my arrival; all which time thou didst not only bear
Thyself without check, but all else, that my lord's brothers were,
Their sisters' lords, sisters themselves, the queen my mother-in-law,
(The king being never but most mild) when thy man's spirit saw
Sour and reproachful, it would still reprove their bitterness
With sweet words, and thy gentle soul. And therefore thy decease
I truly mourn for; and myself curse as the wretched cause;
All broad Troy yielding me not one, that any human laws
Of pity or forgiveness mov'd t'entreat me humanly,
But only thee, all else abhorr'd me for my destiny."
These words made ev'n the commons mourn; to whom the king said: "Friends,
Now fetch wood for our fun'ral fire, nor fear the foe intends
Ambush, or any violence; Achilles gave his word,
At my dismission, that twelve days he would keep sheath'd his sword,
And all men's else." Thus oxen, mules, in chariots straight they put,
Went forth and an unmeasur'd pile of sylvan matter cut;
Nine days employ'd in carriage, but when the tenth morn shin'd
On wretched mortals, then they brought the fit-to-be-divin'd

Forth to be burn'd. Troy swum in tears. Upon the pile's most height
They laid the person, and gave fire. All day it burn'd, all night.
But when th' elev'nth morn let on earth her rosy fingers shine,
The people flock'd about the pile, and first with blackish wine
Quench'd all the flames. His brothers then, and friends, the snowy bones
Gather'd into an urn of gold, still pouring on their moans.
Then wrapt they in soft purple veils the rich urn, digg'd a pit,
Grav'd it, ramm'd up the grave with stones, and quickly built to it
A sepulchre. But, while that work and all the fun'ral rites
Were in performance, guards were held at all parts, days and nights,
For fear of false surprise before they had impos'd the crown
To these solemnities. The tomb advanc'd once, all the town
In Jove-nurs'd Priam's Court partook a passing sumptuous feast.
And so horse-taming Hector's rites gave up his soul to rest.

[1] Shame a quality that hurts and helps men exceedingly.

THE END OF THE TWENTY-FOURTH BOOK.

EPILOGUE TO HOMER'S ILIADS

Thus far the Ilian ruins I have laid
Open to English eyes. In which, repaid
With thine own value, go, unvalued book,
Live, and be lov'd. If any envious look
Hurt thy clear fame, learn that no state more high
Attends on virtue than pin'd envy's eye.
Would thou wert worth it that the best doth wound.
Which this age feeds, and which the last shall bound!

Thus, with labour enough, though with more comfort in the merits of my divine author, I have brought my translation of his Iliads to an end. If, either therein, or in the harsh utterance or matter of my Comment before, I have, for haste, scattered with my burthen (less than fifteen weeks being the whole time that the last Twelve Books' translation stood me in) I desire my present will (and I doubt not hability, if God give life, to reform and perfect all hereafter) may be ingenuously accepted for the absolute work. The rather, considering the most learned, with all their helps and time, have been so often, and unanswerably, miserably taken halting. In the mean time, that most assistful and unspeakable Spirit, by Whose thrice sacred conduct and inspiration I have finished this labour, diffuse the fruitful horn of His blessings through these goodness-thirsting watchings; without which, utterly dry and bloodless is whatsoever mortality soweth.

But where our most diligent Spondanus ends his work with a prayer to be taken out of these Mæanders and Euripian rivers (as he terms them) of Ethnic and Profane Writers (being quite contrary to himself at the beginning) I thrice humbly beseech the Most Dear and Divine Mercy (ever most incomparably preferring the great light of His Truth in His direct and infallible Scriptures) I may ever be enabled, by resting wondering in His right comfortable shadows in these, to magnify the clearness of His Almighty apparance in the other.

And with this salutation of Poesy given by our Spondanus in his Preface to these Iliads ("All hail saint-sacred Poesy that, under so much gall of fiction, such abundance of honey doctrine hast hidden, not revealing them to the unworthy worldly! Wouldst thou but so much make me, that amongst thy novices I might be numbered, no time should ever come near my life that could make me forsake thee.") I will conclude with this my daily and nightly prayer, learned of the most learned Simplicius;—

"Supplico tibi, Domine, Pater, et Dux rationis nostræ, ut nostræ nobilitatis recordemur quâ Tu nos ornasti; et ut Tu nobis præstò sis ut iis qui per sese moventur; ut et à corporis contagio brutorumque affectuum repurgemur, eosque superemus et regamus, et, sicut decet, pro instrumentis iis utamur. Deinde ut nobis adjumento sis, ad accuratam rationis nostræ correctionem, et conjunctionem cum iis qui verè sunt per lucem veritatis. Et tertium, Salvatori supplex oro, ut ab oculis animorum nostrorum caliginem prorsus abstergas, ut (quod apud Homerum est) norimus bene qui Deus, aut mortalis, habendus. Amen."

George Chapman – A Short Biography

George Chapman was born at Hitchin in Hertfordshire in about 1559. There is some evidence that Chapman attended Oxford University but did not obtain a degree, but the evidence is rather scant.

For most of his life Chapman was plagued by debts and was eventually living in near-poverty. It seemed to begin in 1585 when Chapman was offered a bond of surety in order to obtain a loan. Chapman planned to use the proceeds to "use in Attendance upon the then Right Honorable Sir Rafe Sadler Knight". The surety was offered by John Wolfall.

Chapman's designs for Court were short-lived. It appears the money was never received but the papers had been signed and Wolfall used them to pursue Chapman for repayment for many years.

During the first part of the early 1590s Chapman was in Europe, in military action in the Low Countries fighting under the famed English general Sir Francis Vere.

It is from this period that his earliest published works are found including the obscure philosophical poems The Shadow of Night (1594) and Ovid's Banquet of Sense (1595).

By the end of the 1590s, Chapman had become a successful playwright, working for the Elizabethan Theatrical entrepreneur, Philip Henslowe, and later for the Children of the Chapel.

In 1600, Wolfall, still claiming his money, had Chapman arrested over the outstanding debt. In 1608 Wolfall's son, having inherited his father's papers, sued yet again, Chapman's only resort was to petition the Court of Chancery for equity.

To add insult to injury it also appears that Chapman had little time to train with Sadler although he seems present in the Sadler household from 1577–83, and dedicated all his Homerical translations to him.

From 1598 he published his translation of the Iliad in installments. In 1616 the complete Iliad and Odyssey appeared in The Whole Works of Homer, the first complete English translation, which until Alexander Pope's, was the most popular in the English language and was the entry point for most English readers of these magnificent poems.

Chapman does appear to have been diligent in obtaining another patron who would finance his growing reputation.

Robert Devereux, Second Earl of Essex seemed likely to be his patron before being executed for treason by Elizabeth I in 1601.

However Chapman was by now of some renown. It is often said that he worked with Shakespeare, and certainly, in the employment of Henslowe, that could well be an artistic or business relationship pushed upon him.

The great Ben Jonson was also using Chapman's talents in the play Eastward Ho (1605), co-written with John Marston. Both Chapman and Jonson landed in jail over some satirical references to the Scots in the play but both were quick to say that Marston was the culprit.

The friendship with Jonson later broke down, most probably as a result of Jonson's public feud with Inigo Jones. Some satiric, scathing lines, written at a point after the burning of Jonson's desk and papers, provide some evidence of the rift. The poem lampooning Jonson's aggressive behaviour and self-believed superiority remained unpublished during Chapman's lifetime; it was found in documents collected after his death.

Chapman had continued on his great translations of Homer's Iliad and the Odyssey for many years. He had begun their publication in installments starting in 1598. In 1612, his latest patron, Prince Henry, died at the age of eighteen of typhoid fever. He had promised Chapman £300 and a pension on their publication. Whilst publication in their entirety was some years away Chapman felt the money was his due and when the Estate neglected the commitment Chapman petitioned for the money owed him. The petition was ineffective.

Chapman's resultant poverty did not diminish his ability or his standing among the starried gallery of his fellow Elizabethan poets and dramatists.

His talents as a translator were unquestionable. His work on the Odyssey is written in iambic pentameter, and his Iliad in iambic heptameter. (The Greek original is in dactylic hexameter.) Chapman often extends and elaborates on Homer's original contents to add descriptive detail or moral and philosophical interpretation and emphasis.

These translations were very much admired both by those unable to read Greek but inquiring of Homer and by many artists themselves. John Keats, was reverential in his famous poem On First Looking into Chapman's Homer, and other poets from Samuel Taylor Coleridge to T. S. Eliot were equal in their admiration.

Chapman today is under-rated and woefully forgotten. His plays show a willingness to experiment with dramatic form: An Humorous Day's Mirth was one of the first plays to be written in the style of "humours comedy" which Ben Jonson later used. With The Widow's Tears, he was also one of the first writers to meld comedy with more serious themes and thus creating the tragicomedy.

Another interesting creative pursuit of these times was the writing and performance of masques, and they were perhaps regarded as the highest of art forms. Part of this accolade may well be because of the audience being specifically that of the Court and therefore more refined and sophisticated. Obviously with the Puritan's closing the theatres in 1642 and the onset of the Civil War masques ceased.

Chapman wrote one of the most successful masques of the Jacobean era, The Memorable Masque of the Middle Temple and Lincoln's Inn, performed on February 15th, 1613. Another masque, The Masque of the Twelve Months, performed on Twelfth Night 1619 is also now given as Chapman's.

Unfortunately due to their small audience and the cataclysmic events of the era little documentation has survived. What can be stated is that the form developed in various ways, initially in Italy. A masque involved music and dancing, singing and acting, with an elaborate stage design, in which the architectural framing and costumes might be designed by a renowned architect together with performances from professional actors and musicians.

To this other works are now being recognised as Chapman's hand. The lost plays The Fatal Love and A Yorkshire Gentlewoman And Her Son were assigned to Chapman in Stationers' Register entries in 1660. Both of these plays were among fifty or so used for kindling and other uses by the cook of the neglectful collector John Warburton. The lost play Christianetta (registered 1640) may have been a collaboration between Chapman and Richard Brome, or a revision by Brome of a Chapman work.

Other poems by Chapman include: De Guiana, Carmen Epicum (1596), on the exploits of Sir Walter Raleigh; a continuation of Christopher Marlowe's unfinished Hero and Leander (1598); and Euthymiae Raptus; or the Tears of Peace (1609). Some have considered Chapman to be the "rival poet" of Shakespeare's Sonnets.

In truth Chapman's known poetry was not particularly influential; his translations of Homer's Iliad and Odyssey, and the Homeric Batrachomyomachia undoubtedly were.

George Chapman died in London on May 12th, 1634 having lived his latter years in poverty and debt. He was buried at St Giles in the Fields. A monument to him designed by Inigo Jones marked his tomb, and stands today inside the church.

George Chapman – A Concise Bibliography

Plays – Comedies
The Blind Beggar of Alexandria (1596; printed 1598)
An Humorous Day's Mirth (1597; printed 1599)
All Fools (printed 1605)
Monsieur D'Olive (1605; printed 1606)
The Gentleman Usher (printed 1606)
May Day (printed 1611)
The Widow's Tears (printed 1612)

Bussy D'Ambois (1607)
The Conspiracy and Tragedy of Charles, Duke of Byron (1608)
The Revenge of Bussy D'Ambois (1613)
The Tragedy of Chabot, Admiral of France (published 1639).
Caesar and Pompey

Plays – Collaborations
Eastward Ho with Ben Johnson and John Marston (1605)

Plays – Attributed but not Completely Verified
The Fatal Love
A Yorkshire Gentlewoman and Her Son
Christianetta
Sir Gyles Goosecap

Masques
The Memorable Masque of the Middle Temple and Lincoln's Inn (Performed on 15 February 1613)
The Masque of the Twelve Months (Performed on Twelfth Night, 1619)

Translations
Homer's Iliad (1598-1616)
Homers Odyssey (1598-1616)
Homeric Hymns, the Georgics of Virgil, The Works of Hesiod (1618, dedicated to Francis Bacon),
The Hero and Leander of Musaeus (1618)
The Fifth Satire of Juvenal (1624).
Batrachomyomachia.

Poetry

George Chapman wrote several poems. Among his other poetical works are:-

De Guiana, Carmen Epicum (1596)
Hero and Leander (Begun by Marlowe Chapman continued with the work.
Euthymiae Raptus; or the Tears of Peace (1609)

www.ingramcontent.com/pod-product-compliance
Lightning Source LLC
Chambersburg PA
CBHW062148080426

42734CB00010B/1611